MARJORIE HOLMES

The Inspirational Writings

MARJORIE HOLMES

The Inspirational Writings

Lord, Let Me Love

Love and Laughter

To Help You
Through the Hurting

INSPIRATIONAL PRESS

NEW YORK

First Inspirational Press edition published in 1995.

Inspirational Press
A division of Budget Book Service, Inc.
386 Park Avenue South
New York, NY 10016

Inspirational Press is a registered trademark of Budget Book Service, Inc.

Published by arrangement with Doubleday, a division of
Bantam Doubleday Dell Publishing Group, Inc.

Library of Congress Catalog Card Number: 95-78592

ISBN: 0-88486-120-1

Printed in the United States of America.

ACKNOWLEDGMENTS

LOVE AND LAUGHTER

This material appeared originally in *The Evening Star*, Washington, D.C., Copyright © 1964, 1965 by The Evening Star Newspaper Co., and in the following magazines: *McCall's, Everywoman's Family Circle, Guideposts.* "The Family Table" appeared originally in *American Home*, Copyright ©1961 by The Curtis Publishing Company; "A Child's Garden" reprinted from *Better Homes & Gardens*, Copyright © 1947 by Meredith Publishing Company, All rights reserved; "Mother's Wonderful Wishing Book" and "Mother's Apron" appeared in *Today's Health* published by the American Medical Association, Copyright © 1966,1967 by American Medical Association.

LORD, LET ME LOVE

Grateful acknowledgment is made by the author to the editors of the following magazines, newspapers and publishers where many of these prayers and poems first appeared, for permission to reprint:" 'What Became of the Man I Married?' " reprinted from *Better Homes & Gardens*. Copyright © 1952 by Meredith Corp. All rights reserved. "A Song of Praise for Spring," "Give Me a Generous Spirit," "Bathtime," "The New Outfit," "Help Me to Unclutter My Life," "Shopping with a Daughter," "The Stoning, " "Good Roots," "If Only," "Paper Boy," "For Being Cherished," "The Generous Artistry," "Fortify Me with Memories," "Let Me Go Gently," "The Courage to Be Kind," "Bless My Good Intentions," "Hold Me Up a Little Longer," "Don't Let Me Take It for Granted," "Time Out for Love," "Possessions," "The Son Who Won't Study," "Let Them Remember Laughter," "Getting at It," "Let Me Take Time for Beauty," "This House to Keep," "Needlework Prayer," "Forgiving Means Forgetting," "I'm Tired of Being Strong," "The Missing Ingredient," "I Can't Understand My Daughter Any More," "The Box in the Attic," "Give Me the Love to Let Them Go," "I Must Depend on Myself," "A Mother's Wish-Gifts for Christmas," "New Year's Eve," "An American Woman's Prayer" (first appeared in *Ladies Home Journal* as "An American Woman's Bicentennial Prayer"), from *Hold Me Up a Little Longer,Lord,* Copyright © 1971, 1972, 1973, 1974, 1975, 1976, 1977, by Marjorie Holmes Mighell. Published by Doubleday & Company, Inc., and reprinted by permission. "The Cows," "The Earth's Heart Beating," "Let No Job Be Beneath Me," "More Stately Mansions," "Music," "Poetry," "A Potato," "To Love, to Labor," "The Trees," "Two by the Side of the Road," "Why Am I Working Here?" "With the Tongues of Men and Angels," "His Very World Dances," from *How Can I Find You God?* Copyright ©1975 by Marjorie Holmes Mighell. Published by Doubleday & Company, Inc., and reprinted by permission. "A Mother's Prayer in the Morning" as "Mother's Prayer at Morning," "Night Duty" as "Mother Answers Voice in Night," "Order" as "Psalm for an Apron Pocket," "Bring Back the Children" as "A Mother's Arms Aren't Long Enough," Copyright ©1966, 1967, 1968 by The Evening Star Newspaper Company. "I've Got to Talk to Somebody, God," "I've Said 'Yes' Once too Often," "I'm Showing My Age," "I Was So Cross to the Children," "For a Wanted Child," "For an Unexpected Child," "Respite," "Scrubbing a Floor," "Unexpected Company," "The Refrigerator," "The Tender Trap," "The Hour of Love," "The Quarrel," "When a Husband Loses Interest," "The Good Days of Marriage," "A Psalm for Marriage,"

TO HELP YOU THROUGH THE HURTING

Biblical quotes are from the King James and Revised Standard versions. Grateful acknowledgment is made to the following for permission to reprint their copyrighted material: "Come Home" from *You and I Yesterday* by Marjorie Holmes. Copyright ©1973 by Marjorie Holmes. By permission of William Morrow & Company. "Believe and Receive" originally "The Choice," "To Sing So That Others May Hear," "God Only Knows," "The Suffering Few of Us Escape," "If It Can Teach Us to Forgive," "The Crosses," "Cut Back the Vines," "Persecution," "God's Answer to Evil," "For Every Cross I've Carried," "Gone Where?" "Dad's Roses," "Mother's Bible," "Face to Face," "Promises to Keep," "So Short, but Oh So Sweet," "The Procession," and "God Says, 'Get Up!'"from *How Can I Find You, God?* by Marjorie Holmes. Copyright ©1975 by Marjorie Holmes Mighell. Reprinted by permission of Doubleday & Company, Inc. "This Hurt," "He Was So Young," "When Loneliness Is New," "The Lonely Women," "She Sits in Darkness," "The Lovely Solitude," "Psalm for Deliverance," "The Radiant Company," "The Adventure," and "Myself," first appeared in *Who Am I, God?* by Marjorie Holmes. Copyright ©1970,1971,by Marjorie Holmes Mighell. Published by Doubleday & Company, Inc. "The Healing," "Let Me Say 'Yes' to New Experiences," "Don't Let Me Stop Growing" all first appeared in *Hold Me Up a Little Longer, Lord* by Marjorie Holmes. Copyright ©1971, 1972, 1973, 1974, 1975, 1976, 1977 by Marjorie Holmes Mighell. Published by Doubleday & Company, Inc. "The Message," "The Lesson of Loss," "The New Dimension of Love," and "When the Winds Cry I Hear You" from *I've Got to Talk to Somebody, God* by Marjorie Holmes. Copyright ©1968, 1969 by Marjorie Holmes Mighell. Reprinted by permission of Doubleday & Company, Inc. and Hodder & Stoughton Ltd. "We'll Come" first appeared in *Love and Laughter* by Marjorie Holmes. Copyright ©1959, 1967 by Marjorie Holmes Mighell. Published by Doubleday & Company, Inc. "At Christmas the Heart Goes Home" by Marjorie Holmes. Reprinted with permission from *Guideposts* magazine. Copyright ©1976 by Guideposts Associates, Inc., Carmel, New York, 10512. All rights reserved.

CONTENTS

Part I
Love and
Laughter

Foreword

This book is in response to the many requests that have been received from readers of the column, "Love and Laughter," that appears in the Washington *Evening Star*. The author wishes to thank the publishers of the *Star* for permission to reprint these sketches in book form. Thanks are also extended to *McCall's* magazine, *Better Homes & Gardens*, *American Home*, *Today's Health*, *Guideposts*, *Everywoman's Family Circle*, and *Reader's Digest* for permission to include other sketches which first appeared in their pages.

Contents

A Woman and Her Home

I have my own home, to do what I please with, to do what I please with. My den for me and my mate and my cubs, my own!

—Song of the ancient gods of the hearth

IT'S NOT THE DIRT, IT'S THE DISORDER

It isn't the dirt that gets most housewives down so much as it is the disorder. The incessant need for picking up after people. The constant coping with clutter.

It's the hanging up of coats and scarves that are shed on the bench in the hall. It's the putting away of gloves and purses and boots and patrol belts. It's the trotting to the toy cupboards with armloads of dolls and bears and jacks and pieces of jigsaw puzzles.

It's the insoluble daily dilemma over what to do with school papers and drawings and *Junior Scholastic*. It's the eternal hassle with magazines. No matter how conscientiously you assemble them into their proper piles, *National Geographic* invariably goes traveling. *The Saturday Evening Post* gets mixed up with *Life* and *Popular Mechanics*. *Reader's Digest* romps merrily with *McCall's*, and *Esquire* and *Guideposts* get gaily if incongruously together.

As for those brashly ambitious attempts to stack them not only with their proper families, but according to months—what folly! Last year's Christmas issue is bound to bounce to the top in July.

Bathrooms are another place guaranteed to break a tidy housewife's heart. No sooner do you get the towels neatly folded on their bars than flop—they're on the floor. Gleaming basins become grubby puddles before the day is advanced by a few hours. Toothbrushes seldom find their way back to their proper holders. And twisted, tortured toothpaste tubes ooze at you, always minus caps.

Then there is the sheer, cussed, incomprehensible enemy—things lying on top of things. How, oh how does anybody keep the surfaces of tables, buffets, dressers tidy and shiny when an army of miscellany invades them hour by hour and fiercely holds the fort? Mail, trading stamps, pencils, homework, bobby pins, thumbtacks, bits and pieces of broken items—a screw from this, a handle, arm, eye, knob, nail, propeller or feather from that.

You gather them up onto your person; your pockets bulge with them. Trudge, trudge, trudge, you go about trying to find the origin of all these items, to lead them safely home and maybe by locking doors or slamming drawers, keep them at bay. Yet by some evil cunning they have reappeared before you can scarcely turn your back. This sometimes happens even when there's nobody else in the house. They seem to descend from the ceiling, or emerge slyly out of cracks.

"Train your children to be neat," we are advised—and this too is a part of the very problem. How is it possible to achieve and maintain order in a family without becoming a mean old witch? "Don't yell at your children," we are also warned. But how else are you going to get Jimmy to pick up his ball bat, hang up his pajamas, make his bed, feed and clean up after his pets, and at the same time make himself presentable and on time to catch the school bus?

If you don't holler nobody listens. If you do ride herd, well—you're also the one that rides the broomstick!

WAYS TO OUTWIT THE IRONING

What a pleasure it is to finish the ironing—really finish it, down to the last pesky dresser scarf, hanky, and whatsit in the basket. To gaze upon the neat stacks and hangers and foldings of your accomplishment. To think, "Well, for a week at least, the ironing's done."

Ironing has a built-in tendency to multiply and mount. It's so easy to toss a bunch of clothes into the washer and dryer; but such a monumental effort to overcome the barrier that keeps you from getting them wearably back to closets and drawers.

"My ironing resembles a mountain," a neighbor said the other day. "Whenever it threatens to touch the ceiling, I just snatch off the top and iron it." This is true of a lot of us. Or when somebody yells, "I've got to have a shirt," or, "I can't find a decent clean pair of slacks," you dash for the board and get them pressed somehow.

My favorite crack from comedienne Phyllis Diller is—"I'm eighteen years behind on my ironing. There's no use doing it now, it doesn't fit anybody I know!"

Ironing is the primary reason most women hire day help. It's the one job most of us dread. Yet ironing isn't so bad once you get at it, tackle it as if you mean business, and stick to it. And there are ways to simplify and outwit it.

For one thing, if you have a steam iron and a shaker you don't have to go through the long waste motion of dampening. Just steam and sprinkle as you proceed. Or use spray starch. Also, if you wait until after dinner you can iron and yell at people and supervise homework and more or less watch TV at one fell scorch. This diversifying of your attention keeps the job from seeming too much the master, you the slave.

Another good idea is to mend things as you iron them. With button box and sewing machine close by, you can send a blouse back to its owner with all buttons intact, and suture trouser slits. Thus you won't have to start dreading the *mending* once you get the ironing licked.

Another nice thing about *not* having a maid to iron for you is that inevitably a stranger will mix up everybody's belongings so that morning can be a madhouse with people flying from room to room and wrestling through drawers trying to find their own slips or socks.

Yes, indeedy, ironing can be just jim-dandy. Now hand me the classifieds, somebody; tell me a good employment agency. Help! Wanted: Somebody to do the ironing!

CURTAINS

Curtains . . . An armful of ruffled white organdy. A length of lace. Or a thick, lined oblong of material to draw against the dark.

How much of a woman's life is devoted to these innocent-looking tyrants. How many hours in the selecting or making thereof. In the arduous if challenging business of hanging them up and taking them down. In the washing and ironing.

"Did the first people have curtains at their windows?" your little boy asks as you sit whipping up a new set at the sewing machine.

"No. The first people lived in caves with holes in the top to let out the smoke." (Lucky cave women, you think.) "They didn't have windows. The pioneers had windows in their cabins, but sometimes they didn't have glass to keep out the cold. They used paper, I believe I read somewhere."

"Funny papers? Hey, that'd be great."

"No, this was long before comic strips." You shake out the rectangle of ruffled print you are working on. "And I'm sure very few of them actually had curtains until later on."

"Were they too busy making soap and chasing the Indians off?"

"I guess, probably," you laugh. "And I doubt if it was easy to get the material. It was many miles to the nearest store. Most of the material they had, even for clothes, they had to weave themselves. (Come to think of it, you'd rather cope with curtains.) "No, I don't imagine pretty curtains at the windows were a very common sight."

"If they got along without curtains, why don't we?" he reasons, lounging on the sill. With a finger, he begins to write his name on the dusty glass.

"Dear, don't do that."

"Why not? They're dirty, anyway."

"That gives me an idea—you can wash them."

"Oh, boy, can I?" He's still young enough to greet this with rejoicing. With gusto he smears the cleaner and begins boldly to letter his name on that.

"We hang curtains, I guess, because we're used to them," you tell him. "A house looks sort of undressed without its curtains up." And this is true. You recall all the places you have lived, and your parents before you, and those of other people; and how there is always this sense of echoing emptiness until those snug squares are safely in place.

"Also, curtains give us a sense of privacy, so that other people can't see in."

"I *like* to see in. I like going along the street when they have big picture windows and you can see the lamps and the people and what they're doing. Makes it interesting."

"I like to too," you agree. "It's like catching a glimpse of a play on a stage. But they still have draperies, usually, that they can pull when they want."

You snip the final thread, reach for a rod. Anticipation begins to mount as you work the rod through. Nothing like new curtains to brighten up a room. "How'd you like to help me hang them?" you ask. "You may as well learn. You'll be doing it for your wife some day."

THE DINNER HOUR

It happens in almost every house:

At the tender behest of husband and kiddies, Mother takes a well-earned vacation at the home of a cultured, well-to-do, and incidentally childless, girlhood friend.

She returns home not only soothed in body and spirit, but inspired. Meals, for instance. Now there's simply no reason why ours have to be so hectic. Dinner, especially, she thinks. It doesn't take money to achieve an atmosphere of charm and quiet. It merely takes time, efficient management, and the little artistic touches of a woman who simply *cares* enough.

So instead of the more probable pot roast, she lavishes the afternoon on a seafood casserole, replete with herbs and cheese and wine. She crisps up a big green salad, and decides it might even be amusing to start off with little cups of vichyssoise.

As the dinner hour approaches, she interrupts the operations of three vigorously dissenting kite builders on the dining room table, and patiently polishes same. She arranges sprigs of ivy and laurel into a reasonable facsimile of a centerpiece. She gets out the candlesticks.

"Oh, boy, company! Who's coming?" the shout goes up.

"Nobody's coming, but we're all going to *act* like company," she explains. "No arguing, no elbows on the table, just good conversation and good food, with some good music in the background to put us all in the mood."

With an air of sweet resolution, she selects a symphony for the record player. Just a little planning, that's all it takes. Just the props and arrangements of beauty and grace.

But the first fight erupts as she's dishing up. "I get to light the candles." . . . "No, me, no, me!" There is a frantic scrambling, a shoving for position, followed by shouts of anger as somebody blows them out and somebody else burns a finger and goes howling to the bathroom for first aid.

The father, meanwhile, demands, "Why all the ruckus, and why all the dark?" and flicks the overhead lights on.

Oh, well, the candles will still be nice, the mother thinks, lighting them herself and making everybody sit down. And she can't help feeling a proud little thrill over the vichyssoise.

"What's this stuff?" one boy demands, skeptically sniffing.

"A French potato soup. Now eat it, you'll love it." She glances appealingly at her husband, who loyally orders, "That's right, if your mother made it you eat it, whether you like it or not."

This wasn't exactly the reaction she'd anticipated, but no matter. And when the first cup is spilled, and in chain reaction, two more, at least it's a relief from the usual milk. At least if they've got to spill something it's more refined to spill vichyssoise.

The symphony! My goodness, she forgot to put on the symphony, she realizes, leaping up to attend to it, while others dash to the kitchen for sponges, towels, and to summon the dog. Brahms, that's what they needed, a good soothing background of Brahms.

"Turn that thing down," somebody yells as she returns, "I'm on the phone!" The doorbell is ringing. Elbows are on the table and arguments are going strong. The dog provides an efficient but inartistic touch, slurping up the spilled vichyssoise.

She is home.

THE PEOPLE WHO USED TO LIVE HERE

Have you ever felt that sometimes when you buy a house you buy a family with it?

It may be the family that has just packed up and is departing as you (feeling a bit shy and strange, almost the apologetic intruder) move your own crew in. For a little while the ghosts of this former family linger. You find them popping out at you from closets and cupboards—in a sash from a little red dress that still dangles on a hook, a garden hat, a book, a sheaf of accounts, a forgotten toy.

The personality of your predecessor seems to be watching as you get acquainted with her sink, her stove, hang curtains at what were once her windows. "No, no, not that way, stupid," you nevously fancy her scolding. And unconsciously defend, "Look, it's *my* house now, and you'll be surprised at the improvements I'll make."

Then you laugh at your own absurdity—feeling rivals, imagine!—and something warm and nice comes over you as you see that she's left a casserole in the refrigerator, a list of baby sitters, and those bedroom draperies you admired.

In most cases they leave rather quickly, these forerunners who lived here. They fade, they vanish, you forget that this roof and these walls ever sheltered anyone else. No matter how often the neighbors refer to them, or how many preceded you, there is the conviction that this house now firmly and forever has been yours.

Yet in an old house this is not always the case. A very old house that another family built long ago when the neighborhood was new, and lived in fully and richly until they went their separate ways and the house fell into impersonal hands. And though we have lived here twelve years now, I sometimes wonder if the huge old house we occupy will ever fully and completely belong to us? For they were waiting for us in the attic the day we came, those gracious ladies and gentlemen of the past.

They smiled at us from their photographs. And when we plunged into ancient trunks that had obviously been many times around the world, we found even more graphic evidence—for there, enchantingly, were their bustles and bonnets and high-buttoned shoes and tall silk hats.

Many of their letters they left behind them too. Invitations and bits of small talk written in fine and elegant script. Magic lantern slides taken in Egypt, the Philippines, Japan. Diplomas. Citations.

And though they have all been gone for many years now, neighbors—old neighbors who knew them at the height of their prominence, still speak of them. And their words are filled with admiration and affection. "Oh, yes, everybody knew the Corbetts." And people still refer to the house where we live as "The Corbett House."

And one day, to our joy and amazement, some of them, living people, not ghosts at all, but vivid young descendants, came swarming in. And expressed astonishment and delight that we had actually saved some of those souvenirs of their ancestral past.

"Well, we just couldn't bear to throw them out," we admitted. "After building the house and living in it so many years—well, it sort of seemed as if your family, as well as its house, belonged to us."

LONG LOST FRIENDS

It happens in almost every house:

The phone rings and you hear the voice of some friend, relative (or friend of a friend or relative) so long lost you grope to place the identity. "Why—why, how wonderful," you exclaim. "Where *are* you?"

And as they admit they are either in the city or approaching it, "Gracious, we'd just love to see you—" even as you make frantic calculations: How many beds can we make up? Did those towels get back from the laundry? "You—you must come out for dinner." And as they demur that they wouldn't want to put you to any trouble, you not only insist, you find yourself urging that they spend the night. No, no, it won't put you out a bit, you won't do a *thing*.

Hanging up, you gaze wildly about the tumbled house. And food! You can hardly feed them the intended leftovers and it's too late to thaw a roast; you'll have to go to the store. Meanwhile, you start barking orders: "Pat, go clean up your room, they'll have to sleep there—you can have the couch. Freddy, put those puzzles away and sweep the rug. Janey, go out in the yard with Jimmy and see if you can find enough dry branches to start a fire. Also, anything that remotely resembles flowers. Now *hurry*, everybody, they should be here in an hour."

And you go galloping off to the grocery intent only on steak for supper, bacon for breakfast, lettuce, some rolls— and spend twenty dollars. And there's a long line before the cashier, it takes longer than you thought; and as you finally come panting into the homestretch, you see, with sinking heart, the out-of-state car.

They've found a shortcut, they announce triumphantly over the kisses and exclamations—here they are!

And the fireplace that should be blazing brightly is stone cold. Janey comes in with three frostbitten, bedraggled weeds. The sweeper's dead center of the rug while Freddy gazes transfixed at the TV set. And why, oh why didn't you at least put on a skirt before going to the store?

But, still frowsy and frenzied, you strive to be the cordial hostess even as you stash some groceries away, snatch out others. And if your husband is going to have all these relatives why can't he get home and help entertain them? And thank goodness here he is to make the fire and mix the drinks and bolster conversation while you get dinner on.

And between courses you slip to the basement to check the sheets and signal a daughter to iron them before the evening's over, hoping she doesn't get the one with the mended place in the middle. And *where* did you put those thick bright Christmas-present towels?

And you sit up late visiting, showing home movies, getting acquainted or reacquainted, and there is a sense of fellowship, of warmth and goodness and drawing together that compensates for the confusion. And when at last you are all bedded down you whisper to your husband, "They're really lovely, aren't they? I'm really glad they came."

And in the morning you linger over a fresh pot of coffee after the children are off to school. You find yourself urging, "You don't have to go on today, do you? Can't we show you around?" And when the hearty thanks and farewells have been said, you wave at the departing car with a curious sense of loss. "Good-by, good-by, come back soon!" you call—and mean it.

It's been worth all the trouble.

THE FAMILY TABLE

You sit around together, the antique black walnut table that your husband bought with a bunch of junk furniture and lovingly refinished years ago.

It took him months to complete that single project, so carefully did he sand and plane and varnish and wax, until its surface was smooth as glass and hard as stone. It will take the hottest dish and survive the roughest blows. The dog has chewed its legs without much damage; it wasn't too much hurt even when a chafing dish caught fire once and burned up a tablecloth. Long and steady it stands there, opening up for additional leaves when guests are coming, shrinking smaller and smaller as children go away from home.

How many meals have been served there? you sometimes wonder, getting down the plates to set it another time. How many birthday cakes and Thanksgiving turkeys and Christmas dinners has it known? How many kites have littered its broad expanse, how many model planes and scrapbooks and doll clothes?

How many bills have been paid there, how many notes written to teachers, how many income tax forms? For that matter, how many apples have probably been peeled there, how much canning done? For it bore the marks of knives and jars and water buckets when your husband first came carting it home.

And you think back to all those other lives which came to this selfsame table before you. The women, busy at their humble kitchen tasks before clearing it, as was often done, to set it for supper. The men who sat down to carve. And the children, the many children, excited about their birthday cakes, their Thanksgiving drumsticks, their news about love affairs or school.

People. Living people drawn together at a sturdy table. And you think of the laughter and the tears and the arguments and stormy scenes this table has known. They are its essence, a part of it like its grain. And it is this which gives an antique its true value and meaning. It is old and warm and wise with living. It is like a person who only grows more beautiful with age.

THOSE "VALUABLE COUPONS"

Help! They arrive in a plain envelope marked "occupant," and though you're tempted to throw them away unopened, you know it's hopeless. The children will only rescue them exclaiming, "Look, Mommy, why look, here's a letter you didn't open."

And they're even more excited when they discover its contents. Bright-hued coupons that sometimes look like money. Slips that proclaim the wonders of soup or soap, margarine or mayonnaise, and what's more will save you ten cents on your next purchase.

So that you realize, "Dear me, that's right, I really ought to take advantage of this." Arousing in you guilt feeling for your rash improvidence if you don't, albeit a kind of resentment at being so insidiously enslaved.

So the next time you go to market you've got to remember to take the darned things along. And oh, dear, where are they? And so many of them, too—how they accumulate.

So instead of poking pleasantly down the aisles selecting what you want or need, you find yourself on a kind of half-amused, half-determined treasure hunt, scouting out the certain brands (often of items you never use and have a sneaking suspicion you never will). Yet once dedicated to this silly mission you feel morally obligated to track down every so-called bargain, from perfumed starch to fluted sandwich bags.

Now there follows some frenetic arithmetic. In addition to all the coupons clutched in your fists, you are further lured by a sign above the scouring powder which announces, "Two for 27 cents." And wait, as if this weren't enough, another sign upon each can joyously proclaims, "Ten cents off!"

With a gush of gratitude for the manufacturer, you reach for the spoils. Two goes into twenty-seven how many times? Well, let's make it roughly fourteen cents a can (fractions always throw you). Hey, and then there's ten cents off. That leaves it four cents apiece; times two makes eight cents—and you're holding a coupon worth ten cents. Why, at this rate you'll come out money ahead!

The cashier dashes your triumph, however. The ten cents off doesn't apply if you're buying two for one, he informs you. Your dime saving coupon applies only to the super-giant size selling for fifty-nine cents. And half the other coupons expired three months ago.

Too exhausted and embarrassed even to consider trekking around putting things back, you haul them home. Only to find further enslavement tucked diabolically inside each package. A spanking new coupon leers at you: "Fifteen cents off!"

"YOUR HOUSE SMELLS SO GOOD"

Houses are like the people who live in them. They are a showcase of the kind of things people like to have about them. And subtly yet distinctively they reveal their occupants' nature in the very way they smell.

One of my neighbors' houses has such a clean and housewifey scent. It smells of the ironing she's always doing at odd hours—of the flocks of crisp little dresses and starched white shirts that hang over the backs of chairs. . . . It smells of the baby—its formula, its freshly folded diapers, its talcum, and its toys. . . . It smells of the big brown pot roast simmering in the kitchen, and the just baked cinnamon rolls set out to cool.

Some houses smell of sickness and age and mustiness and death. They are dark and unaired and dismal. Yet the houses of old people need not have this odor.

My own grandparents' home always smelled of apples. There were great bins of them in the basement, brought in from the farm. Grandmother kept a huge blue Chinese bowl of them on the dining room table, and our grandpa, who seemed to us a very old man, a man of great dignity and dominance, with a perky Uncle Sam goatee, would pare them for us, the peels uncoiling rosily on the thick white linen cloth. . . . The kitchen smelled of gingerbread and sour cream cookies, and the upstairs of sachet.

Kitchen fans have their place and deodorizers too, I guess. But I don't mind home smells, people smells. The smells of bacon frying, or onions, don't offend me in the least. Or the smell of pets. Or the smell of a father's greasy guns and hobbies.

These odors are the breath of living. They are human. They are good.

A Woman and Her Children

I love these little people, and it is not a slight thing when they, who are so fresh from God, love us.

—*Charles Dickens*

CHILDREN'S HANDS

Children's Hands . . .
   First they are but tiny tendrils, gripping your finger, brushing at your breast . . .
   Next they are plump and dimpled, getting into things so that you must say, "No, no!" continually. Or, "Mustn't touch, naughty hands.". . .
   Then, still small and grubby, they are clutching crayons, scribbling. Or groping awkwardly with pencils, learning to print their names . . .
   Then soon, so soon, they are lengthening—catching baseballs, swinging ropes for jumping, playing jacks . . .
   And a little longer still, anxiously struggling to tie a necktie for a party, or applying a first excited touch of lipstick . . .
   And now, longer and stronger yet, they are being fitted for class rings, adjusting the unfamiliar robes and tasseled hats for Commencement, reaching out to take diplomas from older, surer hands . . .

And after that outstretched so eagerly and confidently for engagements rings, and wedding rings, and jobs . . .

And then, completed, they take up the new, the just beginning, with wonder and pride. Lifting her own child, the new mother marvels, "Isn't he beautiful?" Just look at those tiny hands!

PINK OR BLUE?

You wonder sometimes which is the more lively, the more spirited, the more trouble—little boys or little girls.

Little boys throw things when they get wound up (which is practically always). They are likely to snatch anything from a cap to a ball to a lamp. Or they take swipes at each other, grab each other with joyous abandon, kick, shriek, hurl each other to the ground, and wrestle like noisy, nipping cubs.

They are a threat to everything on the place, including and especially your nerves. Exposed to them for any length of time, you are likely to think in sheer desperation, "Boys are absolutely and utterly impossible. Give—oh, give me little girls!"

Then the little girls come flocking in. Little girls with their squeals, their screams, their giggles. Little girls are less likely to throw things, but they have other methods of wrecking havoc—such as chasing each other wildly around a table. Or hauling out all your pans, spoons, cups, and glasses for a tea party. Or getting into your lipstick, perfume, hats, evening dresses, and high-heeled shoes. Or dumping boxes of "little people" complete with furniture, dead center of the rug. Most of this to the accompaniment of knife-shrill voices calling bossily to each other, plus such side effects as face-making, tickling, hip and shoulder wiggling, and stuck-out tongues.

Let a herd of little girls take over the premises, and rare is the person who doesn't recall his former plea to heaven and implore, "Give, oh give me little boys!"

PARENTAL PUZZLES

Have you ever wondered why:

. . . Though you know exactly what your child looks like and don't find his looks any particular treat at home, it becomes of such vital consequence to spot that beaming being as he marches in with the others for a program at church or school. Or why, once located, he is just about the *only* one your eyes can feast upon?

. . . They always get sick on schooldays, rather than bright, sunny weekends?

. . . When they're little they laugh hilariously at your jokes and beg for more? When they're older they say, "Oh, Mother, don't be corny."

. . . Children are so much more eager to help with the work at somebody else's house than at home?

. . . They always seem to look and act their worst when you're most anxious to show them off?

. . . It's so much easier to see how other people should manage their offspring than to know what to do about your own?

. . . They look so unutterably innocent when they're asleep?

PLAYING JACKS

Oh, what is so lovely as a circlet of little girls playing jacks? Their bright skirts bloom upon the concrete step. Their knees are bare and brown and their sneakers dirty. Their voices rise and fall like the bouncing ball; they giggle with the same merry tinkle as the raining jacks.

Onesies, twosies. Upsies, downsies, babies in the cradle . . . Sweep the floor . . . Pigs in the pen . . . Go to church.

They exclaim and discuss and argue and laugh.

They get as excited about the old combinations as you once did, and introduce more you've never heard of: Fast Chicago . . . Jack-be-nimble . . . Snake in the grass . . . Fly to the moon . . .

And you remember the thrill of new jacks in your pocket, jingling as you scurried to school. The bright coppery glint of those double-x's. The rubber ball, red as an apple; or the nicked but aristocratic golf balls that briskly spanked the stone and shot to haughty heights.

Little crowds, cohesive as a bridge club, dashed to claim the choicest slabs at school. The undisputed champion was a quiet, angular girl, whose skeletal fingers plucked and scooped with a lovely, awesome, exasperating skill. Though you practiced fervently for hours, you couldn't approach that rare, odd, singular grace that conquered all.

Jacks were easily lost. Reduced to two or three, your store was augmented with rough pebbles found along the lakeshore. Humble, yet charmingly, they glinted when tossed onto the sidewalk.

Now again you hear the leaping ball, the laughter and the arguments, the rainy spatter of the tiny objects flung and deftly snatched. You hear the children reaching out in this time of life's early morning, as children before them reached out in ancient civilizations, playing their games of skill.

The voices, the music of the jacks—a timeless song of history itself.

LITTLE BOYS

Your little boy awakes and cries because of a bad dream.

His hot small body clings to you as you sit on the edge of the bed. You feel the firm curves of it through the thin crumpled pajamas. His fat cheeks are moist and the tips of his lashes are moist and fragile, too, against your cheek.

You hold him on your lap and comfort him and know the joy of holding and comforting him, of being his mother to whom he turns when unhappy or afraid.

You think of some fracas in the yard, his demanding in a plaintive howl, "Mummy, help! Billy took my shubble!" And though he is sent back usually to settle the trouble himself, it comes to you with some thrilling sense of wonder and privilege how good it is to be, for this little while, supreme commander of his day. The person omnipotent, who is empowered and entrusted to heal all hurts, answer all questions, meet all his many demands.

And holding and comforting him there in the dark, you think how soon he will be a big leggy boy, remote and roughly shy, not wanting your caresses any more.

And how he will become a man and go away from home and perhaps do splendid things, things of which you'll boast, but in which life gives no mother any real part. How you will become a shadowy figure to him, someone of whom he thinks with fondness and tenderness and concern, perhaps, but no longer vital or essential to him, because that is life's way.

And it comes to you how brief and filled with glory are these early years of parenthood.

How those who are young mothers are creatures of special privilege, for all the trouble and bother and often unutterable weariness we know. How we should live every moment with our youngsters to the utmost, creating bright memories and hoarding them like riches against the inevitable loss to come.

Few, so tragically few of us, have the faintest conception of what other, older women feel.

"This is my son!" they proudly say, taking a photograph from the mantel and speaking of his accomplishments, while we murmur polite admiration.

This night, however, holding your own little fellow, you begin to understand:

He is lost to them. Gone. But in showing his picture to others, speaking of him to people who can't possibly care, they are recreating him for themselves. Bringing back the little boy who woke up crying in the night, who could be comforted, caressed, and held close against his too swift growing up.

THE FAMILY HEARING AID

A housewife has been described as a combination cook, nurse, laundress, and cleaning woman.

The housewife who is also a mother is all these things and more—she serves as a personnel manager. And not the least of her arts in this respect is that of family listener.

Mothers, I am convinced, develop a phenomenal sense of hearing. Perhaps to compensate for the almost total deafness enjoyed by nearly everyone else in the family.

Sitting exactly three feet across the table from each other, children can hardly convey the simplest messages without, "Huh? What'd you say? Whad'you want? Don't talk with your mouth full. Honestly, Mom, you ought to do something about her manners."

"What she means is she wants to borrow your bike, hers has a flat tire and they're going on this bike hike tomorrow," the mother explains, knowing full well that he can't hear because he doesn't *want* to lend his bike and is trying to divert the whole conversation into a hassle over why his sister talks with her mouth full. Multiply this situation by as many offspring as are gathered at the groaning board, and you will find the typical mother as active as any United Nations interpreter.

Her role is not simplified by the fact that fathers often consume their food groping through such clouds of business concerns that they are only vaguely aware of how many people are present—let alone able to hear clearly the remarks directed their way.

"Who? What coach? What'd he want?" the male parent swims briefly to the surface of discussion. "What's all this about, anyway?"

"Jimmy's coach, dear," his wife tactfully tries to elucidate. "Jimmy was just telling you—there's this new rule about going out for track, and Jimmy feels—"

There must be good reasons why mothers find themselves continually passing the conversational ball, running interference. Standing dead center of the family playing field, we not only are usually tackled first on any issue, we develop a kind of sixth sense about it. An intuitive understanding of who really does mean *what*—and a fervent desire that everybody else get the straight of it, too.

But it's wearing, being the ears of a family. If my own

audio powers should ever wane, there will be a hard time selling me a hearing aid!

A CHILD'S BIRTHDAY

Why are birthdays so enchanting to a child? Beside this signal event every other holiday pales.

"When's my birthday?" they begin to ask, almost as soon as they learn to speak. "How long till my birthday?" And they climb on chairs to consult the calendar, argue mightily as to whose birthday comes first in a family and whose is next and who, therefore, has longest to wait.

Although their very *own* birthday is, of course, supreme, they drain every drop of delight from the birthdays of others. Ah, the ecstasy of birthday secrets—shopping, presents hidden, cards laboriously lettered. And the fun of the mailman's coming:

"You got a present! Here, I'll help you open it." And the ensuing struggle—"Honey, no, it's her birthday, remember, let her—"

And the wistful watching as small clumsy fingers grapple with paper and ribbon. "Oh, boy, gee, look!"

And the fun of helping to bake the cake, of trimming it, lighting the candles with quick scared darts of a match. And the final triumphant procession as the winner of the argument grandly carries it in. The shrill little voices singing, "Happy birthday to yoooo. Happy birthday toooo yooooew!" In these ways they reap vicarious pleasure, and preview their own coming reign . . .

For the youngster having the birthday is indeed king or queen. Special, from the moment of waking. His eyes sparkle. He walks in a proud new way. He must be spanked, of course. And measured—heels flat against the wall and a book upon his head. "How much bigger am I than last year?" he eagerly demands. "How much have I grown?"

And he must ask, no matter how often you've told him, "What time was I born?" And his face wears a special wonder as you explain. He ponders the remarkable fact of his being. How exciting. How marvelous just to have been born!

Is that perhaps why birthdays hold such magic for a child? Perhaps far more than the fact of his presents, he thrills to the gift of—himself.

"We are the guests of existence," Pasternak said . . . And a child is so new a guest.

Oh, to retain that early fervor for living. That first rosy blush of being in love with life itself. To find in each birthday a renewal of wonder at our own creation.

THE BLANKET ROLL

"To make a bedroll, put your oldest and dirtiest blanket on the bottom," your Bluebird directs as you kneel on the living room rug.

"Well, our oldest blankets are at the cabin, but this is certainly the dirtiest one. In fact I ought to wash it—"

"Oh, no, this is lovely, it's real nice and dirty," your daughter enthusiastically approves. "Now you're supposed to put the other things on top and fold the ends."

You gasp as she hands you the instructions. "Why, dear, this doesn't say dirtiest blanket, it only says darkest one."

"Well, dirty means dark, doesn't it? Now come on, let's fold in my boots and stuff."

Mother and daughter take ends of the bulky mess and begin. But objects skid around, and your child giggles. "It sure is lumpy."

"It certainly is. Let's unroll it and start over."

"Daddy ought to be here, he'd fix it."

"Well, women can do these things too—it says here. C'mon, roll."

After three attempts, each sloppier than the last, you give up and settle for what you have. "We seem to be getting worse. Let's tie it. Oh, for Pete's sake, a bowline knot—and I never was a good Girl Scout!"

"This is Campfire Girls."

"Well, the knots, I dread to think, are all the same."

"Just follow the directions."

"Directions are something I've never had much faith in, but let's see. 'A. Lay free end over standing part.' Now this must be the free end—" You get a firm grip on the end of a ball of twine. "But I can't see anything standing, can you?"

"Maybe the boots are standing up inside."

"That's not exactly what they mean. 'B. Bring it through this loop from underneath.'" You can't seem to see any loop either, and the illustrations don't help. "Nuts, let's just forget about the bowline till they teach you, and do it up the best we can."

"Sure, anybody that can tie a package can tie up a blanket, Mom."

It's not that simple, however. Suddenly you seem to have two free ends, and the twine has acquired a squirming life of its own. The ball collapses into a mass of loops and coils that gets worse the harder you strive to encircle and bind the long woolly worm of a so-called blanket roll.

"Don't worry, Mother. Here, I'll help you. Oh, golly, I've got it snarled around my feet."

"Watch out, honey, you're making it worse. Oh, dear, they're out there now, they're honking—and the roll's coming apart!"

You grab a sagging end, stuff objects madly back in, and make a quickly strangling pass with the twine. "Here, give me the scissors, I'll just tie it wherever it sags and cut it off."

"Sure, Mother, don't you worry." She kisses you and struggles the massive monster into her arms. "Just so it holds together till we get to camp. Why, this is okay, this is fine!"

Staggering a little under its bulk, but beaming reassuringly over her shoulder, your Bluebird lugs her blanket roll to the car. As yet, nothing comes spilling out—no toothpaste, soap, nor beans nor candy bar. With fingers crossed, and praying, you return her trusting wave good-by.

HOLD FAST

Watch it with wonder, hold it fast—the gangling length of a little boy, the slender, tender dimensions of a fast-growing little girl . . .

You test this state of growing more often than not just after a meal. For you are sitting at the table, and they are just leaving their chairs. It seems you must reach out to them an instant before they go. "Come sit on my lap a minute, let's see how big you are."

And quickly, if sometimes a bit shyly, they oblige. Grinning, they settle themselves upon your inadequate knees. Cocking their heads to show they are really a bit beyond all this, yet with the relaxed enjoyment of animals still taking comfort in the nest, they cuddle, arms about your neck.

"Can't do this much longer, Mother, soon we'll be bigger than you."

"Okay, it'll be my turn then, you'll have to hold me."

They not only fervently promise, the prospect so intrigues them they sometimes insist on clambering down and trying you on their spindly laps for size . . .

To draw near to one another, that is the main thing. To hold each other fast. Physical demonstrations of affection are as needful in the human family as food. To restrain them may be to walk the cold and proper road to adult dignity, but it is also to stunt the emotions and starve the heart.

Hold your children in your arms as long as you can. And when you can't, let them hold you!

TO PUSH A BABY CARRIAGE

A mother tucking her child into a baby carriage is a special and privileged being.

For a carriage arches over something wonderfully new and small and yours alone. Reaching into its cozy confines to check the baby, you too are shielded there, cupped in a safe small shelter that must hark back to the distant days when you were the sleeping infant being made comfortable to his journey into the world of out of doors.

The smell of leather mingles with the scent of fluffy blankets and the sweet scent of a baby just bathed. You arrange the tiny bonneted head on the embroidered pillow, smooth the pretty gift spread. Then down the steps carefully, tilting back, trying not to jolt your precious cargo.

Just to push a baby carriage is a gently satisfying thing. And this too harks back to days distant and half forgotten. The thrill of trundling your very own doll carriage down the street. How maternal little girls feel then; what a sense of power and privilege, to grasp a handle and guide this heavy, protective, joyous, signal vehicle.

There is never a second's loneliness, pushing a baby carriage. Children come rushing up to tag along beside you. Passing people smile and steal a glance. Or parking it a moment before a grocery store, you come out to find someone peeping in. For who can resist the marvel—a human being still so small that he lies sleeping on his tummy in public?

Even walking alone, without contact with other people, there is this secret, quiet, enthralled communion with the passenger so royally propelled.

You smile too, you lean forward to make your presence known. You pause to turn him over, settle him afresh. "See the trees!" you long to say to him, and sometimes do. "See the sky? This is the world, a great big wonderful place that belongs to you too."

The days of pushing a baby carriage do not last long. Some mothers miss it altogether, what with so many errands done by car, and the speed with which strollers appear on the scene. Which seems a pity. Because it's one of the oldest traditions of motherhood, symbolized by a first doll buggy. Just one of those special, brief but beautiful times in a woman's life when she feels complete.

"WHEN I WAS SICK AND LAY ABED"

I wonder if Stevenson had mothers in mind when he wrote the lines: "When I was sick and lay abed I had two pillows at my head. And all my toys beside me lay to keep me happy all the day."

For who provides the fat white pillows and is called to

rearrange them a dozen times a day? As for all the "toys that beside me lay!"

Now according to the picture books Stevenson's ailing patient was quite tidily consoled by a ball, a boat, a bear, and a flock of wooden soldiers. Today's sick-abed son adds to this basic equipment an Erector Set, Tinker Toys, a wood-burning outfit, model airplanes to be assembled, and sometimes a cardboard cupboard filled with dire chemicals.

And no matter *how* sick he is, he not only summons the strength to work with them, but to keep his nurse on a constant trot for such supplies as scissors, paints, pans of water, candles, cardboard boxes, the hammer, the pliers, and the glue.

If the victim (other than you) is a girl, you assemble an entire family of dolls, often with complete wardrobes. And if you've had any experience on the sickroom detail at all, you march right on to your sewing corner to dig out needles, thread, and inevitable scissors, and a bag of bright scraps with which to make additions to the aforementioned wardrobes.

Also you brace yourself for the indubitable call for paper dolls, paint boxes, books, bead stringing sets and sets for the weaving of pot holders, plus such miscellany as pencils, paste, and crayons.

Usually the bed is so full by the time the doctor arrives he can hardly find the patient. You have to make wild scooping motions in order for him to have a place to sit down, let alone write a prescription or hold the medicines.

Ironically enough, by the time evening comes it's the child who feels frisky. In fact, he's usually revived by his day of rest and attention, he tears out of bed so full of vigor it's all you can do to drive him *back* to bed when it's time to be there.

By then you're so tired you're practically praying for somebody to prescribe a couple of days' complete rest for you.

No wonder a mother secretly groans when a child complains of a morning, "I dooon't feel good." Conscientious though our concern, as we anticipate the day's trotting, we dooon't feel goood either!

SO YOUNG, SO BUSY

How busy children are.

"Mother, where's some paper? I simply must have some heavy paper for my dollhouse."

And she burrows through toy cupboards and drawers, hunts down the scissors, the paste. And you see her and her companions on their knees vigorously laboring away.

Or they get out their coloring books and work as fervently as if they were preparing for a show at the gallery. Or they tackle their stick-em books or their embroidery cards. Or, with many pleas for help ("Thread this needle, will you?" "Tie the knot—" "I can't cut it out very well—") make doll clothes.

Or little boys will sweat and pant and heave for hours fashioning a tree house, a fort, a play car out of an old box with roller skates for wheels.

Or they will bang and saw earnestly away, creating a fleet of toy boats, wooden airplanes, or nameless "scientific" gadgets made out of a piece of board, scrap tin, nails, and spools.

However our society may have spoiled them with plastic toys and model kits that stifle half the creative effort, they still manage to fill their hours (and clutter the house) with the things they are continually making, drawing, contriving. Nature has endowed her human young with sheer creative energy which must be expended, whatever the society in which they live.

It is a constant struggle to know what to do with these efforts as you strive to keep order in a house. Throw them all out, the result of so much living labor? It seems too cruel, somehow. Also, there is the ever-present prospect that some treasure will be missed and demanded the minute it's gone. A mother must be constantly facing such decisions. How much longer will Johnny cling to that insane clutter of lances, sabers, and shields he and a pal have fashioned? After all, they don't play with them any more.

But you know, as you pause in your closet cleaning (and can't help marveling at the ingenuity of the arsenal) that the actual use they have been put to is not the test. They have already served their major purpose, the ships and swords and pictures and paper dolls. And though you cannot resist tucking a few away to be saved, yourself, from sheer sentiment, the majority must be cast out.

However painful it is to be the one who must destroy, you know that something far more vital is constantly being preserved: The experience, the practice, the small but many steps taken forward in the long march of learning.

After all, you think, regarding the house that must be constantly cleaned, the laundry, the dishes, the cooking to be done over and over—woman's work is an endless procession, with each day's result consumed. And the same is true of man.

Perhaps, as children dedicate themselves so avidly to their self-imposed creations, they are only preparing for the routine of life's labors. And discovering, en route, that the reward is in the doing.

A CHILD'S GARDEN

Every child should have a little garden all his own.

Let it be close enough to the big folks' garden so that he will feel secure, squatting on his haunches there, becoming intimate with clods and angleworms. But let it be far enough that he may learn the utter loveliness of grubbing the ground alone.

Let it be his kingdom, where he is absolute swaggering potentate. And let it be his farm where he can plant and tend his crops, and reap a bountiful harvest—of radishes, and weeds, and lettuce and carrots and snails, and little jingling rocks, and dreams.

Let his equipment for this patch be his own bright rake, and a red-handled shovel, and a hoe, a trowel, a watering can. And a mother's love. And a dad's sage advice.

Let him have, of course, many gaily colored packets of seeds, to rattle and show to his friends—and open, and spill, and strew in his wobbly rows. And let these seeds be good lively seeds, eager to reach their roots into the soil, quick in their climb toward the sun.

But first let the child know the sweet agony of waiting. Of anticipation. Of a daily rush to look for the miracle. And then just before he loses heart, let the fragile green stripes reward him. Let him drop on all fours to touch the tiny, newborn spears with his fingers. Let his eyes shine. Let him cry out in high, proud excitement, "My garden's up! It grew!"

Let the earth in every child's garden be rich and good, to nurture the things he has planted, and nurture as well his life. . . . Let it smell loamy and lush after a watering, or rain. Let it have a dry baking tingle for his nostrils in the heat of noon. And oh, let him sniff with delight at these earth scents, breathe them deep into his being. Let him sense in some buried core of his own awareness that it is earth's fertility and finality that makes him kin to God.

Let the child get dirt on his hands and streaked across his face. Let him sweat as he hacks with his hoe and pulls at those thrillingly wild and stubborn enemies, the weeds. Let him learn what it is to be tired and hot and dirty with labor and never to be ashamed.

And let the beetle bugs come, and the foraging rabbits, and all the countless creatures, winged or footed or crawling, that with such innocent, driving purpose take unto themselves a portion of what men grow. Let a child discover their ways, along with the ways of seeds and sun. . . . Let him lie for a dreamy spaceless time upon his tummy, watching the progress of a furry caterpillar. And hearing the soft, bullet thudding of grasshoppers; the swift scurrying of bunnies and chipmunks—and maybe a thieving elf, or a sprite or two. For overhead, let the sky be so blue, the clouds so whitely gliding, all things in children's gardens take on a magical quality.

Let the child reap the results of his efforts. A fistful of saucy-tailed radishes. Some spindly carrots, too thickly planted, of course, and not thinned. A saucepan of peas, half-spilled before reaching the house. Long, lumpy green pendants of beans. . . . Let at least one meal be glorified by a mother's boast, "Joey raised nearly everything on the table." And let the child know that most splendid fulfillment of all—producing enough of something to give away.

Let every growing child have a garden all his own!

A TENT

Children must all be the descendants of nomads, for they would live their lives out, if you let them, in a tent.

They discover the joy of this triangular shelter when they are very young. Let any mother start airing blankets on a line, and her offspring are sure to come scurrying between the blankets' flapping sides.

"A tent! A tent!" they shout in delight. "This will be my tent and that pink one yours. We'll be neighbors and live in our tents."

Sometimes they prevail on their mother to string up a line especially for the purpose and over it drape an old unused spread or quilt. Staked to the ground with little sticks, it makes a lovely tent. There, with their dolls and their dishes and their little toy stoves, they set up housekeeping, crawling joyfully in and out to obtain crackers and jelly sandwiches and to pick tiny bouquets of clover or dandelions. They urge you to creep in on all fours—into this cozy, sun-fragrant, grassy haven, where they crouch in such delight.

When they are older, they must have a real canvas tent to make their pleasure complete. A waterproof tent, where they can be snug even in a shower. A place where they can sometimes "sleep out." A tent to take on camping trips. Every summer, their dad digs it out from under the porch and aids in setting it up in the yard.

And there, for a few days, it becomes the social center of the neighborhood. Club meetings are held there, and tea parties, and fights. And the inevitable pleas bombard you: "Oh, please, may we sleep out tonight? Let us sleep in the tent!"

This, too, usually brings on arguments. The little ones

want to join the big ones and their friends, which is un-thinkable: "We want to *talk*! Besides there isn't room." The boys want it the same night as the girls. "And don't forget whose tent it really is," some long-forgotten claim is laid. "I got it for Scouts, remember. So it's *my tent*!"

And when some of these matters are settled, the most elaborate plans go oft awry. Mosquitoes, a hoot owl, an unexpected fright ("We heard this *terrible noise!*") will send a covey of girls tearing to the house, clutching their sheets. And even when they do finally settle down and get to sleep, *you* can't. They're so crowded, how do they stand it? And it's chilly. Have they got enough blankets? You toss and turn and worry and finally steal outside with a flashlight. Cautiously, you lift the flap and peer in.

And there, crammed together on the hard ground, they are blissfully snoozing. Close to nature, close to their primordial ancestors, no doubt, they are sleeping the sleep of the wild, the free, the innocent; the peaceful sleep of the young, when all the world is new and summertime is eternal—in a tent.

"PLEASE MAY WE GO SWIMMING?"

Those who claim that all life began in the ocean must surely have children.

Even infants have an affinity for water that must spring from deep wells of the past.

The baby, still too wobbly to hold up his head, loves to be lowered into his bath. And it becomes the major event of his day when he is old enough to be able to play and splash.

Then when the wonderful world of water is discovered outside the home his ecstasy is boundless—and adamant. Observe the small fry in any wading pool. Except for the occasional youngster who is terrified, the only screams you hear are those of pleasure—or of angry protest at being hauled out.

As they grow older their love for water seems to become more desperate, a need. "Oh, please may we go swimming?

Please, please, please!" And heaven help the parent who for reasons of his own must deny that frenzied imploring, for it is like bucking some natural force that is as strong as the ocean itself.

Almost no child will ever leave water of his own volition. He must be called, exhorted, threatened, and sometimes dragged bodily from its liquid embrace. And rare indeed is the time when he is too cold, or too sunburned, or too waterlogged to stay out if there is the slightest chance to go swimming again. In fact, barely is he dried, fed, and diverted toward some other course of action before he is beginning to whine, then to argue, then to plead.

My own would go swimming five or six times a day, if allowed. In fact, they seem to draw some peculiar sustenance from the water, some nourishment that makes mere meals unnecessary.

Sometimes when they are swimming I have the eerie feeling that they must be watched lest in some moment when I'm not looking they sprout fins and disappear.

And whenever I hear myself saying things like, "No, you can't go swimming, it's too cold—" Or, "Now you come right in this minute or you can't go tomorrow—" echoes of my own parents' voices rise in my ears. I remember so acutely it is like pain, standing on a dock that rocked beneath my feet, and gazing down, down into the gray-blue wonder of it all. And knowing that if I were not allowed to plunge into it at once, to merge with it, explore it, identify with it completely with body and spirit, my soul would die.

A child's need and love for water is instinctive and eternal.

THEY'RE ONLY LITTLE ONCE

Two small naked boys splash wildly in the big white tub, their bodies shiny under the bathroom lights. The older flails the water and hurls it into his little brother's excited, uplifted rosy face. He doesn't mind. Blinking, rubbing his face and eyes, he shrieks with delight and tries vainly to hurl the water back.

They thresh about, grabbing for the soap; they throw their sodden washcloths. Their hair plasters their heads like the feathers of drowned birds.

Patiently and helplessly you sit waiting with the towels, urging them to stop, to get out, with a kind of rhythmic hopelessness. Finally you pull the plug, though they still flail about like seals, sliding down the tub's edge, trying to chin themselves on the towel bars. The younger laughs, makes faces, imitates his big brother's every antic.

Finally, meaning business, you haul one out bodily, and the other hastily scrambles. The older seems suddenly long-legged, rangy and limby beside the younger's chubby curves as—with much cavorting, he sketchily dries himself. You grab more towels and give both a vigorous rubbing, from the head down. You don't risk letting them hold the talcum powder, not tonight! Lifting high the can you give them each a brief dousing and shoo them out.

"They're only little once," you remind yourself for the tenth time, mopping up.

Thank goodness!

PACKED SUITCASES

Life is a long long journey, marked by a line of luggage through which you can almost trace a woman's biography:

There are her first childish belongings put excitedly into a satchel for that first visit to Grandma, or to spend the night with a friend.

And after that the slightly larger bag that she fills with such eager anticipation for a sojourn to camp.

And then the trunks to be arranged and rearranged, with a mother's hovering help, then carried on a father's stout shoulders, as she prepares for college.

And the shining dignity and wonder of cases that she fills with all the secret lovely things for her wedding journey.

And the small bag packed, often weeks ahead, patiently awaiting the joyous dash to the hospital to have her first baby . . .

Somehow all this comes flooding poignantly back as we supervise the packing of our own children's bags:

A small boy eagerly stuffing his new, very own suitcase with his toothbrush, his favorite pajamas, and a rabbit dirty and worn from loving, getting ready to go to the hospital to have his tonsils out.

The earnest inventory of socks and sheets and swimming suits as a son or daughter also pack up for camp.

The hauling down of dusty trunks from the attic to see if they'll hold the countless things that our offspring must carry away to college.

The suitcases lying open upon a bed, being filled by another starry-eyed girl before another wedding trip.

The catch in the throat as you come across it later, standing patiently waiting in another hallway—the small bag filled with the tiny garments for your grandchild's first homecoming . . .

Life is all too swift a journey!

The Man You Married

There is nothing stronger and nobler than when man and wife are of one heart and mind in a house, a grief to their foes, and to their friends great joy, but their own hearts know it best.

—Homer

IN DEFENSE OF AMERICAN MEN

Don't tell me the average American male is becoming soft. There have been a spate of articles decrying this so-called "trend," and personally I resent every one of them.

Recently I climbed down off the roof where I was helping my husband build a house, to relax and read. Here I'd had a lot of fun swinging a hammer and even mixing cement, all the while visualizing myself as a sturdy pioneer woman helping her mate wrest a home from the wilderness. According to this article before me I'd been all wrong: Men should be men, and women women—and never should their traditional duties overlap. Above all, and particularly, men should be above such menial pursuits as helping with the housework or putting a bevy of kids to bed.

Then there are the patently false stereotypes of Dad foisted on us by stories and cartoons that depict him as a kind of ineffectual nincompoop. But these seem to me no more false than the stereotypes of the stern Victorian father who never deigned to dry a dish, and rules the roost. If we were transported to the Good Old Days I suspect that we'd find far fewer of these archetypes than is popularly supposed.

My own father's boast was that he'd washed dishes for my mother the night they met and been doing it every night for forty years. I also cherish happy memories of his bathing his little flock, then with one on each arm of his squeaky rocker and one on his lap, singing us all to sleep.

My mother was not a dominating woman, and she practiced no career. My father worked long and hard at very masculine labor. He did these things for the selfsame reason that thousands of good men do them still: Because he loved his wife and children. And these tasks were the most enjoyable way he knew of to express that love.

American men are not sissies. They're simply wonderful husbands!

HOW TO MAKE A HUSBAND HAPPY

It's the little things that speak subtly yet most reassuringly of love in a home. When it comes to husbands, we so often take them for granted.

We are so busy mothering the children we forget that men are secretly but grown-up little boys inside, and they'd sometimes like a bit of inconspicuous mothering and looking after, too.

Here are some of the little things a woman can do for hers:

Make sure his shirts are done the way he likes them, whether by yourself, the maid, or the laundry. And if the laundry, that they're taken and delivered on time. Also that the buttons are on . . .

Press and have clean and available his favorite ties . . .

Occasionally (though don't make a habit of it) shine his shoes . . .

Take care of his clothes. See that his suits are safely gotten to and from the cleaner's and in good repair . . .

Refrain from attempting to take care of his stamp or coin collections, his fishing or hunting gear, or his tools . . .

Buy food and cook it with his preferences in mind. Surprise him sometimes with a special dish . . .

Make just as much fuss over his birthday as you like him to make over yours. And on your wedding anniversary, buy him a card . . .

Keep the day's mail in a convenient place where he can find and enjoy it when he gets home . . .

Don't let the children dissect the evening paper before he can get to it . . .

Train them not to bombard him with pleas and problems the minute he walks in, and don't do so yourself. Wait until after dinner when he's relaxed and more in a mood to cope.

FATHERS AND MOTHERS—DIFFERENT GOALS

What most parents want above all else for their children is happiness and success.

And while generalizations never fit all cases, it seems to me that mothers are more often striving for the happiness, the fathers for the success.

Women are with their children so much that we become keenly attuned to their moods and emotions, their secret (and often not so secret) desires. Women are like sensitive instruments that not only continually pick up and record their offspring's heartbeats, but react in kind.

When they hurt, we hurt. When they rejoice our own spirits soar. When they need or desperately want something, we often want it for them even more.

Women, in the interest of their children, are continually anticipating, laying plans. It is the mothers, usually, who arrange for dancing or music lessons, preview a neighborhood to gauge its social suitability for their young, arrange to get tickets for children's concerts, interview teachers, do what they can for good schools.

And men have a great and genuine share in all this. It is the men who cheerfully pay the bills, haul the progeny to their mother-maneuvered destinations, physically participate. Because men, bless them, want the good life too, for their sons and daughters. But in a subtly different way. Men want to be proud of their children; they want them to succeed.

It seems to me that a woman's approach is primarily emotional. While children's "happiness" is of less immediate concern to men than the knowledge that they are soundly prepared to meet and triumph over life's vicissitudes.

A DAD, A BOY, AND A CAR

It begins when they're about fourteen, this curious disease of wanting to drive, work on, own a car.

There is no inoculation against it, and no medicine as yet discovered that will ease its pangs—either for the victim or his father. Nor are there any vitamins that will fortify these two males for the long struggle ahead. But patience will go a long way. And love. And on the father's part, a large dose of remembering how he suffered when this particular malady struck him.

Some of its early symptoms are the pleas: "Let me steer." "Hey, I'll back it out of the garage." Or long puzzling periods when the boy will merely sit in the car, fumbling with its controls.

A slightly later manifestation is the desire to take a car apart. The average car-struck lad will want to peer under hoods, examine parts, by his hand at taking spark plugs out. The desire does *not* always make him want to change a tire or wash the thing, though if he is very far gone he will do so. Constant throughout is the frenzy simply to ride in cars. To go along with guys who have their drivers' permits, or those dashing heroes who own their own cars.

Constant too is the amazing ability to identify the make, model, and characteristics of every vehicle that passes. A boy who can't remember who discovered America, or when, or correctly identify any three parts of speech, will rattle off: "There was this 1958 blue hardtop convertible Mercury coming from the right, and there was this guy in a '64 Mustang trying to pass from the left—" Cars are the topic of conversation from dawn to dark.

The father may as well teach, or have his son taught, to drive as soon as it's legally permissible. If he does this himself his offspring, he finds, already knows most of what to do—or thinks he does, and the results can be even more harrying than trying to teach his wife. A hired, emotionally uninvolved instructor is heartily advised.

Once the boy is licensed, the most painful phase of the whole affliction sets in. Two burning issues rock the household now: "Can I have the car?" And, "When can I buy a car?"

The first is never really settled, but must be resolved in soul-searching misery time after time. The second involves a merciless bombardment of propositions: "There's this ad in the paper for this '59 Olds—all I need is two thousand dollars—" It means arduous, anguishing discussions of jobs, budgets, payments, upkeep, and insurance.

Once the deed is done, the parent is due for a whole new rash of pains and problems. Dad, who's been comforted to think, "Well, at least it's not a piece of junk," is likely to look out the window and go into mild shock. The beautiful, civilized, just-bought car is being stripped of its chrome, having its rear end lowered, subjected to the indignities of leading, and a paint job of passionate purple. The whole topped off with a Confederate flag and a flying girl-friend scarf.

As if this shuddering spectacle weren't enough, Dad must gird his loins afresh to do battle with hours, homework, and possible traffic tickets. As for the insurance—that alone consumes hours as he copes with the question: How best can he protect the safety of this young driver, and that of the public?

It's a curiously American manifestation, this of the car-happy adolescent. It comes about because of a culture of prosperity, perhaps. And freedom. And of men and boys who used to fight a wilderness, but now fight—traffic. And sometimes each other. Perhaps there is no explanation for it, just as there is no real cure.

But it's sure to strike almost every family. And there's something zesty and wonderful about it, at that. About the whole combination—a dad, a boy, and a car.

DADDY CAN FIX IT

Father can fix it. Or Daddy, as little folks call him. Or, as they get older, Pop or Dad.

Whatever his title, there's nothing like that remarkable do-it-yourself but do-it-for-everybody-else male parent.

Often his ingenuity surges to the front even before his offspring arrive, as he fashions a crib, a feeding table. More, today's dad enjoys bathing and feeding his babies some-times, rocking them, telling them stories. And when they come running in with a broken toy, how many a lucky wife can console, "Don't cry. Wait till Daddy gets home. Your father can fix it."

Daddy can fix it. Anything, everything. Radios, clocks, a bike, a pair of roller skates. A doll, a leaky boat, an eyeless stuffed rabbit. Or those antiques his wife is always dragging home from auction sales. Patiently, cleverly, with glue and tape and nails, and paint and love and imagination—what-ever the object, if it's dear to its owner, somehow, some way, he'll devise the means of its salvation.

Father can fix it. Often he will even build it. A playhouse, a picnic table, a fireplace, a wall, a patio in the yard.

Handyman—yes, he's usually that, but more important, he's the family handyman in matters of the heart. Report cards. Budding romances. Times of illness, worry, family strain. That complication in the Cub Scouts, that looming problem at church, at school—don't worry, talk it over with Dad. Dad will analyze the whole thing wisely, come up with the proper solution, make you realize it's not so grave a complication, after all. Or if it proves to be—well, your father will be standing by.

Daddy can fix it. Dad will get it for you. That costume for the play, though it means a trip clear across town. The supplies you need for the bazaar. That last-minute birthday present. Those pretzels and cold drinks for the teen-age party. And regularly, with the car crammed with little folks, groceries at the supermarket on Friday night.

Father can fix it. Find it, get it, pay for it, help you figure it out. Here's to him, bless him—the one who lives at our house, and at yours. The American dad!

FATHER'S DAY EVERY DAY

"Your mother's a wonderful cook," my father use to say—sometimes in her presence, but just as often not. Or, "Isn't Mama pretty? Really, she's one of the best-looking women in town."

And time after time she would remark of him: "Dad's so good to all of us. We certainly should be thankful to have a father like him."

Neither of them had the faintest idea of influencing their children by such comments; they were simply statements straight from the heart. Yet subtly, constantly, such words were helping to shape a pleasant and goodly image of the other parent in their children's minds.

All too often in the battle of the sexes offspring are sought as allies. "Just look at that mess," a woman will berate her husband. "Daddy's so careless, he never picks up a thing." Or, taking out her own frustrations and disappointments, "We could have a beautiful home too if your father had a better head for business like Uncle Bob."

Or a woman will use a father as the perpetual expender of punishment and bogeyman. "You'll be sorry, just you wait till your father gets home!"

Men are less prone to attack their wives in this back-handed manner, and when they do it's often disguised as a joke: "Where's your baseball bat? Why, Mom probably threw it out—you know how she is when she gets on a cleaning spree." Or, "I know how you feel when she nags you, boy, look how she picks on me."

All parents have their differences; there are things about each other they'd very much like to change. And there are sometimes occasions when one may treat a youngster in a manner which seems to the other outrageously unfair. Sometimes, in the cause of sheer human justice, the other must take a stand.

Even so, criticizing one's mate to his child is fraught with danger. It not only seems disloyal, it's building within that youngster a feeling of wretched ambivalence. He is divided, pulled this way and that. Instead of loving his parents fully, completely, as a unit, he feels impelled to choose up sides, and often he pits one against another.

Regardless of all this, mothers and dads can do a great deal for the children by forming the habit of sincere appreciation, voiced spontaneously and frequently: "Just listen to Mother, sewing away on that dress for Jane to wear to the party—what a wonderful person she is." . . . Or, "Wasn't it nice of Dad to drive this whole gang to Scout camp? You kids should be very grateful to have a father like that."

THE ART OF COMMUNICATION

Complaints run rife these days from husbands and wives who seem to have lost the art of communication.

Why, women demand, don't their husbands go to as much effort to make good conversation at home as they do at the office or their clubs? Why don't they ever tell us anything? And why, men echo the outcry, can't women learn the essential technique of really listening to or talking with a man?

For marriage may be said to be a blend of both sound and silence. When a sense of unity and fellowship pervades both phases, the marriage cannot help be firm and good. But when the sound is all one-sided, or the silence of either too prolonged, loneliness and subtle estrangements set in.

Here are some suggestions for both husband and wife to consider in closing the breach:

1. Be understanding. Don't try to wrest conversation from a person who's obviously tired. "Women simply have no idea what a man's up against out in the business world," as one man says. "Often he comes home not only acutely worried but exhausted."

2. Show interest. Give your undivided attention to what the other does tell you, even though the soup be scorching or you're missing a vital play on the televised football game.

3. Be an enthusiastic audience, but don't interrupt to show it.

4. Don't criticize. Be tolerant of the other's speech faults.

5. Find out what your own are and correct them.

6. Never betray a confidence. Keep all intimate discussions about business, the neighbors, or your own personal problems strictly between yourselves.

7. Keep your emotions under control. Lots of times men don't confide in their wives or vice versa because the other is likely to react too strongly to what he or she is being told.

8. Share the other person's interests. Learn everything you possibly can about his or her profession, sport, or hobby.

9. Cultivate new mutual interests that will give you common food for discussion.

10. Try to keep alive a free, unself-conscious expression of vital issues. People who know each other intimately often grow embarrassed about exposing their deepest thoughts. Yet most of us need spiritual companionship even more than we need small talk.

ARE YOU DEBIT OR CREDIT?

"Every wife is either a credit or a detriment to her husband," says my sister Gwen emphatically, "there are no in-betweens."

As the veteran wife of a school superintendent, she has witnessed a long parade of women who either help or hinder their husband's careers. There is the bossy wife who tries to dominate the system and the town. There is the meek and mousy wife who never takes part in anything. There is the jealous wife, the homesick wife, the social-climbing wife . . . Against these there are all the good, wise, personable, and often talented wives of whom the man, his boss, and even the school board can be proud.

Having disposed of educators' wives, we got to talking about wives in general. Particularly the woman who seems to have no special gifts. My sister Gwen insists that such a woman, to be a genuine credit to her husband, should develop talents of her own.

Be a good homemaker, which doesn't mean getting obnoxious about ashtrays and dirty feet. But at least hurl yourself into the joys of keeping a tidy, attractive house, so that if a business associate drops in your husband will be able to entertain him in a neat living room.

Be a good cook. Not necessarily a gourmet, nor a woman who toils her life away under the impression that the way to a man's heart (or success) is through the kitchen, but cook so that his meals are hearty, appetizing, and reasonably on time. Or be a wife whose husband can invite the boss to dinner, or expansively offer to have the staff party at his house, knowing you'll come up with something not only delicious but fairly original.

Be his personal valet. See that his clothes are back from the cleaner's when they should be, with all buttons intact. See that his shirts are flawless, his ties on the ready. That he gets a haircut when he needs one, even if you have to nag or threaten to shear him yourself.

See that his children are presentable most of the time—not only physically as clean as children are sensibly supposed to be, but that their manners do him no discredit. A man's prestige sags almost tangibly when he's embarrassed by a brat. See that it's never said, "I like old Harry and his wife, but take those kids away."

And when you go out with him, be as chic and charming as it's within your power to be. This doesn't mean striving to be a beauty or a fashion plate, but at least that your clothes are not too hopelessly dated, and that you are tidily groomed. (No dandruff on the collar, no tortured stocking seams.)

Also, bone up on what others are likely to be talking about. Be a good conversationalist—but not so good that you outtalk everyone else. Especially your husband.

As for the wife who is talented in other fields, who has outside accomplishments—she has to be twice as good in all the foregoing so her husband and his friends won't think she's neglecting him.

TWO LITTLE SOMEDAY-MEN

Every day about three the doorbell rings and they come bounding up the steps to pay you a visit—two little second grade boys.

Their mothers don't mind. The one who works acknowledges that she's glad there's somebody to give Randy a hug and maybe a cookie after school. Someone to make a fuss over his papers and drawings. As for the other one, she understands if Tony's a few minutes late. "Thank goodness," she says, "there are a few people left in the world who still like little boys."

Who still like little boys . . .

Boys with their shirttails out and their pant legs trailing. Little boys with their shining eyes and their big ear-to-ear smiles. Little boys who smell of crayons and bubble gum and dirt and grass and out-of-doors.

True, they are sometimes pests, these two-legged beginners in the mysterious and troublesome business of living. They track and spill and fight and break your lamps with their baseballs. They trample your lawns and climb your trees and snitch your apples and play havoc sometimes with your flowers. They write on sidewalks; they throw stones, they yell, they boast, they argue, they tell tall tales, they quarrel.

There are times when you could cheerfully bash their heads together—your own small male offspring and those of the neighbors. Times when you wonder why their Maker didn't simply skip the phase between their strollers and their first automobiles. For their own sake you sometimes wonder. For it must be hard to be a noisy, untidy, scolded, berated, unwelcome little boy.

They seem tough, it's true, these little guys. They don't seem to mind when people order, over and over, "Now you stop that, get out of here, go away!" They beat a hasty retreat, still jaunty, undaunted. But I wince whenever I see or hear it.

Little boys . . . little boys . . . So young, so new, so unsuspecting of what tomorrow has in store.

So soon to be candidates for the awkwardness, the secret agonies of adolescence. Soon, all too soon, to have their hearts broken by girls. And soon, oh much too soon, to be rebels, fighting for their identity in a confused and troubled world.

And soon—so terribly soon to be put into uniform and sent away from home. So far away, some of them, where they'll know loneliness and fear, and even give their lives, some of them, in the conflicts we manage to be involved in, whether or not we're at war.

And after that the cares of marriage will be upon them all too soon. The adult male longings, the sometimes impossible dreams: To be loved and respected by their wives. To have children they can be proud of. To provide well for their families in an age when families demand so much. To succeed.

Sometimes you see not the spindly, pesky, lovable, noisy little fellow—you see in his stead the tall, strong, yet somehow tragically burdened man he will one day be.

And so when the doorbell rings and they call, "It's us!" you call back, "Well, good, come on in. If there's one thing I like to see about this time of day it's two little boys."

"DAD, I NEED SOME MONEY"

To me, one of the most touching gestures a man makes is that old familiar one of reaching into his hip pocket and drawing forth his leather wallet.

"Touching is right!" he'd probably say, laughing, if you mentioned it. For day in and day out, he's been touched for money.

"Dad, this is cracker-money day, and also I've got to have a new notebook." . . . "Dad, I've got a big date tonight. How about getting my allowance early?" . . . "Don't forget to leave me some money, dear. The maid's coming today, and I think I'll take advantage of that shoe sale downtown."

Cheerfully, patiently, automatically, he produces that faithful source of supply. Without complaint, he doles it out—the change for the children, the pay for the cleaning woman, the cash you specify. "Now, you sure that's enough? Here's a little extra, just in case."

Sometimes he's forced to protest. If the bank account is low, he has to say so. But you know that it hurts him to do so, and he'll put it off as long as he can. He'd far rather cut corners and do without himself than deny his family the things they need or would like to have. For he cherishes that age-old American tribute—"a good provider." To be able to take care of his own is a matter of masculine pride.

He also likes to hold up his end of things with other men. How often during the day he reaches for his wallet—to pay a cab fare, pick up the check at lunch, donate to some cause or drive. And then, when he gets home at night, the whole family campaign starts up again: "Honey, the paper boy is at the door." . . . "There's a man collecting for the Salvation Army." . . . "Judy's leaving for her music lesson. She'll have to have three dollars for it."

And watching the hand travel to the familiar spot, you realize: "This is the hand that works for us."

And you remember your father's big brown calloused hand making that selfsame journey, to produce an old-fashioned snap purse, from which he brought forth funds. And you think of all the hands of men throughout the country, going back and forth to the hip pocket, like faithful pendulums, in this timeless cause.

"Dad, I need some money." How many billfolds that plea wears out! No wonder husbands so often need new ones for birthdays or Christmas. The billfolds get tired and worn and thin; eventually, they give up.

But the men? Tired and worn though they too may become, somehow they can't just quit, and they seldom give up. They are made of tougher, finer leather, sewed with sinews much too strong. So long as there's life in their bodies and love in their hearts and somebody to say, "Dad, I need some money," they manage to keep on filling the wallets. And reaching for them.

HE LEADS HIS FAMILY HOME

The motor begins to sputter one night on the lonely road to your country place. "Oh, no, don't tell me we're out of gas," your husband says. He cuts the motor and coasts downhill, everybody straining forward as if to lend strength. As the car comes to an inexorable stop, he roots through the glove compartment and groans afresh: *"Who took that flashlight?"*

Naturally, nobody can imagine. "Well, you sit here and wait. I'll walk up to the next cabin to see if they can lend us some gas. Or some kind of a light, at least."

He trudges off through the shadows, while you huddle together in a kind of snug alarm. "What if a robber should come along?" the children scare themselves. "What if a bear should come out of the woods? Maybe the dog should've gone along to protect Daddy!"

"Now hush," you tell them nervously. "He'll be right back with some gas—we hope." Guiltily you remember the flashlight back home in the closet where you were using it digging out winter wraps.

A little eternity drags by before a welcome eye comes swinging back down the road. "Well, everybody out, we'll have to walk. They didn't have any gas, but at least they lent us a light to see by."

"You mean *walk*? All the way? It must be a mile!"

"Be thankful it isn't two. C'mon, you kids each grab a cat. And don't let 'em get away," he warns. "If they get lost in these woods they might never find their way home."

The dog bounds ahead, barking lustily. "Good for Belle, she'll scare away the bears," somebody says. "Or the snakes."

"Snakes!"

"Now there's nothing to be afraid of," the head of the household says firmly. "See how bright the stars are. And notice how good the trees smell."

The stars indeed are glittering overhead. The earth has a spicy fragrance. The night things begin to sing a kind of marching tune. And almost before you know it, there is the cabin on its rise of ground, its dark shape a welcome friend as it keeps vigil beside the shining lake.

"Well, here we are," your husband says. "Now all you kids and cats get to bed while I carry some gas back to the car."

Cheerfully he sets off alone, carrying the heavy gas can. And as the small eye of the flashlight disappears over the hill you think of men the wide world over doing the tough, the lonely jobs that keep a family going—and lead it safely home.

The Wonderful World of Women

Their tricks and craft have put me daft,
They've ta'en me in and a' that,
But clear your decks, and—here's the sex!
I like the jads for a' that.

—*Robert Burns*

A NEW BABY AT THE NEIGHBOR'S

The secret world of women . . .
You call on a neighbor and her new baby.
The house smells of talcum powder and milk
and diapers and confusion and love.
The other children come running, eyes big and shining, overflowing with reports and details: "She's got long black hair, just like I had and she weighs eight pounds." . . . "Mommy let me hold her already, and when she gets a little older she's going to let me give her a bath!" . . . "Daddy is *so* proud it's a girl—"

Your friend too regards you with that excited welcome and wonder that is characteristic of someone just returned from some miraculous journey. Her hair is untidy, her figure not yet normal, but she moves with the grace of her own achievement, she smiles with the beauty of one who has glimpsed rare horizons.

"Wait till you see her!" Her voice is touched with a soft marveling pride.

Together you steal to the bassinette, gaze down on the tiny scrap that lies, a hint of pink cheek outlined against the white sheet, a touch of downy black hair.

"How tiny. How adorable—" You exclaim the usual trite but fervent things. "Oh, don't wake her—"

But it must be lifted up, this newcomer, gently raised for exhibiting. "It's time to feed her anyway, and she needs to be changed," the excuse is given. The mother sits down to execute these blessed tasks, ever new, ever strange and special, while the younsters dance about "helping," enjoining your further adulation. "Isn't she darling? Look at her teensy feet."

And they cast shy hinting glances at the gift you have brought, and are allowed to open it, with much scrambling, and are lavish with their own words of praise. "Mommy, look, just look. Sister, look what you got—a present!"

Your neighbor shoos them out and you sit together a little while discussing it, the whole experience—the secret world of women in which such a thing can be. And you hold the baby a minute yourself, so impossibly tiny, a hot bundle in your arms. Then you hand it back and say good-by, and return to your own domain with memories stirring, and a sense of joy in your heart.

THOSE PASSIONATE PERFUMES

To me, one of the craziest things that has ever happened to an innocent bit of femininity like perfume is the way today's scents are named. To leaf through any magazine bearing the ads of their manufacturers is to run a course that sounds about as sexy as *True Confessions*:

Shocking . . . Possession . . . Love Me . . . Desire . . . My Sin . . . Intimate . . .

All this came to mind the other morning, cutting roses in the garden. Their petals were soft and pink as a baby's skin. The dew sparkled on their cups like crystal, clean and shining, and they filled the air with such a delicate yet heady essence it was sheer perfume. And I remembered my mother's dressing table filled with its exquisite bottles . . .

Attar of Roses, wasn't that her favorite scent? And there was Lilac, Heliotrope, Lily of the Valley. For in those days a name good enough for a flower was good enough for a perfume.

But now perfumes are named after passions . . . Cutting a long-stemmed beauty I held it close and breathed deep. The most expensive bottle I own could not improve upon that fragrance which was and is and always will be pure glorious Rose. Yet if those roses were distilled and bottled they too would promptly lose their virtue.

Scarlet Letter, they'd probably be called . . . Or Feverish Embrace . . . Or Crimson Crime.

A DAY DOWNTOWN

How wonderfully good it is to get out of the house and go shopping after being tied down for a long time with small fry. What a great big glorious world it seems.

Just to see women walking along in skirts instead of slacks, and with hats upon their heads instead of scarves. To glimpse the latest fashions being worn, and realize with a little smack of surprise that women are truly women instead of merely trash-toters, grocery buyers, cooks, nurse-maids, and domesticated machines . . .

And to gaze upon the wealth in windows and stores. Such jewelry, such furs, such flowers, paintings, all exquisitely displayed. And oh, such table settings, colorful and charming, with arrangements of glass fruit and candles and mats that give you inspiration for table settings of your own.

And the furniture arrangements—now why didn't you think of that idea? A dry sink banked with potted plants sitting gaily before a window draped with gingham that you could just as well duplicate. You scurry into the dress goods department in search of the same gingham, and there see a dazzling cocktail suit that you could also copy on the trusty sewing machine.

How wonderfully good to meet a friend on this excursion, and have lunch in the dining room. The silver, the linen, the soft music. And the steaming shrimp and mushrooms—what a welcome respite from a baloney sandwich gulped while perched on a kitchen stool.

And to be actually waited on by people who act as if they were born solely to serve you. Never suspecting, poor dears, that your usual role at this time of day is wiping noses, refereeing battles, and dispensing peanut butter and jelly sandwiches. For this hour, at least, you are poised, relaxed, chic. For this precious, signal hour you are a queen.

And then at last to go home with your packages, that you spill all over the sofa as you relate the day's activities. Whom you saw and what you did and the bargains you found. And the youngsters dance around you, elated and marveling. For you have brought them more than sweaters and jeans and T-shirts on sale. You are giving them a personality refreshed, revitalized, stimulated. A new self that is heightened and is even made prettier by that simple thing, a trip downtown!

JUST TO PAINT A TABLE

Some of us wouldn't shy so at the labors of life it if weren't for the preparations.

You decide to paint a table. But first, your husband reminds you, you're obliged to scrub it down and sand it. "But why?" you plead. "Since it's only going to be all covered up."

To which he patiently explains the obvious: "So that it'll look nicer in the end. Of course, if you don't want to do a good job—"

Naturally that clinches it. What might have been a happy hour's achievement becomes an arduous Project.

But even if you have the good sense to do what painting you're inspired to when a man is safely off the premises, there is still no escaping a long, petty but painful obstacle course of preparations.

You've either got to have the paint already, or go to the

store and buy it. Usually you spend half an hour rooting through half dried-up cans. Then you have to find something with which to pry loose the lids. The screwdriver is best, if at hand, which of course it never is. A kitchen knife snaps off, and a nail is too blunt. Finally, you run down the screwdriver (in the sandbox where an offspring was using it to fix a dump truck), free the resistant force, and are faced with the problem of trying to find something to stir it with.

Another trip to the yard produces a few sticks, which are likewise too brittle and break. And the only thing you can wrest from the woodbox is too thick. Feeling guilty, you sneak a kitchen spoon (a deed that would cause family excommunication for anyone else), begin hopefully to dig at the gummy crust, and ultimately to mix and blend.

Meanwhile, you realize that you've got to spread papers down and do something about a brush. Your husband is really very sweet about cleaning out the brushes you invariably leave to harden. But of late, once he's restored them to some semblance of life through long loving soaks in various mixtures, he's taken to hiding them.

The last time he had them cached away behind the furnace; another time underneath the tool chest. After a long maddening search you give up, and stamp feverishly through the children's rooms. At last something resembling a paintbrush is found in a can of red enamel where a son has been working on a Cub Scout tomahawk. It's warped and crusted, however (why *won't* they learn to wash their brushes *out?*), and when you've scrubbed it with various concoctions and dip it gingerly into your sunshine yellow, its red blood spills and its black whiskers fall out.

Nearly frantic with frustration, you begin to yank out drawers, and lo! The numerous fates that have conspired to thwart you have changed their minds. For here is a lush new packet of paintbrushes—all shapes and sizes. Take your pick.

Now at last, blissfully, you are prepared to paint. But after a few blithe strokes the drippings remind you—oh, my goodness, you'd better spread the newspapers. So you grab several from the stack the Brownies are saving for their drive, and open them up, spotting at once several vitally important articles you'd missed. And by the time you've finished reading them there on your knees, the telephone rings. Bikes buzz up the driveway. Doors slam, dogs bark, the kids are home.

And who can possibly paint a table *now*? Better leave it for your husband. After all, it would be a shame to cheat him out of all those other silly preparations.

A WOMAN IN THE SPRING

A woman's moods are subject to the changing seasons. Especially do women relate in some mysterious fashion to the burgeoning earth in spring.

The heart is stirred within us at the scent of growing things. The pulse responds. Subtly, deep in our beings, we feel that a secret is about to be revealed. Some core of truth that only a woman could fathom, some mystery akin to all creation . . .

And a woman feels a restlessness, a giddy, inexplicable aching in the spring. Old hopes rise from a long, long sleeping. For a little while, watching the buds break, hearing the birds' bright promise, we feel them stirring gloriously too— our young, forsaken dreams.

And oh, how we miss people in the spring. Such small things will quicken the image of the loved one lost or merely away. Sunlight on new green grass, the smell of lilacs, a spade on the garden path, a battered hat . . . How they surge back at such moments—mother, father, sister, friend. Or a child. A daughter whose brown legs used to run so lightly down the steps, her soft hair flying. A son whom the wars have claimed . . .

A woman's heart always breaks a little in the spring. But spring offers its own ways of healing. Hoe the row a little deeper. Kneel on the ground and dig the roots. Gather armfuls of bright yellow flowers. Or take the house apart and put it back together shining clean.

THE GREAT GLASSES HUNT

It finally comes to all of us—that time when it seems that books and newspapers are using smaller print, and they're shrinking the eyes in needles. You find yourself holding your work farther and farther from you, and making the trite complaint, "It's not my eyes, just that my arms aren't long enough."

Ultimately you yield to the inevitable and wind up with a pair of "reading glasses." Now practically nobody sits reading all day, which brings you eyeball to eyeball with a grave decision: Will it be bifocals, or the take 'em off and lose 'em kind?

If you're the average, red-blooded American female (who'll admit being the mother of grown children, but never to being a day over twenty-nine) you are *not* likely to buy the kind of half-spectacles that made Ben Franklin famous. Thus, having been chief sleuth for all missing caps, gloves, homework, keys, and PTA notices, you yourself now become a contributor to the store of things-that-can't-be-found.

The only alternative is to buy and attach one of those chain things to the elusive lens. However, this too gets a stranglehold on glamor, and literally hangs it by the neck. Also, the noose proves a nuisance. The glasses keep bumping into things. Or you spill cocoa on them. Or the contraption springs the bows when, in excitement, you snatch them on or off.

After the third set of frames in as many months, I went back to the old routine of the glasses hunt. Now the familiar cry, "Has anybody seen my glasses?" echoes through the house. Having one pair for each floor doesn't help much. It's too easy, when you take off the ones you're wearing, simply to transport them with you to some other usually illogical spot. And it's maddening to realize that at least two pair are hiding out on the same level.

My glasses have been found reposing on paint cans, in and under beds, behind catsup bottles, amidst baskets of laundry about to be sorted, in bags destined for Goodwill. Once I chased a truck halfway down the block and made them stop and let me go through a half reupholstered chair—and sure enough, there were my glasses.

Usually glasses disappear just when you need them most: When you have to write a check for a C.O.D.; or mend a last-minute tear in a skirt for a daughter whose school bus is appearing around the corner; or catch a plane for distant parts. Then the whole family flies into frenetic search, fanning out to cover the house inch by inch, like a squad of volunteers hunting down a lost child. It's usually the husband's eagle eye which spots them in some appallingly obvious place.

"Here they are, right where you *put* them," he makes his inevitable, if redundant presentation speech.

Generally you're too relieved to respond, "But of course they're where I put them. It's just that somebody always hides or makes me forget the *putting place!*"

TIMES WHEN WOMEN WEEP

Life is not all pleasure for a woman. Far from it. There are times when women weep:

When children are seriously ill . . .

When the burdens of housekeeping seem simply overpowering . . .

When money problems seem insoluble . . .

When there is estrangement between fathers and daughters or sons . . .

When in-laws all seem to be against you . . .

When you're tired, half-sick, and discouraged, and it seems nobody loves you at all. Times when even a husband can't understand . . .

No, there are times when it's *not* fun to be a woman. When, like a child, you want to hide in a corner, or run frantically away, or bury your head on your arms and simply weep your burdens dry.

Crying may be a childish outlet but it is sometimes a very

good thing. We often rise cleansed and refreshed by the storm. And while it's usually wrong to subject the family to these outbursts, there are even times when a sudden, rare but brimming bucket of tears from that mostly stoic soul, Mother, is good for everyone.

INVENTORY

It's easy so much of the time to feel sorry for ourselves. But the good days we mostly take for granted. Now and then it's fun to take inventory of the things we *aren't* at the moment miserable about. To wit:

I don't hurt, ache, or feel even mildly ill anywhere . . .

I can't think of any pressing problem to worry about . . .

I'm not mad at anybody and can't think of anybody who might be mad at me . . .

The children are well . . .

My husband is well . . .

I haven't pulled any bad bloopers recently to be blaming myself for . . .

I'm not too far behind on my duties . . .

I don't feel guilty . . .

I guess I must be happy!

CONCERTMASTER, MOTHER

Almost every woman goes through life moved by a constant chorus of things clamoring to be done.

Her house or apartment is a perennial stage set for this ceaseless background chant—beds begging to be made, tables to be cleared, dishes to be put away, sinks to be scrubbed, papers and magazines to be straightened, clothes to be sorted, ironed, hung up.

All this, not counting the tasks beyond her doors—the marketing, the committees, the meetings, the dental appointments, and such lessons as dancing, music, horseback riding, painting, judo, guitar for her young. Or, if she has a yard—

garden chores. There too things creep, crawl, leap, spawn, and toss their green and tattered heads pleading to be hoed and dug and transplanted and fed and mowed and pruned.

She is a kind of concertmaster who can never coordinate, never create any real lasting harmony between all these aggressive, yet appallingly patient voices (they will always wait for her, they never give up). There is simply no controlling or subduing them to a point where they all conclude on time, however desperately she dances from one section to another, waving her broom or trowel or iron. And when she drops spent into her bed, she can hear them slyly tuning up their instruments or running little scales for tomorrow. Even there, she puts herself through rehearsal:

"Be sure to call the milkman . . . the front steps need scrubbing before Jimmy's teacher comes to see about the pageant for Sunday School . . . and he'll need a clean shirt by Friday . . . and I wonder if Bob got that spray for the roses—which would be nice on the platform if the beetles don't eat them first . . . and I'll have to bake a cake for the refreshments—remember to get vanilla when I drop Lucy off for tennis . . . and will my blue linen be okay to wear for the reception?" So that she is for a little while in her mind creating at least one little segment of song that makes a totality, however divergent its various elements.

Thus, when Jimmy has marched onstage to pleasant applause and she in her blue linen is serving cake at the reception, with a rose on her shoulder and more on the table, and the teacher is saying, "He did so well, and you have such a pleasant home," then, perchance, she is aware of it. If only for a minute. It's a little thrill of accomplishment, one small but memorable melody within the eternal dissonance of living.

TIPS FOR A GLOOMY DAY

Your hair's a mess and the house is another. The children are cross and the sun won't shine. In fact, the whole earth seems to have taken on a veil, a gray one, sad and forlorn.

The easiest thing to do is to give up, give in, wrap the selfsame woeful veil about you—and in so doing, lose forever out of life's bright store, one whole irretrievable day.

Instead, why not try to beat those blues? Here are some suggestions guaranteed to help:

1. Put on your brightest lipstick. Do something about that messy hair. Wash it, set it, or whack it off if you're so inspired.

2. Get out of that sloppy outfit, hop into something comfortable that also makes you feel lithe and nimble and gay.

3. Let the children take over one room they can't hurt too much, and there make as big a mess as they like with blunt scissors, finger paints, old magazines, and toys.

4. Whip through the rest of the house as if company were coming and you had to make at least the surface appealing, even if you have to dump things into drawers and behind closet doors.

5. Go into that sodden gray dripping yard and try to scare up a few bright branches, break off a handful of laurel, a chunk of ivy, a few truant flowers.

6. Build a crackling fire.

7. Feed the offspring by themselves and resettle them for naps or play. Then get yourself something really tasty for lunch and use your favorite dishes. Better yet, invite a friend.

8. If the friend can't make it for lunch, have her in for coffee later in the day.

9. Do something you've really been wanting to— curl up with a new book, paint a picture, dye your hair.

10. Put your favorite music on the record player so you can hear it while you work, whether symphony or rock 'n roll.

With a little effort and imagination, that dreary dullard of a day can be rescued and rejuvenated. Try it and see!

THE SECRET OF STAYING YOUNG

"Act your age," we're traditionally admonished. And there are those who ridicule efforts to hang onto at least the appearance of youth.

"No hair dyes for me," women will often say smugly. "And if I'm fat, so what? You don't catch me starving to try and look like the girl I was when I married."

As for men, the male who actually watches his waistline, considers touching up his hair, or investing in a toupee is considered not only absurd, but somewhat suspect.

Yet isn't the desire to look young a healthy, happy thing? Doesn't it relate to the new, the hopeful, the strong, the vigorous, the affirmative in life? Psychologists tell us that action precedes emotion. As we behave, our glands respond.

A youthful look is, therefore, more often than not, linked to a youthful *outlook*. And the man or woman who thinks young even feels young. His step is light, his body usually agile. He is less prone to the aches and pains and illnesses that plague the human species as the years accumulate.

True, we can't all stay sixteen forever. Perish the prospect! Perpetual immaturity would be intolerable. Growth brings not only mental and spiritual rewards, but its own form of beauty. Yet surely this beauty is far more discernible in the woman who is actively interested in beauty. Who refuses to be resigned to the dowdy, the dull, the colorless, the obviously "matronly."

Yet there are those who—quite consciously, I believe—begin to talk old, think old, even walk old, once they reach the middle-age mark. Sometimes they refer to themselves as "the old man," or their mates as "the old lady."

I believe with all my heart that this is folly, and those who do so are actively encouraging their own downhill slump. Once we lose touch with the dreams and delights and outward manifestations of youth, we are courting age, and ultimately—death itself.

And while age and death must come inevitably to all of us, it is a healthier, happier, and more constructive thing to cling to the best aspects of our youth as long as we can—for to do so is vigorously to cling to life!

RESOURCEFUL SPECIMEN, WOMAN

How tough and sturdy is the stuff of which a modern American mother must be made.

Her resources must be endless; her physical stamina rival that of the ancient Amazons; her emotions (however subject to trial and temporary explosions) basically shatterproof.

How is it that she can rise from her sleep night after night, sometimes for weeks, to attend sick children, comfort one who's frightened from a bad dream, feed babies, cover those who've kicked the covers off, counsel one who's come in late and wants to talk—and still go cheerfully about her labors by day?

How is it that she can make and serve hot cocoa for school patrols on a nippy morning, help with the health program, serve as a lunchroom mother, shepherd a bunch of Brownies to a concert, cook dinner for her family, supervise homework, call people on her PTA committee, and hostess another committee for her husband's club—sometimes all on the same day.

How is it that not only her body but her emotions are able to withstand so many blows and upheavals and remain intact, if not exactly serene? That she can be worried sick about one child's cough, another child's grades, have a stormy fracas with a son about a car, a misunderstanding with a neighbor, a disappointment in the mail—and yet powder her nose, don a perky hat, and go to a charity luncheon where, if called upon, she can rise and make a convincing little speech?

For all the gadgets that have simplified her laundry, her cleaning, and her cooking, the demands upon her time, her temper, and her sheer physical energy have multiplied. She herself is one of the marvels of our streamlined age—a kind of pre-packaged combination public servant and private attendant to numerous other human beings; a keen, efficient, resilient quick-mix of tenderness and strength which today's family and today's society have come to accept and depend upon quite as much as we do planes or cars.

A NEW HAIRDO

Nothing more seriously affects a woman's personality than the state or the style of her hair.

To the complete mystification of men who are either less emotionally linked to the state of their pates, more efficient in shampooing arrangements, or less vocal about it, any one of us is likely to burst out at any time, "I've simply got to do something about this hair. I can't stand it another minute!"

Whereupon we drop whatever we're doing and dash from the room. Sometimes to the telephone to make an appointment, sometimes to the bathroom to wash the offending mop.

No matter who attends to the matter, in the very act of being sudsed and ducked and rinsed until we squeak, we are purged of many of the minor miseries that beset us.

In the shearing of our craggy locks we are trimmed of at least a few of our trials.

Even in the curling that makes us resemble monsters, there is the temporary illusion of having our problems neatly skewered into place.

A woman's hairdo also has a genuine influence on her sense of well-being. Each of us nurtures a secret image of herself—be it clean-cut career woman, gracious hostess, sultry siren, or just plain Mrs. Suburbia, mother of four.

Imagine then the dismay when the gal who fancies herself a flirt emerges from the dryer resembling, instead, a stable matron with neatly waved blue hair. Or the career woman who wants to remain severe gets a load of herself in the mirror with a frisky poodle cut.

Such mistakes are sufficient to shatter a psyche. . . . On the other hand, stuck in the rut of a certain hair style (that we may fancy expresses the real Inner-I), we can be catapulted into an exciting new creature by some change we finally are reckless enough to try.

Men escape all this. Their hair types are straight, curly, or bald, and they have practically no choice either way. Except for the big decision as to whether or not to get a crewcut, they usually are stuck with one hairdo for life.

Small wonder then that they regard our harried, hairum-scarum doings with a slightly puzzled eye.

A WOMAN'S VOICE

"Her voice was ever soft, gentle and low," wrote Shakespeare—"An excellent thing in woman."

An excellent thing, indeed. Especially when that woman is mother or teacher, for these are the voices that guide and shape the lives of children; their immediate effect is powerful and their influence may last a lifetime.

Think back a minute; remember: Which teachers spring most fondly to mind? Those whose tongues scolded and clacked and clattered? Those who shrieked and railed? Or those who managed to keep order through the quiet dignity of their own presence, enhanced by the voice itself?

Dewey Deal, eighth grade English—will I ever forget that deep, rich voice, so darkly royal it was like walking on velvet rugs. Or Miss Heflin, home economics, whose sweet, flute-like tones sang out above the machines on which we struggled to sew a straight seam. Or in college, Essie May Hill, who had a chuckle in her throat, a joyous, bubbling spring even explaining the Pleistocene Age.

Voices . . . Voices in the schoolroom, voices in the home.

A child awakes in the morning—is it to a pleasant greeting, or a screaming tirade? Which is most likely to set a happy, healthy tenor for his day?

A child eats, goes off to school or play—what is his accompaniment as he goes about these things? A firm but quiet voice chatting, admonishing, advising—or a constant harangue punctuated by outbursts so loud, so coarse, at times so uncontrolled that if it weren't his mother one might think the woman insane. But no, it is only his mother, and though he flinches as from a blow, or scurries guiltily to correct his infraction, or merely becomes inured to it and pays no attention, there is a mark on his spirit, nonetheless. These scars go deep, psychologists tell us, and do their damage unseen.

It's hard not to yell at children, especially when they are small and the problems of housekeeping (or schoolteaching), the budget, and a dozen outside emotional factors are complex. Upon their hapless heads it is all too easy for a woman to vent her disappointments and frustrations, her own sheer weariness.

Yet they are so helpless and small to be the victims of what is actually cruelty. However we try to justify it, to shrug it off, it is exactly that.

In fairness, most women don't *want* to be the harpies we often sound. It is mostly a matter of habit. Of self-control. Of getting oneself firmly in hand. Of practice—yes, and of prayer.

A young mother told me, "I'd hate myself so when they were asleep. I've actually gotten down on my knees beside a crib and cried. And since I was there anyway, I asked for help. And I'm getting it.

"I've learned to keep my voice down, to speak so quietly it's almost funny—they've got to pay attention to hear. And now when I hear a woman screaming at her children, I think, 'Oh, don't. It sounds so hideous to them, to your neighbors, to your husband—and if you'll just listen a minute—to yourself.'"

... *Her voice was ever soft, gentle and low, an excellent thing in woman.*

THE TENDER TRAP OF MARRIAGE

Not long ago a single woman said to me, "When I was younger I used to regret not being married. There is a kind of stigma attached to being a so-called old maid. Though my married friends were sweet about it, and though I had turned down several proposals in order to stay at my career, the inference was that I'd been left out.

"But now that I'm older and have made a success of my work, I find myself feeling sorry for them. So many of them are frustrated intellectually. None of them are free to travel as I do, and few of them have any independence about money, however well off their husbands may be.

"Sure, they have what's called companionship, but I notice that it's often a pretty hectic kind, filled with noise and confusion and arguments. I notice too that they're forever having problems, if not with their husbands, with their children. Taking a good long look at it, it seems to me the price you pay for being married is misery."

Before such telling arguments what can a mere matron say? In fact, looking at such women from the dusty drudgery of housework or the depths of the very troubles she cites, these arguments sometimes come unbidden. Along with the realization that she herself may have married for all the wrong reasons: Prestige, security, infatuation, a romantic notion of living happily ever after.

But once involved in this "tender trap," she is no longer an individual whose wants and desires come first. She is a wife, a mother, and though she may balk at the sacrifice sometimes and weep copious tears of self-pity, if she's any kind of a woman at all she gradually ripens and deepens in the very process of coping with all these other people and their problems whom marriage has somehow dumped on her soul's doorstep. Poor though she may be in material things, in trips and intellectual contacts, she is rich in the substance of living. A substance which nourishes even as it depletes.

She is rich in responsibilities which, however burdensome, she would not care to miss: The knowledge of being vital to the welfare and happiness of others. Of hearing a small boy yelling, "Mother, Mother, where are you?" when he comes banging in from school. Of frightened voices summoning her to a bedside at night. Of voices pleading for her counsel or guidance over the telephone . . . She is rich in secrets shared, confidences grave or amusing. Rich in a thousand and one opportunities to comfort, share, rescue, direct, and shape other lives.

The wife and mother knows that, for all her disappointments and discomforts, she is deeply cared about. She knows that when she is ill or absent the wheels of the family well nigh stop. She knows that if anything should happen to her she would be tragically missed. More important, she knows that in that instance she will have left behind something valid and significant in the whole scheme of human affairs. People of her own creating, without whom the world would not be the same.

Above all, right now, today, she is caught up in a strenuous but stimulating tide. She is heart-deep in living. Living that sometimes hurts but that is full and meaningful and good.

Little Small Young Things

All my life I've been tagged and trailed
By little small young things, both boys and girls;
Kittens and chipmunks and rabbits that ailed,
And birds to be doctored for broken wings,
And limp little blind fallen squirrels—

—M.H.

HOW DO YOU BURP A SQUIRREL?

What is this chattering as you come up the walk? What is this hopping and jumping and switching of skirts and book bags and pony-tails?

"A squirrel, a squirrel!" they inform you as, puzzled, you push through the little flock. "We found it on the playground and the teacher's been letting us feed it all day."

"And I'm the one that's s'posed to keep it overnight," your daughter proudly announces. "And you're s'posed to feed it every half an hour."

The cage, leaking grasses, is carried into the kitchen. Milk from a tiny carton (left over from their morning milk break) is warmed, and one cradles the scared little quaking creature while another pokes an eyedropper into its mouth.

"Not so far, not so hard, he can't suck it!"

"He's not supposed to suck it, silly, you're supposed to squirt it in."

"Here, I know how, let me!" . . . "No, me, it's my turn. Here, Christopher, come to Judy—"

"Christopher?" you ask.

"Yes, we put all these names on the board and voted. Wasn't it lucky Miss Meyer already had a cage? And we covered him with this old red sweater from Lost and Found."

The corps of little nurses keeps busy till time to disperse. Never has one squirrel gorged so much milk from so many. "Dear, are you *sure* it has to be fed so often?" you inquire as squirrel belches begin to disturb the dinner hour.

"Oh, yes, the science department said so. My goodness, it's time for some more!"

By bedtime Christopher is not only bulging, he has practically passed out. Except for continuing hiccoughs he lies inert on his grass nest, eyes glazed.

"Don't anybody worry, I'll get up with him," the eight-year-old announces, though her brother valiantly volunteers for the night shift. "Let's see, how d'you set the alarm clock for every half hour?"

"Every half hour nothing," you declare. "What this guy needs is a little rest from so much Tender Loving Care."

Over anguished protests she settles down. "But I'm *responsible*," she warns. "I promised the whole room I'd bring him back tomorrow!"

Of this fact you and your husband are only too well aware. He is gazing at the still limp if hiccoughing Christopher when you come down.

"Poor little thing, sounds like he's got the colic. Maybe a hot water bottle would help; it does with babies."

"If he'd just stop making that noise. Sounds like he's needing some relief for sure. Say, how d'you suppose you burp a squirrel?"

"Same as with babies, I guess."

Laughing, your partner lifts the little charge to his shoulder and begins to stroke it. With all the anxiety of fond parents, you listen for the welcome blast. To your delight it comes at last, and in a few minutes Chris is curled up fast asleep on a hot water bottle.

At dawn you hear the alarm clock the little one has slyly set. "Gee, I hope it lived through the night," your husband sits up to mumble as heels go pattering downstairs.

In a few minutes you hear a happy tap at the door. "Boy, was he hungry! I think I'll stay up now—remember he's supposed to be fed every half an hour!"

SPOOKY

"No, no, we have enough trouble without a dog!"

"But the children, dear—and these people have a litter of Labradors—"

The debate wages lively, but who always wins? Mother yields. Mother herself drives into the country to view the candidates.

The first time this occurred in our family, I blush to admit my ignorance. Labrador retrievers, I'd gathered from my husband, were hunting dogs. Which to me connoted a picture of a beautiful white creature standing in profile, one paw raised.

I remember distinct dismay at seeing the jet black mother and her two remaining offspring. "This is the gentler of the two," the owner said. "See, she's a little scarred—the others have picked on her, but the marks will soon go away."

How shy, that quaking black bundle. How scared. And to compound her terror, Ornery, the cat, who was king of the household, dominated her shamelessly until they learned to play.

Perhaps that's why we loved her so, to start. I'll never forget how the six-year-old, whose birthday surprise she was, swept her into his arms, face working. And without a word, strode off down the street with her to show his friends. Or the sight of that little black face bobbing baby-like over his shoulder.

Spooky, we called her. And within the year she was satin-sleek and tall. She loved to swim in the stream that flowed by us, and that was fine. She loved to chase the ducks, however, and neighbors' cats and squirrels. She was desperately contrite when caught; she would hide her face in her paws, or squirm frantically under a chair.

She shadowed the children everywhere, but was never one to cavort with other dogs. There was something exclusive about her; when a fellow canine would approach, she would rise and move haughtily away. She was gentle; like a well-bred woman, she spoke only when necessary.

Yet let a doubtful stranger come up the walk, or a sound disturb the night, and her cockles would rise, she would growl, and with three short barks give warning. I could wheel the baby's carriage into the sun and know that this four-legged nurse would faithfully keep vigil.

Three times she had babies of her own. Each time we planned to supervise her nuptials, but invariably some suitor got there first. The first time, we took her carefully to the kennels, and had the "purebreds" all spoken for.

On Mother's Day morning, appropriately, we heard the exciting whimper of new life in the basement. And the whole family rose and tiptoed down. "Stand back," my husband said, flashing a light on the nest. And we'll never forget his gasp, half of amusement, half dismay. "Well, they're *not* Labrador retrievers!"

She loved them, however, her babies of many hues, and so did we. And after that it didn't matter. The household was lively with puppies, and with children begging them. And we gave them all away.

How healthy she was, how strong. We fed her anything and everything and she thrived. Almost her only contact with a veterinarian was when we boarded her during vacations. And these were the only times she ever grew ill—from grieving.

But nature does not vouchsafe a dog the long life man can enjoy. By ten Spooky's sleek black jowls were frosted with gray. When she was past eleven, she suffered a stroke. The tail still wagged mightily, but she was inclined to veer and had difficulty breathing. The doctor did what he could, and night after night we got up to try to make her comfortable.

But finally her misery was too much for those who loved her to bear. We delivered her into kind hands that would gently put her to sleep.

Bidding a loyal dog good-by is a strange experience. It is saying good-by, as well, to a long, memory-filled phase of your family's life. That, too, is why you cry.

TO CATCH A BAT

"Mom, where you keep your paper sacks? Big ones that'll come down over our ears—"

"What for?"

"We're going bat hunting, me'n Johnny, and man, we sure don't want 'em to get in our hair."

"If they did you'd be bats in the belfry," you contribute the little gem as you hand them the sacks, which they draw fetchingly down almost to their chins.

Clutching their homemade butterfly nets—contrived out of old lace curtains and bent hangers affixed to broomsticks, they dash off to the school playground.

"Those kids actually think they're going to catch some bats," you inform your husband in bemused tones, and settle down on the porch. "It's wonderful the faith children have."

"I'll say." He jerks upright presently, at the sound of wild screams. Pale with fright, you both race down the steps. "We got one, we got one!" They are clutching a twisted net, and at its bottom, making a queer sound, is something black and small and desperate.

"How did you do it?" you both gasp, relieved.

"We threw rocks. They'll dive right down at rocks. Get a jar, quick. First we'll put him in a jar, then we'll make a cage and keep him as a pet. Might even charge people to see him. Daddy, you be the one that puts him in the jar. But be careful," your son warns helpfully. "If that thing gets in your hair—!"

You wince. "If that thing gets in the house—!"

You get a fruit jar from the cupboard, punch holes in the

lid. Gingerly, the floundering black bunch is eased from the net to which it wildly clings. The lid is clapped on, all gather round to observe a live bat at close range.

"Eeeee—I don't like it!" the little one squeals, diving her face into your skirt.

It isn't exactly pretty—quite small, very black, with an ugly but pathetic baby face, and hunched up wings.

"Poor little thing," you say. "You've got to let him go, he'll only die if you try to keep him."

Reluctantly persuaded, they race off to exhibit the prize to Johnny's mother, who screams, "Get that thing out of here!" and to disrupt the usual hush of the corner library.

"Aren't bats harmful?" your husband ponders during their absence. "Aren't they supposed to be destroyed?"

"Oh, my no—oh, goodness, they just—haunt houses, I believe."

Presently they come trudging back, flushed with triumph, satisfied.

"You let him out, Mom. We sure don't want any bats in our hair."

Shivering, the bold venturers back away. Watch from a safe distance as, with a not too convincing determination, you walk a few paces into the yard and cautiously unscrew the lid. Holding it at arm's length, you tilt the jar. With a scraping of claws, the small dark body slides out. For a sad instant it lies absolutely still.

"Oh, you poor little thing, are you scared, are you hurt? Fly," you beg as it flops on the grass. "Fly, fly!"

Suddenly up it swoops, so fast you jump back several feet. Cutting graceful arcs, it goes bending and blending into the night.

The small boys regard its going with a sigh. "Well," they inform each other, "we can always say we caught a bat!"

WE LOST OUR MITTENS

Such a dear little kitty he was, warm and fluffy and new, gazing at you with his pointed baby eyes. His mew was a comical yeep, his purr a toy motorboat rumbling. How daintily he would wash himself, and how he would play, patting at dangled string with his new little paws, rolling over and over, nipping at his own bewitching tail.

And now he is lost! You have taken him to the country and brought him out into the sunshine to roll and play and chase things in the grass. And become busy with company and when finally one of you remembers, he has vanished.

Where, kitty, oh where in this vast world of weeds and wilderness and water—where are you hiding? What perils have you perhaps already met?

"Kitty, kitty, kitty—" The whole family takes up the call. "Go find Mittens." Even the dog is dispatched. And with quick understanding, the sensitive black nose goes sniffing along the ground.

"Mittens, Mittens, come back, come home!" Its mistress is a forlorn little figure as she trudges up the road. You run and take her hand. Together you search, off side trails, along banks, calling, calling, with a mounting sense of urgency and despair. And after troubled conferences, take the car, asking neighbors, "Have you seen a little gray kitty with white paws? We call him Mittens, though he's almost too young to know that."

So young and dependent. And evening is coming on. Feeling almost guilty, you finally eat supper, setting out first a bowl of milk, just in case.

But it stands untouched. Even the dog, formerly prone to wolf it down, skirts it, crouches on the floor dejected. Oh, Mittens! You all fan out again, searching, until its owner must be put to bed, distraught. "Oh, it's cold out there, it's lonesome, it's hungry—oh, Mittens, forgive me, please!"

You wake several times in the night, listening. Is there a scratching at the door, the faint tinkling of a little bell? But it's only the wind, and toward morning, the rain. And you can't bear the picture of its wandering, bewildered—and that one little gesture it made, of a white paw lifted as if to test this strange new world. And how is it that such an infinitesimal creature can cause an entire family this terrible sense of responsibility and failure?

Morning, your little girl rushes to the door. But the bowl of milk is there, and the little rug you've put out. Taking up her burden of grief afresh, she swallows her breakfast and gets on her coat.

"I'm going out to look for him now."

"I'll go with you," says her father, and together they set off. And you think—at least she'll have the memory of companionship in her first loss.

At last they return empty-handed. Gravely, she hangs up her wraps. "Mummy, tell me honestly, do you think it will ever come back?"

"Honey, I wish I could."

"But why did it have to happen? Why—why?"

"Because life is like that. We make mistakes. Even when we're big and know better we still make them and things are lost, many things dear to us. Mistakes and loss are a part of the way life is. They come to everybody, honey, and we've got to—accept it."

She still prowls the premises, occasionally calling out, "Kitty, here kitty." But gradually there is a new note in her voice. And after a while you hear her playing with her dolls, even singing. And—thank goodness, you think. We do get over things. That, too, is the way life is.

BOTTOMLESS BELLE

"Chicken bones!" a friend cried the other night as I was about to feed our Dalmatian. "Surely you don't give a valuable dog like that chicken bones?"

He couldn't understand why the whole family burst into laughter. Not until we related the story of Belle. Belle, and her freakish appetite.

She had already been named when we brought her home. And though Belle seemed a dignified, dowager sort of name for such a cunning bundle of squirming black and white polka dots, it stuck. She frolicked about the premises as puppies will, making puddles—and the first assaults on possessions.

Shoes were reduced to a pulp. Crayons she masticated daintily, then swallowed, leaving her jowls colorfully trimmed. She tore into and thoroughly digested the biggest, meatiest, most expensive books. She would eat cigarettes, and then, rather brightly the children thought, the matches to light them with.

Unblanching, even unbelching, she would eat not only her dinner; she would go right ahead and eat her feeding dish.

It was definitely no lack of food, we saw to that. Nor was it a lack of toys of her own—she ate the balls we gave her to play with, the rubber bones and squeaking frogs.

Nor did it help to scold and spank. She would simply gaze back with a comical and bewildered expression in her odd unmatching eyes. For one is an innocent baby blue. The other an impish brown. And the result is a kind of weird, ridiculous blamelessness.

It isn't funny, though. Not when you find her contentedly licking her chops after a meal of your best new sample hat.

In sheer desperation we try to put everything out of reach, as you would for a toddling child. Only this four-legged toddler has thrived so on her depredations she has but to rear up on her hind paws and blithely sweep the desired objects to the floor.

On our son's birthday she celebrated by gulping down an entire baking chicken that had been set out to thaw. It must have gone down whole, for we never found a scrap. In fact, we wouldn't have thought to blame her as we hunted for it, had we not caught her helping herself to the just decorated cake.

"This is nonsense," said the vet. "Get her a muzzle."

Which we did. To her delight, for she promptly ate it off!

"Get her another one," he advised on our second appeal. "And grease it with this stuff. I guarantee she won't like that."

Like it? She loved it. In fact, she found this second juicy morsel of muzzle so tasty, she went nosing around until she found the can of grease itself to lick.

One day our daughter was given pills by her doctor. Five

dollars' worth. Belle got to the opened bottle first and downed them every one. When we went to refill the bottle the druggist laughed.

"You know what these pills are for, don't you?" And as we shook our heads—"Appetite stimulants!"

THE TURTLE RAFFLE

Turtle Road, they call it. This place not far from your country cabin where they like to go exploring. And it must be Turtle Suburbia, for they never return with fewer than two of its helmeted residents, and the last time twenty-four.

"Good heavens!" You regard the boxes of clicking, scratching creatures clambering over each other. "You must've scooped the whole village, what are you going to do with them?"

"Race 'em, man. Take 'em back to town and sell them to kids for racers. I figure to get two bits apiece for the fast ones, fifteen cents maybe for the babies."

"Not the *babies!*" The littlest wails and clutches a couple of the unlovable looking reptiles to her bosom. "I get to keep some of the babies for pets."

You nip the ensuing fight in the bud and trust that this enterprise will meet the death of waning enthusiasm you've observed before.

No such luck, however. When you return to civilization, the car is crawling with turtles. At home, the car is demoted to the driveway while the garage becomes a turtle racing stable. Pans of water, dishes of egg, lettuce, stale bacon, and dead flies are daily trotted out to the stolid steeds. And small fry from all over the neighborhood arrive to aid, admire, and take their favorites on trial runs.

Turtles, however, seem to be a commodity few kids care to pay cash for. Even prices shamefully reduced and special two-for-one offers fail to produce the anticipated revenue. Meanwhile, back at the ranch, you and your husband keep reiterating, "You've got to get those monsters out of the garage!"

Then one day the manager of the whole turtillian scheme comes home from school inspired. "We'll have a raffle, sell numbers—"

"Dear"—you hedge, with vague visions of rearing a racketeer—"is that exactly legal?"

"Why, sure," he assures you cheerfully, "churches do it all the time."

He has you there. And after a couple of days working the fifth grade and even the playground, he's richer by forty-six cents. "I figure a penny a chance would make it easier for everybody. And," he adds with a grin, "get rid of the turtles."

He's right. After school at three that day kids of all sizes swarm the yard. The big tycoon holds them at bay while he sends little sister in for a hat and his duplicate set of numbers.

You can't help laughing as you look out. The gamblers to whom you could scarcely give a turtle before, are jumping and shoving against each other in their eagerness to win. Mounted importantly on a box, holding a hat and yelling for silence is your son, while your daughter draws the lucky numbers.

There is considerable argument and confusion, of course. Especially when your littlest one insists on taking her babies and stalking off with them. But the lucky winners trudge triumphantly home in the end.

"Well!" Your son ruefully juggles his take. "Now if I'd just charged two cents a chance. Say, when we going back to the lake? How soon can we go back up Turtle Road?"

PSYCHOLOGY'S NO SOLACE

Mothers of children with pets should comb the last remnants of college psychology out of their hair. Ax your Adler, junk your Jung, and forget you ever heard of Dr. Sigmund

Freud. Never, but never, listen to anyone who speaks in terms of secret motivations, wish fulfillments, and hidden urges innocently acted out. To do so is to open up ghastly new vistas of soul-searching and futile self-reproach.

For whose fault is it all too often when pets escape? Invariably, yours. Who left the cage ajar enabling the mother of all those newborn hamsters to skip out? You, of course. And if you're the self-analytical type you get to probing:

What in the world made me *do* it? Some hidden urge to punish the children for all those noisy wheels going all night long? Or a martyr complex, maybe? You wonder as you sleepily warm milk for the yapping worm-sized babies and fill the eyedropper for the next feeding. Or—good heavens, the possibility strikes—even some secret urge to become *more* the mother than you already are?

This seems so preposterous that even you laugh in self-derision. But still—!

Or take the late lamented departure of Chipper, the baby squirrel. Remember all the arguments you used when the rescue squad came toting him home? Squirrels had everything from worms to to rickets. Little creatures fallen from their nests were hard to raise—much better off if left undisturbed. But they won, as they usually do. And somewhat to your surprise, the little guy thrived, even to leaping nimbly about the house snitching peanuts, or perching on a shoulder.

Who was it decided that he needed some fresh air and sunshine? Who put him on a sunny spot on the porch and then was lured into a lengthy phone conversation? You, you monster! And however you grieve and try to make amends, and justify your intentions—isn't it just possible that deep down in your dire demonic subconscious you *wanted* to lose him in order to vent hostility, dominate, prove them wrong?

And when it comes to the lengthy list of lost cats. . . . The behavior patterns— But don't get started on that. In fact, when it comes to parenthood and pets, better send your psychology back!

THE MOST PRECIOUS MOUSE

"Oh, Mommy, Mommy, come look, come quick, help me catch him—a little gray baby mouse."

"I'll catch him all right—in a trap. It must be him and his family that've messed up the cupboards and nibbled everything in the drawers."

She regards you, innocently appalled. The beginnings of understanding flickering about the small eager face. "Oh, but he's a *nice* mouse, I saw him—he's way too little to do any harm. If we catch him and I can keep him I promise to train him not to hurt *anything*."

"Darling, we couldn't keep him, he's a wild mouse. He belongs in the fields. He just comes into the cabin down the chimney or through a crack."

"But maybe he likes it in here where it's warm and there's all the crumbs. I could make him a little shoe-box house and feed him toast and cheese—" She wheels, shrieking with excitement. "Quick, quick, there he goes, into the bathroom, let's run in and shut the door."

Without reasoning, you are in absurd pursuit. the miniature culprit has ducked behind the shower curtain and is wildly circling the slippery stall. Spurred by fanciful Disneyland visions—Mickey, Minnie, and the Beatrix Potter mouselings, suddenly you too want your little darling to have a mouse of her very own.

But Mickey, or Minnie, or whoever he is, is no "wee sleekit, cowrin tim'rous beastie." When you do finally corner him and cup his tiny trembling satin body in your hands, he pays you off, but good.

"Ouch! Why you little—ingrate." Away he scoots, while you regard, in righteous astonishment, the blood on your finger. "He—*bit* me," you announce. "See, honey, mice don't want to live with people, they want to live with their own mommies."

"Not once he got to know me," she insists mournfully. "I'd have taught him such nice mouse manners. And I was going to call him—" She sighs mightily and gazes wistfully out the window, considering. "Golden Diamond Twinkle

Star Mouse—because he would be the most beautiful, precious mouse in the world."

ABSOLUTELY NO MORE CATS

"Absolutely no. No more cats!" you say when the striped little stray tries to adopt your family. For so many have been lost or met with misfortune. "We have such bad luck with them and you children always feel so bad."

But she simply won't go away. With a kind of wistful patience she awaits the saucer of milk they slip her, and soon is sleeping on their beds. But she is such a little lady, quiet and well-mannered. Never scratching, like some of her predecessors, and simply ignoring the dog.

You don't suspect her condition until one day your little girl rushes in, ecstatic, the bland-eyed subject in her arms. "Tammy's going to have kittens! A girl just told me, she can tell—no wonder she's been getting so fat!"

"Oh, no!" you protest afresh. But suddenly you too are filled with a great tenderness and rejoicing. And all the family shares it. "No wonder she was so anxious for a home, poor little thing."

Tammy assumes a precious new importance as the days pass. Extra milk now, warmed, and vitamin drops. And at night a box in a closet. "They like a nice dark place to creep into, the pet book says."

She walks with a graceful bulging beauty, and lies down with caution, arranging her burden in the gentle circle of her paws.

Her condition complicates your weekend trips to the country, however. She is so restless en route, crying and pawing at the glass. Holding her, you worry, "Just hope she doesn't have 'em on my lap!"

"Animals usually have their young at night," your husband tells you. "I seem to remember from the farm."

But it is on a Saturday morning at the cabin that the stork of kittyland descends. "She's acting awfully funny, come quick, come quick!"

"Now calm down, honey," you tell the child whose personal pet she is. You rush to where the bewildered would-be mother is racing wildly about, and put her in a box. Your husband carries it to a quiet room and builds a fire to keep her warm.

"She's had her first baby," you return to tell the child who is trembling with excitement. "Would you like to come to see it? Tammy doesn't seem to mind an audience a bit."

Enthralled, she tiptoes down, stares into the box, and asks, "D'you think there'll be any more?"

"First litters are usually small, but she looks as if she might."

You return to your book and your breakfast coffee and she keeps vigil, dashing in every now and then to announce, "Now we can sing the 'Three Little Kittens'! This one's so tiny and black, some see!"

So you go to pay your respects. And later again. And again, until the count is five.

"I'm keeping the black one," she firmly says. "Well then I get the gray one," somebody else pipes up. "I want the tan—"

Your husband looks down at the box with the squirming inhabitants, its proudly drowsing mother, and then with a grin at you: "What was that I heard you saying about no more cats?"

Once Upon a Lovely Time

I remember, I remember
The house where I was born,
The little window where the sun
Came peeping in at morn—

—Thomas Hood

THE WALK TO SCHOOL

I have always felt sorry for children who miss the experience of walking to school.

When I was a small town youngster we walked at least a mile each way, whatever the weather. And the distance was fraught with wonder, no matter how familiar its landmarks became.

On certain corners there were magic talismans to be invoked—simply lettering on the sidewalk immortalizing some builder's name. Yet the first one to stamp on them and shout, "Good luck!" was sure to be protected from evil all day.

And there were houses that loomed with significance en route. There was the Flower Lady whose entire yard was a riot of blossoms and who might give you some for teacher if she felt in a generous mood . . .

There was the sheriff's house; he could arrest you and throw you in jail if he chose, the older kids claimed . . . There was the Witch's House, an ancient red brick with cupolas and towers, where a daft old lady lived; she sometimes sang from a window, or scurried out in her little white cap to ask if you'd seen her angels who'd flown off again.

There was the Presbyterian Church with its mighty chimes and clock, and its bubbling drinking fountain . . . There was that whispering treasure house, the public library. On the way home you could stop and borrow exactly two books, no more. But by starting them as you sauntered along, you could have them read by tomorrow and borrow two more.

In the fall there was the scent of apple orchards and the dusty scuff and rattle of fallen leaves. You picked up the loveliest samples, scarlet maple, golden beech, to show your teacher, then pin on a paper to trace.

When the first snow fell, you raced joyously through it, trying to catch the cool lacey flakes on your tongue. Drifts did not deter you. They were an excuse to wade.

Snow and ice held the earth fast most of winter, followed by a miracle when the warm days came. For now the gutters ran wild with the melted waters and sidewalks mirrored an upside-down world of sky and clouds and trees. And gazing down, down, you felt a breathless transporting.

You were one of the five foolish princesses who ran off at night into the world beneath the world and danced their slippers to shreds.

You spied the first robin on your way to school. And the first crocus, and it was news. And there were seedpods to be stepped on; how they squirted. And the fuzz of cottonwoods to catch, and dandelion fluff to be blown. And violets to be gathered in a shady wood, and clover to be braided. And you bounced balls, skipped ropes, and raced to join friends who were waiting, or they rushed up to join you. And you argued and philosophized and giggled and dreamed big dreams as you made this daily pilgrimage.

There was time for these things, to think and wonder and truly be a child on these long walks to school.

WHEN FAMILIES READ ALOUD

Who remembers a dear and memorable family custom, reading aloud?

In most households fathers did the honors. But in ours it was Mother's role. She had the most beautiful speaking voice in the world, we thought, and she read with "expression."

We were not scholars; few people were in our little Iowa town. No Dickens or Shakespeare or Thackeray for us. We borrowed the popular authors from the public library. Or Dad, taking a stroll downtown after supper, would come home with a striped sack of chocolates from the Candy Kitchen, and a shiny new copy of *The Saturday Evening Post*.

"How about reading to us, Mama?" he would suggest. And heads would fly up from doing homework around the dining room table. "Hurry up, hurry, Mama's going to read!"

The hard-coal burner clucked softly and shed its rosy glow on our faces as we all sprawled around it on the floor.

We gave ourselves over to the spell: Alexander Botts and his Earthworm tractor; the hilarious exploits of Florien Slappey.

Jack London's magnificent stories of the Klondike. The dog stories of Albert Peyson Terhune, Zane Grey's rousing and very pure westerns. Edna Ferber, Kathleen Norris. Gene Stratton Porter's *Freckles* and *Girl of the Limberlost*. Booth Tarkington's *Seventeen*.

We had never seen a real live author and we never expected to. We hadn't the remotest notion of the human beings who labored to give us such delight. To us their names on a book or story were simply tickets to enchantment. They never failed us. That they were not profound never occurred to us. We *enjoyed* them.

They gripped our fancy, transported us into lands and loves and lives more dramatic than our own. Therefore, we loved them. And loved Mother's voice as she sat in the creaking rocker, usually with a sleeping baby on her lap— her voice, the instrument of all this wonder.

Gone, long gone those enthralling hours. Hi-fi and radio and television have drowned out the voices of mere mothers and fathers. Mechanical marvels speak for us. And who needs imagination when everything is acted out for you on a screen?

And even if such were not the case, if all the radios and TVs were suddenly banished, where indeed would the good books be? Can you imagine gathering your kiddies around you for a cozy evening with James Jones or Grace Metalious or John O'Hara?

WHATEVER HAPPENED TO THAT TWILIGHT TIME?

Who remembers when . . .

Children played Run, Sheep, Run, beneath a corner light?

The crowds began gathering right after supper, in that lovely twilight hour just before the streetlamps came on. Fathers had just begun to rock on porches over the evening paper, the smell of their pipes and cigars wafting across the yard to mingle with the fragrance of new-cut lawns.

Mothers joined them shortly, still drying their hands from the dishes; and little girls, with a final swipe at the sink or the kitchen floor tore wildly out to join their brothers, who bossily had already selected their captains and were choosing up sides.

Who remembers the dark breathless thrill of the huddle as signals were decided on? The conspiracy, the plotting, the secret codes.

"Now Tornado Potato means we're going the other direction. But Devil's Pitchfork means we're headed your way, lay low!"

And slipping off across back fences and gardens to hide. And cowering in the darkness, with the stars beginning to blossom overhead . . . the sound of a freight train rumbling through town . . . the lonely barking of dogs. The whole night was mysterious, delicious with danger as footsteps came closer, voices arguing, and your leader called out those signals privy only to you.

Then at last the wild and glorious release of it—"Run, Sheep, Run!" Screaming like banshees you came tearing out of your hiding place, wild horses pounding toward base, not sheeplike at all. For your goal, the sole center of your living, breathing existence, was that serenely shining beacon on the corner, the pale and patient streetlamp.

Who remembers the gnats and mosquitoes swarming there in dinning circles like the children? And the moths that hurled themselves blindly to destruction in that fragile lady's burning eye beneath her scalloped hat. And the great night beetles—June bugs, you called them—fat and shiny, that dropped with horrible plopping clicks, and that the boys would thrust down your back if they suspected your revulsion.

Who remembers the parental voices calling for you to come in now? Insistent enemy orders that you pleaded with in vain. And the slow sweaty trudge back to your own porch steps, panting, tired, but too exhilarated to go to bed. And the cold blessing of a cup of well water, or a glass of your mother's tart iced lemonade.

KITES, OLD AND NEW

They buy them at the dime store now, in frail and slender oblongs, the kites that you used to fashion, kneeling with brothers and sisters on the kitchen floor. Is their pleasure the less for the simplified putting together? You wonder, as in a scant five minutes the kites are made.

"The string, where's some string? Oh, goodness, we forgot to get any kite string."

"Nonsense, who needs kite string?" you demand, producing plain white wrapping cord from a kitchen drawer.

"Mom, you can't fly kites with that, it's too heavy," the whole tribe hoots.

"Yes, you can. We always did. Now get busy and help me tie all the ends together."

Grudgingly, with a certain wry bemusement, they obey, and at least one flimsy kite acquires a lengthy launching cord. The littlest (likeliest victim) gets her coat, and to prove your point you accompany her into the yard. "Run, now run," you order, "unrolling the ball."

Excitedly, she obeys. A brisk breeze cooperatively snatches the kite, does its utmost. It wavers, struggles, almost makes it, flops to the ground.

"We told you the string's too heavy," the older ones insist. "That's all the matter is. You've *gotta* have lighter *string*."

"That's nonsense," you stubbornly claim. "Just a silly idea you kids have to spend more money. You think you have to buy everything these days."

To prove it, you grab the contrary little winged ship and plow frantically across the lawn. Again, like a feeble bird trying its wings, it struggles, flails the air, and shamefully falls.

Someone meanwhile has gone to the drugstore. Several fine new balls of kite cord emerge from a paper sack. (No string!) No one bothers to argue. The remaining fleet is efficiently attached and soon soaring.

"Well, I guess you win," you admit with a grin.

Your eyes follow the strange triumphant sails growing smaller above the trees. Your heart feels the old excited tug. For whether it be store-bought or fashioned in a kitchen, whether its cords be thriftily pieced together or unwound from a ball, a kite is always a mystery and a marvel, no matter what one's age.

HOW THOSE CEREALS HAVE CHANGED

Who remembers when breakfast cereals were blessedly few?

At our house there was little choice, we got the cheapest—cornflakes or oatmeal. But nothing tasted better than those crisp golden flakes spilling into a bowl, or the oatmeal laced with raisins and brown sugar on a cold winter's morning. Especially if you got "First of the milk!" which everybody started yelling almost as soon as he popped out of bed.

For that was before homogenization and cartons of Half-and-Half in the grocery store. The cream rose like rich furry neckpieces on the throats of those cold but pleasant ladies, the milk bottles on the porch.

On Sundays and special occasions we got shredded wheat or the puffed kinds that were beginning to be sold. But whatever the kind, the cereal boxes sat on the table to be thoughtfully studied while you munched. Though mothers sometimes got fancy and yanked them off, especially when company came, those cereal boxes on the family breakfast table were an American commonplace.

Small fry learned their letters from them; little jokes and games and puzzles could be made. Recognizing this, the companies began to print the jokes and games and puzzles. And soon thereafter the amazing offers which have led the modern American parent to the brink of nervous prostration, beset by youngsters tearing the tops off these boxes, fighting furiously to root out the prizes, and meanwhile spilling their contents all over the kitchen floor. Or besieged by them for "only a dollar" to be mailed with the boxtop for membership in a secret club of twenty million members, with a sheriff's badge for identification, or a genuine magic ring.

Breakfast cereal companies have become gigantic business empires that often control the destinies of radio and TV stars. And they knock themselves out continually to come up with something new. The jaded appetites of our offspring are tempted by presugared cereals, cereals that taste like chocolate candy, cereals in the shape of the alphabet, space ships, animals at the zoo.

In fact, today's housewife faces such a bewildering battery on the grocery shelves, and is so put upon by the varieties requested, that her head swims. She thinks enviously of her mother, whose income was more limited and whose choices were few and hearty.

WHEN ATTICS WERE IN STYLE

What a pity, it seems to me, that in this era of ranch houses, so few children have an attic in which to play.

That "storage space" with a pull-down ladder has been made to substitute for what was once a marvelous boon both both mothers and small fry.

"Oh, go to the attic and play," harried parents used to be able to say to noisy offspring on a rainy day. Or, "Please, may we play in the attic?" the youngsters themselves would beg, as a special treat.

What family room, however efficient, or rumpus room, however gay, can offer the adventure, the enchantment, of the attics of yesteryear?

If possible, I would tack an old-fashioned attic onto every modern house. And the specifications would be:

A door that squeaks a little when a child's hands turn the knob. Stairs that are castle-steep and narrow as canyon walls. A window that looks down from the landing like a dusty, slightly scary glass eye . . .

A mellow and slightly eerie smell for this world of just-under-the-roof. Stale and stuffy, yes, but mysterious and promising, with the tang of the rough unpainted lumber that tops the house and is intimate with the sky . . .

Long empty alleys for running and yelling and noisily pounding feet. Dark little cubbies for hiding in. Floors thick enough to muffle the racket. Yet cups and hollows of space to echo the wild fruity music of children's shouts . . .

Secret attic sounds of its own: A squirrel scurrying along the eaves. A tree shaking hands with the shingles. The wind whistling by. And on rainy days the rhythm of drops on the roof, cozy as popping corn.

Many things should, of course, be stored in this attic: Hallowe'en costumes. Easter baskets. Great boxes bulging with bells and tinsel and Christmas trimmings. Flags from the Fourth of July. All the accoutrements of a magical children's calendar that boasts only holidays . . .

And there should be mysterious souvenirs to wonder about: Thick plush photograph albums, fastened with silver clasps. Bundles of ribbon-tied letters. Pressed flowers. Tissue-wrapped locks of hair. A child's own baby clothes . . .

And in this attic too there should be treasures for playing house. Porch furniture. Old bridge lamps. Bedsteads. A grandfather's clock. And for the dressing up, trunks of old hats and evening dresses and fancy shoes . . .

Lucky the child who has such an attic for exploring. Lucky the parents. Every house that really means home should have an attic on top!

MOTHER'S WONDERFUL WISHING BOOK

"Look, children, see what's come in the mail," I summoned my young one day. "A big fat mail-order catalog!"

They rushed up to see what I was so pleased about. And reacted with about as much enthusiasm as if I'd just presented them with a big fat telephone directory. Its plethora of riches failed to impress them; they see all this and more in store windows every day. And who ever heard of sending away for something you haven't both seen and been fervently exhorted to buy on TV? Politely, they listened to my promises that when it got a little older I'd let them cut it up for paper dolls—and escaped.

Somewhat saddened, I stood sniffing its elusive, nostalgic scent of thin inky pages and thick glossy ones, letting myself be whisked back to the days when the arrival of mail-order catalogs signaled spring and fall. Like spying your first robin, or a scarlet maple leaf. *Sears, Roebuck. Montgomery Ward.* What magical names! For if you lived in a small town or out in the country, they brought the whole thrilling world to your door.

This was important in several ways. For those often snowbound, without much choice in merchandise in the few available stores, these vast packages of print and pictures spread before dazzled eyes almost everything known to the needs of man. Entire families were often clothed and outfitted from their pages. Whole houses were furnished by mail—curtains, rugs, parlor set, nickel-plated stove, and even the kitchen sink. But more, the catalog was a source of information, of contact, a glimpse of fabulous people at work and play. It was a springboard for hope, the touchstone of dreams.

To children, its arrival was as if Santa Claus himself had walked in the door. We fought over turns to explore it, lying enrapt on the floor. We spent hours poring over its pages, especially before Christmas, greedily drawing up long impossible lists from the section marked "Toys." Desperately though we yearned, fervently though we believed in the miracle of possessing, I don't think it was the *getting* that really mattered. In these orgies of imagination we were fulfilled.

In the same way we spent thousands of nonexistent dollars fervently filling out discarded blanks as we "ordered" the most expensive items—furniture, jewelry, furs.

Most important of all were the paper dolls. With the advent of a new catalog we were free to race for the scissors and start cutting up the old. Having each chosen a basic beauty, we would then whack off the heads and feet of other models in order to equip her with a wardrobe worthy of a queen. True, the arms were often in curious positions and the garments didn't always fit; no matter, the dolls continued to beam and that was good enough for us.

Again, we would choose someone we wanted to be. Gloria Swanson, Aunt Tressa, the minister, the mayor, a town belle—and hunt until we found a fancied likeness. We then cut out families for them—dolls that suited and matched their real or imagined circles. My brother dubbed these our "Hippity People"—perhaps because of the way they danced across the floor in a breeze or a blast from the hot-air furnace. Each of us picked a corner of the dining room where we set up housekeeping with our chosen family.

They became vitally real to us one long cold winter when we were housebound with a succession of measles, mumps, and chicken pox. Gloria Swanson visited back and forth with Uncle Horace, the minister, the judge's family. Their children went to parties and dances, had weddings, and when one of them got torn in two, had a funeral. (We found everything in the catalog but the casket.) Then one day when the snow was melting, my brother took the lot of them outside for a boat ride. He was gone a long time. Returning, he confessed. The boat had upset and all our

Hippity People were drowned. We all cried. Somehow, it spelled the end of our catalog paper dolls. And the beginning of our growing up.

Yet we never outgrew our awed admiration for the beautiful creatures in those books. What grace they had—standing hand on hip as they chatted with each other—what charm, what style. On them even a housedress looked enticing. And the men were so suave and handsome they glorified even a pair of Big Huck overalls. In the never-never land they inhabited there was no dirt, no dishwater, no floors to scrub, no spilled oatmeal. Everyone was radiant, young, enchanting, and it seemed that if only you could obtain their garments for yourself or your parents, somehow your own dull, small everyday world would become enchanting as well. How was it possible to believe otherwise, especially when you read the poetic prose in which they were described?

Though Mother, too, faithfully studied and loved her catalogs, she seldom sent away for things. "It's hard to tell how things really look from a picture," she said. "And besides you can't always be sure they'll fit. Also," she reasoned, "we should support our hometown merchants. They've been good to us." ("Good to us" meant letting us have credit when times were hard.) We found her attitude frustrating in view of this sure-fire magic. She didn't have many clothes, and my sister and I longed to send away and get her a dress.

A dress was simply beyond our means, after weeks of saving, so we decided to settle for a hat. We picked out the prettiest we could find, not a very big hat, but one richly adorned with fruit and flowers. Eagerly we filled out the order blank, stealthily emptying our banks and slipping off to the post office to buy a money order. We could hardly wait. We wanted it in time for Easter. Our suspense was agonizing as the weeks slipped by. Every time she longingly fingered a hat downtown, or spoke about trimming an old one, we were tempted to tell her.

At last the mail truck stopped before our house. As the driver marched up the walk and knocked we thought we would explode. "But we didn't order anything," Mother protested, even as we began to shout: "Surprise! Surprise!" Baffled, she opened the box, lifted it out of the tissue paper, and there it was in all its glory. Even more gorgeous than we had imagined, rosy and shiny, velvet-ribboned, it was a veritable cornucopia of fruit and flowers.

"Oh, my!" Mother exclaimed, looking slightly dismayed. She picked it up gingerly, turning it around on her hand. "This is for *me*?" She'd never worn anything but the plainest of hats; obviously she was almost too overcome with joy to speak.

She went at once to the mirror and put it on, with some difficulty, over her generous mounds of hair. Her hair was her crowning glory. The hat sort of rode on back of it like a ship perched upon a wave. Until that moment it had never occurred to us that the hat might not become her. In our loving dreams she would be transformed before our eyes into a likeness of one of those dream-creatures of the catalog.

Instead, Mother turned to us looking stricken—half sad, half amused. "Oh, girls, girls, it's the most beautiful hat in the world!" she cried, embracing us. "Just wait, I'll curl my hair Saturday night and Sunday I'll have my powder on. It'll look just—fine!"

It did. It almost did. We all complimented her profusely when she was ready for church, and so did her friends when she got there. But something was wrong and we knew it with a queer wrench in the region of our stomachs. It was our first troubled sip of that wry brew, disillusionment. I think we grew up a little that day, as we had on the death of our paper dolls.

Mother loyally wore the hat—how long I don't recall. After a while it didn't look funny on her any more, it simply became a part of her, like her dependable blue crepe dress. When its flowers began to wilt, its fruit to wither, she even doctored them up and wore it some more. She was actually regretful when at last she was forced to abandon it. "I'll never forget this hat," she said, and she spoke for all of us.

I think of it now on that rare occasion when a catalog comes in the mail. I thought of it as I tried to rouse in my children the sense of delight that a catalog used to bring. But a catalog cannot be the passport to wonder to them that it was to us. These children who are so rich in material things that they are desperately poor in the need for make-believe!

No, really to thrill to the magic of a catalog you must live in the country or a little town. And be a pigtailed dreamer in the days when winters were long and lonely . . . and paper dolls came alive, and a hat was truly a Hat to be worn lengthily, head high, by a mother who loved her little girls.

THE TENT SHOW

Sometimes, waiting for the curtain to go up at the theater, I remember my first exposure to this magical experience when I was a little girl in Storm Lake, Iowa.

Spring and fall were the most thrilling times of the year, because Sweet's Famous Players came to town for a three-day stand. The brown canvas tent with the scalloped edges would blossom on a lot beside the railroad tracks.

The dazzling limousine of the Sweets was to be seen parked in front of the hotel. And all day long and into the twilight, the wistful, wildly appealing notes of their music wagon would sing up and down the shady streets, making it positive agony if you could not go.

There was the smell of trampled grass as people crowded up to buy their tickets under the striped canvas marquee. Perched in the wooden box selling them would be George D. Sweet himself, a grave and portly man usually wearing a handsome pearl-gray hat and smoking a cigar.

"Hi, G.D.!" those who claimed to know him would call eagerly; and no honor swelled the bosom more than to receive his nod of recognition and be grandly waved in free.

Sometimes it was Mrs. Sweet who reigned, white-haired, diamonds flashing, like some grand duchess of fairyland. She was rich-voiced, rollicking, flattering, but she seldom let anyone in without paying.

We always sat in the bleachers; they were cheaper than

the reserved seat chairs, and actually children could see better there. The orchestra would be playing and the actors, already made-up, were selling boxes of candy in which, if you were lucky, you found a number entitling you to a fabulous prize. (Lamps, dishes, jewelry, temptingly displayed and awarded just before the final act.)

The real suspense, however, was to await the curtain's rise. Finally, when you couldn't bear it any longer, the lights would blink, the actors duck backstage, and the curtain roll up on sheer enchantment.

The three-night stand always included a romantic comedy, a serious drama, and a mystery. All very wholesome. If they were truly Broadway hits (we wouldn't have known the difference), as George D. claimed in his flat little curtain speeches, they had been rigorously scoured of sex and ridden of the oaths that pepper such today. In fact, George D. Sweet's was known in the trade as the Sunday School Show.

Mrs. Sweet was the undisputed star. When she swept onstage people rose cheering to their feet. Always a messenger dashed down the aisle with a mass of red roses which she acknowledged, blowing kisses to make the heart soar. Boldly and inevitably she stole the show, especially in character parts with a thick Irish brogue. The only person to whom she gave quarter was her daughter Marjorie, a Shirley Temple of her time, who later went to Broadway, succeeded, and returned during the depression to lend her talents to try and save the show.

People had radios by then, and talking movies. And cars made it easier to get to the city. Crowds were still good, though lacking the enthusiasm that used to greet the little traveling company. And it was harder to get good plays.

The Sweets had always scorned "Tobies," those cheap farces which are easier to produce and cost less in royalties. Now they were reduced to using them. And to Mrs. Sweet's surprise and secret consternation, the audiences loved them. The rowdier the better. It hurt her pride, her belief in people and all that the show had always stood for.

Then one of her worst fears was realized. She had always been passionately afraid of storms, worried lest one of them blow the tent away. During their last season together a tornado not only destroyed the tent but seriously hurt one of the canvas boys. George D. rounded up another tent from a circus, and the show went on. But his wife never got over it. And when George D. himself was killed shortly afterward in a car accident, she sold the show.

I have seen many famous actors and actresses since those days. But none has ever created the spell of Mrs. George D. No moment has ever equaled that when she received those roses, or the grip on the heart when the great George D. quietly stepped before the curtain to wish us good night and farewell.

DOING DISHES WITH A DAUGHTER

"Goody, the dishwasher's broken," a daughter said the other day, "now we can wash dishes and talk!"

Wash dishes together and talk, I thought . . . And I remembered the marvelous discussions over the dishes that my mother and sisters and I used to have. The dreams that we dreamed aloud as we washed and dried. And the confidences exchanged. The mistakes, regrets, hopes, ambitions. And oh, the problems to be solved.

There is something about the click of dishes and silver, a kettle of scalding water, a drawerful of fresh dry towels, and a dishpan full of suds . . . Something that breaks down barriers between members of the female sex.

Listen to women working together after a church supper. Or a bunch of women relatives in the kitchen after a family dinner. You can scarcely hear the sound of their labors for the vigorous clatter of their tongues. How they laugh together, consult each other, argue, noisily discuss.

And this is particularly true of a mother and her daughters. The kitchen is a place where they can retreat. They feel safe in its feminine confines.

The stove, the sink, the cupboards—these are eternal symbols of womanhood. And as we scour them, wipe up counters, wash and dry the vessels in which we have cooked and served a family's food, all that is truly womanly in our nature seems to come to the surface.

Dishwashers are wonderful. They simplify immensely the after-meal cleaning up. By whipping the dishes into them at the end of each course the dishes are half finished by the time the meal is done. And even if you wait, one individual—even a child—can do alone what it often took several women working together to achieve.

Yet something else is lost. Something that is meaningful and precious to women: Companionship. The chance—yes, the excuse—to draw together in useful, strictly feminine tasks—and talk.

THE OLD-FASHIONED CHRISTMAS EVE

Who remembers small-town Christmas Eves that were always celebrated with a pageant at the church? And the snow that fell so softly, as whole families headed toward this focal point.

Under the corner streetlamps the flakes spun and twinkled like fairies trying their wings. The whole earth wore a jeweled wrap. And your feet made little squeals on the hard-packed walks, like all the voices of excitement clamoring within . . .

The church smelled hot from the furnace. The spicy tang of the tree mingled with that of hymnals and galoshes and coffee brewing somewhere in huge granite pots . . .

Voices hummed, packages rattled, Sunday School teachers frantically assembled children in their proper rows. You swished your head, magnificently kinky from braids unbound, and imagined everybody was thinking how beautiful you were . . .

Shadows moved behind white sheets hung up for curtains. Garbed in bathrobes and turbaned in towels, your father and other men became strangers saying, "Let us go now even unto Bethlehem and see this thing which has come to pass." . . . And the click and swish of the sheets being pulled. And at last the revelation: For there stood Joseph beside a manger with real straw. And Mary cradling a baby—sometimes a big doll, but once a real baby. The minister's new baby! You could hear it crowing and glimpse a moving hand. It lived! For a breathless, rapturous moment, the living breathing Christ Child was right there in your midst.

Who remembers the programs, with their songs and recitations? The desperately pounding heart as you swished forward in your crackling taffeta and new glory of curly hair. The horror of having to be prompted, the triumph of doing well . . .

And the smell of the tiny candles being lighted on the tree, twinkling tallow stars to signal that something magic was about to happen . . . And the jangling of sleighbells in the hall, and the superintendent asking, "What's this? Do I hear somebody?" And the wild and frenzied screaming, "Santa! Santa Claus!"

As you grew older he began to look familiar—like Grandpa Griffith or old Mr. Samsel, or sometimes your dad. But no matter—when he patted you on the head or handed you a bag of hard candies he became the droll elf of the eternal fairy tale of North Pole and Make-Believe.

And the Ladies Aid served cookies and coffee. And parents visited, and children, mad with anticipation, begged to go home for the stockings yet to be hung . . . And at last you all poured out onto the steps that had been paved with ground diamonds.

"Good night, Merry Christmas, come to see us!" voices called as families set off along the cold sparkling streets.

The snow had usually stopped by now. The night was still and clear. All the stars glittered. But there was always one bigger and brighter than the rest. A great gem that seemed to stand still as if to mark the mystery. You gazed at it in wonder all the way home.

MOTHER'S APRON

"Oh, Mother, buy an apron, please let's buy an apron!" my children urge at church bazaars. Aprons have a special fascination for them; they are forever tugging me toward that table where other women swarm, picking and choosing from among the bright displays. The aprons dancing saucily overhead, or piled in colorful heaps upon the counter. Striped aprons, ruffled aprons, old-fashioned checkered aprons trimmed with rickrack and braid and appliqué. Smart modern ones of orange burlap, hand-painted with abstract designs. A froth of cocktail whimsies of impractical, unwashable net, all bead-and-sequin trimmed.

And suddenly, though an apron's the last thing I want, a little fever of excitement touches me; I too begin to root through this female flower garden and pluck a bright bouquet.

I sometimes wonder why aprons are still so popular, when so few of us actually have much use for them any more? Now there was a good excuse for aprons in our mothers' day. In that blissful pre-cholesterol era hardly anybody broiled or pressure-cooked; no, foods were fried lengthily, smokily, often sputteringly, in good old-fashioned lard. While to bake a cake you coped long and lovingly with flour and eggs and maybe clabbered milk, pausing to shake down the ashes in the old coal range, smash more kindling across your knees, and shovel in more cobs or chunks of rich black dusty coal. An apron was not only part of a woman's uniform, it was protection.

But today, with our instant mixes and frozen foods, only the dedicated cook spends much time in her easy-clean push-button kitchen. And even when she does, her usual costume is shorts or slacks. So who needs an apron?

What inspires us then to make and buy and bestow aprons upon each other, or acquire them for ourselves? Is it mainly that an apron is so—womanly? That apron strings are subtly entangled with childhood memories—the days when mothers stayed home to sew and clean and cook and can. The days when a mother was always *there*.

Women dressed like women then, and anyone who didn't was considered either sinful or slightly cracked. Mothers prepared for their day's assault upon the premises by donning layer upon layer of garments, culminating with a "housedress." A "housedress" might be vaguely pretty, with a bow or a few buttons on it, but mostly it was plain, functional, washable. The costume was crowned with a dustcap, often of sturdy gingham to match the dress. Or it might be a perky concoction of lace and ribbon rosettes. In any case, it protected the hair from the dust that mothers whacked or shook or swept from the house. And always, over all, as a kind of extra fortification, a mother wore an apron. She put it on in the morning and didn't remove it until she cleaned up for the afternoon.

Women were better organized then, perhaps because they had to be. They didn't have cars to whisk them off to meetings or the supermarket while the clothes washed and dried. My mother certainly never did the impulse cleaning to which I'm prone, nor popped a pie in the oven or started an ironing after dark. Each day was sacred to its appointed tasks—the laundry, the baking, the scrubbing; what's more, she arose early, accomplished the scheduled undertaking, and was ready for the sacred rite of making herself presentable by two o'clock. (To be "caught dirty" any time after three would have been sheer disgrace.) This involved at least a sponge bath with a kettle of cistern water heated on the stove, the neat doing up of hair with a number of pins and tortoise shell combs, putting on a "good" dress and silk instead of cotton stockings, finishing off with a touch of rice powder and a dab of cologne. She might receive callers or lie down with the latest installment of a Kathleen Norris serial.

This brief span during the afternoon was the only time she was minus an apron. When she arose to start supper, did she change, as we are wont to, into something comfortable if sloppy? No, indeed, she simply protected her dress with a nice fresh apron. Sometimes a big apron, that encircled her neck like loving arms; sometimes one that tied at the waist in a bow that brothers or your dad would yank when they wanted to tease her. If company was coming, it would be a fancy apron, all organdy frills, the kind women still wear for serving dinners and sociables at the church. But family apron or company apron, it was always crisp and pretty and clean, and she often wore it to the table.

Frequently she continued to wear it on into the evening after the dishes were done. Standing at the back fence visiting with a neighbor, strolling about the yard to see about her flowers, or sitting on the porch in the twilight watching the children catch fireflies. And if the air was chilly, she wrapped her arms in her apron to keep them warm.

It was big enough to shelter you too sometimes if you were cold. There was always a handkerchief for you in one of its roomy pockets. It was a part of her lap.

Her apron gave you assurance. Rushing in from school or play, even if you didn't see or hear her, you felt better just from finding that apron hanging behind the kitchen door or dangling across a chair. Her apron, smelling of cookies and starch and Mother. It comforted you. It made you feel secure. It was a part of her—like her laugh or her eyes or her big black pocketbook.

Sometimes I worry about us a little, we busy, often absent mothers in our slacks. What do we leave behind to greet the child when he comes seeking us? What consoling reminder of our presence?

Maybe that's why our youngsters instinctively want us to own aprons. Lots of aprons. And to wear one now and then. Why we ourselves can't resist buying them at bazaars. Perhaps we still feel the strong sweet tug of apron strings.

Beauty in Your Own Backyard

Every year of my life I grow more convinced that it is the wisest and best to fix our attention on the beautiful and the good, and dwell as little as possible on the evil and the false.

—*William Cecil*

"SWAN LAKE"

Even the ducks can't sleep on nights when the moon is full. Sluggards by day, often drowsing far into the morning with their heads curled under their wings, on moony nights they rouse, making raw little sounds of discovery and agitation. With a stretch of necks and flap of wings, they waddle to the edge of the black satin water and sink into it, to come coasting, like luminous white ghost ships trailing their reflections.

"Look at the ducks," the children say. "They're heading for the moonpath!" And true, they sail directly toward that diamond-riddled bar. Across it they glide, back and forth, tracing their own silvery patterns and making gay, raucous sounds, as if in retort to the frogs in the rushes.

"I'll get some bread." A child streaks bare-legged into the cabin and returns with a bulging sack. "Let me, let me throw some!" Others join her, squatting moon-traced on the float to fling the crusts.

The ducks circle in unison, their movements in such liquid precision that someone remarks, "Swan Lake!" For that is now the picture; they are a quartet of feathered dancers, snow-white, effortless, making their greedy yet graceful arabesques to the music of frogs and crickets and humming night things. While silently flooding the stage from above them the huge round spotlight of the moon shines down.

A NECKLACE OF LANTERNS

You bundle the toddler into his bright blue jacket and little peaked cap. "Now let's bell the kitty," you say, and thrust his arms through the red harness with its jingling bells, and turn him loose outdoors.

He kicks delightedly through a pile of dry leaves, laughing to hear them rattle. He squats, hands solemnly on his knees like a little old man, to examine things on the ground.

Industriously he fills his shiny green dump truck with sticks and leaves. Then, yawning, he sprawls sidewise in his little painted chair, cheeks as rosy as the leaves, chin wet and drooling, eyes the bland contented blue of the sky.

The October breeze catches the cold wet sheets you are hanging on the line. Leaves fall, and trees keep up a gentle undulating dance of branches, like old people nodding their heads in resignation as the children leave home.

The little one trots up, rises to futile tiptoe as he grasps for the fluttering sheets. Ah, the fat bulging clothespin bag is nearer. Fingers go probing, discover the fascinating shapes. Vigorously he hurls them from him—into the leaf pile, into the stream.

"Hey, you!" You rush to the rescue—and turn to find him happily straddling the clothes props for a pony ride.

Japanese lanterns hold the sun in orange cups against the white garage. You break off several branches, and some bright-berried stems of a vine. "F'ower!" These too the plump little fists would clutch. Laughing, you string a chain of the flaming lanterns about his neck. They jiggle, delicate and lovely against the vivid blue suit. He laughs too, and grasps them with both hands.

Dumping the whole treasure into your empty basket—baby, berries, and bright fall leaves—you go with a merry jingling into the house.

SQUIRRELS IN THE FALL

This is the season when the squirrels run freely among the bared branches of the trees.

They are like impish actors cavorting on a stripped stage. All props are gone, no leaves curtain their antics. They chase each other with clownlike abandon, performing their blithe acrobatics unimpeded upon the naked fretwork of the trees.

Their fur is as silvery as the season; their tawny bodies catch the light. They wear their little gray-brown disguises with an air both of blending to their background and of showing off.

Their tails are jaunty question marks. Fluffy plumes.

They are like little ladies waving their fans at a party—or housewives, busy about their marketing. You can almost see them with their shopping baskets on their arms, elbowing and wriggling their way toward the bargains at a supermarket. Then, anxious as parents returning to see about the children, they come scurrying home, sometimes bearing a nut or a bread crust, retrieved or boldly thieved.

Now too their houses are open to behold. Their great leafy nests, shielded all summer, have come plainly into view, rocked securely in the crotches of the trees.

Squirrels are truly free spirits. To watch them running about so lightly, so nimbly, is to feel one's own spirit oddly lifted and heightened, one's own heart lightened and freed.

AUTUMN SHADOWS

Shadows come into some new, brilliant individuality on a sparkling day of fall.

Setting off to the store on a bright October morning, you find your own shadow, like the useless imp of Stevenson's poem, tagging gaily yet persistently along behind.

Sidewalks are striped with the inky shadows of your neighbor's picket fence. While farther down the street a steel one meshes the sunlit grass like a woman's hairnet.

The whole neighborhood is wearing a lilting mantilla of shadowlace. The trees reprint themselves in a shadowy blur upon the pavement.

Nor are they in the least exclusive, these lovely shapes. They sprinkle their charm along back alleys with their trash barrels and heaps of brick. They splay like a fairy fountain across the silvery gray sides of a lumbering garbage truck.

Yet there are strong shadows, too: The long lines of a house lean down to reprint its sturdiness upon the grass. Tree trunks rise in a singing sculpture more powerful than stone.

All the small life of the morning is likewise shadow-linked. A cardinal spurting from the hedge, a bluejay tilting on a branch, a squirrel scampering across a sunny roof, a flock of children playing. Each wears his little shadow as proudly as Peter Pan.

WINTER TREES

Trees are like people. Alike in so many respects, but each so different, so varied, so singular, so strange . . .

This is the season when trees seem to be saying, with that eloquent silence that only trees can assume, "Look, oh look at me."

How their trunks soar upward, strong and joyous with the freedom of boughs uncluttered by leaves. They are like tall-bodied women dancing unclothed in the tingling embrace of sky and wind . . .

And how the branches reach out to admire themselves. How they curve and lift and turn, jut upward, droop low, each in a sculpture unique. Look down any avenue of trees, no matter how similar, and you will find no two the same . . .

Trees stand pure against the sky these days. Only the frail penned pattern of twigs intervenes—and it in a delicate, wispy fashion, as a veil enhances the charm of a woman's face . . .

The trees stand strong, spare, magnificent, and serene.

SNOW COMES BY NIGHT

Snow comes by night—a quiet magic. A secret tiptoeing down while people sleep.

Only a creaking door, a stirred branch, speak of its coming, and they so hushed and careful it is like the accidental rattle of paper packages on Christmas Eve. Only the outdoors is privy to the snow's secret coming, and it does not reveal the surprise . . .

And now—morning. The first one up in a family cries out, "Why, it snowed last night!" Standing there before the window in excited wonder, he gazes out across the muffled back yard.

The snow lies smooth and untrodden, its white expanse unmarred by any print save perhaps the delicate tracery of a rabbit, as soft and secret as the snow itself. The snow glints with a million little points that grow brighter as the sun rises, as if pleased with itself, growing more bold in its delight.

All the trees are furred with it, the smallest branches bearing their precious ermine carefully against the wind. Now and then glinting veils of it come cascading down, and the trees become graceful dancers, half hidden, half revealed through wheeling draperies.

Snow banks the creek, which flashes along through this white expanse, its black taffeta surface reflecting the sheeted world, and flinging back the light. All its peering rocks wear white fur caps, and its edges are frilled and fluted with ice . . .

Snow comes by night, to fill grown-ups with wonder, and children with enchantment. The youngsters are wild to possess it. They will scarcely eat their breakfasts. They scramble into boots, mittens, scarves. With an urgency and an intentness as instinctive as that of homing birds, they drag their sleds behind them across its white bosom. They fling themselves into its soft yielding flesh. They root and burrow to touch its white heart.

Soon the snow is patterned with their footsteps and the twining, twisting ribbons of their sleds. It is trampled and tumbled and marked up like a scribbled page—but not defiled. For snow is God's own invitation to children, written softly across the world.

THE RAINS OF MARCH

Gray are the rains of March. Not nimble and prancing with a promise of petals, like April showers. Nor even bearing the soft twining beauty and brilliance of snow. No, they come humbly out of gloomy skies, as if unsure of their welcome or their purpose in falling at all.

They are sometimes but a mist in the eyes of a troubled world, a cloud over its brow. Their tears flow mostly in silence, or softly, as if for sorrows remote but haunting from some far past.

You must listen for their sounds, the whispered sigh, the patient drip from eaves. Only now and then, wind-roused, do they bestir themselves to come battering at the roof in a sudden frenzy, or dancing their dismal dance upon the walks.

Gray are the rains of March, yet paving the streets with silver, mirroring the lights of passing cars, and soaking the trees black as shining knights in suits of mail.

They fill the earth from a vast cup of grief. And it gives back quivering puddles and rivulets that go searching through the old sodden grasses and leaves.

The rains of March are brooding, like a woman bowed with despair. Yet there is a gray beauty in this sorrow, a gentle giving over to temporary despondency. All is not hopeless and lost, this too will pass—we know, we know—but meanwhile let us weep what we must.

SUDDENLY IT'S SPRING

Spring comes as subtly as snow in the night. It slips up on you with its vague powderings of green.

The maple trees, naked and wind-tossed one day, the next are beaded with buds and standing like princesses serene. In a few more, the tiny, half-seen pricks, no bigger than pencil points, have swollen and become a mass of rosy near-bloom.

The ground is suddenly brash with grass, the forsythias leap into yellow flame. Their fires are purest gold, like fronds of sunshine congealed, thin as lace. And as swiftly as if a wrap had been tossed across their gray-brown shoulders, the hedges turn green . . .

And now the maples begin to rain down their rosy blossoming until the ground is carpeted pink. One day you take your work onto an upstairs porch where the sky is a blinding blue, and you are sheltered by the arched arms of the trees. And as you labor, the rosy bud-flowers keep falling . . . falling . . . with a soft whisper upon your white papers, in a fuzzy plopping rain, like caterpillars . . .

Then, but a day or two later, only the finest, lower fronds of these rosy bud-flowers remain. Above them, like white-green candles, proudly jut the tight-curled leaves.

THE SPARKLERS

Three little girls at bedtime suddenly remember they haven't burned all their sparklers, hoarded ever since the Fourth of July. Clambering out of their bunks at your country cabin, they come pleading to be allowed to finish off the fireworks then and there.

Their faces are rosy from too much sun and water; their noses and cheeks clownlike with white dabs of healing cream. They wear shorty pajamas made in an old-fashioned bloomer style, and their long hair is in their eyes.

Finding no objection, you shepherd them down to the patio where a tiny new moon is shining, little and young and thin like a fledgling girl herself. You strike matches and cup your hands against the breeze, to light their precious sticks.

Squealing and chattering, in tune with the creatures that chirp and squeak from the trees, they begin to prance joyfully about, waving wands of brilliance. They are unreal in the pallid light, like figures out of a medieval fairy tale. Not quite child and not quite witch and not quite sprite, with their blowing hair, their curious garb. Their merrily dabbed faces are grotesque in the glow of their sputtering stars.

"Wheee . . . wheeee . . .!" Their voices blend with the night birds' screech. Behind them is the recitative of crickets and locusts, the heavy thunk-thug . . . thunk-thug of frogs in the rushes. The wind tosses the streaming hair of the willows along the bank, and the strands of hair across their glittering eyes.

ANGLING FOR THE MOON

Everybody else is going to have fat-dripping hamburgers for supper, but your husband, who's on a diet, must settle for something harboring fewer calories.

"I know what, I'll catch you some fish," you announce. "And we'll roast them over the coals after the others have finished."

You fly down to the dock and confidently bait your hook. And sure enough, no sooner has the minnow gone diving into the water than the bobber follows and you pull up a lively bluegill.

"Okay, now go get his brothers," you tell the still vigorous bait. But to no avail. Not another nibble do you get.

Determinedly, you sit on the float facing the cabin porch where the others proceed with their fare. You hear their voices, laughing, arguing. You smell the tangy charcoal smoke that sifts up white against the lilac twilight sky.

The small log house on the hill admires its own face in the olive-green water, and beside it are mirrored the long-limbed trees. They lean there like slender ladies draped in shawls of dark Spanish lace. And one of them wears a great yellow pearl in her hair!

Your line reaches straight into this shimmering loveliness. Each time you withdraw it, it is as if you're about to catch one of these lace-shrouded figures—a curious kind of Spanish mermaid. Or perhaps pull in the very gem itself, round, gold-white, glowing.

At last regretfully you retreat. Bearing your lone fish, you climb back up the rock steps. "Hope you're not very hungry," you tell your patiently waiting mate. "This is all I got—but I almost caught the moon."

HOW BEAUTIFUL IS A FISH

"But who cleans them?" people ask when we wax enthusiastic about all the fish we catch at our cabin on Lake Jackson, Virginia. And I am continually baffled by the number of women who act either amazed or vaguely horrified when I admit that I actually enjoy cleaning fish. I might as well, since the sink is usually full of them, and I just can't bear to see the poor things flopping and gasping about.

Fish don't suffer, some people claim. But unless a fish can personally assure you he doesn't mind choking to death I recommend giving him the benefit of a knife. Having severed the head, you can easily yank out his neat little vitals. You then have a handy pocket in which to get a grip while stripping off the scales.

Men, for some reason, save the head till last. "How would you like to have somebody stick a finger down your throat and skin you alive?" you scold. But they insist a fish doesn't feel a thing; in fact he lies so still it could be he likes it.

Techniques aside, our fish are so beautiful. The crappies, the bass, the bluegills. The fat spunky little bluegills especially, armored in gold and silver, with the deep blue scallop behind the eye. And the arched, silver-sheathed crappies. And the heavy yet slender bass, who are a deep olive green yet also a dull luminous gold. Each scale, aligned in lovely precision, is a thin golden coin outlined with a dark pencil.

And the dusky green-gold tapers off to the creamy white V of the belly.

When, except while cleaning it, do you really see how exquisitely a fish is made? The pinky tones around the fins and lip and tail. And the eyes, blank, staring, like glass buttons stuck on. To scale a fish is to feel and see a fountain of crystals flying. Or it is like stripping off a sequin sheath and finding beneath it an ever purer, more luminous satin-smooth silver that reproduces the fish's colors and all its markings.

No circus performer in spangles, no princess adorned in the finest fabrics and gems can surpass the sheer shimmering beauty of a humble fish lying in the kitchen sink.

DRAMA IN THE NIGHT

The doorbell rings one night, and a slim helmeted youth informs you you'll be without electricity for a while. "We're working on the transformer across the street."

Instant excitement pervades the house, a sense of impending drama. Candles are brought forth, ancient oil lamps lit. Bathrooms take on strange new shapes and shadows as small fry splash and dry themselves by the eerie light.

"Oh, how beautiful," a daughter calls from the front steps. "Mother, Daddy, come look!" And there it is before you—pageantry and drama on the darkened street.

Crowning the brows of two great throbbing trucks are ruby lights; and from them ruddy fingers jut, painting the wet shining grass with scarlet, sloshing gold on neighboring windowpanes.

Figures move about in this shifting light, purposeful workmen in tropical hats.

Looking curiously like a misplaced professor, one in eyeglasses perches on the curb, bending over a big notebook. A generator churns. From the equipment truck juts a long white arm that bends back upon itself and swings a rectangular "bucket" up and up.

"It's an aerolift," the foreman tells you, a gentle-faced older man who stands arms folded, chewing gum. "Originally used for cherry picking, but ideal for jobs like this. They make them now of fiberglass, which is a non-conductor of electricity."

"Where is everybody?" a neighbor demands, striding from her own dark house. "If it was an accident or a fire there'd be a crowd." And you sit together remarking on human nature that will gather at scenes of catastrophe, yet ignore the drama and beauty of constructive things. And speaking of these humble heroes of the night— men who work at skilled and dangerous jobs, unknown, unsung.

You see the head of the man in the bucket emerge, the thrust of his broad shoulders and his arms, heavily sleeved and gloved as he goes about the intricate task of tackling the ailing transformer. Another man scales the pole and dangles below him, assisting.

Cables are hoisted—lovely shining loops. Like a lean, slightly ungainly monster, the lift maneuvers, shifts. There is a flurry of sparks as wires are cut.

"This I've got to see close up!" You train field glasses on the sweating faces, hard and clean and strong, lit by the casual coals of their cigarettes. They are like the faces of workmen in Grant Wood paintings, the courage and strength enhanced in the shifting scarlet and amber lights.

At length their intricate manipulations cease. The old transformer drops swiftly to the ground. The silvery rectangle of the new is hoisted high. With slow grace the lift with its manned bucket continues to maneuver, the motors to sing and chug. While in the trees insects shrill and scold in a kind of background chorus. Stars flake the sky, dimmed by the dazzling lights.

Astoundingly, it is after two in the morning before the white arm bends back upon itself and gently draws its occupant to the ground. Already, as if life blood has been restored to the dark dead house, the lights spring on.

"Well, we got 'er fixed!" the foreman calls.

BERRYING AT DAWN

You arise some morning to go berrying at five o'clock. It is still dark as you eat breakfast, so you dawdle over second cups of coffee, watching the coming of the soft creeping pink.

"We can see it better if we turn off the light," your husband says. And sure enough, the room achieves a new personality, mysterious and strange. The windows are rimmed with silver, and in them your jugs of ivy, the pitchers and pots are set out in entrancing silhouette. You marvel over this, and wonder how much of your home you are missing by not getting up to greet it in that cool changing hour when the night is closing shop.

The yard has a damp sweet breath as you open the door; birds are already cheering from the trees. The woods smell minty and wild as you trudge behind your husband along the path. You think of pioneer women who braved dangers with their mates to forage for their young.

"Gee, just look!" Giving shouts of delight at the abundance, you begin to pick. The blackberries glut the bushes, big as walnuts. You have only to stretch out your hand and a wealth is at your fingertips. They are fat and wet and ripe, they rain into your pails at a touch, or plunge into the tangles at your feet.

The brambles tear at your legs as you progress slowly from spot to spot. The sharp fingernails of the vines claw at your hair. You think how lavish nature is with her gifts, and then, sly witch, how she sets up dragons to make them hard to get.

You are conscious of the world beginning to wake. "What time is it?" your husband reluctantly asks. "I really ought to get going to the office, but it's so hard to stop." Finally, gloating over the heaped pails, you tear yourselves away, trudge back along the now sun-bright path.

Your toddler is awake and peering at you from the door, a sopping cherub in a trailing nightgown. He gives a shout of welcome, grabs for the berries and stuffs them into his mouth. He is laughing and purple-chinned as his father tosses him toward the ceiling. Other children trail sleepily in.

"Where you been? Oh, boy, blackberries for breakfast!"

"'By. See you tonight." Your partner kisses you as you wash and sugar the bright fruit for the children. He too pops a few into his mouth.

"Good-by, we'll have blackberry shortcake for supper." Holding the baby, you wave as he dashes through the bright new morning to the car.

GREATEST DECORATOR

Nature is the master decorator, but then she has the finest accessories at her command. Curtains and draperies of silvery mists and rain and multihued clouds; the swags and fringe and vivid accents of leaves. And the rugs she unrolls—floral patterns, the lush green of lawns and pastures, the shimmering gold of the fields, or the deep white fur of glittering snow.

There are no discords in nature. An art teacher once called our attention to the fact that in nature colors cannot clash, as they can on canvas or fabrics. For outdoor light has a quality that blends their native loveliness, whatever the hues. Architects finally discovered that the most beautiful, livable houses are those which allow nature to do much of the decorating through windows which frame the landscape and draw the outdoors in.

And in a small, quite amazing way, that decorator, nature, often lends to individuals a helping hand. I used to nag about a rusting oil drum at the lake, which nobody seemed to get around to disposing of. And lo, nature tossed a trumpet vine across it, using it as a trellis for the long lacy leaves, the flowers with their flaming throats. The vine spilled over it with such charming concealment that people remarked on its effectiveness.

And once we lived in an old house where the kitchen window was so close to the stove that curtains would have been a hazard. Yet my husband never seemed to get around to building the scalloped cornice boards I visualized in their place. Then one day the ivy that choked the walls outside came poking through a crack, like a cluster of perky little green faces curious to see what was going on. Before we knew it, they were clambering up the sill and framing it—a living ruffle!

Though a neighbor clucked that such goings-on would ruin the house—that ivy covered up a multitude of sins, both inside and out; and so far as I know the ancient testimonial to good old-fashioned ivy still stands. One thing sure, the finest draperies, the best bought kitchen curtains have never elicited the comment, the admiration, that greeted those gay green "curtains" that nature capriciously decided to hang inside.

THE FORGOTTEN HOUSEKEY

You run home from a neighbor's gathering on a cool white night. Your heels ring on the silent walks. You turn in at your own and ring the doorbell, for you've forgotten a key. The sound shrills into the darkened house, but there is no response.

You call under your daughter's window and even throw stones. They make a merry rattling against the glass, which remains blank and still. You begin to feel foolish and a trifle concerned, though the empty garage tells you your husband is still at his meeting and you know he will soon return.

Meanwhile, you cross the shining, dew-wet grass and gaze down at the stream. The moon pours its milky brilliance the length of the water and gilds the stone bank beyond. It spotlights the still stubbornly healthy roses, the chrysanthemums and other late flowers.

They come alive with a clarity never seen by day. You can almost trace each petal and stem. Your neighbor's house stands stately as a castle, its slate roof silver-shingled, rimmed with the same fairy light.

You walk up and down the banks in your light coat, and

feel like a spirit returned. Like a woman taken from home and family who comes back to wander about by moonlight, shut out but still keeping watch over the place and the people she has loved.

The water visits softly with itself as it races past. You hear an occasional car or voice on the neighboring streets that branch up and away. The trees rustle their dry shedding leaves in the silvery light and the breeze.

Presently the burning eyes of another car swing into your own driveway. Your husband springs out, puzzled, and crosses to the place where you stand.

"Good lord, I couldn't imagine what that white prowling figure was! I thought you were a ghost."

"I am a ghost," you tell him. "I'm locked out, so I'm haunting the yard and seeing it all with the ghost-eyes of the moon."

The Family Holidays

By these festival rites, from the age
   that is past,
To the age that is waiting before—

         —Samuel Gilman

THANKSGIVING

It's good to be a woman when your husband and sons come home from the supermarket, staggering under Thanksgiving provender: candy, cheeses, celery leafing from a sack, fresh pineapple, great net bags of apples and oranges.

The kitchen is a wild clutter of pots and pans and mixing bowls. Little boys hover, snitching samples—a hunk of sticky mincemeat, handfuls of nuts and raisins, a finger lick of the spicy pumpkin you're striving to pour into a pie shell. Little girls clamber on kitchen stools to "help" by stirring and spilling and vigorously shaking flour sifters.

Cranberries bounce into a pan. They make a sound of toy bullets popping as they boil. Children beg to be lifted up to see.

Your husband makes a triumphal entry with the turkey, and the rite of preparing it begins. There is the old-fashioned, country-kitchen smell of singed pinfeathers. You scrub the white firm flesh until it's as clean as the baby's skin.

It's traditional that he prepare the dressing; practically a tradition that he can't find the recipe. Finally, he assembles the ingredients with the fussy concern of a Waldorf chef. You rejoice to contribute the sack of dry bread you can never bear to throw out, but never know quite what to do with. Soon the rich odors of sage and onions flavor the air.

You collaborate on the trussing, the anointing with oil, the binding of the wings. Now into the old family faithful, the speckled roaster, and out to the chill back porch, to await its baking hour.

You sleep late, have a lazy breakfast, then rush to get everybody ready for church. You return spiritually refreshed from this gathering with others, which gives focus and meaning to this whole festival of blessings.

The fire feels good after the tingling outdoor air. Your husband mixes a fruity punch. Children dart in and out, to the reechoing order of "Shut the door!" They present you with a bulging sack of pinecones for a centerpiece, and a spray of berries no rosier than their noses. A teen-ager shoos them from underfoot as she helps you open wide the table and spread it with your longest, loveliest cloth.

The fire dances. The wind rattles a shutter. Your big black Labrador growls and cocks a troubled ear. The mad and merry racket of a football game blares through the house.

Fragrances grow richer and more intense, in the dramatic tempo of a play. Lids tap dance beneath their nodding plumes of steam. The turkey is growing nut-brown, and crackles to your fork.

Small fry keep flat-nosed vigil at the window, watching for company. "They're here, they're here!" . . . "I saw them first, I'll open the door—!"

Aprons are whisked off, fires turned lower. "Now, boys—"

Greetings ring out. Relatives and friends swarm in.

"Everything's about ready. Children, wash your hands. Boys, get chairs to the table—"

Loved ones sit down together, bow their heads. "Dear Father, we thank Thee—"

MOTHER'S DAY

"Sometimes I wish they'd dispense with Mother's Day," the woman said to the teen-ager. "I know my children love me; I wish they didn't feel they have to go out and spend their money on cards and gifts.

"Then, too, as an adult I love my own mother dearly and enjoy doing things for her, but Mother's Day makes it an obligation. Not because she expects anything or would be hurt if it weren't forthcoming, but because the advertisers have made it almost a must."

The girl looked back with a kind of troubled astonishment. "Why, I suppose," she said, "I just never thought of it like that. I mean from a young person's point of view it's fun. I like buying my mother a gift—especially now that I'm earning my own money. This year I'm getting her a lovely slip and a corsage. I've been thinking about it all week, looking forward to getting paid so that I could."

And suddenly the event falls into new perspective. Why, of course. Mother's Day, like practically every other holiday—is for the children!

The dancing eyes, the secrets. The giggling, "Stay out of my room!" . . . The pot holders woven at school and hidden under a bed . . . The kindergarten's crepe paper carnations.

And a small girl's sly, "Have you got some material I could use? I mean *big* material, big enough for a big person to wear if somebody was going to make that person a dress?" And submitting to being measured around the waist and draped in an ancient rose print you've dug out of the attic. And warning, "Dear, it's pretty hard to make a dress. I mean you ought to be older and have a pattern."

And the blithe reply born out of the miracle of faith and love, "Oh, I don't need any pattern, I can see it in my mind just as plain—how pretty you'll look in this dress." Aghast at this revelation, she claps her hand over her mouth while you pretend not to have heard.

And a son's dragging you to the drugstore to "look around" while he slips proudly up to the cosmetic counter to spend a whole dollar on cologne.

No, there's no out for us. Even the people who originally thought up Mother's Day probably got a greater glow out of it than their mothers. Gazing at the heap of presents, nibbling burned toast eagerly served in bed, many a mother will secretly agree, "It is more blessed to give than to receive."

But her heart will be full, nonetheless. For she in her own way knows the pleasure of giving pleasure—by simply being the object and center of all this.

This is her secret on Mother's Day. This is the part she plays in the sweet conspiracy of love.

FATHER'S DAY

Moments when a woman admires the father of her young:

Sunday mornings when he gathers the littlest ones on his lap or the arms of a chair, and in his own chipper, comic way reads them the funnies . . .

When he tells a worried youngster: "Now don't fret about that test, just go in there and do the best you can." . . .

When he backs up another who's in a jam: "Just tell the truth and you'll be okay. C'mon, I'll go with you to explain." . . .

When, groaning but game, he agrees to take on another office in the Scouts or PTA . . .

When you see him contriving safety devices for windows, scouring the yard for glass or nails, testing new toys for possible hazards, and firmly fixing anything that could go wrong . . .

When you hear his hammer banging away in the basement late at night, building a playhouse for your little girl . . .

When he hastens home from the office early to help with a birthday party . . .

When he adds an extra ten to the check he's sending a child away at school . . .

When he piles not only his own flock but several extras into the car to take to an amusement park. And when their mothers come rushing out with money, he grandly shoos them off . . .

When, dead for sleep, he snoozes fitfully on the davenport, waiting for that teen-age party to be over so he can pick up the kids and drive them home . . .

When you surprise him quietly going through his old suits, and discover he's hoping to make them last another season so that all the rest of you can have new clothes . . .

When you see him laboring over accounts spread across the dining room table, and know that he's striving to keep up the insurance, manage money for college educations, make sound investments for the future, and balance a badly strained budget—and all without causing you too much concern.

They're not glamorous, any of these things. They probably never entered your head when you were canoeing with him in the moonlight, yelling him on to make the winning touchdown, or dancing with him at a prom. But they're the things that really count. The things that fill your heart when that man you married becomes the man you honor on Father's Day.

THE BIG SURPRISE

The door bangs and he rushes in from kindergarten, your rosy-nosed, cowlicky beginner, with his shirttail out and one pant leg trailing. "Mother, Mother!" He hunts you down and hurls himself against you, smelling of paste and crayons and little boy. "I got something for you—don't look, don't look."

Frantically he hides it behind his back and squirms away, eyes shining. "It's something we made at school. It's a surprise."

"A surprise? Oh, my goodness, give it to me quick."

"Wellll—it's for a special day, but it isn't that day yet."

"Dear me, well then I guess I'll have to wait."

You feel his eager anxiety wrestling with the problem. Plainly, he can't bear it. "Oh, no, I *think* it's all right to give it to you early. The teacher didn't say. But first you have to guess. It starts with V," he helpfully confides.

"V—V—oh, dear, there aren't many words that start with V. This will be hard. Vinegar—velocipede—"

"I'll give you another hint." He is ecstatic with his superior knowledge, vaguely sorry for you. "Val—val—come on, try."

"Valance—valuable—I'm afraid I'm stuck."

"Give up? Give up? Here, I'll give it to you anyway." Triumphantly he thrusts it at you, the lopsided red heart with its lace paper doily trimming. "It's a *Valentine*."

"Why, it's beautiful, darling. And you made it all yourself?"

"Well, the teacher helped us just a little, but it's my very best coloring and printing." He heaves a long, proud, rather wistful sigh. "It's fun being big enough to make something for somebody, especially when they like it and are *really* surprised!"

LINCOLN WOULD HAVE UNDERSTOOD

"We're off from school today. Boy, am I glad Lincoln was born! Hey, can I go to the movies? There's a neat show, about these bad guys—"

"Bad guys? On Lincoln's Birthday? Oh, honey, no—"

"Yeah, but the good guys always win."

"I know but—how would you like to go downtown?" you suggest on impulse. "How about visiting the Lincoln Memorial?"

"You mean it? Hey, that would be neat, we could take some of the guys." You reel slightly as he begins rattling off the names of half the Cub Scout troop.

You remind him that you don't have the car. "Let's make it just us today."

"None of the other kids? Just you and me?" He exults before this unlikely situation. (For some reason, solitary possession of a mother's company is something highly to be prized.)

But little sister has overheard and climbs purposefully down from the table. "Me, too. I wanta see Aber-ham Lincoln."

"You're too little. You don't know anything about him, you stay home."

"Oh, honey, no she's not. Let's take her."

A slight Civil War ensues. Vanquished, big brother scolds and bosses in compensation all the way downtown. His small blond target sits unresistant, too entranced before the spectacle outside the bus windows to mind.

At last, after numerous transfers and directions from policemen, you approach the great white marble temple rising majestic and serene in the sun.

"Now you gotta be *quiet* in here," the brother warns as you climb the broad white steps.

"Can't I even talk?" asks the little girl clinging to your hand.

"No, you can't."

"Can't I even *whisper*?"

"Don't worry, either of you," you intervene. "It's just a statue, a big white statue of a truly great man."

"But I thought he was buried here," your son exclaims, obviously let down.

You gaze up at the enormous seated figure which seems so very much alive. The eyes, though grave, seem to twinkle as you attempt to explain that this isn't a tomb but a shrine. And the small uplifted faces sense the kindliness. The boy relaxes, actually grins. "He sure was a homely man." The little girl looks as if she'd like to climb upon his knees.

"Was he a daddy?"

"Yes, he had several children. He had four sons."

"Didn't he have any little girls?"

"No, but he loved all children. And he freed the slaves."

Other parents and youngsters stand about, gazing up. Cameras click, light bulbs flash. People speak in low tones.

You feel the breeze, brisk and cold and clear. Below you the reflecting pool wears a sparkling wrap.

The littlest has lost interest. She goes to try the steps, climbing three or four down, three back. But the boy, in his hooded jacket, stands as if transfixed. His lips move. He reads: "In this temple, as in the hearts of the people for whom he saved the onion, the memory of Abraham Lincoln is enshrined forever."

You postpone the correction, though your lips twitch. Abraham Lincoln, who loved jokes and children, would have understood.

THE EASTER EGGS

"Well, dear," your husband says heartily, hieing for the store, "I suppose I ought to get a few extra dozen eggs."

"Couldn't we skip that part this year?" you plead, remembering previous orgies of Easter egg coloring. "Let's settle for the candy kind. That's what they really like best. At least to eat."

"You mean not color any? Why, honey, it wouldn't be Easter unless we did that. I mean—you and I—"

You laugh and say, "Okay, I guess it wouldn't." And you remember how your parents used to stay up half the night playing egg artists with watercolors. And the years you two have perched side by side at kitchen counters dipping those pesky white ovals and tracing names and little messages with crayons and exclaiming over each other's cleverness. And how they always smell so good that you invariably peel a couple and eat them with salt and pepper before you go to bed.

And you guess there is something about an egg; an old-fashioned, elementary, hen-laid egg that has something to do with the basic values of Easter. That reflects its true significance far more than baskets and bunnies and jelly beans ever can. Because, no matter how you fancy it up, there is nothing artificial about an egg.

Maybe that's why, even if they don't eat them, children

want to touch them and hold them and work with them, and find them in the nests along with everything else on Easter morning. An egg, like the grass and flowers and birds that have suddenly burst into being all about us, is directly related to life and newness. An egg is the very beginning.

THE FOURTH—AND UNCLE FRANK

The Fourth of July is always associated in my mind with Uncle Frank.

He lived in a distant and to us fabulous city, and it seemed appropriate that he come to visit on an occasion of boom and blast and bust. He was a bachelor, which somehow lent him luster. He was enormously fat, but a snappy dresser, given to white vests and pin-striped suits. He wore a derby hat perched jauntily upon his slightly greenish toupee. He had little shining eyes in a ruddy face which fell away into pleats and folds. He had a fat and genial mouth, wrinkled like a prune. In it was always stuck a huge cigar, which strewed ashes down the vast arch of his belly.

He had an oddly dainty, secretive little manner of speaking from the corners of those plump lips, although his voice came out in a glorious cannon boom. He carried a cane, partly to enhance the picture of the potentate descending, partly upon which to lean his massive bulk, squeezing it through doors, or easing it into chairs. His slender frog legs, destined evermore to be parted by his girth, reached down into small feet, elegant in spats and highly polished shoes.

We thought him stupendously rich, involved in big deals—gold mines, oil wells, real estate, and inventions. He was always seething with plans for less-favored members of the family to make a killing. He seemed on the coziest possible terms with the wealthy, the influential; and his voice rang out with such conviction about the state of national affairs that we were certain he must be a power behind the political throne.

The thing that struck straight to the hearts of his nieces and nephews was his astonishing largess. The first thing he did when he had lumbered down the steps of the train or into your house, was to extend one of his great pink paws. Solemnly pumping your hand up and down, he would pay you lavish compliments: "My gracious, what a beautiful child. And smart too, I hear. Say, your folks should be mighty proud!"

And as, dazzled with praise, half numbed by the grip, you withdrew your hand, you always found in it a shiny silver dollar. Not a dime, not a quarter—a whole dollar to be spent drunkenly on pop and candy bars and other madness that afternoon.

He was through with you then; the audience for his sonorous pronouncements on world affairs, his sure-fire schemes, did not include children. Fussily, he would shoo the small fry from the room.

But we always adored him and breathlessly awaited his coming; and when we learned of his death, it was as if some vital force related to fireworks and celebration had gone out.

He didn't leave any money to anyone. He died broke in a spare little rented room. But he left a legacy of bigness and grandness and generosity that I still feel swelling up inside whenever I smell punk and gunpowder and cigars. And when skyrockets go spinning toward the stars—I think of silver dollars, and of Uncle Frank up there, probably selling God a sure-fire scheme!

EVERYBODY GETS IN ON HALLOWE'EN

All through dinner the eight-year-old pleads desperately, "Can't I go out just a *little* while? I won't do much, just soap windows and stuff, please!"

"What's with this Mischief Night?" your husband frowns. "Tomorrow night's Hallowe'en. Then you can Trick or Treat."

"They get you going and coming," you tell him, echoing the annual confusion. "Some kids go both nights, one to play tricks, the next to ask for treats. Or vice versa."

"Well, not ours. That's no fair," he says sternly, avoiding your eyes. For both of you are remembering the days when All Saints' Eve was a far less civilized event than it is now . . . The thrill of prowling the night in search of excitement or downright devilment . . . The delicious shocks of the morning after as you witnessed the havoc wrought—the outhouses upended, the wagon wheels on the schoolhouse roof.

Thus the juvenile delinquents of yesterday. But nobody carried knives then, you rationalize righteously. There wasn't the widespread vandalism and crime there is today. Pranks were simply that, innocent and free. Still—our parents were just as hard to convince, even so.

The smaller boy has been echoing every plea. He wriggles with eagerness. His round eyes shine. He flings down his fork and dashes to the window to peer out at imaginary spooks. As the doorbell rings he goes wild, shrieking after the tricksters, who have already disappeared.

"See?" the older one triumphs. "Other kids are allowed. I tell you what—" He suddenly becomes earnestly concerned. "Just let me into the back yard and gimme the hose, I'll squirt everybody that tries to do damage to our property."

Surreptitiously, you confer in the kitchen. "Let's give them each a little bag of corn and let them attack a few windows," your husband suggests. "That's harmless enough. I'll tag along in the background to see that they don't get into anything else."

"Okay, and I'll call their Sunday School teacher and some of the neighbors to come out and pretend to be very scared, or very mad. They'll love that."

Giggling, enamored of their own wickedness, the boys scramble into their wraps. Clutching their sacks of ammunition, they dash into the starry night.

"I know what would be fun," says an older sister, beginning to clear the table. "Let's dress up like ghosts or something and go out and scare *them*."

You agree. Feeling a silly excitement yourself, you leave the dishes in the sink and dart upstairs to dig out sheets. Giggling, possessed by a sense of some impish intrigue, you wrap yourselves. Then you too steal into the frosty, bon-fire-scented outdoors.

Dry leaves make the brittle sound of wrapping paper as you scuttle through them, to hide behind the trees. The last late flowers send up an acrid tingling. As the small boys and their dad come back, breathless and joyful from their antics, you rise, flapping and moaning.

The boys screech and give elated chase, capturing you at length and ripping aside your disguise. "Why, it's Mommy, it's Sister. Hey, this is a *real fun* Hallowe'en!"

THE FAMILY CALENDAR

This is the season of calendars. They make their bright bustling invasion even before the old year is laid to rest. Flat in their envelopes, the mailman leaves them, or tightly rolled in cardboard cylinders. Or husbands tote them home in bulging briefcases, and children gather around excitedly, to inspect and admire.

"How d'you like this?" Father asks. A large, impressive one is unveiled, with colored scenes of sailing ships. "Or this one? It hasn't so many pictures, but there's sure lots of spcae to write dates."

"I want the kitty one!" . . . "Dibs on the one with air-planes." . . . "Hey, no fair. You had that one last year. You take the one with the foreign countries. Use it for geogra-phy." . . . "He can't have that one. Daddy already promised me!"

Calendars, you think, taking down the old one in the kitchen, to replace it with the new. And you remember how this same scene was reenacted over and over in the years of your growing up. Big hearty Dad, with the calendars adver-tising coal, hardware, the barbershop, insurance—and the family eagerly gathering around the dining table.

Were calendars even more profuse in those days—and prettier, you wonder? Or does it only seem so now? Those purple mountains. Those waterfalls. Those Indians. Those cupidlike girls. Women often saved the pictures and framed them. Today, with our gay prints and draperies and mural wallpapers, it would be silly to save a calendar picture.

Yet, with a tinge of regret, you hold it a minute longer. You know it isn't the illustration that makes you reluctant to part with it. It is the scribbled notations: *Surprise party at Engelbach's . . . Dentist, Johnny, 4:00 . . . Get box off to Susan . . . Mark's wedding . . . Graduation . . . Cake to PTA.*

Some of the spaces are crammed with appointments and with reminders. Others bear witness to a child's eagerness: MY BIRTHDAY. (*Pony?! Hint, hint!*) and a picture of the pet he's dreaming of.

It is tattered and smudged, this packet of papers you hold in your hand. It is fingerprinted and jelly-smeared. Yet it is a rich document of living, for fixed there with pencil strokes are all the things that mattered, the occasions so eagerly anticipated: the parties, the plays, the dances. The contests and football games that ended in such glorious triumph, or such defeat. The hopes, the disappointments, the tragedies. Finished now, over—only a few of them to remain alive in memory.

And gazing on the new one, so bright, so clean, un- marked, you ponder: What record will be written there before another year has passed? What shining events to be looked forward to? What trivial tasks dutifully cited; what joys, or sorrows?

For the calendar that hangs in the kitchen is so much more than a sheaf of dates—it is your family's history.

Apron Pocket Philosophy

It's nice to be important, but it's more important to be nice.

—Old Saying

SHUT THOSE DOORS BEHIND YOU

"Shut the door behind you!" my mother used to remind us as we all came banging in. And, "Shut the door!" I hear myself, like countless other mothers, calling out to my own flock.

Shut it to cut out the draft, the cold—yes, that's generally what we mean. But in the larger sense, those words can be significant. For the habit of shutting doors behind us is invaluable to happiness; we must learn to shut life's doors to cut out the futile wind of past mistakes.

The man or woman you didn't marry. The house you didn't buy. The job you didn't take. That long-gone injury that is so much better forgotten. That loss, that devastating sorrow, that failure.

Forget it. Put it firmly away. To leave the door of memory even a little bit ajar is to provide passage for grief, remorse, regret—a flock of deadly enemies that can only damage the bigger, better, forward-looking people we should be today.

Look ahead. Advance, proceed. Reach out your hand toward the new doors waiting to be opened, the new dreams and opportunities. They are the doors that should concern us, not those through which we've passed along the way.

Shut that door behind you. Lock it and throw away the key. The only doors that matter are those that we open today!

LIVE WITH IT A LITTLE WHILE

"Live with it a little while," a dear friend Helen, who stayed with us during the war, used to say. The lamp you weren't quite sure of, the picture hung in a new spot, the piece of furniture—"Live with it a little while and see."

And what good advice it proved to be. Because in a day or two perhaps, a week or so, the answer was usually quite evident. Either the object had settled down cozily into its surroundings to complement or enhance them, or it jabbed and harried you until one day you'd exclaim, "I just can't stand that picture leering at me a moment longer—it's got to go!"

And she'd laugh and agree, "You're right, it just doesn't *do* anything for that corner. Try it somewhere else."

Unfortunately, we can't make the same maneuvers with people, with a husband or children. Whether children prove to be blessings or little beasts, we're stuck with them.

Even the neighbors have a certain inescapable permanence. I've never met one yet sufficiently accommodating to pack up and move somewhere else if it was plain he was never going to *do* anything for me.

No, there are many things in life that we've got to go right on living with, regardless. People. Troubles. Problems. But the funny part about "living with" that which can't be changed, is that we adjust to them. After a while they don't seem so bad. In fact, we get so we'd be lost without them.

SERENDIPITY

Serendipity . . .

I had never heard the word until the president of Iowa's Cornell College, Dr. Arland Christ-Janer, used it at an alumni meeting. Serendipity—finding something better than what you were looking for.

Being a born word-hound, I proceeded to search for it in my battered dictionary. Then my Thesaurus, which doesn't have it either. So I called a friend, who rushed over with an armload of references. And though we never did find the word—there among her offerings was some rare and wonderful data I'd been madly hunting for an article.

We could only regard each other in amazement—the proof seemed so clear. *Serendipity.*

We take so much in life for granted. We complain so often of its cheatings, denials, shortcomings. Yet actually life is so richly laden a tree that it's almost impossible to reach out to pluck an apple without getting baskets full to overflowing.

College itself, for instance. We go for so many reasons—because it's a status symbol, or an avenue to the professions, or "necessary," they tell us, "in order to get ahead." And lo, the mind awakes, the sheer adventure of knowledge stirs, and off we sometimes gallop on careers undreamed of, or a lifelong love of arts previously unexplored. . . . And the friendships made, particularly with beloved professors.

Two of my own, Toppy Tull, English, and Judge Littell, Political Science, became father figures to an enormous family of students, who form little clans in cities wherever they find each other, so that what began as something casual on a campus has deepened and ripened to something permanently dear.

Serendipity . . . Something better . . . Every commitment that we make holds this built-in potential.

Marriage, which begins with the supreme and sole desire of two people for each other, expands almost inevitably to include children, relatives, friends—love that multiplies in shining circles around this first self-sufficient unity, enhancing and enriching it far beyond its original scheme.

Parenthood is so much more than just "having a baby," which is as far as most couples visualize at first. It involves the whole agony and ecstasy, mystery and marvel of creating and rearing new human beings. And though our off-spring seldom fulfill all our first fond specifications, they often so far surpass them later that we are amazed.

Serendipity. It's at work for all of us in large and little ways. Shopping for a dress and finding a whole outfit. Inviting a foreign student for dinner, and finding yourself in turn a guest of the ambassador. Taking a shortcut which turns out to be a longer but far more beautiful way.

Buying a house—whether you seek a spanking new rambler or a crumbling mansion—invariably you get so much more than you bargained for. Headaches, drawbacks, yes, we get those too. But they seldom hold a candle to the unexpected blessings of new friends, church, school—a veritable rainbow of opportunities arching across shining new horizons toward unanticipated pots of gold.

Serendipity. Steadily, all unseen, it's functioning for us every day. Surely it works best for those who are serene enough to receive it. Perhaps that's the secret of its power, as well as the source of its name.

SOLITARY CONTENTMENT

Peace is a rare experience for a busy wife and mother. Quiet is almost an unknown commodity. Generally the only way to acquire a precious hour of silent solitude is to wait until the entire family is bedded down. Even this takes a bit of doing, and often you're too tired to enjoy it once you succeed.

Or, hopefully, patiently, slyly, you browbeat the young fry through their homework and start the bedtime treks a few minutes early, only to be caught in the net of your connivance: "But it's early yet—I've got to get a bath—I've got another chapter to read—hey, *no fair!*"

Even on the nights when with luck you succeed and are prayerfully about to settle down, the ensuing quiet may be shattered. Somebody wants another drink of water; somebody else has a nightmare; or, most dismal of all (making you feel a meanie), you are summoned instead to the night nurse shift as a plaintive voice calls out, "I don't feeeel gooood!"

But again—ah, again, somehow the simple, homely, blessed miracle is achieved. They are silent, every last one of them. No voice cries out, no footsteps go pounding along the hall. The house is yours, a strangely changed and promising place in which to do what you will. The hours stretch forth in a soft shining vista, their possibilities limited only by your own endurance.

What first—a bath, a book, or both? First the long sweet soaking, then a book—or a stack of magazines waiting like riches on the coffee table. Or possibly the TV—a late movie or a program to be savored in the sheer luxury of just being alone. It is almost too much, you must taste these pleasures one by one. And so you poke the fire, heat the coffee, turn the set on low, and take up the book, or dip into the enticing stack of unread magazines. Or, if you're so inspired, you uncover the portable typewriter and write long letters to dear ones, or possibly poetry. . . .

The night is all around you, close and comforting. It is like a good friend, someone so understanding it does not intrude but only rests quietly by your side. Its eyes shine through the window, its voice murmurs gently in the whisper of the fire, the breath of the wind.

You are your own person now entirely. For a little while you have escaped all demands. You are your own.

CORDIALITY

Of all human traits, I believe cordiality to be my favorite. That warmth of greeting, that enthusiasm which makes everyone, friend or stranger, feel welcomed, wanted, liked, and enjoyed.

Maybe this is partly because I was lucky enough to grow up neighbors to some people named the Johnsons. What the house lacked in luxuries it more than made up for in this rich quality. You felt it like a gift, a kind of happy bestowal, the minute any one of its members opened the door.

"Well, come in, come in. Say, but it's great to see you—hey, Dad (or Babe or Jack or Lois)—look who's here!"

It made you feel special, that greeting. It made you feel like someone they'd actually been hoping for. Nor did this cozy, glowing sensation leave, no matter how long you stayed. They talked with you, they laughed with you, they focused their attention upon you with interest and warmth and joy. And they never seemed to want you to go. "Ah, come on—listen, you just got here. Wait now, have another cup of coffee, let's talk some more."

That everyone who entered got the same treatment didn't diminish the value of your own reception a bit. You knew, somehow, that they were sincere—they *did* enjoy people. All kinds of people, attractive or not so attractive, rich or poor. Cordiality was not just something assumed out of kindness or courtesy, it was unconscious, spewing naturally out of an innate delight in human fellowship. Therefore you accepted it, trusted it, knew with an overwhelming certitude that, whatever your own shortcomings, you were truly welcome here.

Cordiality . . . Cordially yours . . . It is not a lost art; there are many who still practice it, if only because it's their nature, they can't help it. Yet I wonder sometimes if sheer old-fashioned cordiality hasn't gone out of style? People so seldom sign letters "cordially" any more. The occupants of some homes seem to have lost the hang of it. Despite the perfunctory courtesies, even some of the most excessive attentions, you feel uncomfortable. As if, "I shouldn't have come," or "I mustn't stay long," or "How soon can I politely leave?"

What a pity! Doorbells were meant for ringing. Houses for the entry as well as the departure of visitors. True, often we are so harried, preoccupied with personal concerns, that the unexpected arrival of some caller is not a thing of joy.

And yet . . . if we could only all be Johnsons. Able to sing out, and truly mean it, "Well, come in, come in—look who's here!" And, "Oh, stay just a little while longer, it's so *good* to see you, please don't go." Our own hearts would be the richer.

DON'T BE AFRAID TO BE FRIENDLY

My father was a bold and jolly man. He "never knew a stranger," as the saying goes. He used to embarrass my mother—in fact all of us—by his habit of addressing people he'd never seen before, on public conveyances, or at fairs and celebrations on the street.

"Nice day, isn't it? Say, this is some crowd." And he would introduce himself and pleasantly ask, "Where you from?"

"'Fools rush in where angels fear to tread,'" my mother would despair of him, shaking her head. But I think she envied and admired his lack of inhibition, for it freed him for rewards not enjoyed by more timid men.

For almost invariably the face would light up, information would be vouchsafed, often an interesting story volunteered. Sometimes for only a few casual moments, but often much longer, he would have made a friend.

"Everybody really likes to talk if he'd just admit it," Dad used to say. "Half the time people are dying for somebody to pay a little attention to them." He would smoke his cigar and chuckle, his bald head shining under the parlor light. "The way I figure it, life would be mighty lonely if there weren't some of us willing to break the ice now and then."

His philosophy makes more sense to me the longer I live. Propriety, good manners, good taste, the fear of being conspicuous, of being rejected, our motives misunderstood—such are the locks behind which too many of us quake, lonely, bored, and too shy to make the first move.

I once rode a hundred miles on a bus beside one of the most fascinating women I have ever met—before either of us had the courage to speak to each other and discover a common interest which kept us talking avidly during the scant half hour that was left. We all have been at cocktail parties where, overwhelmed by numbers, and failing to find a familiar face, we spend a miserable time—until somebody, some total stranger, takes pity on us and speaks. When, by the mere act of introducing ourselves, starting up a conversation, the evening might have been successfully launched. Not only for ourselves, but for someone else.

Shyness is actually a form of selfishness.

HOSTESS TO LIFE

Sometimes you think you can't stand the chaos any longer: The telephone's incessant ringing, often before you are out of bed. ("Is Susy there?" . . . "Can you take over lunchroom duty?" A den mother. Your son's piano teacher . . .)

And the errands: Doctor and dental certificates to be signed. Socks to buy while you're near the dime store (how is it humanly possible to lose so many socks?); and a birthday party present—and ribbon, paper, card. The bank, the bakery—and home in time to wash and dry a slip for a daughter to wear to the party . . .

And the deluge after school: "Make me a sandwich, will you? I've got to get back to football practice." . . . "I can't find my trumpet!" . . . "Where's the Scotch tape? Where's the card?" . . . "Wait'll you hear what that mean teacher did today—!" . . . "We're having Scout inspection, I've got to have my uniform pressed and the emblems sewed *exactly* one inch down." . . .

Little folks chasing each other in full cry. A lamp upset. A quarrel settled. Extra kids for dinner (will the meat go around?). More phone calls shattering the meal: "May I please speak to Bill?" . . . A friend apologizing, "I hate to bother you, but did you ever cook venison?" . . . A man about the insurance . . . A dancing studio gaily announcing, "Congratulations. You have just won a free cha-cha course."

Then the wild scramble for TV programs. People shooting in all directions to meetings. More people popping in: The paper boy. A stalled motorist. A prospect for one of the puppies. A neighbor wanting to cut out a rocking horse on your husband's power saw . . .

Papers on the floor. Schoolbooks. Blocks, crayons, a headless doll, a baseball bat. Coke bottles on an end table, pretzels on the piano. The cat whining to be fed. The dog barking. The power saw dimly screaming; every radio and record player going.

Oh, to escape! you sometimes think. Oh, to lead the quiet life of contemplation in the woods—or better yet, a good hotel.

Then the motorist, thanking you for use of the phone, looks about and grins, "This house really looks lived in."

"Lived in is putting it mildly," you agree.

He leaves and you bend to your tasks—straightening things up, turning noises down. And you think about his remark—how right, you realize. For your household is constant host to that priceless thing called *life*.

This is life that flows in and through you, battering you with its demands. You are the channel for the strong, vigorous blood beat of a living family.

And though it fatigues and harasses you, sometimes almost beyond endurance, through it too you are strengthened. It is the tonic that keeps you going. It is your very reason for being.

"NOBODY KNOWS THE TROUBLE I'VE SEEN"

There is a popular belief that it's a good thing to talk out our troubles. That it is the quiet, self-contained souls who more often wind up in institutions, because they lack this safety valve for letting off their emotional steam.

Yet women are far too prone to pounce upon this warning and use it as an excuse for pouring out problems to friends, relatives, neighbors, in a continual stream.

Now one close friend may be fine for this purpose. With the kindred spirit who knows us wisely and well, it is sometimes a downright pleasure to disclose our secret selves. The trouble is that many women have too many such seeming soul mates. They run from one to the other being desperately self-revealing. Until suddenly this ceases to perform its original function—the desperately needed outlet—

and becomes instead a habitual orgy of self-analysis and shoulder-weeping. And in it the person so beset begins to find greater satisfactions than in quietly meeting and coping with his problems, in salvaging such happiness as he can from life as it is.

Another danger is that in such outpourings the individual refuels his resentments. He recharges the batteries of his misery. He—or more likely she, gets all worked up afresh. Because "Emotion follows action." And it is usually true that the minute we begin to reenact, through recital, the dramas of our woes, the nerves and heartbeat respond, the tears are eager to flow from their abundant well.

Even physically this can do very real damage. It adds to the wrinkles, the pouches under the eyes. While emotionally, what might have begun as a really glowing day turns, because of this sorrowful reenactment, into an exercise in misery . . . Reenactment. It is said that some of those who participated in the Civil War Centennial battles actually got mad all over again at the long dead enemy!

Sometimes that's how it is with us. The enemies—past slights, hurts, betrayals, have long been dead, many of them. Why disinter them? Or if sometimes we must—well, there is always that patient listener and counselor, the pastor. Or, if you can afford one—a psychiatrist.

LOOK OUT—YOUR PUNCTUATION IS SHOWING!

Did you ever think of people as resembling punctuation marks?

There is the period person, for instance. His judgments are decisive. His pronouncements final. There's simply no use arguing with him, period. He always has the last word.

Or take the quotation marks personality, who carries on almost his entire life's conversation in quotes. Impressed by his vast reading background, and the rich storehouse into which his retentive memory can dip, you seldom stop to think that he produces almost no ideas of his own.

The comma person is hesitant, meek, and a trifle pedantic. Careful pauses mark his sentences, as if compelled neatly to hook each thought before proceeding.

The colon or semicolon type is first cousin to the common comma, though a bit bigger, broader, often trailing an advanced degree and a Phi Beta Kappa key. His pauses are less those of the uncertain and tentative than of the organized thinker who lovingly groups his often complex ideas. No mad rush of words for him; you can almost see the structure of his concepts impressively laid out.

The CAPITAL LETTER individual Thinks Big, Talks Big. He is a name dropper, and the bigger the Name the better. Yet he is robust and entertaining, for everything he describes is Epic in scope. He can make a trip to the market to buy a pound of liver sound like an African safari; or if female, a polite thank you to the man who picks up her gloves on a bus, the beginning of a mad romance with a VIP.

No use trying to relate *your* adventures to the Capital Letter Kids. They're simply too enthralled with their own, you don't stand a chance. But they can be fascinating.

Then there is the species of human being whose entire approach to life seems to be shaped like a question mark. He concludes his simplest statements with, "Isn't that so?" "How about it?" "Wouldn't you say?" He doesn't converse with you, he tests his ideas on you in a kind of earnest interview. Which can be flattering, of course, but also disconcerting.

The no punctuation at all personality talks a blue streak racing from subject to subject without pausing for breath and seems to have been born talking and will die talking and is hard to get away from especially on the phone but he's often warmhearted and wonderful.

His (or more often her) next of kin is the parenthesis person, who eventually gets *back* to the original idea, but only after wandering down a bewildering labyrinth of side trails. "This was when Arnold was five years old (Arnold, by the way, was my husband's little brother, who'd been adopted by his stepmother, his stepmother was one of the Flying Filberts—did I ever tell you about their act?) Well, it seems—" And eventually, "Now where was I? Oh, yes, Arnold—"

My favorites are those people whose whole approach to life is best expressed by an exclamation point! They have the gift of enthusiasm. To them everything is vital, exciting, stimulating. They are vigorous, not only in their own speech, but the manner in which they listen. They are not afraid to exclaim.

"An exclamation point in writing," said F. Scott Fitzgerald, "is like laughing at your own jokes." Well, me, I like people who laugh at their own jokes. And at other people's. Who aren't ashamed of their own emotions, or unwilling to share yours.

Exclamation mark people! Give us more of them!

PATIENCE

Perhaps the hardest lesson to learn in life is patience. To wait unperturbed while the child in the highchair does everything with his food except eat it. Quietly to hear out the interminable tales and complaints of the harried neighbor, the long-winded friend, or the very old. To give earnest attention to a son or daughter as he describes in minute detail the movie, or an episode at school.

Not to interrupt. Not to cut the other off. Not to explode. To curb the forces within us that would hurry, hurry, hurry. To hush the frenzied voices of rebellion. To still the frantic and usually futile impulses that would result only in hurt feelings and unnecessary distress . . .

These few minutes lost—what actually do they amount to in the long span of living? Are they worth one tantrum? One wounded spirit? One rejected soul?

True, the baby must be induced to get at least a few bites of the carrots or spinach down. The son and daughter—yes, they must be steered back into the course of homework, duties. The neighbor, friend, the aged—there are times when somehow we must have the courage to bring the encounter to an end. But meanwhile—patience. Patience.

Withdraw the emotions, practice detachment, kindly interest, self-control. With the conscious effort comes a strange calm, a sense of being not the prey of outer forces, but in command of some subtle yet significant inner forces of one's own.

TO TRIUMPH OVER FEAR

What a triumph it is to overcome the fears and aversions that beset us. What a sense of self-mastery it gives.

Some things we simply outgrow: Not to be afraid of the dark any more; nor to fear going into a lonely attic, the hiding place of ghosts. What a thrill for one child to say to another, "Come on, I'm not a-scared, nothing'll hurt you—" and to see him take a friend by the hand and lead him into the place of imagined threat.

Yet some of us take years to overcome our aversions. As a child I was once teased with a snake. Thereafter the mere word in a book was enough to make me skip the passage, a picture was a horror. Once at the Smithsonian, accidentally finding myself in an area where the creatures were realistically mounted, it was all I could do not to bolt the place, screaming.

The first year we summered in the country I lived in constant misery lest one of these ancient anathemas appear. What's more, every child was fitted with boots, which he was ordered to wear whenever he set foot outdoors. By the end of the second summer, however, the silly rule had been pretty well forgotten. In the first place it was an unenforceable nuisance, in the second—expensive. Everybody kept outgrowing those high-priced boots. Furthermore, my mortal enemies were so scarce as to be a rarity.

And gradually the subtle miracle of nature had begun to penetrate: Harm does not lurk behind every boulder and blade of grass. Such hazards as it harbors are far less than those of busy city streets, and more than compensated for by its peace and beauty and wonder. If you can't trust it and accept it on those terms then you belong elsewhere.

Meanwhile, the children's enthusiasm for all living things, whether they flew, hopped, swam, or crawled, began to draw me into their world.

The first time our four-year-old came running excitedly up holding a twining length of living ribbon, it was all I could do not to gasp, "Put that horrid thing right down!" But I did not want to curse her with the phobia that had enslaved me. Furthermore, I was stopped by the sheer pleasure on her face.

After that, little by little, the V-shaped silver patterns that an occasional water snake drew in its gentle course became a source of pleasure rather than alarm. I was able to join the family and watch with fascination instead of aversion the behavior of one of them as it engorged a fish. I could not only face a snake book without flinching, I began to study such books, along with the others, so we'd know the poisonous ones when and if they ever came around.

We learned that black snakes are actually friends—they keep down rodents; what's more, harmful snakes for some reason are seldom found in a black snake's territory. So when a fine stout black snake adopted our Point the better part of one summer, it actually added to my sense of security. And when some strangers came along one day and killed it, I was indignant. How dared they destroy "our snake," which we trusted and which had never done anyone harm?

Thus gradually we can overcome some of our deepest aversions. It's a slow process, and takes a combination of both will and willingness to learn. But in the end it spells freedom—and often new enjoyment.

ANTIDOTE FOR MISTAKES

Sometimes we think we're the only people who make mistakes. "How stupid of me!" we berate ourselves. "How could I have been such a colossal idiot?"

And we regard, appalled, the extent of our blunders:

Expensive purchases that cannot be returned. A seemingly impossible assignment assumed from which there is seemingly no escape. Wrong choices, commitments, decisions that we may be stuck with for years—sometimes for life.

Because, while some mistakes can and will be corrected, to a very large extent most of us have to live with our mistakes. Worse, other people often have to live with them, and it is painful to know that because of our own errors in judgment they too must endure.

And then to our vague surprise and consolation, we discover that we're not the only ones! Other people err too. Often wise and admirable people whose judgments would seem to be infallible.

Dispirited recently over what seemed to be a bumper crop of bloopers, I was heartened to fall into conversation with a learned judge. He was kicking himself all over for a list almost as lengthy as my own: "We bought the wrong house in the wrong neighborhood at the wrong time and there's simply no getting out of it. It's the only place big enough to take care of my wife's parents—and taking them in to live with us was another mistake that can never be undone."

While I was sympathizing with his predicament, my own spirits were curiously assuaged. It isn't alone that misery loves company; rather that our follies don't seem so abysmal when we are reminded that mistakes are the common lot of man. We all make them. Little ones and big ones. Whatever their size or shape they're pretty much inevitable. And punishing ourselves only compounds the problem. Instead, we should face up to them and make the best of them.

For lurking somewhere in the body of every mistake there are compensations that we find only when we stop scolding ourselves long enough to look for them!

TAKE TIME FOR OLDER PEOPLE

There's a man in my life I can't forget. He doesn't know it. He never will—that's what haunts me.

No, he isn't romantic or handsome. Just somebody's

grandpa, who was standing in the corridor one day at school. Not a daddy any more, busy about setting up tables for the fair, or there to see about a child's homework. Not president of the PTA, or even a member, just—there. And I should have paused, if only for a second, and said "Hello." Should have found out who his grandchild was, made him feel welcome. But no, I rushed on about my business, and he stands there still in my mind—ignored, lonely, feeling in the way . . .

That's what's so cruel about aging. One day you're racing about the business of life, harried but vital, a part of its machinery. Then gradually but inexorably you are left out, until one day you find the machinery tearing along without you—and nobody even notices. Your worries may be behind you, but so is your importance, your sense of involvement and of having a right to be where the younger people are.

And the younger people ought to remember that we too may be standing bewildered and embarrassed in a school corridor one day . . . Or sitting forgotten in a corner while bubbling young matrons discuss their children or the last dance at the country club. Hoping to participate, to contribute from our rich fund of anecdote or observation—but fearful of intruding. Only nobody bothers to notice.

Actually, elderly people are often fascinating. They're so filled with wisdom and experience. And so gratifyingly pleased when you show an interest in what their lives have been. Older men particularly. One question alone serves to bring light to a retired man's eyes: "What was your profession?"

Before these magic words a man warms, expands, unfolds. His life's work! It may be far behind him, but whatever it was he's usually proud of it: "I was a doctor . . . an accountant . . . I worked for Standard Oil . . . I was a union leader . . . I was an engineer."

And the attention of any woman makes him feel masculine once more. I used always to serve lunch to the old gentleman who tuned our piano, and you never saw anyone so pleased. Once he brought along a comrade from his boardinghouse, and I got out the good silver and made a casserole and warmed them with sherry. There was a sparkle in their step they hadn't had when they came.

How I wish I'd served up at least a friendly word to the man I remember at school.

LIFE TAKES A LITTLE NERVE

When I was a child there was a certain girl my parents liked but never really approved because, "She's got such a lot of *nerve*."

I've come to believe, however, that the example of Nicky's nerve—her uninhibited daring before new people, new experiences, was really good for the shyly squelched rest of us. That often fools who rush in where angels fear to flutter get places angels don't.

At least they have a more interesting time of it.

Certainly the simplest achievements of life, as well as the bigger ones take—a little nerve.

It takes nerve for a boy or girl to go out for football, enter a speaking contest, run for class president. A dread of being conspicuous, of "not going over," plus a kind of comfortable laziness keeps many a promising youngster from trying out for the paper, the class play, things they may really long to participate in and have real aptitude for. And this same combination of fear and laziness must be overcome in order to blow the lid off their own talents.

A woman who is today a concert pianist told me that after winning a scholarship in high school she was terrified at the prospect of leaving home, traveling to the distant academy of music. "The mere business of a train trip, of living in a big city appalled me." Only by a desperate summoning of sheer nerve was she able to resist the easier, more comfortable course of simply staying home.

What defeats so many of us is that it's so much easier to give in to the humdrum way of living, not even to try. One day when we lived in a small Texas town, I was enjoying a leisurely breakfast when I read that Dale Carnegie had arrived on a lecture tour. "Why not go down and try for an interview?" something urged me. But the coffee perked enticingly, and after a few hours at the typewriter I was going to play cards with the girls. Why spoil things? I was very young and inexperienced as a writer, he'd probably be too busy to see me. Besides, what would I say?

Yet nerve can be very stubborn sometimes. Dreading the whole thing as a foolish, self-inflicted ordeal, I went. And was not only graciously granted the interview, he hired me to substitute for his regular secretary who was sick, and gave me much valuable material and help.

It takes a little nerve to make friends. To introduce yourself in a new neighborhood, to be first to call greetings across the yard. But it pays fantastic dividends.

It takes a little nerve to be kind sometimes, when being kind also means being conspicuous. Yet one kind word to that lost or lonely stranger can change his day—and quite possibly his life.

Anything worth doing takes a little nerve. If you're one of those bored, "nothing ever happens to me" people, ask yourself if it's simply nerve you lack. Go after that job, that audition, that interview, that friend. Consoling as it is to think that all things come to him who waits, it's a lot more practical and interesting to go after them. Or when opportunity knocks, have enough nerve to open the door!

A Woman and Her Friends

A friend is, as it were, a second self.

—*Cicero*

FRIENDS ARE NOT A ONE-WAY STREET

A few weeks ago in New York an old and valued friend remarked, "I don't bother with anyone who bores me. I have cut down all my contacts to a minimum, I see only those people whom I really enjoy."

With the instantaneous reaction of the very busy I thought for a moment, how wonderful. To have matters so arranged that one would be spared the countless contacts that often seem frantically and futilely time-consuming.

And yet, on reflection, I'm not so sure.

Aren't friendships, on whatever level, a part of human fortune? Friendships can be infinitely varied. And by their very differentness the whole pattern of one's days can be enlivened, and in so many ways rewarding.

Sift through your friendships; sort them.

There is the rich inner circle of those people who are dearest to the heart. Usually these are the persons to whom we can most honestly express our deepest selves. And even though we may not see them for days, weeks on end—even years—the bond remains strong and special and true.

Yet would we not be the poorer without the infinite variety of others?

Friends can be friends for so many different reasons. There is the wonderfully helpful neighbor who is always willing to give you a hand with the children, or whip up a skirt for you.

There is the witty one who can always make you laugh.

There is the one who sends over bones for the dog, and is generous with praise for your growing crew.

There is the quiet soul who occasionally comes up with a startling gem of philosophy.

It takes patience sometimes to appreciate the true values in the people with whom circumstances have surrounded us. It takes awareness to recognize these values when they appear.

Yet almost everyone has something uniquely his own to contribute to our lives—and equally important, a place in his own life that perhaps we alone can satisfy.

The heart has many doors. Don't be too quick to bolt them.

REAL FRIENDS ARE NEVER FAR APART

One of the sad ironies of our busy metropolitan lives is that the friends we love and most enjoy are often those we seldom see.

In small towns where everybody is your neighbor, your friends are but a few blocks away. You meet them almost daily on Main Street, at church affairs, or PTA.

In cities, however, friends are physically parted for miles. It takes so much effort to get together (what with transportation complications, the problem of baby-sitters, not to mention the sheer strain on the budget that such arrangements entail) that frequently we simply forego the pleasure. Except for a luncheon date in town when both of you have to be there anyway, or a specific dinner invitation, you may go months on end without ever seeing the person your heart may hunger for.

In short, what kindred spirits so often miss through the accident of urban living is spontaneous communion. That quick delight of drawing together when you have exciting news to share; or problems that only this person who loves and understands you can help you solve, if only by lending a sympathetic ear.

Yet one of the compensations of true friendship is that people who are truly congenial *don't* drift apart. Anyone who has traveled very much, or lived in different parts of the country, discovers this. From among all the countless people one knows at each place, there rise to the surface one or two couples or individuals who remain steadfast.

And though time and distance reduce your contacts to perhaps one letter a year, when and if your paths do cross again, you find yourselves excitedly picking up the threads of friendship precisely where you left off. Because what united you in the first place was something that went beyond mere place or circumstance.

And even deprived of such reunions, there is still the telephone. The other day mine rang, and a dear voice came singing out of the past. A voice I hadn't heard in twelve years. "For goodness sake where are you?" I asked. "Come right on out."

"I'm afraid I can't," she laughed. "I'm still way down here in Texas. But I just suddenly got lonesome to talk to you."

And we found ourselves talking our heads off just as we used to do when she lived next door. And this has happened on other occasions with people too far away to see, but never too far away for real communication.

The same is true of city friendships. Neglect doesn't kill them; it simply deprives us of the happy hours that otherwise we might share. But even so robbed, our hearts remain filled with them, the consciousness of their devotion, their sincere interest in our concerns.

A teen-age girl going away to college for the first time expressed this very well: "If you don't miss me too much,

Mother, I'll consider it a compliment. When you really love somebody you're so filled with them you're never too far apart."

THE FACE OF A FRIEND

You are among strangers. At a party perhaps, or in a press of people at a public function. And suddenly, out of all the meaningless, faceless faces, there blooms like a bright light—one!

It may be the face of a friend whom you see so frequently that—like the face of a husband, or your own features in a mirror—you no longer really see it any more. Yet lifted from its familiar setting, suddenly it is new and clear to you and excitingly defined.

"Why, she's beautiful," you recognize in a burst of awareness. "I hadn't realized before how striking she is."

Or it may be someone whom you seldom see, but love. In this case too the face appears like an unexpected vision. The blood beats faster, the thrill of recognition is like that of finding a celebrity in your midst.

But better. Because the celebrity can give you no sense of identification. The celebrity will not call out to you in delight, nor can you call out to him. The celebrity furnishes no warm, welcome little island toward which you can draw in the choppy waters about you, and know that there you will be comfortable and safe. How lovely is the face of a friend!

MANY HANDS, LIGHT LABOR

It's good to be a woman when the friend who's offered to "get some of the guys from the office to come down and help" arrives at dawn one morning with the promised crew!

"Hey, I didn't expect you in the middle of the night," you hear your husband's astonished but glad protest. . . . And drifting blissfully back to sleep you are dimly aware of the hearty male voices kidding and conferring in and through the smell of perking coffee. Then the tramp of feet . . . the clank and bang and bump of rocks and lumber and hammers. Followed by the rhythmic chugging of a cement mixer borrowed from Frank, your dependable neighbor, whose old gray monster has coughed up concrete for almost every place on the Point.

When at last you arise from this seeming dream, they are hard at it. Figures crouch and measure at the balcony rail. One holds a ladder while a confederate saws away at the leafy branches of a tree. Others, stripped to the waist, are wrestling rocks at the sunny lake bank, where the walls need reinforcing. A duo are shoveling sand, mixing concrete, staggering under a loaded wheelbarrow, which they steer toward the patio.

All day, fortified by coffee, cold drinks, laughter, and comradeship, the activity continues. It is all you can do to persuade them to stop for a swim, a boat ride, a charcoal steak. At last, sweaty, grubby, but triumphant, they survey all they have achieved: The trees trimmed, the floats repaired, the bank more sturdy, the balcony sporting new rails, a beautfiul new flagstone floor hardening on the patio overlooking the water—and they still don't want to quit!

"No, no, you've done enough—too much—it's a little miracle, all you've accomplished. And the work you've saved us—we'll never forget it—it's one of the nicest things that's ever happened to us."

You are all sitting around the long pine table on the porch now, refreshed from a swim, relaxed. The sun is going down in a golden glow behind the trees. A heron glides grandly across the sky and settles in the rushes. A coal oil lamp shines on the tired but still eager faces. There is the sweet earthy smell of woods and water, the first tentative tuning of the chorus of little night things.

"Ah, well, when you get a bunch of guys working together it goes fast and everybody enjoys it." A strong hand lifts a mug of coffee, eyes look thoughtfully into the still glowing and silvery dusk. "And after all, that's what got this country going. Take the first settlements, the house-raisings, the threshing parties—people helping each other."

WHAT PEOPLE DO TO US

Have you ever wondered why most of us can be so many people? Not only in the mélange of personalities that quarrel in the privacy of our beings, but in our relationship to others.

A woman is one thing to her husband, often quite another to her children. To one neighbor she may appear a regular Phyllis Diller; to the next someone as serious as Margaret Mead. The cop on the corner sees her as a trifle frumpy parent hastening dutifully toward the school, while to the visiting executive who gives her a whirl at the club dance she's a creature so ravishing she ought to be on TV. She may represent half a dozen different versions of femininity, depending on the beholder.

And running the gamut of her contacts, without consciously contriving or even willing to do so, she finds herself enacting the role in which each one has cast her. For, curiously, different facets of our makeup are aroused by different personalities.

With some people we seem doomed to show off our worst features. One of my most admired and gracious relatives turns me into a blithering idiot. Never have I been in her presence that I didn't drop something, spill something, lose something, or say something stupid.

Another person to whom I am deeply indebted, and on whom I long to shower appreciation and praise, calls up instead some absurd and alarming demon determined only to shock and annoy her.

A certain couple to whom my husband and I are very close, are so prejudiced on some issues that they make both of us want to stand up and fight. Yet we feel that it would be rude to argue when they're guests at our house, and even more rude when we're guests at theirs. So we keep a cowardly silence, meanwhile fuming that these otherwise delightful friends can turn us into such simpering mealymouths.

Whether it's a matter of physical chemistry, or some secret disparity of the spirit, there are just some human beings with whom each of us can never hope to harmonize. People whom others enjoy, but who make us feel lackluster, and wanting in all charms. I used to consider such people a challenge, and deliberately sought their company in order to prove myself—and disprove nature.

I can tell you it was a waste of time. It's pointless to try to get in tune with people who don't give you the chance, when life abounds with others who inspire the gay, the good, the bountiful-best in you. Some friends touch the true and secret self on sight. These become your Best Friends. They are almost like your own blood (often they understand you better than your family). They see all the varied facets of your nature and package them into one human being who is precious to them. Just as you summarize their many attributes and hold them close to your heart.

FRIENDS ARE LIKE BRACELET CHARMS

It was a party, in the truest sense of the word. An assortment of interesting people, small enough so that strangers could become acquainted, old friends could talk. Yet large enough to be full of laughter and music and pleasantries and stimulating new contacts.

On impulse I remarked to our hostess, Peg Howe: "You certainly have a lot of lovely friends."

"Oh, yes," she laughed. And lifting her braceleted arm she remarked, "My friends are the charms on my bracelet of life."

The charms! I thought. Why—yes. The enhancements, the adornments—that extra shining something. If you truly love and enjoy your friends they are a part of the golden circlet that makes life good.

When you gather them about you, you feel happy—and proud. Their accomplishments add a glow to your own being. What's more, you want to share them: "He's a distinguished surgeon, and his wife makes a home for all these foreign students—you must meet them." . . . "They both do little theater work, you'll just love them, they're both so alive—" . . . "He plays folk songs on the guitar and sings in three languages—" . . . "Now that the children are in school she's studying law." . . .

But not only their accomplishments, their qualities: "Helen is the most generous person I've ever known." . . . "Grace has the most beautiful brown eyes—when she talks they just shine—" . . . "Jim has a laugh that makes you feel good all over. And you can depend on what he says, he'd never let you down—"

The person who can feel and speak this way about his friends is truly blessed. His life is rich in meaningful relationships. His "friends" are not a source of criticism and carping and jealousy and gossip. They are people truly dear to him, so dear that he can't refrain from singing their praises to others. And in so doing he is always making new ones. For the way a person feels about his friends is a pretty accurate indication of the kind of person he or she is.

The man or woman who treasures his friends is usually solid gold himself.

FINE STRANDS OF FRIENDSHIP

Never underestimate the deep attachments children form for each other. They are meaningful and real. In their purity and strength they are part of the sweet mystery of childhood, something that is seldom found in the later complexities of the adult world.

Little girls are particularly prone to form these alliances. (Perhaps because the female of the species is created to be more tender, more utterly giving of her emotions than the male?) Little boys have best pals, but often their closest buddies are likewise their direst antagonists. They fight, verbally and physically. And I have never known one to grieve deeply over the loss of such a friend, either by moving away, a final smashup, or even death itself.

When a very little girl has a best friend, however, she is likely to worship her. They laugh, they whisper, they share secrets, they go around with their arms about each other. They write each other notes and think up surprises for each other. And when they are forced to separate they are inconsolable.

Nancy was such a child in Texas; a dear little blonde with a bone disease. When we moved away our daughter was heartbroken. "What'll she do without me?" she wept. They corresponded for years and sent each other gifts and saved up Christmas money for phone calls.

Other mothers have witnessed this same manifestation. One showed me the touching postcards that her daughter's favorite small friend had mailed from every stop en route to California: "This is the first time I've ever been away from you. I'm crying so hard I can hardly see to rite."

Most of us outgrow such attachments, drifting apart emotionally and physically. If we meet in later life it's usually as strangers. Yet sometimes circumstances themselves are kind, and two who loved each other as youngsters cuddling dolls or swinging on a fence remain dear to each other throughout life.

Aunt Tressa was such a friend to my mother. She lived far away, but they never let the lovely strands of friendship fall apart. Every few years she would come to visit—small, dark, sparkling, with hands that could make a piano sprout wings and fly. And to hear them laughing and chattering away was to hear echoes of a far but never quite lost springtime when both were bubbling young.

Age could not change the essential spiritual communion they had with each other. A thing that children sense. For children, little girls especially, are close to nature, close to love. Instinctively they recognize that this joyful, unquestioning rapport with another human being is one of the most beautiful, significant things in life. That is why they rush headlong to claim it when it comes to them, and grieve for it so profoundly when it's gone.

Your Family—Your Cornerstone

Nothing is more important to human happiness than to be part of a fractious, forgiving, warm, tightly knit family.

—*M.H.*

THE FAMILY CORNERSTONE

The roar of the cement mixer stops. The rocking, loud-mouthed monster gives a chugging sigh, as if to rest before spewing another thick gray load.

Your husband wipes his brow. The sunlight rippling on the water reflects on his face as he says, "Well, now we're ready to start the supporting columns. Say, this is kind of an event, at that, building our cabin. Maybe we ought to lay a cornerstone."

"Hey, yeah, how about it?" Your tall bronzed son turns from the pile of cinder blocks.

The little one, who's been busily "helping" by hauling little tin buckets of sand, demands, "What's a cornerstone?"

"Well, it's a kind of ceremony they have sometimes," you lamely attempt to explain. "When they put up public buildings, well like colleges or post offices or churches, sometimes they put souvenirs in the corner block. Say a coin or a newspaper, and their names."

"But what for?"

"Well, so that years later if the building's torn down, people will know who built it."

"But who'd ever want to tear our cabin down?"

"Help!" You turn to your grinning spouse.

"It's a kind of celebration, honey," he says—and instantly the word is taken up. "Hey, kids, c'mon, everybody, we're going to celebrate."

Already our daughter has dashed off to return triumphantly clutching assorted contributions—jacks, paper dolls, puzzles, the dog's collar.

"Oh, no, honey, not all that junk," her father groans.

Others with similar notions are weaned from the dramatic idea of burying treasure in the walls.

You settle for a new penny, the daily paper, a baby boot, and a tiny document gravely passed around and signed. All are stored in a cigar box, tied with a ribbon from the little girl's pigtail.

"Now we put it in the corner block—"

"Wait, wait, that picture I drew of the horse!" It seems so vital to the artist, a pause is arranged while the wobbly purple horse is likewise proudly interred.

"Now what?"

"Well, at this point they usually make speeches. If Mr. Ryland were here, he'd say a prayer. We'll just say a silent prayer in our hearts that we're glad we're all together and have come this far with our cabin, and hope we'll be able to finish it and be happy here."

Your husband deposits the box, applies the mortar. Together with his son, another cinder block is lifted into place.

"Now don't they hit it or something?" somebody pipes up. "With a bottle? I've seen pictures."

"Silly, that's only with ships. Besides, who's got any champagne? Though boy, oh boy, I could sure use some Hawaiian punch—"

"That's right, when do we eat? After all, it's no fun to celebrate unless you get something to eat."

"I'll see what I can scare up." You rise from your perch on a pile of lumber. You climb the rock steps. You see your family below you, silhouetted against the water—your quarreling, laughing, laboring family. And you think—that is what counts. This is what lasts when the rest of it is all over. Your family—your cornerstone.

"LISTEN," SAYS YOUR HEART

Your little boy plunges onto your lap where you sit reading the paper, a warm damp bundle after his bath. Another child perches on the chair arm, still small boy enough to caress in a restless, hunting fashion.

"Read to us, Mother."

You put down your paper and take up the storybook. The rain pauses to rest as you sit there together. A golden-green light floods the sky, gilding the new featherings of the leaves outside the window, silvering the shingles of your neighbor's house, making a shining chariot of the family car parked in the drive.

Then the sky turns to rose, deepens to a rumbling purple, and the rain begins again, rhythmic and purposeful.

"Horsey! Camoool," the younger child interrupts the story now and then to point the pictures out. But mostly he lies relaxed, moist of chin, two fingers in his mouth.

His brother listens intently, palm cupping one cheek, or leaning down to clasp a pink heel and pick vaguely at his toes.

Their dad, in his robe, has heated up a cup of coffee and sits on the hassock at your feet, reading the paper you've discarded. "Hey!" he protests, as the younger child takes a sudden notion to crawl over your shoulder and snap off the light.

"Bad boy," scolds his brother. "Turn that right back on!"

"No, wait." You pull the baby back down. "This is cozy. It reminds me of when I was a little girl. My mother used to gather us all close like this, in a big chair in the dusk, and listen to the rain. . . . Listen—"

"Listen," whispers the older one. "Listen to it come down, boy, a regular cloudburst!"

"Listen to the lake," says your husband. "This keeps up it'll rise several inches by morning."

"Listen," the awed baby chimes in. His head is cocked. "I hear the fwowers."

Listen . . . listen . . . says your heart.

THE NEW CAR

Your husband calls one afternoon with that certain half-reluctant, half-reckless lilt in his voice that betokens surprise.

"Honey, you know how we've been worrying about that old car?"

"Yes?" you say eagerly, fingers crossed, letting him take the lead. "You think maybe we should get a new one?"

"Well, I've been looking. How'd you like to come help me pick one out?"

Through childhood's mysterious antennae the signal has already been flashed. "A car? New car!" They streak from all directions, big-eyed.

"Now not so fast, we're not sure yet."

You shove the vacuum into a closet and exchange your shorts for a skirt. "Now everybody wash up, but if you go along, no teasing. It's Daddy's money, remember, and his decision."

The old one seems suddenly dear and faithful when he drives up. You begin to fight an emotion that strikes whenever you've had to move, or a piece of furniture has to be replaced. An impulse half sentimental, half economic.

"I know." Your husband pats the dented hood. "She's taken us a lot of miles. And the engine's perfectly good."

The children emit a mass wail. "We are going to get a new one? You said—"

"Now nothing's decided yet. Be still."

Doubtful, but with rising anticipation, you are ushered into showrooms and begin your gingerly inspections.

"Now be careful of the seats, don't fingermark the glass—"
. . . "Look, Mommy, a big shelf where I can have a doll bed—"

. . . "Boy, push-button windows!" . . . "Man, oh man, I can't wait till I get my driver's license—"

Test rides are taken. Then, "I don't know. Which one do you like, honey?" your husband asks.

"She'll take the blue one," grins the salesman who long has served your family's needs. "I remember, your wife always wants blue."

"But the blue one hasn't got spinners," protests the thirteen-year-old. "Hey, Mister, you put on wheel spinners, no extra charge?"

The salesman laughs. "That kid's going to do all right. Sure, son, I think it can be arranged."

You drive home in the old one while minor adjustments are made. The kids keep the phone busy, too elated to eat. "Hey, we're getting a new car!"

He's still there when you return, this man who never seems to eat or sleep or have a life of his own apart from these shining vehicles. "Well, folks, hope you enjoy it."

"Pile in, everybody. Now, now—Mother's sitting up front with me."

"Dibs on this window." . . . "Dibs—dibs—" . . . "Hey, no fair, I said dibs first—"

"Now no fighting, and be careful of the upholstery."

"That's right, sit down, don't put your feet up, don't touch anything. Mom, look, he's already made a mark—"

Anxious, preening, vaguely guilty as you glimpse the old one standing abandoned and rather forlorn in the lot, you glide off. Smooth as a cloud it rides, quiet as a confidence.

"Let's take a ride, let's go to a drive-in, have some ice cream to celebrate."

You smile at your husband and at your young, sitting for this first rare period so quiet and pleased, almost too impressed to move. You know it can't last, this harmony, this newness, this sense of joy and value and beginning. But it's wonderful when it comes. You're glad you took the plunge.

You're glad you live in a land where it's possible for everyday people to go sailing down the highway in a snug house of glass and steel and power—a new car!

MY SISTER GWEN

Just about the nicest thing I could wish for everybody is that
they have a sister Gwen. My sister Gwen is gay, comical,
friendly, exciting, dramatic, and beautiful. To be with her is
to live with laughter; she is a fountain of sheer fun.

Her voice, though sweet, is rather loud; it rises in propor-
tion to her enthusiasm. She would have made a good evan-
gelist, for she is forever converting people—to clubs, causes,
new hairdos, new decorating schemes, new interests and
challenges. But she's as generous with her energies as her
advice, joyously whacking out their slipcovers, papering
their halls, dyeing their hair, teaching them to drive. Her
visits strike with all the zest of an electric storm. The breeze
of her personality rocks the house.

She is an insatiable sightseer. However often she has
been to Washington, she must consume it afresh, right
down to the rind. She loves the White House, swap shops,
jewel collections, the Smithsonian, Congressional hearings,
old bookstores.

On a recent stay she took in the White House twice to
absorb the changes, engaging every guard in conversation,
taking notes, pondering. Then off she rushed to comb sec-
ondhand stores for similar dusty treasures, donning jeans
and a bright bandana to refinish them for us.

Tender and devoted to our mother, she is also the spark,
the catalyst that keeps her active and spiritually young.
"Now come on, Mama, it won't be any fun without you,"
she insists. And carrying her coat, and finding her a chair,
she forestalls the fatigue of age.

She was determined that Mother see the John Glenn
parade. I'll pack a lunch and take a folding chair and we'll go
early and get a good place." When rain made the plan un-
feasible, she came up with an idea that would never have
occurred to me. "The Congressional hearings! We can see
him better there anyway." And sure enough, they sat directly behind all three of those first astronauts and came
home glowing. My sister Gwen was especially elated, for

she has made it a personal passion to learn everything possible about the space age.

She has a special technique of sightseeing with children, left over from rearing her own: "Always take along a jug of water and something to eat." This provender she stows in the car, portioning it out just before the mass assault on the Washington Monument or the F.B.I. "It's when they get hungry and thirsty that they get tired and cross. Also, a good stoking before you start means you don't waste time trying to find places to eat." They love to go with her, maybe because she's more interesting than anything they see!

Nothing's ever the same after my sister Gwen has gone. Your hair may be a different color, your house completely rearranged. But she's shined up your spirit along with the silver, hung rosy new curtains on the windows of your heart. You feel excited, exhilarated, revitalized.

WHEN A FAMILY FACES TROUBLE

The true test of a family is trouble. Will it be shattered by this grave blow, or will it survive to become even stronger than before?

Under the first impact it may stagger and falter, and for a brief appalling moment feel its own structure slipping, its very fate in doubt.

Then quickly the good family recovers, unites, feels itself somehow stronger than before. Qualities unsuspected in its own members come rushing to the fore: The ability to understand, to weigh and analyze a problem, and advise; the willingness to share each other's burdens, the capacity for sacrifice.

Members formerly at odds may be drawn together in the common cause of helping to overcome this thing which threatens the precious whole. Goodness and kindness cement the cracks, tighten the slipping bonds.

If a family can meet trouble together and triumph over it, then nothing can overcome that family. And each of its members will be able to cope with his own life a little better than before.

STARGAZING

"Come down on the dock and look at the stars with me, Mother," the middle boy begs. "Let's go stargazing together."

"Oh, dear, it's so chilly," you hedge. "And it's getting kind of late."

"That's good, that's all the better. The later it is, the more stars. And we can take a blanket, you can put on a sweater."

"Oh, goodie, can I come too?" the littlest pleads, flinging down a toothbrush and grabbing for a robe.

"Not you. It's too cold," her brother protests.

"Oh, now, let's all go, shall we?" you urge. "After all, the sky's a big place, there are enough stars to go around."

Grudgingly the trip's proponent agrees. Trailing blankets and wraps you all grope down the rocky steps toward the float. The sky is blacker than it has been in weeks, the stars a fiery peppering. Some of them seem almost near enough to touch—the rungs of a shining ladder. They are more than reflected on the water, they are doubled and tripled in brilliance as the wind stirs, as if combing them through its black hair.

The broad wooden float is cool and damp as you cuddle down, Indian-fashion. The smaller ones creep inside the clumsy enfolding tent, nuzzling like ponies vying to be close. The older ones sprawl about, importantly citing constellations.

"I see the Big Dipper."

"Aaah, anybody can see that. I see Orion, the Big Bear, and Venus."

"I see the Three Bears and Goldilocks."

"There isn't any such constellation as that, is there, Mother? That's just a story."

"Well, I can still *see* it, can't I? You can see anything you want in the stars."

"That's right," you soothe. "That's how the constellations got their names in the first place. People who watched the stars thought they looked like pictures and made up stories to fit."

"It's still no fair, but tell us some more."

"Some people used to think the world was a huge room, and the sky a vast ceiling where the gods hung out the stars every night for lamps."

"Tell us some more. Tell us how you used to play out at night when you were a little girl."

And so you tell them—about Old Gray Wolf, and Redlight, and Run, Sheep, Run. "It was a small town, of course, and safe for children to play games under the stars. And we had this superstition—whenever we saw a shooting star we thought someone had just died, and we'd all get scared and run for home."

For some reason this strikes them as hysterically funny. But even as they are laughing, a streak of fire traces the sky.

"Hey, see that?" somebody gasps. "A shooting star!"

The laughter suddenly stops. They gaze at you, impressed. The little ones huddle closer. The bigger ones get to their feet.

"See what you started, Mom? I know it's silly, but—*beat you to the house!*"

IF MOTHER GOES TO JAIL

You're sitting on the float one evening feeling benign toward the world. Above you perches the cabin achieved through faith, hope, and sheer togetherness. While your husband was wrestling boulders for the walls, you and the small fry were swinging pick and shovel.

The float itself was another family project. From it you've been diving, fishing, and chatting with people passing up and down the lake. "Nice place you have there," they call, these pleasant-looking men in the boat.

"Thank you," you beam. And are pleased as they cut the motor.

"Pull in," you invite. "My husband will be right back, I'm watching his lines for him."

They glance at the two rods and then at you. "Catch many?"

"They're not biting too well right now, but gee, I've sometimes brought in thirty or more. My husband only caught two tonight."

He comes loping down the steps and you present him. "Though I didn't catch your names," you say apologetically.

"Well—" They exchange glances. "We're the game wardens."

"All three?" you gasp.

"Yes, Ma'am. And we're checking on fishing licenses. You folks got licenses, I suppose?"

"You bet." Your husband digs for his wallet, which is gravely studied. "That's yours, how about your wife?"

"Who, me?" You feel astonished, acutely betrayed.

"She doesn't need one, does she?" your husband asks. "Why, she's the lousiest fisherman on the lake."

"I am not. Remember that time I caught—?" You gulp, look meek.

Patiently but grimly they explain. Yes, indeed. Out of state. Even property owning and paying taxes don't make no difference. 'Course if you were fishing from your own property, sitting on the bank . . .

But this *is* your property, you protest, and it's attached to the bank. Like that gambling ship they couldn't do anything about because of the gangplank, only this is legitimate.

"Lady, you can tell that to the judge." One of them is writing. Fixing you with a steely eye, he reads: "You are hereby charged with violating fishing laws of the State of Virginia, and summoned to appear in court—"

You gape at him, heart pounding. He must be kidding! Such a nice young man. Surely he can't do this to you.

"Sign here." He really means it. Still astonished, you wonder what would happen if you refuse. But there are three of them, all huskies, against one paltry dame. Resisting arrest would hardly do.

"Listen, this is no fair!" you sputter, wanting to cry. "I'm a good wife and mother. I—I—tonight I wasn't even fishing."

"If you're on a dock with a fishline in sight, Ma'am, you're technically fishing. See you in court." They pull away.

The children come trooping down the bank. "Who was that? What happened?"

"Your mother just got arrested," their father laughs. "Listen, this should be fun. If you argue with the judge the way you can argue with me, I wouldn't bet a nickel on him."

"Well—it'll be an experience." You're beginning to see the possibilities. "And I've always wondered—Listen, will you treat me to a baby-sitter if I decide to go to jail?"

"Honey, I sure will."

"You really mean it, Mom? Oh, boy, wait'll I tell the guys!"

"Can I go stay with Gracie? And wear my new pink nightie? Can I tell my Sunday School teacher?"

"Think of the peace and quiet. I'll take my typewriter along and write a protest. I'll write a book. And let's face it— any woman who's been raising a flock of children would enjoy a few days off, even is she has to spend them in jail!"

COVER THE CHILDREN, IT'S COLD

The cold is a great animal that bestirs itself by night and prowls the earth, blowing its chill breath through the walls of your country cabin. You feel it first against your face, your nose, and burrow instinctively deeper into the nest. Then responsibility, as subtle but as strong, intrudes: The children. . . . No, no, they're perfectly all right, if not they'll call you . . . But you cannot escape the nagging of that second beast, conscience. Children, it insists, never really *know* if they're cold.

It routs you at last. In sleepy protest you crawl out, go padding across the chilly floors.

The fire has almost died out. Only embers light the rustic room. Shivering, you stir the coals, pile on another log.

Then you go digging into closets for more blankets and those odds and ends that can be made to serve where it is dark and style means nothing; where there is no motive except to combat that primitive adversary, cold.

Fron bunk to bunk you proceed. The children lie huddled into nature's own position of protection, curled up like hibernating cubs embracing themselves against the cold. Gently you unwind them, pile on the additional bedding. And as they groan against your ministrations, you insist, "Call me if you need any more, it's cold."

The mission completed, you go back to see about the fire. The logs lie sullen, refusing, beyond a scant fume of smoke, to cooperate. Kneeling, you bait them with papers, which instantly spring into a joyous flame. You break fresh kindling across your knees and thrust that too beneath their stubborn weight. There is a welcome crackling. The room is rosy now with leaping light. Even the big logs want to get in on the party. Grumbling at first, then enthusiastic, they catch, begin to burn. And it is so suddenly pleasant, so merry, this fire in the lonely night, that you long to make a pot of coffee, to sit by it and just enjoy it for a while.

But you know that despite its splendor and show of strength, it will prove no match for the antagonist outdoors. For he has summoned up the wind to join his forces; the wind is shouting taunts and battering mightily at the windows. So you too must call up allies. You go about flicking on heaters that begin to sing softly and play their own rosy glow across the floors.

You stand a moment more, soaking up the warmth, reluctant to leave. Then you go plunging back to your own nest, pull up the covers. Let the contest continue—the brash wind blow, the hearth fires answer. All your babes are snug now, safe, protected, and you can sleep in peace.

THE MERRY-GO-ROUND

You come upon it unexpectedly as you drive through the little town. A park with picnic tables. A pool. A few booths with their games of chance. And oh, the magic circle turning with its necklace of colored lights—a merry-go-round.

You consult your husband as the clamoring of the children begins. You know their fate hangs in balance as adult considerations are weighed: Should you stop, can you spare the time? Your suspense is almost as great as theirs. However, you assure him, "It's all right if you don't think we should."

A childlike relief surges up within you as he pulls up by the side of the road. "C'mon, everybody out that wants to ride the merry-go-round."

You walk across the trampled grass with its nostalgic memories. Up to the little booth. "How many?" (How many tickets to enchantment? How many cardboard stubs to touch the stars?)

"You take them on it," you urge. "I'll hold the baby."

"Me too, me too!" The child reaches out to the spinning loveliness, trying to grasp its essence as he strives to touch and taste the moon.

"No, darling. When you're older. See, we'll watch Daddy and the others ride."

It is slowing, the chipper metallic tinkling of the music is slowing down. People surge forward, and this too you remember—the frightful anxiety as they rush to catch a horse.

The rearing black one with bulging eyes—no, taken.

The low-diving sorrel with the silver tail—it too is gone.

Help them, oh help them to find and capture the ones they want!

Ah—you sigh, for they are all together: the boys—one casual and rather clumsy as he clambers on, too big for this kind of thing, his manner firmly announces; the younger with his shining eyes and tousled hair; the ecstatic little girl.

The child in your arms watches, transfixed. His wave is almost automatic. He is pondering this mysterious revolving toy. What is it?

What is the secret of its rapture, this melodious plunging up and down? These colored lights like fruits that you cannot touch or taste—what do they mean?

And you too ponder as you watch it work its wonder on the faces all about—other parents who stand watching blissful children spiral past on flying steeds. Is it that all life is a mystery and a marvel, hurling you now high, now low, but forward, if only in a circle that echoes the revolving of the globe?

You don't know, you cannot say. Only that a child on a merry-go-round has captured Pegasus himself and soars above the world.

THE SWING

What can equal the joy of an old-fashioned rope swing?

To a child it is at once his homely friend and his most royal possession, gracing his castle yard like a throne. In mellow dignity it occupies its chosen place, the ground beneath the firm board seat worn bare, leaves and stirring boughs and sky its wondrous canopy.

It is the focal point for gatherings and games. It is the king's chair, to be conquered, abdicated, or occupied in soaring majesty. It is a place of refuge when the child is lonely or hurt.

A swing, to assume its true and rightful identity, must hang alone. It shouldn't be part of a playground set strung up on bars along with seesaws and rings. It can't be one of half a dozen in a park—public, impersonal, chained to iron posts. It has to belong to someone who loves it. Its strong rope fists must grip bark. It must claim its special tree.

An old-fashioned rope swing is usually hung by a father who remembers the swings of his own childhood. He chooses the toughest coil of rope he can find and a sturdy board to be notched with a jackknife for the seat. The hanging is gaily and noisily accomplished, with youngsters laughing and yelling directions and bouncing with impatience, thick as blackbirds.

An old-fashioned rope swing is something to be shared. Everyone must try it, even Mother and Dad and aunts and uncles. Children come running from blocks around to take turns in it, fight over it, beg to be pushed in it, to be "run under," and know the glory of the world's dipping and their feet rattling the leaves.

A rope swing is fun to pump in, standing up singly or by twos. It's fun to climb hand over hand, and to slide down, palms burning. It's fun to wind up and spin in. And its seat is a pleasant place to lean on, to dreamily watch the lazy glide of the ground below.

A swing is the instrument of a child's imagination—a ship's rigging, a circus trapeze, a rocket to the moon . . . Its song is made up of rope creak and leaf rustle and birds twittering . . .

A rope swing is like a blessed presence that is taken for granted. And when something happens to it, when the seat breaks or the rope frays away, or a child rushes out after a rain to find that it has shrunk foolishly high, he feels a sense of shock and loss. Almost of betrayal; there is a loneliness about it, akin to that when Mother is sick or gone.

Children often fight over such a swing, sometimes fall out of it, or are hit by it. That too is part of its nature, that makes it almost a human thing. The tears and bruises and parents scolding. As if the swing were giving a small preview of the eternal marvel and the peril of life.

Rooted in earth, but headed for heaven. A wonderful thing, a swing!

THE FRAGILE BALL

On a glorious golden Sunday the older children cavort with their wives and sweethearts and friends on the dock. You hear the music of their voices, their laughter, their playful tormenting. "Another crack like that and I'll throw you in."

"I dare you!"

At a tremendous splash the little ones prance about in delight, begging, "Me, me, throw me!" Vainly above the skidding commotion you yell for them to stop, it's dangerous, now quit.

The boys are young and brown and rippling with muscles,

the girls slim-legged in their vivid suits. Turquoise, tangerine, emerald, and strong primary colors, yellow, ruby red. All these weave their patterns against the steel-blue water and the vibrant blue of the wet dock.

Your husband has bought a beach ball that is transparent, a globe of sheer dazzling pink, through which the sun shines as they toss it, playing "Keep away." It bounces on the water and the Dalmation dives after it, nosing it ahead of her frantically, for the airy globe is not to be caught.

"Watch out, if she gets a tooth in it she'll break it."

"She can't, it's too slippery." A young body slices into the water, snatches it away from the pursuing snout; then together boy and dog wrestle in a wild splashing that sends a fountain of fire into the air.

Inner tubes, glossy black circles, lie about. Orange life jackets hang from posts. The red and white boat rocks beside the pier. On a rock one boy stands fishing, calm and detached from the noisy merriment, his line a delicate tracing as he casts.

Another boy is intent on skipping stones. He chooses flat ones, and leaning slightly back pitches them across the glossy expanse. *"Sssspt! Sssspt!"* comes the sound as the stone kisses the water and leaps forward toward new lips. Bracelets of silver follow its course; swift, bright, spreading and blending they multiply.

Boats go by, making huge waves which come rolling, glassy-backed. The float bangs and rocks, throwing people off balance, making the young ones cry out, "These are great, come on, dive in." They plunge into the heaving water, and with each contact, as with the stones, there is a mad new multiplication of light.

The fiery patterns are infinite—and moving on into infinity. They are elusive and not to be caught by the wondering eye.

They are like the bright pink ball that flies at the touch of the fingers and cannot be held except in destruction and collapse.

They are like youth and love . . . They are like life.

A Woman and Her Faith

The Lord is my shepherd; I shall not want—

—The Twenty-third Psalm

A FIRM FOUNDATION

*L*ucky is the woman who can come to her marriage with her faith intact, and her will to practice it strong. And lucky is her child. For, often with her husband, sometimes single-handed, she provides what every child needs most: Order. Structure. A sense of being sheltered by forces older, stronger, and sounder than himself.

She equips her children, from their earliest memories, with the greatest weapon, consolation, and aid they will ever have—prayer. "Bedtime, now let's say our prayers." . . . "Timmy, you can give the blessing." . . . "Don't worry about the exam, honey, ask God to help you—and I'll say a little prayer." This amulet against danger and evil, this comfort in times of disappointment, this touchstone of hope. Nothing else that she could give them by way of luxuries or attention could last so long or help them more. Deep in their beings she is embedding a power that they will never be without, no matter how old they grow or how far they stray from her principles and beliefs.

And all about her family the woman of religious convictions rears the rafters of her faith, roofs it with her love of God, and furnishes it with the activities of worship, organized and otherwise, and ushers her dear ones in. Her church is often an adjunct of home, which children embrace, accept, or reject, according to individual age, nature, or stage. For youngsters go through many phases:

The first excitement of Sunday School with its flannel board stories and little red chairs ("Jesus Loves Me, This I Know!" . . .). The mystic ardors of adolescence when they may yearn to go into convents, become missionaries, or study for the ministry . . . The often searing and turbulent times when they begin to kick at the very structure that has given them shelter. ("How do we know? You can't prove anything by the Bible.")

This period can be painful. The other day a friend told me, "Bill's reached the age where they stop picking on God and start picking on you." As I looked puzzled—"You know, they almost all go through it. When they decide they're atheists. Since there's no God to blame for things any more they've got to blame somebody, so they blame Mother. The wold is all your fault." This hurts. But after a child or two, the woman whose faith is strong knows that "this too shall pass." While stubbornly, proudly, even merrily, she and her stand survive.

And this too is her priceless gift: She will not be moved. She will listen to their logic, she will agree where agreement is just. But basically her faith holds fast. It has sustained her through all the storms of family living, and it will sustain her now. And even as they challenge and scorn it, children are glad that she will not give in. Bigoted, old fashioned, narrow-minded—yes, they may call her all these things (or think them). Yet she inspires awe as well as exasperation. She believes in something.

She is someone they know and trust and respect—and she believes. She is no stranger to the cruelties and injustices of life—and she believes. While others flounder and grope for answers—Mother believes. In a world where so little else is stable, this is no small thing.

So there she stands, in the old-fashioned house of her faith. So patient, so small and yet so mighty, holding the lamp of her love for him. In all the shifting, foundering world, the child knows that this one thing will not change. He can turn toward it whenever he's ready. He can come home.

FAITH IS A PRIVATE AFFAIR

It takes years, often a lifetime, to reach one's religious convictions, or at least a workable philosophy to live by.

It takes trial and error, despair, and even bitter rejection as you follow false paths, find yourself at dead ends, and retreat, rest, and wait. Then a new spark is touched in you—by something someone says, an example, a demonstration, another book (of the many, many books you've read), and off you go again. But each time a little more secure, less likely to grope and grapple in vain.

What eventually evolves may be a special combination of principles, precepts, and convictions that has never met in anyone else before—and that can't be transferred to another. Yet if it enhances your joy in living, makes you a better person, and sustains you in times of trouble, that is the test.

I don't think anyone is truly happy until he has worked out some private pattern, not only for getting along with people but for getting along with God.

MOM, I COULD HEAR MY HEART

Dialogue with a young philosopher . . .

"Mom, I could hear my heart beating against my pillow last night. It was thumping away so loud it almost scared me."

"We all hear our hearts beating that way sometimes."

"Y'know, it's funny we don't hear it more often. I mean it's funny that we've got all this junk inside of us, all this machinery going and we can't hear it at all."

"Well, we're pretty well insulated—all that flesh and skin."

"Yeah, but it's still funny. The lungs breathing and the heart pumping and all that blood rushing around. And the stomach working away at your food, and all those valves and whatever they are opening and closing and so busy—it's like a factory, it still seems like we could hear it."

"Yes, I guess it does."

"When people make things you can hear them. Factories make a lot of noise. Motors make noise. Trains, airplanes, ships—nearly everything that people make makes noise."

"That's right. Even watches tick."

"But hardly anything that God makes makes noise."

"How about animals?"

"Sure, they growl and all that, but that's only when they're mad or hungry. That's their speech; the machinery part of them is just as quiet as ours. And the trees are quiet except for the wind. And grass and flowers and butterflies and birds and worms and spiders—why, just about everything else you can think of is quiet."

"That's right—the sun's quiet, and so is the moon. Except for the wind and rainstorms just about everything in nature is still. I'd never thought of it before."

"Neither had I, but it's true. And I thought of it!" He regards you for a moment of shining silence. "You know it's pretty exciting to think of something nobody else has ever thought of maybe. I mean nobody else in the whole world."

"Even thoughts must come from somewhere," you remark.

"Yeah. So they must come from God. Maybe thoughts are the most important of all the silent things God makes. And it makes you feel wonderful when He sends a really good one straight to you."

MOTHERS ARE SELDOM ATHEISTS

Men say there are no atheists in foxholes. Women can testify that there are no atheists in delivery rooms.

For never is a woman so close to her creator as when she is giving birth. Never is she so at the behest of forces beyond herself, nor so in league with life. And when she hears her baby cry, or holds it for the first time in her arms, she knows that she has been party to a miracle.

A woman doesn't waste much time quibbling about God in moments of family crisis, either. I doubt if there are many atheists in ambulances rushing an injured son to a hospital (or a husband who's just had a heart attack) . . . Or awaiting a doctor's pronouncement outside an operating room . . . Or just watching for the blessed swing of light into the driveway late at night, signaling that a daughter is safely home.

A MINISTER'S TRUE ACHIEVEMENT

This doesn't apply to all ministers, fortunately, and certainly not ours. But I've often wondered why some ministers, in relating their successes, so often speak of material things: Of mortgages reduced or paid off altogether, of new buildings, or old ones impressively improved. Sometimes I've even heard them refer to the physical framework in which they function (the church itself, the parish hall, and whatever other adjuncts that accompany it) as a "plant."

A plant! Acceptable jargon to the pros of the cloth, no doubt; but to the layman—well, it has a cold and clanging sound. Smacking somehow of assembly line efficiency—of canning souls in mass production.

Conscientious ministers, even more than some doctors, are on call at any hour of day or night, seven days a week. Their personal responsibilities and sacrifices are monumental. How sad then that pride or modesty or maybe some people's sensitivity prevents them from acknowledging their true achievements: "We succeeded in comforting and helping so many. We healed the sick and aided the poor. We brought hundreds of people into a closer relationship with God."

THE AFTERGLOW MEANS HOPE

My mother always loved sunsets. This is true of many people, but Mother had a special feeling for them; she kept almost daily appointment with them, and she savored them until the last glow faded from the sky.

We lived in a small Iowa town which boasts a long and lovely lake. And though our house was small, it overlooked a tag-end of the water where the sun seemed to fling its gaudiest banners at the end of the day.

"Oh, just look at that sunset!" Mother was always urging. "You can do those dishes later—your lessons can wait." We must stop whatever we were doing to follow her pleased gaze upward. "Isn't that the most beautiful sky you've ever seen?"

She always acted as if a sunset were something new and glorious and amazing, and we must observe it with as much intensity as if no sunset were ever to appear again. And though we often teased her about it, I realize now that those flaming sunsets compensated for many things we lacked during those grim depression years. They were her daily luxury.

Later when the bright hues had melted into the dusk and there was nothing left of the sunset but a last lingering band of burning rose, she would return to the porch a minute and stand there, arms wrapped in her apron sometimes against the chill, and murmur: "The afterglow means hope."

Hope. The afterglow means—hope! . . . The boy of your dreams would call . . . The test grade would be high . . . You'd get that scholarship for college . . . The job you wanted so desperately would materialize . . . The great big wonderful world of love and wealth and achievement would open up to you . . . For these are the faces of hope when you are young and looking up, eagerly seeking answers in a band of final color across a darkening sky.

As for her. Dimly I sensed the meaning of hope to my mother: The problems of all those about her would be resolved. Wounds would be healed, family frictions smoothed . . . The doctor's report on Dad would be favorable . . . The company policy would be more generous. There would be enough money to go around . . . Her children's often turbulent lives would get straightened out— the boys would find themselves, the girls would marry the right sweethearts—in time they would all be happy, make good.

For while the hooks upon which a youngster hangs his hopes are intensely selfish and personal, those of a mother are multiple; they encompass the entire circle of her family. Her dreams are no longer rooted in self, but in these others.

Yet standing on that porch together long ago, each of us saw in that smoldering band of light a symbol of happier, brighter tomorrows.

Hope. "The afterglow means hope." I don't know whether she had heard the phrase or coined it out of her own indomitable spirit. But I think of it whenever I see the quiet rosy afterlight that follows the blazing sunset. As if a few stubborn coals remain against the coming darkness, little fires of faith that cling long after the sunset is gone.

A BUSY MOTHER'S PRAYER

Dear Lord—

You know it isn't that I don't have enough love to go around. It's just that there are so many of them, and my time and strength won't stretch that far.

Today, for instance, I was so busy coaching Bill on English that I couldn't go along with Jeanie to dancing school. She's having trouble with that new step for the recital, too; she wanted me to watch.

But if Bill doesn't pass this special English course he won't get into college. And you know how important that is, especially after losing that time in the service. Yet Jeanie looked so pathetic going off alone with her little suitcase that I felt guilty . . .

And their dad. So often I forget to do the little things he asks me to. I didn't save those clippings. I let the kids get into his tackle box. I'm sometimes so preoccupied in the morning I'm not even sure whether or not I've kissed him good-by. This isn't right. A man needs a good send-off to face the day quite as much as the youngsters do . . .

Choices—all these choices! Between being a den mother for Tommy or a Girl Scout leader for Ruth. Between all the conflicts of music lessons and dental appointments and birthday parties and homework and just plain talking with them seven days a week, sometimes far into the night. No woman can possibly keep up with it all, no matter how hard she tries. Somebody's bound to feel neglected, to think, even if he never says so, "You don't love me as much—"

But you know it isn't any lack of love. It's only lack of energy, of strength, of time. So give me a little extra, please, if possible. And while you're at it, patience, so that I don't get cross and make the problem worse.

Amen.

(And oh, yes, if you could possibly work in an hour or two of peace and quiet and rest for me I'd be so grateful. In fact, it would help all of us a lot!)

SO POOR, SO RICH

Dialogue with a colored cabdriver:

"There were twelve of us children and we were very poor, only our mother taught us to be rich. 'What d'you mean poor?' she'd say whenever we'd complain. 'Your father gave you two good eyes to see with, and two good hands to work with, and two good feet that'll carry you wherever you want to go. That's being rich, son, that's being rich.

"'There are plenty of people that can't see—you can use your eyes to help them, that's how rich you are.

"'There are some people that can't even walk—you can walk to them and lift them up. Some people have to bear the burdens in this life and some people have to be carried. You be the person that learns to do the carrying. You be the strong—that's what really counts, that's what makes you rich . . .'

"Mother was a gentle-spoken woman. I never heard her use rough language, and neither did any of her six sons. 'A person is judged,' she always told us, 'by what comes out of his mouth.'

"And she always had an answer for everything. When my sister would say, 'It don't pay to be good, Mama—look at our neighbor, what a wonderful woman she was, and she's dead. And how some of the worst people just live on and on,' my mother would say: 'If you had company for dinner what flower would you pick for the table? Wouldn't you go into the garden and pick the best? That's the way it is with the Lord—he don't want the old bad ones. No, no, he says, let them be, maybe if I give 'em some more time they'll improve. But I want the loveliest, the nicest, the best—even little babies sometimes.'

"My mother didn't need Thanksgiving to remind her to be grateful. She was grateful every day of her life for her husband and her church and her children, and for living in a country where everybody can be free. And if he looks at it right, he can be rich!"

Part II
Lord, Let
Me Love

Contents

Preface

This book is about love.

Human love. Our love for each other. Love for this incredibly exciting and beautiful world. Love for the precious gifts of self. And God's love for us.

It is composed of selections that have appeared in magazines or some of my previous books. Pieces that readers tell me *they* have loved.

Putting it together was a joyous but in some ways painful labor of love. So many pieces begged to be included, so many had to be left out. (It was a little like having to shut the door on your own children.)

I hope you will find your favorites here, or others you missed but now can love. For it is through words, spoken or written, that the circles of love widen, or that we touch and share more deeply the true meaning of life with those we love.

Young Love

WHEN I'M A MOTHER, WILL I?

*L*ord, when I'm a mother will I . . .
Try to pick my daughter's boy friends, and always think that those who dress and talk and act the nicest around a girl's parents are the ones you can trust, the ones who'll be best for her? . . .

Want her to be best friends with daughters of *my* friends, and with cousins she can't stand? . . .

Worry when she doesn't have dates, and worry when she *does*? And wait up and ask for explanations when she comes in late?

Lord, when I'm a mother will I tell her how much harder I had things when I was growing up, and what a considerate, generous, helpful, obedient daughter I always was?

Will I forget all the bad parts of being my age now and

remember all the good parts and try to mold my daughter into some beautiful memory of myself?

Lord, will I make as many mistakes with my daughter as I think my mother makes with me?

I suppose I will, Lord. But whatever I do, just let me love her as much as I know my mother loves me.

HE THINKS I'M BEAUTIFUL

Oh, Lord, he thinks I'm beautiful! This boy thinks I'm beautiful. At least that's what he says, and when I look in the mirror I think he could be right.

My eyes are shining, my hair is lively and shining too, my smile is suddenly brighter. I'm standing straighter, and I feel—oh, lovely and strangely alluring. I feel graceful. Even my clothes look better on me.

I feel, and suddenly believe I am, some of the things I've always longed to be—at least attractive, worth looking at.

Thank you, Lord, for this awareness of loveliness in myself. I want to be beautiful for him. I *will* be beautiful for him—and for all the other people I'm going to meet in life.

I will be beautiful for this boy and for those other people, yes. But also—for myself. It gives me so much self-confidence, it makes me feel so good. The whole world looks wonderfully different.

Thank you for this transformation. (Help me to hang onto it even if he looks a little closer and changes his mind!) Thank you that for once in my life I am beautiful in somebody's sight.

TO WALK IN BEAUTY

No garment is more becoming
than love. No vitamin more invigorating.

No lotion, potion, or cosmetic more
glamorizing. The exciting secret of true
beauty is love.

Some say that when beauty fades, love
goes. Isn't it the other way around?
Beauty only fades when love is gone.

If you would walk in beauty, stay
in love! You will see the loved one as
beautiful. You will see yourself as
beautiful. All the world about you will be
beautiful. And the people in that world
will seem more beautiful, for they will
reflect the shining warmth and beauty
you radiate.

THE BETROTHAL

He, Joseph, had only his love for Mary. She was his Temple,
his wealth and his wisdom. And to her he would bring all
that he possessed, every stitch, every penny, every eagerly
hewn bit of wood. Every fiber of his strong young body,
every thought that did not first belong to him who had
made her for him, their God.

He was awed by the honor of his undertaking, but he was
not humbled. He knew that the gift of total commitment is
never small.

Joseph worked feverishly even the day of his betrothal. It
would help to pass the hours until sundown. Furthermore,
there had been a slight upsurge of business, as if already his
union with the house of Joachim might become an asset to
his family. He did not want to be found wanting, and he
wanted to prosper. Soon he would have a wife to support.

Suddenly he could not believe it. The daze of sheer blind
yielding, moving forward, ever forward in harmony with

his fate deserted him. Something might happen even yet. Hannah might still hurl herself between them. Or some awful caprice of God might strike. His mother had gone up to help with the baking; any moment she might rush in, her eyes cold with horror. Or Timna would never return at all. The day would simply go on forever, with Mary ahead of him like a mirage on the desert, or a port toward which he was forever doomed to sail.

"My darling, you're still working?" His mother's hand parted the curtains, her concerned face peered through. "It's growing late, I'll fetch the water for your bath and lay out your garments." Flushed and perspiring but smiling, she pulled off her kerchief. Hannah had bade her come up with the aunts and other kin to join in the joyous preparations. Kneading the dough and baking it in the ovens dug in the yard, setting out the vegetables that were now bursting in such abundance, polishing the bright fruit, checking the wine. And all the while they worked, caught up in the glittering net of women's talk. They had praised each other's efforts and each other's children, favoring her especially, as mother of the groom.

Home now, she looked about with her familiar anxiety for her husband. But Jacob was fine, Joseph assured her; only sleeping. "Good," she sighed, "he'll need the rest. We'll be up late. You should have rested too." She pressed his arm.

Joseph bathed and dressed and anointed his hair with olive oil. His confidence was returning. As the water had washed away the grime and sweat, so it cleansed him of his nervous, foolish imaginings. He felt the splendor of his own body in its pure white linen; he felt the wonder of his youth pulsing, urgent and eager. One small thing troubled him exceedingly—his hands. Although he scrubbed them nearly raw and rubbed them with the precious oil, he could do nothing about their callouses or the scarred, broken nails. He wanted to be perfect for Mary. He did not want his hands to be harsh, clasping hers, or to snag the betrothal veil.

His father puffed in and out, bumping into him, borrowing things, asking Joseph's help with the tying of his girdle.

Jacob could never manage and his wife was busy with the girls. "And do I have to wear shoes?" he pleaded, exhibiting his poor swollen feet with their bunions. Squat, ruddy, his wispy hair combed futilely over his baldness, he looked uncomfortably clean and dressed up and rather pathetic. Yet it was he who reminded Joseph of the things that in his agitation he might forget: the purse of long-hoarded silver dinars, the ring, the presents.

Together they set off at last, Joseph lugging the heavy table. Jacob limped along in his unaccustomed sandals. A brisk breeze set the palm trees clashing and blew their robes about their legs. The dusty cobbled streets seemed strangely empty, as if life had been suspended for this gravely impending hour. Behind a tumbled-down rock fence a camel lurched growling to his feet, a donkey worried a bucket and brayed. They trudged along the steep narrow corridors in a strange silence. They were miserably aware, the nearer they drew to their destination, of the inadequacy of their offerings.

Ahead of them in the fast falling darkness they saw the newly whitened bridal house in its clump of prickly pears. Fluttering from it like a beckoning arm was the pennant that proclaimed its festivities to passers-by. As they approached they saw that Joachim had stepped outside to light the torch of pitch-soaked rushes at the step. It blazed up suddenly, revealing his face with its unguarded look of grief. However quickly he jerked his head there was no denying that naked sorrowing. Because of me? Joseph wondered, or only because his dearest child has so little time left to be under his roof? Promptly Joachim recovered himself and turned to welcome them. Courteously ignoring the gifts they carried, he led them inside.

The room had been transformed. This was no house now, but Eden; the women had gathered up armsful of Eden and brought it inside. The white walls struggled to hold up its colors—the shining green of dampened leaves, and blossoms that rose in a bright riot, to wind even into the rushes of the ceiling. Purple iris, scarlet carnations, pink and blue cyclamen, the ruddy cups of tulips, heavy-headed poppies, already beginning to swoon in the heat of the lamps that stood like little floating stars.

The largest lamp, burning the finest oil, was placed at the head of the table where the bride and groom were led. Joseph found himself there as in a dream. Mary seemed unreal beside him, though her sweet flesh at times brushed against his. The scent of her was more heady than the overpowering fragrance of the flowers. He was stiff with guarding his emotions, remote from her, afraid. Her eyes had a fixed shining, she was smiling, smiling, laughing and smiling before the lavish compliments that each guest paid as he laid his gifts at her feet. Bolts of cloth, baskets, jugs, skeins of flax, countless tools for keeping house. The guests deposited them and then returned to their seats which were bedecked with olive boughs.

Finally an expectant hush; the scribe came forward. The rabbi nodded to Joseph, whose heart was large in his throat. With unsteady hands he drew from his girdle the purse containing the marriage fee, and turned to Mary, whose face floated before him. Not smiling now, but grave and as white as one of the pure white roses in her crown.

"And have you brought a token to give the bride to signify that this covenant is made?"

Nodding, Joseph unwound his girdle. His eyes did not leave Mary's as the rabbi took it and placed it across her uplifted hands.

"And have you other gifts?" the rabbi asked.

"Yes." If only there were more. . . . But nobody seemed to think ill of them, the shawl he had for Hannah, the fine hand chisel for Joachim. And for Mary—ah, for Mary, the sewing box, the soft little doeskin slippers, and the table that would be the first piece of furniture for their house. Plainly she loved them all, especially the slippers. She cried out with delight and thrust out her feet to their measure. There was an awkward moment for it seemed as if she would have him kneel there in the presence of everyone to put them on her. He flushed and people laughed at his discomfort and the rabbi made stern noises in his throat. For the scribe sat waiting to pen the terms of the contract.

And when it was finished, Joseph spoke aloud the pre-scribed words: that he would work for her and honor her in the manner of Jewish husbands, and that all of his property would be hers forever. Thus did he openly take the vow already made within his heart.

It was over now, all but the draping of her face with the betrothal veil. But the children must first be called forward. They had been bouncing with impatience for their treats; now the rabbi beckoned, and the mothers who had been restraining them let them go. They came in an eager swarm, shrieking, hands outstretched for the nuts and cakes. The eyes of Mary and Joseph met, and between them ran a shining thread of wonder, for despite its festive nature, this too was a grave thing, this matter of bestowing the sweets. For it symbolized the fact that she had kept herself for him.

In the commotion he almost forgot the veil. "The veil, the veil!" various ones were whispering. "Quiet the children." An aunt shepherded most of them outside, the others clung to their mothers, eyes focused with a placid interest on the bride.

As Joseph had feared, his fingers caught on the delicate gossamer stuff, and his hands shook placing it with an-guished care so that it fell before her face. Yet pride upheld him. This was his victory; he knew that he stood before them tall and comely, humble yet mighty, a man claiming his true bride.

A vast tenderness swept him, and a great reverence. Now she belonged to him and her face was his to shield. In regret and joy he draped her, his personal Torah, which now must be returned to the ark to await their covenant.

Mary could not sleep. Affectionately she had thanked her parents for the betrothal feast and bade them goodnight and crept into the chamber from which they had removed the younger children, in deference to her new state. Long before the revelry was over the little ones had collapsed one by one, to be carried, limp as the drooping flowers, to pallets in various corners of the house. There, heavy with food and spent with excitement, they slept the deep sleep of the innocent. Her parents slept too at last! She had lain rigid during the long hour when they had murmured together. But finally the voices and the creaking of the mattress ceased. There was heavy silence broken only by Joachim's snores.

Slowly, luxuriantly, she let her knotted fists uncurl, her whole being go limp. And as she did so the memories came flooding in . . . Joseph. *Joseph!* The proud tilt of his head throughout the ceremony. The trembling of his hands—she marveled that he hadn't dropped things as he had once dropped the towel. She ached for him; all that he did was inordinately precious and must be looked at in the fresh new light of herself, alone in her chamber and yet bound to him, awaiting their hour.

And it was all mixed up with that longing which made her toss and turn, which is why she had held herself back until her parents slept . . . Joseph! The grave little smile upon his face as people shouted blessings and wished them well. And his eyes upon her in the glare of the torches in the garden. Those passionate, pensive gray eyes. And the songs that he had sung only for her, quietly, next to her at the feast table, looking straight ahead almost as if she were not present. Singing to her softly, secretly, wooing her with his lips and his remoteness while the others danced and sang.

"Thou hast ravished my heart, my sister, my spouse; thou hast ravished my heart with one of thine eyes. . . . How fair is thy love, my sister, my spouse! how much better is thy love than wine! . . ."

Some of the village boys had brought up lutes and a timbrel, and they too sang and danced, but like shadows, a spectral chorus whose faces flared and fell in the roistering light. Abner had been among them, a trifle tipsy with wine even before he came, striding about making noise, which was alien to his shy nature, and by that giving his heartbreak away. Poor Abner. And poor Cleophas, who had gone off to console himself in Magdala, she had learned. She grieved for them, yet always her being turned back to Joseph. He was the only one she had ever wanted, and he was hers. Hers by law. If he were to die she would be his widow. And if she were to die he would be her widower. And if she were to betray him he would have to give her a bill of divorcement.

But no—no, how could she entertain such thoughts on this night of her betrothal when the moon was shining for good luck? It was still fairly early; the working people of Nazareth could not spend much of the night in celebration, for they had to rise at dawn. The moon was still so bright they had scarcely needed torches going home. It was flooding her little room and she couldn't bear it, this restlessness, fed by the moonlight.

> *By night on my bed I sought him whom my soul loveth; I sought him, but I found him not.*
> *I will rise now, and go about the city in the streets, and in the broad ways I will seek him whom my soul loveth. . . .*

She found herself at the window. The moon possessed the sky. It traced every tree and twig and bush and branch in silver, laying inky shadows, giving everything a stark clarity seldom seen by day. "Joseph. *Joseph!*" she whispered toward that blandly smiling and triumphant face. Was he sleepless too, perhaps pacing alone in this unutterable light, or gazing up in a frenzy of longing? And all because she had indeed set forth on the streets like the bride in Solomon's dream:

> *. . . but I found him whom my soul loveth: I held him, and would not let him go, until I had brought him into my mother's house, and into the chamber of her that conceived me. . . .*
> *My dove, my perfect one, is only one, the darling of her mother. . . .*

Hannah. Poor brave beaten little Hannah, who had been finally reconciled. Who slept in the next room by her husband's side. While the bride . . . the groom? Mary shuddered and pressed her hands to her breasts.

"*A garden enclosed in my sister, my spouse,*" Joseph had gone on singing from those selfsame songs, *"a spring shut up, a fountain sealed."*

Joseph. Joseph. She gave herself over to the final memory, held back to savor utterly. The moment in the garden when both her mother and father had been busy with the guests and they two had drawn a little apart. He had gripped both her hands within his own. "Would to heaven this were our wedding night!"

"Yes. Yes," she whispered, swaying toward him. "But we must be patient, and it won't be long, I promise. Just as I persuaded my father before, I'll surely be able to persuade him not to postpone the wedding for long."

Yet even as they gazed at each other in the nakedness of their yearning, she had begun to shrink from the task ahead. Having yielded thus far, her parents might feel it a point of honor not to yield again. Besides, they loved her, she was their firstborn. She knew that they would keep her with them as long as possible.

JOURNEY OF DISCOVERY

Every experience in love is a journey of self-discovery. The more we learn about the one we love the more we learn about ourselves. And even though the love may cool and we may go our separate ways, we have gained in knowledge. We understand at least one other person better. And we cannot help but better understand that intriguing, groping, puzzling companion we are destined to live with forever: the secret inner self.

Strangely—fortunately—seemingly unlovable people do have those who love them. But only the lovable and

loving ever enjoy the true delight and
wonder of love.

I don't think love is "never having to say
you're sorry." If we're human we all hurt
each other—even when we don't mean to.
True love is understanding and being
willing to say, "I'm sorry."

Married Love

A PSALM FOR MARRIAGE

I am married, I am married, and my heart is glad.
I will give thanks unto the Lord for the love and protection of my husband. I will give thanks for the blessed protection and satisfaction of my home. I will give thanks that I have someone of my own to help and comfort and even to worry about, someone to encourage and to love.

My husband is beside me wherever I need to go. My husband is behind me supporting me in whatever I need to do. I need not face the world alone. I need not face my family alone.

I need face only myself and my God alone. And this is good. This is very good.

Whatever our differences, whatever our trials, I will give thanks unto the Lord for my husband and my marriage. For so long as I have both my husband and my God I am a woman complete, I am not alone.

THE PRICELESS GIFT

Lord of life, creator of man and woman, thank you for the priceless gift of sex. Sex as you intended it long ago in the garden at time's beginning, when they saw that they were naked. Innocent, without responsibility, they hadn't realized. But in their hard-won wisdom they saw, and covered themselves.

I don't think it was their shame, God. It was the instinct you gave them, their basic common sense. For the marvel of their differentness was enhanced by the shielding leaves.

They achieved mystery for each other; they achieved a sweet excitement and new worth. And they achieved another very precious thing—personal privacy. The right to keep to oneself the most important part of oneself.

In this way I think you conveyed to man and woman the true wonder and beauty of sex. Secret not because of being shameful but because of its infinite value. Something too significant in the scheme of human happiness to be lightly exposed.

Lord of life, creator of man and woman, thank you for the joyous fulfillment of sex. When this marvelous secret is shared between two people who deeply love each other. Shared freely, generously, completely, without shame.

Thank you for this most perfect of all human delights, most profound of all human communions. This that regenerates both body and spirit.

The most vital act of life, the very core and source of life. Help us to appreciate and revere it always, the priceless gift of sex.

A WOMAN'S NAME

Listen, Lord, please listen . . .

I miss myself sometimes, I even miss my name.

How is it, I wonder, that I have become just "Mother,"

"Mom," or "Honey"? Words that are tender and kindly but simply don't conjure up *me*. The person I really am.

I sometimes long for the sound of my whole given name. And my last name too. The name that first marked me as belonging to my parents, blood of their blood, name of their name.

You know how truly grateful I am to be a good man's wife. Entitled to stand before the world as *Mrs.* Glad that I bear my husband's name. A name of honor and achievement; and that I am proud that he is the summary and epitome of all the qualities of that name.

But isn't something vital lost when, even through marriage, anyone assumes another person's name? Isn't that the first subtle erosion of a woman's identity? To be known no longer as herself but as merely an adjunct to a man?

Cleave to each other, we are told. Become one flesh. And in most matters let the man be master.

I agree with this, Lord. I believe this is not only your will but good sense. However we may rail against it, seek to escape it, it is wise because it is natural. It works. It makes for a stronger home.

Yet how can a woman ever discover how her own soul's value if she is nothing but echo and shadow of a man?

Lord, you know I love my husband and cherish the protection and even the status of his name. But don't let me forget who I am. Let me cling to myself, too.

Please don't let me ever lose the precious individuality you created, if only through the simple symbol of my name.

"WHAT BECAME OF THE MAN I MARRIED?"

There is one luxury that any man, rich or poor, can give his wife. It costs him nothing, yet it is, curiously enough, the one thing that his wife wants more than anything under heaven. But, by some perverse force of fate, it is also the one thing the average American male puts the least stock in.

The American husband has many virtues. He is a good provider. He works faithfully and hard. He buys more insurance against illness, accident, old age and his own demise than any man anywhere in the world. What's more, he is fundamentally loyal. When the telephone rings and a husband sighs, "I won't be home for dinner, dear, I've got to work late," 99 women out of 100 can believe him implicitly.

He can be counted on not only because he's basically decent but also because he's simply too unromantic to kick up his heels. Give him a comfortable home, a place to pursue his hobby, a wife who feeds him well, sympathizes with his problems and takes good care of the children—and home is the one place he'd rather be than anywhere else. And he's usually too busy reading the newspaper or puttering about the basement to notice or care whether or not his dream girl still wears that cute curl and is a svelte size 12. She's with him and he's with her. And that, to him, is proof positive of love.

That this attitude is the direct opposite of every phase of courting never bothers him. As Dorothy Dix said, "when you've caught your streetcar, you don't go on chasing it." Relieved of the frantic need to rush after his heart's desire, he settles down to the business of her support, not even suspecting that he's neglecting her nearest and dearest desire—romantic love.

Yet romantic love is, to every normal woman, quite as important as material security and faithfulness. It is, in most cases, the reason a woman marries in the first place. What man ever won fair maiden by promising, "I will hoe the garden, pay the bills on time and take out life insurance"? No. He pleads, "Darling, I can't live without you. I want you forever in my arms." And she believes it.

Wrapped in this shining cloak of adoration, she is swept ecstatically into marriage. But, unlike the male of the species, she is not content to drop the cloak and start scrubbing the kitchen as all-sufficient proof of her corresponding passion. Her home duties are proof of devotion, but they seldom assume for her the same role that her husband's work does for him—namely, a substitute for ardor. To her, love is a continuing emotional state. It does *not* become simply an established fact when two people join their lives.

The average woman is, I believe, love-conscious and love-anxious at least 60 percent of the time. Nature has designed her to be emotionally responsive, yielding, warm, sympathetic and sensitive. For these are the qualities and emotions that make for motherhood, that go with its very equipment—the womb that shelters, the breast that nourishes, the arms that comfort and carry. And they are also inevitably linked with a woman's major need and function, love.

I realize that there are plenty of stupid wives, nagging wives, wives who become dowdy and dull and break all the well-known rules for holding affection. On the other hand, more women would strive to be stimulating and beautiful if they tasted the sweet heady flavor of adulation more often. Love is a more potent beautifier than any cream, lotion or charm course on the market. Nearly everyone has observed some drab little creature who became downright stunning simply because some man thought her so. And nearly everyone has seen some truly gorgeous woman gradually fade because her man was so unobserving or chary of compliments that beauty itself became joyless and without meaning.

The husbands who really do care about their wives' appearance would find a little old-fashioned flattery doubly rewarding. They'd have partners to be prouder of on Ladies' Day at their luncheon clubs, and they'd actually save money. Lots of women buy clothes they don't need in the vague hope that if they change outfits often enough their husbands will eventually notice they exist. The man who's smart enough to convince his honey she's a knockout in anything she dons isn't likely to find her too bitter about wearing make-do's. No Schiaparelli original can make a female feel so robed in glory as the admiration of the man she loves.

Maybe this doesn't fall under the classification of romantic love. Maybe it's just old-fashioned bread-and-butter married love. But basically it's what every woman wants—to be cherished, to feel herself adored, to be drawn richly and consciously ever closer to her man.

Another thing the average American husband doesn't understand is the way women feel about sex. Women differ in their needs and responsiveness, just as men do. But more women are more passionate than a lot of men suspect, simply because the women are too modest to let on. I don't honestly think, however, that sexual satisfaction is in itself nearly so important to a woman as the feeling of reassurance the relationship gives her—the reaffirmation of the fact that her husband has wanted to be close to her, to hold her in his arms, to be complete with her in a way that shuts the whole world out. Impotence would be a lot less common in men if they could understand that. Women don't so much seek physical thrills and bodily fulfillment as they seek a time and place of nearness, of going spiritually back, just two people alone together—to those far-lost moments of the past when each was supremely important to the other.

If I were a man, I would make it the first and last acts of my day to take my wife a few moments into my arms. I would make this drawing together so much a part of the fabric of our daily lives that either of us would feel lost without it. It would be the symbol of that blind hurtling together we first knew, a moment of closeness and strength exchanged with which to launch the day. And no matter how many other things had come thrusting between us, it would be a final seal of unity and communion at the day's end.

THE HOUR OF LOVE

Oh, God, thank you for this beautiful hour of love.

My dear is asleep now, but I am too filled with the wonder and joy of it to sleep just yet.

I stand at the window gazing up at your star-riddled sky. I lean on the sill and gaze down upon your quiet earth.

How rich and fruitful it smells, how fragrant with life and the promise of life.

I see your trees reaching out as if to each other. For even trees must have mates to mature. Then they cast down their seeds and the rich fertile earth receives them to bear afresh.

I see the fireflies winking, hear the crickets and the locusts and the frogs. All are calling, calling, insistently, almost comically, "Here I am! Come. Come to me!"

"Male and female created he them," I think. For everything must have its opposite and meet with its opposite to be fulfilled.

Thank you, God, for this remarkable plan. Thank you for the hours of love it means.

I am as happy as one of those crickets singing in the grass.

I feel as tall and strong and lovely as one of those outreaching trees. I fell as complete yet filled with promise as the earth teeming with its seeds.

Thank you, God, for making me a woman.

FRUIT OF LOVE

> *No woman is ever so full of love as*
> *when she is carrying a child.*
> *Whether she planned the circumstance*
> *or not she is trapped—literally locked*
> *into a remarkable role: that of carrying*
> *love. Man's love, her love, God's*
> *love, all joined—united to fashion this*
> *precious growing product: Life! Life, the*
> *literal fruit of love.*

THE QUARREL

God, we quarreled again last night, and today my heart is sore. My heart is heavy. It is literally heavy, as if a leaden weight were hanging in my breast.

And part of its weight is that he is bowed with it too. I

keep seeing him, his head low, his shoulders actually bowed under it as he trudged off to work.

I can hardly bear the image. I could hardly bear it then. I wanted to run out and stop him, say nothing is worth this awful estrangement, say I'm sorry. But I didn't. I let him go, afraid more words might only lead to more quarreling.

I turned my sore heart back into this house, so heavily haunted by the quarrel. I drag myself about my tasks here, trying to forget the things we said.

But the words keep battering away at my sore heart and aching head. However I try to turn them off, they repeat themselves incessantly, a kind of idiot re-enactment of a play so awful that you keep trying to run out of the theater. Only all the exits are locked. The play goes on and on—and the worst of it is I keep adding more lines to it, trying to improve my part in it, adding things I wish I'd said.

God of love, please let this play end! Open the exists of my mind. Let the blessed daylight of forgiveness and forgetting pour in.

Bless him wherever he is. Lift the weight of this quarrel from his heart, his shoulders. I claim peace for him now, this minute. I claim and confirm your peace and joy for both of us when he returns.

"WHAT BECAME OF THE GIRL I MARRIED?"

LOST: *One gay, sweet bride. Girl who thinks I'm wonderful and tells me so. Chief characteristic: Appreciation! Ample reward offered by one discouraged guy.*

Countless husbands could have composed that ad.

In the main, we women do a good job on our homes, our children, our community undertakings, and making ends meet. We don't come off too badly on the score of personal appearance, and most of us love our mates with depth and loyalty and passion. But far too many of us fall flat on our faces when it comes to showing those mates any real understanding or appreciation.

We fail in the first place, I believe, because we were not realistically prepared for marriage. Most of us floated down the aisle believing that our particular orange blossoms would never fade. Many a wife, instead of accepting her quite human but often quite wonderful husband for what he is, remains stubbornly in love with the prince of the fairy tales. And she will shove, shame, nag, weep, plead, and connive to try to fit her bewildered partner into the princely mold. That she knows it's impossible is beside the point. For she has also fallen in love with another deadly mirage: her own sense of having been wronged.

The woman who has formed the habit of thinking herself neglected is reluctant to relinquish the role even when she can! The very invitation she has been clamoring for, a date to go dancing or out on the town, is rejected: "You know I haven't anything decent to wear." (To come right down to it, she'd rather stay home than give up that precious: "You never take me anywhere.")

More women would find their longings fulfilled if they realized that romance is a two-way street. The wife who sits dourly at one end of it expecting love to come to her had better be prepared to sit a long time! But she who is willing to hop down from her high horse and come running halfway (and a little more) will find all her marriage relationships enriched.

For men like attention too. There are almost no men who do not feel a responsive leap when they are praised by their wives, told: "You're wonderful; I'm proud of you; I'm glad you're mine."

Before complaining too loudly of neglect, women should ask themselves honestly—who has the best of it? We may bear the children and rear them. We may wash, iron, clean, cook, quickfreeze, sew. But most of us have conveniences to make the going easier. And no law says we have to do these things.

A man, on the other hand, becomes an economic slave the minute he signs the marriage license. He is linked forever not only to the girl of his dreams but to his desk, or whatever means he has for her support. Because support her he must—and likewise any children she bears him. Morally and legally, he alone is responsible, and little short of death itself will ever free him. For even in case of separation or divorce this burden continues.

Just as a woman is under constant advertising pressure to be "alluring," a man gets constant financial pressure. He is attacked in his most vulnerable spot—his wife and kids. Take them vacationing in this roomier car; make them cooler with air conditioning, safer with fencing. And the most potent pleas come from the family itself: "The Beckers have bought a summer place, *why can't we?*"

Small wonder that so many men bury themselves in the financial pages, instead of whispering sweet nothings to their wives.

It may be true that husbands too often take love for granted, but women too often take for granted the responsibilities men assume for them. Ask any widow who is suddenly faced with the need to carry on alone. "When you have a good husband, you just don't realize how much he does," she will tell you. "Not until you're actually in his shoes can you appreciate what he's been up against. Then it's too late."

But for most of us it's not too late. Thank your husband for taking such good care of you—starting now. Praise him to his folks, his friends, and his offspring. Be grateful for his every little kindness—and show it!

If you are one of those who have been in love with your own misery, there is a good way to end the affair: Write yourself a letter. Turn a searchlight on your own faults, and list them honestly. Then set down every lovable trait, accomplishment, and quality of the man you married. You'll find such positive action a revelation in values, and you'll rise from it a far more appreciative, hence *lovable* wife.

Understanding and appreciation. The woman who can rediscover those virtues won't have to worry about romance. She'll have her share of it, and something even better—a guy who'll be saying, in his heart:

"FOUND: *the girl I married.*"

THE TENDER TRAP

Oh, Lord, I'm so tired and lonely and blue I'm a little afraid. I'm so sick of housework, sick of the children. They get on my nerves so I could scream (and do). I'm even sick of my husband right now—I wish he'd go away on a trip.

Or I wish *I* could get away for a change. My husband says okay, go; go visit my sister. But that's not it. Even if I managed to leave the children I'd be around hers. . . . No, I want something else that has nothing to do with women and children. I want to be somebody else for a while. Maybe the girl I used to be, or maybe a woman I haven't even met yet. A beautiful, poised woman with a mind and life of her own.

Only I can't. There's never any going back to what you used to be. And right now there is no going ahead. There is only the present which sometimes seems such a trap. As the play called it—*The Tender Trap*. Only it was funny in the play, and it was the man who felt trapped.

Maybe my husband feels trapped too, going day after day to the same job. Maybe the people he has to deal with get on his nerves too (only a man can't scream). . . . And the women who leave their houses and fight traffic or crowded buses to get to work every day. Maybe they're screaming, too, somewhere inside.

Lord, help me to realize how lucky I am here, right now, within this tender trap. Turn my fantasies of escape to some purpose. If there's a woman I haven't met yet, locked somewhere inside me, let her out.

Bless that person you surely meant me to be, instead of this self-pitying drudge. Recreate me in her image. Help me to see that she is not some superior creature that would evolve out of other circumstances, but that she lives inside me.

Lord, I now affirm and claim her. I claim her poise, her calm, her patience, her cheerfulness, her self-control. I claim her beauty. I claim her awakened mind.

I claim her for my children. She will be a better mother.

I claim her for my husband. She will be a better wife.

I claim her for all women who are feeling the confines of their tender traps. Bless them and help each of them to find her too.

WHEN A HUSBAND LOSES INTEREST

My husband has lost interest in me, Lord. I feel it. I know it.

I am less to him than his easy chair. Less to him than his dinner. Less than the TV set or his friends or his hobby or his newspaper.

At least such things comfort him or give him enjoyment. But me—it is as if I am invisible to him, He does not see me. He scarcely ever touches me. Even at night he has no need of me; he is asleep before I get to bed.

Lord, where have I failed that he takes me so for granted? Is his blindness and indifference perhaps a reflection of my own blindness and indifference to myself?

If I am no longer physically attractive, let me improve. Give me the time, energy, imagination, yes and the money, to become more appealing.

If I have become dull and boring, wake me, shake me, let me read more, think more, do more to be a better companion.

If I have nagged or scolded or complained without realizing it, show me these faults clearly, help me to change.

Dear Lord, please awaken my husband to my presence once again. Make him see me, touch me, know me, love me as a woman once more. With your help I can become someone more worth seeing, touching, knowing, loving.

Thank you for revealing this better self.

FOR BEING CHERISHED

Lord, thank you for this simple yet priceless thing: Being cherished. For that old-fashioned word in old-fashioned wedding ceremonies, a word we take so for granted. Yet in reality how beautiful it is.

I'm untidy, my hair's a mess and so is the house. But the littlest fervently hugs my middle, and an eight-year-old presents me with a fragrant necklace of braided clover . . . A daughter banging in from school exclaims, "Hooray for anybody who can make gingerbread smell like that!" and gives me a kiss . . . My husband, toiling wearily in, perks up at sight of me and give me another.

And suddenly, in a burst of awareness, I am overcome with this shining wonder: I am cherished!

I'm sick. Dizzy without warning. Trembling, not only with fatigue but a chill. Somebody says, "Go lie down, I'll finish the kitchen." I am being steered toward a hot bath, an already turned down bed. Cool hands are on my head.

I hear them making the phone calls I should be making, attending to things, sense their anxious tiptoeing about. And as I drift off there is something deeply sweet about even the misery that set all this in motion: I realize that I am cherished.

We'll be late for the reception. As usual there's the last-minute search for the mislaid address; as usual I can't find my bag. And halfway down the block I set up a wail—a runner!

Patiently my husband turns back, waits with motor running while I rush inside to change . . . And when I return, breathless, he leans over to pat my knee and say, "You're a lot of trouble, honey, but I guess you're worth it." And my heart leaps up in a little prayer of gratitude, God (I hope you hear it) just to thank you for being cherished.

WHEN A MAN IS AWAY

How many noises there are in a house when a man is gone!

Tickings and tappings and mysterious creakings. Slight rattlings and rumblings and thumpings heard at no other time . . . Maybe doors opening? . . . Footsteps approaching? Only don't be silly, don't be scared, everything's locked up tight . . . relax and go to SLEEP.

But the house refuses to be quiet. And the very night beyond its doors seems to want to come in. Branches scrape windows, leaves scurry across the steps, the wind fingers the shutters like a nosy woman shopping, and the rain whispers "Please."

Then the rain begins to rap, knock with a bold insistence. And though you smile and snuggle down thinking, "Goody, I'm safe. Burglars and suchlike surely don't work much in the rain," yet the house seems to stir with new interest.

The cat begins to prowl, bell tinkling, but refuses to go out when you get up—not in the rain. Refuses even to cuddle down cozily at your feet . . . The dog begins to snore—great guttural blasts that almost drown out the cacophony of other noises (some protection SHE is!).

Since sleep seems to be hopeless, you turn on a lamp, make a cup of cocoa, and sip and read (something very soothing) until you're just too drowsy to hear them any more—these orchestras of night that seem to tune up only when there's no man in the house.

THE GOOD DAYS Of MARRIAGE

Dear Lord, thank you for the good days of marriage. The days when we wake up pleased with each other, our jobs, our children, our home, and ourselves.

Thank you for our communication—the times when we can really talk to each other; and the times when we understand each other without so much as a gesture or a word.

Thank you for our companionship—the times when we can work together at projects we both enjoy. Or work in our separate fields and yet have that sense of sharing that can only come when two persons' lives have merged in so many other ways so long. Thank you that we don't feel cut off from each other, no matter how divergent the things we do.

Thank you for our times of privacy. Our times of freedom. Our relaxed sense of personal trust. Thank you that we don't have to clutch and stifle each other, that we have learned to respect ourselves enough to respect the other's individuality.

Thank you, Lord, that despite the many storms of marriage we have reached these particular shores. Help us to remember them. Help us to hold fast to them, Lord.

Family Love

FOR A WANTED CHILD

Oh, God, thank you for the child I carry.

I am in love with it as I am in love with my husband and my life—and you.

I walk the world in wonder. I see it through new eyes.

All is changed, subtly but singingly different. The beauty of sunlight upon the grass, the feel of its warmth along my arms. It is cradling me in tenderness as I shall cradle this child one day.

I am mother and child in one, new as a child myself, innocent, excited, amused, surprised.

I marvel at my changing body. It is as sweet and new to me as when I was a little girl. Even its symptoms are less of misery or fatigue than signals of its secret. "See how important I am," my body claims. "Feel my insistence as I make and shape this child for you."

God, I am happy. God, I am sad. God, I am vital—alive, alive. Life has me in its hands. Life is moving me in an immutable direction that I don't want to resist and couldn't if I tried.

It is almost comical, this sweet and stern insistence. It is like night and day and the changing of the seasons. "Stop, stop!" I might as well cry to the winds or the sea.

No, no, I am in for it now, and I rejoice, though I am also a little bit afraid. The labor, the delivery, the care. But it is an exciting kind of anxiety. It is part of the privilege of being female.

Oh, God, bless this body in which the mystery of life is working. Let it be equal to its job.

And bless the tiny marvel it is responsible for. Your handiwork! Oh, bless my baby too—let it be whole and beautiful and strong.

A PRAYER FOR FATHERS

God bless fathers, all fathers old and young.

Bless the new father holding his son or daughter in his arms for the first time. (Steady his trembling, Lord, make his arms strong.)

Give him the ambition and strength to provide for its physical needs. But even more, give him the love and common sense to provide for its hungering heart.

Give him the time and will to be its friend. Give him wisdom, give him patience, give him justice in discipline.

Make him a hero in his youngster's eyes. So that the word Father will always mean a person to be respected, a fair and mighty man.

And God bless older fathers too.

Fathers who are weary from working for their young. Fathers who are sometimes disappointed, discouraged. Fathers whose children don't always turn out the way they'd hoped; fathers of children who seem thoughtless, ungrateful, critical, children who rebel.

Bless those fathers, Lord; comfort them.

And stay close to all these fathers when they must tell sons and daughters good-bye. When kids leave home, going off to college, or to marry, or to war—fathers need to be steadied in their trembling then too, Lord. (Mothers aren't the only ones who cry.)

You, our heavenly father, must surely understand these earthly fathers well.

We so often disappoint you, rebel against you, fail to thank you, turn away from you. So, in your infinite love (and infinite experience!) bless fathers, all fathers old and young.

BATHTIME

No matter how busy I am, Lord, let me be thankful and find joy in bathing my baby—he's growing so fast. No longer tiny and helpless, almost lost in a long white nightie, but now full to my arms, with a rollicking will of his own.

Thank you for the sight of his back straight and sturdy in the tub, and the perfect peach globe of his head. (Please keep him always straight and strong.) For the sheer bright abandon of his antics—his mad splashing, his impassioned clutch of floating ship and ball. For the foolishness of a chewed washcloth dribbling daily down his chin, and the flirtatious peeking of his eyes over the tub's rim.

My son, Lord, my plump brazen elf of a son to be soaped and rinsed as he scolds and sings and chatters in his own expressive jargon. My son to be gathered warm and wet into a big towel, to be patted and powdered and oiled.

I lift him up in a joyous little gesture of offering, and he dances on tiptoe with nimble nakedness.

Thank you for this son to be wrestled into a diaper. For he keeps flopping over, scrambling to his knees—it is like trying to put pants on the wind! Yet you made mothers strong-fingered and determined. We must win the kicking contest against shoes and stockings, we must subdue our offspring into clothes.

And our reward is to carry a son at last, sweet and fresh, clasping our neck, riding royally down to his dinner like a king.

Thank you for this child and this happy daily struggle that is half duty, half delight. And whenever it seems a chore, help me to remember how awfully fast little boys get too big to be bathed . . . or maneuvered into *anything*.

A SON

A son is surely the most remarkable thing that can happen to a man and wife.

A man usually wants a boy first, to be sure of carrying on the family name. Men need this firm symbolic title to the past. They want it spelled out, printed, inscribed on documents, carved in stone. They don't want the chain broken. It is their lifeline.

A woman doesn't need this reassurance. She takes her measure of immortality with every child she bears. Yet it pleases her to think—some day their son will bestow this proud name upon his wife! Like herself and John, *they* will be the Smiths, the Andersons.

But long before this can happen, the subject has to be taught, trained, hauled places, exhorted to study and to practice, conferred about with teachers, coaches, Scout leaders and the neighbors. In his behalf there are innumerable meetings to endure, programs to applaud, dinners to down. His tonsils must usually be deleted, his teeth fixed, his feet fitted into an appalling parade of ever bigger more expensive shoes. Even shoes run second, however, to the incredible number of pants that a boy is able to ruin, outgrow, or even lose.

There is all his equipment to be procured. His ball bats, camping gear, football helmets, fishing tackle, swim trunks and track shoes.

And his means of propulsion! Today's boy takes to wheels as soon as he can straddle a tricycle, and is seldom separated from them until he takes off in a jet plane or a rocket to the moon. Between these points the parents spend enough time in arguments, discussion, trips to the doctor, the insurance agent, and sometimes the police station (not to mention the hours of lying awake worrying) to have personally paved at least ten miles of local highway, or written most of Shakespeare's plays.

As for the pets and projects . . . The escaping hamsters, the injured birds and wormy squirrels, the dead butterflies, the cats, dogs, rabbits, snakes, racoons—and eventually, girls . . . The courses in hypnotism and taxidermy; the hikes and hideouts and tents and secret clubs. The stamp and coin collections, the chemistry experiments.

A mother's reward for all this is the thrill of finally discovering a compound that will take the stains out of the sofa, and the relief of being told at the hospital that he didn't get his neck broken falling out of the tree house. If you're lucky (and strong-willed) you also have someone to carry out the trash, run errands, and (police brutality) rake and mow the yard.

Less definite but dear returns are: A snaggle-toothed grin from a school bus . . . A limp bunch of violets . . . An unexpected hug . . . The shout, "I got an A!" or "I made the team!" . . . A neighbor's remark: "He's the best paper boy we've ever had." . . . A trumpet's stubborn tooting . . . A football game where he makes the winning touchdown (or they at least call him in to substitute) . . . The look of a thin neck and tender young shoulders going off in a white jacket with a corsage box under the arm . . . A voice sweeter than all others in the choir . . .

Finally he gets his diploma (where's yours?) and sometimes follows in his father's footsteps, but more often goes striding off on paths of his own. Sometimes he falls by the wayside and doesn't seem to be going anyplace. And these are times that try parental souls. But eventually (if you just live long enough) he picks himself up and rushes forward toward achievements beyond your fondest dreams.

A son may worry you, disappoint you, keep you broke. Or he may excel, fulfill every ambition, make you so proud you think you'll explode. Anyway, he leaves a cluttered trail on his way to manhood—schoolbooks, papers, marbles, fish hooks, tennis racquets, souvenirs, and autographed pictures. He abandons a lot of gear, outgrows a lot of trousers, and wears out a lot of shoes. But he will always carry your hope in his hip pocket, and he can never lose or wear out your faith in him, or your love.

He's stuck with it. It's his heritage, his lifeline—as permanent as his father's family name.

I WAS SO CROSS TO THE CHILDREN

Oh, God, I was so cross to the children today. Forgive me.

Oh, God, I was so discouraged, so tired, and so unreasonable. I took it out on them. Forgive me.

Forgive me my bad temper, my impatience, and most of all my yelling.

I cringe to think of it. My heart aches. I want to go down on my knees beside each little bed and wake them up and beg them to forgive me. Only I can't, it would only upset them more.

I've got to go on living with the memory of this day. My unjust tirades. The guilty fear in their eyes as they flew about trying to appease me. Thinking it all their fault—*my* troubles, my disappointments.

Dear God, the utter helplessness of children. Their vulnerability before this awful thing, adult power. And how forgiving they are, hugging me so fervently at bedtime, kissing me good night.

And all I can do now is to straighten a cover, move a toy fallen out of an upthrust hand, touch a small head burrowed into a pillow, and beg in my heart, "Forgive me."

Lord, in failing these little ones whom you've put into my keeping, I'm failing you. Please let your infinite patience and goodness fill me tomorrow. Stand by me, keep your hand on my shoulder. Don't let me be so cross to my children.

A CHILD'S HAND IN YOURS

What feeling in all the world is so nice as that of a child's hand in yours?

It is soft. It is small and warm. It is as innocent and guileless as a rabbit or a puppy or a kitten huddling in the shelter of your clasp. Or it is like living clay to be molded. It is the essence of all trust.

"Here I am," it seems to tell you. "Shape me. Guide me. Lead me."

If you stop to consider, the responsibility it imposes is almost too much. But you don't. "Here, take my hand while we're crossing the street," you say, and concentrate on the immediate business of getting him safely to the curb. Or, "Hold onto my hand, Mother will see that the dog doesn't bite you, don't be afraid."

Or you take the feverish, betrayed little fingers in yours after the tonsils are out and say, "I know it hurts, darling, but it won't last long. Just hang onto my hand until you fall asleep."

A child's hand in yours—what tenderness it arouses, what almost formidable power it conjures up! You are instantly not only the symbol but the very touchstone of security, wisdom, and strength.

Though you may secretly know yourself to be lacking in all these things, miraculously the child endows you with them as he reaches up. As he clutches your own hand so unquestioningly, he is giving back the very qualities that he draws from that hand to comfort himself.

He is making you taller and stronger and wiser. He is leading you just a little nearer to the person he imagines you to be.

And a child's hand in yours is something more. It is your

link with life itself. For each son or daughter is a projection of those who created him.

A mother clasping her little girl's hand, a father gripping the fingers of his small son—each is leading his own dreams forward, holding fast to his own tomorrows.

I SPANKED MY CHILD TODAY

I spanked my child today.
She'd torn her dress at play
And tracked across the rug
and peered at me in such a smug,
Defiant, impish way,
I sort of lost my head.
I spanked her till her little
Spanking place was red.
But now that she's in bed
I don't know what to say.
It's. . . . hard. . . .
A sleeping child
Is such a chokey sight,
The face so very small
Against the pillow white,
The hands upthrown,
A toy on guard,
The fair hair mussed. . . .
If I've betrayed
My sacred tiny trust,
Oh, Lord of little children,
Please forgive
And let me give
The scales of love
An extra disc of patience
To outweigh. . . .
I wish I hadn't
Spanked my child today.

I'M TIRED OF ALL THE EXPERTS

Listen, Lord . . .

I'm tired of all the experts.

People who try to tell me how to raise my children, how to run my marriage, how to be a better person, how to save the world.

I've listened to them far too often, been intimidated by them too often. I have underestimated my own instincts and common sense—and you.

I am going back to the Bible for some good old-fashioned guidance: "Honor thy father and thy mother." "Bring up a child in the way he should go and he will not depart from it." "Love thy neighbor as thyself."

Yes, and the Ten Commandments, and a whole lot more.

I'm going to rediscover this long neglected gold mine. God. I'm going to see how it stacks up against the advice of today's so-called experts.

(And while I'm at it, I'm going to be a lot more careful about posing as an expert myself.)

LITTLE GIRLS TOGETHER

How delightful is the friendship that exists between little girls. Small females somewhere between the ages of six and ten.

When they are smaller they will quarrel over toys. They cry and get mad and go home. When they are older they compete. They will hurt each other's feelings. Many times they talk mercilessly about each other, even the closest chums. They can weep their hearts out on a pillow over a real or fancied snub.

But when they are first grade playmates, or second, or third or fourth, then they are still exactly that: Companions in play. In secrets. In giggling games. In merry undertakings which include everything from baking a package cake to selling cold drinks, or organizing a back yard show or a Witch's Club.

Their laughter is as sparkling and without malice as a bright morning shower. Their jokes are bold, obvious, usually old as the stars, and utterly without guile. They make up insane songs with which to accompany their rope jumpings, or the bouncing of a ball. They call each other up mornings and evenings to giggle, exchange lengthy lists of what they hope to get for their birthdays, and make vast impossible plans for building a playhouse or buying a horse.

Spending the night together is a thrilling undertaking which involves lugging along a bulging bag of stuffed animals as well as their best pajamas, robe, slippers, bubble bath, and at least one doll with complete wardrobe. They climb joyously from bed to bed, bounce, throw pillows, and keep each other awake with scary stories.

At last, after many remonstrances and warnings, they collapse into the profound sleep of childhood. Stealing in, you find them sprawled in incredible positions. legs dangling over the bedside, pigtails or curls awry, covers trailing the floor. They are usually awake at dawn, singing, cavorting, and buzzing like bees over their marvelous plans for the day.

Little girls playing together in this wonderful morning of their lifetime are like young birds chirping, or butterflies winging lightly among the flowers. They need each other in a way that is instinctive and joyous; they are nourished by each other's presence, they thrive and grow strong in the light of each other's warmth, as plants grow unconsciously upward in the light of the sun.

FOR AN UNEXPECTED CHILD

Dear God, it's true, we're going to have another child. And I am aghast, I am stunned. I didn't expect this, I didn't want it, and there's no use pretending—to you or to myself—I don't want it now.

With so many childless women longing for babies, why

have you chosen me? You, who are the Author and Giver of Life, as the prayer book says—why not one of them? Why me, why me?

I don't need or want this gift. I am not grateful for it. I don't understand your ways.

"Some day it will be a great comfort to you," the doctor says. And some deep abiding instinct assures me he is right. But that is small comfort *now*.

Then there is that other cliché, "The Lord will provide." And you will, financially you will, you always have.

Yet I don't want to have to wait for that proof either. Provide for me *now*. Provide for this child. Provide me with love and joy and a feeling of welcome for this little new unexpected life.

THE NURSERY

There they lie, in their little glass garden, these fragile new fruits of human love. And of your love too, the eternal love that flows through the universe, creating and re-creating these exquisite creatures in your image.

There they sleep, God, in the blessed sleep of their newness. So fresh from the mystery of their beginning, so warm and moist and sweet from the waters in which they were cradled.

Resting from the rude shock of birth they lie. . . . Resting . . . resting for the long journey ahead.

Though one or two awake and start yelling—lustily, comically demanding the rescue that quickly comes. Hands, gently efficient, to change and feed and comfort them. To hold them up before the pleased eyes of the people gazing in.

There they sleep, God, or are displayed, wrapped in the most complete and absolute love they will ever know.

Then one grandmother, old and broken with living, smiles faintly and shakes her head. "Poor little things," she remarks as she turns away. "If they only knew what's ahead."

And my heart gives a little start of sorrow. I too am suddenly stricken. For I see these children rising and walking, stripped of protection, of warm blankets and sheltering arms.

I see some of them cold, frightened, struggling—against danger, violence, physical abuse, drugs. I see them tempted, I see them shaken. I see them bitter with heartbreak, confusion, despair. And my whole being cries out to you, "No, no, spare them, keep them here!"

But I know you wouldn't have it so. *They* wouldn't have it. They are as hungry for the life struggle as they are for milk. It is their right; they are savagely insistent upon it.

They sleep now . . . However sweetly they sleep now . . . they must rise up and go. But oh, Lord, when the blissful sleep is over and they take their first faltering steps, give us patience, give us wisdom. Show us how to help them.

For now, bless them as they lie resting for the journey ahead.

NIGHT DUTY

Oh, Lord, I hear it again, that little voice in the night, crying, "Mommy!"

At least I think I hear it. It may be my imagination. It may be just the wind. Or if not, maybe it will stop in a minute, the child will go back to sleep. . . .

(Oh, let it be just the wind. Or let him go back to sleep. I'm so tired. I've been up so many nights lately. I've got to get some sleep too.)

But if it's true, if it's one of them needing me and it isn't going to stop, if I must go—help me.

Lift me up, steady me on my feet. And make me equal to my duty.

If he's scared give me patience and compassion to drive the fears of night away.

If he's ill give me wisdom. Make me alert. Let me know what to do.

If he's wet the bed again, give me even more patience and wisdom and understanding (and let me find some clean sheets).

Thank you, Lord, for helping my weary footsteps down this hall.

Thank you for sustaining me too as I comfort, and care for the child.

Thank you for my own sweet . . . sweet . . . eventual sleep.

LUCKY IS THE WOMAN WITH DAUGHTERS

Lucky is the woman who has daughters.

They're so lovely when they're little, with their bonnets and bows. Fun to sew for, to bathe and cuddle, to dress. Boys resist much of this; whereas daughters whisk you back to your childhood. Daughters are your dolls. And daughters increase in value as they grow older, because there are so many things mothers and daughters can share.

A daughter is made in your image. As if to enhance this happy marvel we go through a phase of mother-daughter outfits (luckily, short-lived). But hard on its heels rides the wish to turn out a product which is pretty and popular, witty, wise and good. A kind of impossible package mix of all that we probably were NOT at her age. We watch the clock praying she'll have a good time at the party, and know an ancient heartbreak when she weeps, "It was awful, only one boy danced with me and he's a fink!" Or, when she rushes in starry-eyed, we waltz to a secret tune.

At about this time we discover the mixed blessings of mother-daughterdom. There is a continual pirating of perfume, nail polish, lipsticks, rollers, sweaters and hose. Which grows, with their acquisitions, into a kind of female mutual fund. "I never have anything I can call my own," a mother may lament, adding, "But I've doubled my potential supply of accessories and clothes."

Also, daughters come in handy once they've taken home

economics. Now they can fit and fix some of your things, as well as their own. And there's nothing more satisfying, if rather touching, than to hear the sewing machine humming as a daughter sticks gamely to the cause of making her own prom dress.

By now it's no longer Mom who's passing on the tricks of glamor—it's the girls. They're suddenly so good at hair, they're doing yours. Also, helping you make up your eyes before a party, advising you which hat to wear and for Pete's sake to hold your stomach in. For scarcely have they put their toys away, it seems, than today's daughters become wonderfully wise in the feminine arts.

Alas, perhaps too wise! For daughters can be wildly exasperating to shop with. They detest everything you like, making you feel about as hip on fashion as The Girl of the Limberlost. But they're also fun to pause and have a snack with when you've almost come to blows.

Mad as little girls are about "helping Mother" scrub, iron, cook, by the time they're old enough to be some use around a house, they're usually off somewhere, or on the telephone. And their rooms are invariably a mess. Preoccupied with the lengthy rites of bedtime, and the preparations as if for a beauty pageant before taking off for school, they leave in their wake a welter of open drawers, horses, Beatles, stuffed animals, strewn garments, and unmade beds. I know of no cure for this except for the girl to join the Marines, go away to college, or get married. And when this happens you miss them so acutely you'd rather have the chaos.

Yet mothers and daughters occupy a secret country of the feminine where you can giggle, gossip, discuss your ailments, share your dreams. That's why the misunderstandings between them are so painful, quarrels so devastating. And yet inevitable. For nature, at whatever cost to both of you, decrees that your bright, your beautiful, kind-cruel daughters must cast you aside, break free.

My own mother used to say: "A daughter is just her mother's heart walking around outside her." I know now what she meant.

A MOTHER'S PRAYER IN THE MORNING

Thank you, Lord, for this glorious day.

Bless the carpet beneath my feet and the bombardment of hot and cold water that freshens my waking skin.

Bless the breakfast I am cooking for my family, and the special music of morning around me—doors banging, the clatter of forks and plates, the rattle of lunch boxes, children demanding "Mother!"

Thank you for my healthy available presence that is able to cope with them.

Bless the husband who provides all this. Be with him as he sets off for work; fill him with a sense of his own worth and achievement, enrich and enliven his day.

Bless the school buses and their drivers, let them transport our children safely.

Bless the teachers and that marvelous institution that claims my offspring for the next important hours. Please let them be good there, happy there, bright and able to grasp the lessons there, and oh, thank you that they're well enough to *be* there.

Now bless this quiet house—even its confusion and disorder which speaks so vividly of its quality of life. Thank you that I have the time and the strength to straighten it.

And thank you for the freedom to sit down with a cup of coffee before I begin!

FOR A CHILD ADVENTURING

At two:
Into the perilous world you'd trot,
With never a backward look.
Into the teeming traffic,
Into the rushing brook.
"Come back!" I cry, and snatch you,
Small bird, against my breast,

To cuddle and caress you
And keep you safe in your nest.

At twenty:
Into the dazzling world you stride
With scarcely a backward glance,
Into the cruel, competitive race—
Into romance.
"Come back!" cries my heart.
  "There's danger."
Knowing it does no good,
Knowing I'd never dim your dreams
Nor keep you if I could.

LET THEM REMEMBER LAUGHTER

Lord, whatever else my family remembers of me (the mistakes, the tears, the temper) please let them also remember my laughter. Guard me against ever becoming a grim and cheerless mother unable to see the funny side, even when things go wrong.

Lord, keep my laughter especially on tap when I'm the culprit in the case: When I've locked us all out of the house or the car . . . When my lovingly molded mousse skids onto the kitchen floor . . . When I've pulled some awful boo-boo with the president of the P.T.A. or the grande dame of the neighborhood . . . When I've dyed my hair the wrong color, or ruined a dress I was making, or gotten us all hopelessly entangled in wet wallpaper . . . help me to see the comedy of my errors.

Instead of stamping and storming, let me give my children the healing gift of laughter.

Lord, let me be a mother who can laugh with her children.

Don't let me ever laugh *at* them when they're trying to please me, no. Never when they're awkward, discouraged or troubled. But remind me to laugh more freely, gaily at their antics and their stories. Yea, though I've witnessed such clowning so often, heard the same jokes before, equip me with patience and a convincing show of enthusiasm. They need an audience so much.

Let me applaud with my heart as well as my hands. Help me to give them the sweet gift of laughter.

The same thing goes for my husband, God.

He needs an audience too, he needs a cheering section (and goodness knows after all these years *his* comedy routines are familiar). But mainly let him remember me as laughing more often than crying the blues.

I know that a family means problems, Lord. A family means troubles large and small. Troubles I can't always expect to "come smiling through." But with your help no troubles can overcome us, and laughter helps too.

Lord, let no day pass that my family doesn't hear my laughter.

GOOD ROOTS

Help me to give my children good roots, God.

As I work with my plants I can see that the sturdiest, and those which bear most freely, are those whose roots go deep, gripping rich soil; they have a base from which they can grow tall and beautiful and sound.

Let this household furnish that kind of soil for my family, God. Enriched with good music, good books, good talk, good taste. But above all, goodness of spirit. Goodness of action.

So that those who come here feel welcome, and those who leave here feel warm. And those who live here know, in every fiber of their beings, that they belong to people who, for all our faults, are good people. People of decency and honor, who would not willingly hurt or cheat any living thing.

Let my children grow freely, God, in whatever direction

their nature directs. But give them root strength, too. So that they will never deviate too far from their own beginnings.

Help me to give my children good roots.

HER ARK AND HER COVENANT

It has been said of man that his home is his castle. But what of woman? Strangely, few phrases have been coined to express the significance of home to her, the person who presides over its every function. What, then, is home to a woman?

Often, to be quite honest, home represents chaos, confusion, and quarrels. It is a place so hectic that sometimes, if we are human, we long only to escape. Time and again women, good women, have said to me, "I reach a point where I actually have insane thoughts of running off. Just any place to get away!"

A great deal of the time home to a woman is just plain old-fashioned work. Meals and dishes and ironing curtains and cleaning the closets and washing clothes.

Frequently it is entertaining. Everything slick and shining, and heavenly smells from the oven, and counting the silver, and baths early for everybody so that fresh towels can be up. And flowers and mints and nuts, and the sheer delight of pleasant voices exclaiming, "My, what a beautiful home."

A lot of the time it's worry—four walls that hold more concentrated concern than it seems any soul can bear: Will your son pass? Is your daughter really serious about that impossible boy she insists on seeing? Why can't the doctors find out what's wrong with John? Why doesn't money go further? How will the budget stand the added strain of college?

A great deal of the time it's fun. Small fry prancing about, so comically sweet in their antics you must scoop them into your arms. Teen-agers doing card tricks, dancing, playing the piano. Neighbors popping in for coffee. Your husband cornering you in the kitchen to tell you that funny story he heard at his luncheon club.

Her home is all these things to a woman, and a whole lot more. Something intangible. Something deeper. Something impossible to capture in a phrase.

Home is both the place where she is sheltered from the world, yet where her weaknesses and failures are exposed. Both the prison from which she cannot escape, yet the place where she is freest.

And here, for all its turbulence and burdens, she is its keynote. The touchstone for other people's progress. The focal point from which the spokes of their lives radiate.

As such, her home is not a matter of rugs and linens and beds and the washing machine and the kitchen stove. It is not the walls that surround it nor the contents of its rooms. It is both an ark—and a covenant.

Her ark for her protection. Her covenant with the future. It is her destiny.

DAUGHTER, DAUGHTER

How straight she sleeps, how slender-tall,
Daughter, daughter, recent small.
Gone the braids and pinafores
And paper dolls across the floors.
Party clothes across the bed,
Her hair spills shining free instead.
An orchid floats within the dish
That once held turtle, snail and fish.
Gone the tomboy, gone the child,
A woman dreams here, life-beguiled.

The bough must break, the bud must flower.
Daughter, daughter, soon the hour
When you, like others, come to wife.
This the pattern, this—life.
But let me stand one moment brief
Cupping again the uncurled leaf

So small, so safe upon the tree—
Daughter, daughter, close to me.

HOLD ME UP A LITTLE LONGER

Hold me up a little longer, Lord, just a little longer.

I've been up since before daylight and it's so late and this P.T.A. speaker drones on and on. Just keep me awake until he stops (please make it soon) and revive me enough to help serve the doughnuts and coffee and get home.

The miles I've put on the car stretch behind me like a trip through eternity instead of a single day. To market and music lessons and the vet's. To the laundromat after our machine broke down. To the doctor's after our son got hit with a baseball bat. (Thank you, oh thank you that it wasn't serious, after all.)

What else, Lord? I'm too tired to remember. I just know that off somewhere there's a hot bath waiting. A bed waiting . . . my own dear sweet bed is waiting and the time will actually arrive when I'll sink gratefully into it . . . It will even be morning . . . tomorrow . . . next week!

Thank you for this image of respite, Lord. Of rest and energy renewed. Right now, this minute, prop me up, revive me.

Hang onto me just a little longer, Lord.

PAPER BOY

Oh, Lord, his alarm's gone off, I can hear it ringing . . . ringing . . . as I lie here so snugly in bed. Please let him hear it and get up without having to be called. (Maybe if I just slipped in, without waking his father . . .)

There now, thank you, he's stirring, it's stopped, he's dressing. (Please let him put on a warm shirt and his boots instead of sneakers, it's so cold, it's snowing.)

Now his door is opening, I can hear him clumping downstairs (thank you, Lord, that he's wearing his boots). Please help him to find his heavy gloves (they're right there on the hall table) and please, please make him wear something on his head for a change, that wind is fierce. (Maybe I should get up and help him find it. Or try and persuade him . . . And fix him some breakfast, only he'd probably have a fit.)

Now he's getting his bike from the driveway. (I can't help it, Lord, I just had to come to the window to watch—and sure enough his head is bare, and the bike's all covered with snow, he's got to brush it off . . . Why, *why* won't he put it in the garage like he's been told?)

Lord, help him, please help him as he lugs the heavy bundle from the corner where it's been tossed. And the wind's blowing so hard, help him as he stuffs the papers into his bag and struggles the whole thing onto his shoulder. (Maybe I should throw on a coat and run down to give him a hand . . . Maybe I should even go with him.)

Should I, Lord? Tell me, help me . . . only it's too late anyway now. There he goes wobbling off down the snowy street. I might as well crawl back into my own warm bed . . . But, oh Lord, keep him safe. Don't let him get too cold or make too many mistakes this morning, and please get him back in time for a good hot breakfast before Sunday School.

And now, Lord, forgive me all this worrying. Let me go back to sleep knowing you will protect him, you are with him, you will put your loving arms around him.

Thank you that he wanted this job and for the lessons he's learning. Thank you, Lord, for my son and his paper route.

"SUPPER'S READY!"

Whatever happened to the family dinner hour? Or "supper" as we called it in our small town? That time at the end of the day when everybody was summoned to wash up and sit down together to share a common meal. A time not only to eat but to talk to each other, even if you sometimes quarreled. A time and place where you could laugh, joke, exchange ideas, tell stories, dump your troubles. (Yes, and learn your manners.)

Surely its disappearance has a lot to do with the much lamented disintegration of the American family. We've traded it in on the TV set and a freezer stuffed with prepack foods. We've exchanged it gaily for the cocktail hour. We've let it get lost in the flurry of meetings, lessons, parties, and activities to which we have mortgaged our evenings today. None of these things are particularly harmful in themselves, most in fact are essentially progressive and pleasant. But nonetheless an insidious encroachment and ultimately the destroyer of a daily custom that could not but contribute to family solidarity.

"Suppertime!" The last meal of the day . . .

Only city folks or people who put on city airs called it dinner. To us dinner was at noon, and we didn't mean lunch, we meant *dinner*. When we spoke of three square meals a day we meant three square meals. During the morning, along with everything else she had to do, a woman was also getting dinner. Tending the pot roast or pounding the beefsteak, cooking the vegetables and potatoes, making a custard and opening a Mason jar of pears or home-canned applesauce. And promptly on the stroke of twelve it had to be ready. For at that point the town's activities would come to a sudden halt with the blasting of the noon whistle at the firehouse.

On that instant stores and offices closed, school got out. A few doctors and lawyers and businessmen ate at Martin's Cafe or the Bradford Hotel, but most men headed for home. Since we had no school cafeterias or buses we walked home too—only the country kids, whom we envied, were allowed to bring their lunches. Winter or spring, fair weather or foul, we walked; and since our house was more than a mile away, it was stow away all that food and start back so you wouldn't be late. (To be tardy was a disgrace.) Anyway, noon dinner in our town was an hour of suspended activity, except for a sense of clicking dishes and earnestly munching jaws.

Supper was different. More leisurely. Less a time of common refueling than an hour when everybody gathered at the day's end to summarize and share what had gone on. And it varied with families. You'd begin to hear the calls, "Hey, kids, come on now, time to help get supper—" or the announcement, "Supper's ready!" all over the neighborhood anywhere from five o'clock on. People like the Renshaws ate early; Mr. Renshaw worked the night shift at the creamery and liked a long evening with his family before he donned his white overalls and departed. Judge J. Rutherford Jensen was to be seen stalking up the steps between the white Corinthian columns of his house at 5:15, expecting his food to be on the table and his children ready to sit down. Mrs. Flanders who liked to gad and was sort of slapdash about her cooking never managed to round up her brood until nearly seven o'clock—to the horror of some women and the distress of many kids, because most of us had finished the dishes by then and were ready to play out again.

But whether you ate at five or six or seven, one thing we had in common: Everybody had to *be* there. And in most households everybody had to help.

We thought the boys got off easy after we'd converted to cooking with gas. Before that they'd had to chop the kindling for the range, carry in the baskets of mealy red cobs, and from dusky bins in the basement haul up the snout-mouthed coal buckets. Theirs too the duty of trimming the wicks on the oilstove, cleaning its yellowed isinglass chimneys, and filling its tank with kerosene poured from a can with a potatao stuck on its spout. Since Mother didn't quite trust her gas stove, especially for baking, they still sometimes had to. And after supper they had to carry out the scraps.

Even very little girls were summoned in to put the teakettle on and start the potatoes. Potatoes were as essential to supper as the silverware. Boiled potatoes or fried; for company scalloped or mashed: but inevitably potatoes. And since you'd usually had them boiled for dinner and there were generally plenty left over, the cold, boiled globes were chopped up, salted, peppered, and fried.

Mother was not an impassioned cook. She felt a defensive, half-guilty distress for women who spent most of their time in the kitchen. "All that work just for something to put in your mouth and swallow, just to fill your stomach, just to *eat*." To her, food for the soul was just as important, and she feasted richly, if indiscriminately, on Tennyson and Tarkington, Shakespeare and Grace Noll Crowel and Harold Bell Wright. A true "book drunk," as she described herself, she would often become so absorbed that it would be late afternoon before she came to, shocked to discover from the redolent odors wafting up and down the block that other people's suppers were cooking. "Oh, dear, what'll we have?" she would worry vaguely, and start summoning offspring for calculations and tasks.

If in summer, someone would be dispatched to pick, pull, or dig whatever was ready from the garden, and fingers would fly, snapping, shelling, or peeling things. Meanwhile, tapping her gold tooth, she would achieve a small list of items for when the phone would ring and whoever was downtown would ask, "What do you want for supper?" Often she dismissed the whole business with a cheerful, "Oh, I don't care, just whatever looks good."

Dad didn't mind and he bought with a lavish hand when he could. If times were plentiful the meat was invariably thick red beefsteak, and the sack would be full of surprises like Nabiscos and coconut-topped marshmallow cookies, along with cherry pie from the bakery, and white grapes. And maybe a fresh hairy coconut, which we broke open with a hammer, drinking its flat tasteless milk and prying out its sweet if tough white heart.

We were always ravenous by suppertime, and no matter what was served we fell on it with relish. Especially on the days when the bread was fresh from the oven. Though Mother would never win any ribbons at the county fair and didn't want to, she did make good bread. And like everbody else (except the elite who could afford the extravagance of bakery bread) she was forced to bake it once a week.

The batter had to be mixed and set to rise the night before. A great, yeasty, bubbling batch in a huge granite pan. Potato water was saved to combine with the scalded milk, salt, sugar, and lard, and into this she sifted white cones of flour. We often knelt on kitchen chairs to watch, begging to help by shaking the heavy, squeaking flour sifter. When the dough was thick and smooth it was covered with a lid and left to rise on the lingering warmth at the back of the stove. If the house was cold, Mother would tuck it down as cozily as she could under a heavy towel.

By morning it would have blossomed tall and white, only to be stirred down and forced to accept more flour. Now she must dump it onto a floured board and knead it, flopping the tough yet delicate mass over and over, pressing out the air bubbles that made little squealing protests, caressing it, yet maneuvering it to her will. And thus subdued it was set to rise again.

By afternoon it was ready to be kneaded once more and molded into loaves. When we were small she always pinched off enough dough to let us play with and to fashion into tiny loaves of our own. They were usually grubby from our hands, but they looked beautiful waiting on the sunny windowsill in the little lids that served as pans. When the loaves themselves had risen, she brushed their plump heads with melted butter and popped them into an oven so hot that sometimes the lids on the range were as rosy as rouged cheeks.

Slowly the heavenly smell of baking bread began to drift through the house. When you came in from school or play your jaws leaked and you began to tease, "When will the bread be done?"

"Well, it should be soon." Opening the nickel-plated door, she would reach in and snap an experimental finger on the brown cracking crust. "Just a few more minutes." Finally, clutching a dish towel, she would reach in and carefully draw out the large black pan. The loaves were dumped on the table, to stand tall and golden as the sheaves of wheat from which the flour had come. Promptly she brushed them with more butter, and they took on a satin sheen. When she broke them apart, their white flesh steamed.

"Now don't eat too much," she would warn as people

begged for more. "Hot bread isn't good for the stomach. Besides, I don't want you to spoil your supper."

On rare occasions she diverted part of the batch into cinnamon rolls, a special treat. But the fresh bread itself eaten straight from the oven with butter, or slavered with honey or strawberry jam or apple butter, was enough to rouse the envy of the gods.

In a day or two it was simply bread, no longer so white and a trifle heavy, to be cut on a breadboard with a saw-toothed knife before each meal. And you disloyally wished you could buy bakery bread like some people, it seemed so light and spongy beside your mother's sturdy product.

Mother also made a marvelous bread pudding dignified by the name of "chocolate soufflé." Dry bread soaked in scalded milk; sugar, cocoa, vanilla and a couple of eggs added. Baked in a moderate oven until a knife came clean and its rich chocolaty promise was scarcely to be borne. The crowning touch was the hard sauce, which one of us always made. Confectioners' sugar was stirred into about half a cup of butter, added and pressed and added and pressed until you achieved a fat white ball that could literally take no more. (Also a few drops of vanilla.) Then you made it into individual balls, and stamped on each, with the bottom of a cut-glass toothpick holder, the imprint of a diamond or a daisy or a star. Bread pudding? Nonsense. These creamy balls, melting down over each crusty steaming dish, achieved ambrosia.

But whatever we ate for supper, whether the fare was feast or famine, certain rules prevailed: The whole family ate in the dining room, on a linen cloth with linen napkins. Nobody ever sat down before Mother. And nobody ever left the table unless she excused him first. Nor did we ever begin until everyone was present and until the blessing was asked. Also, we all had to sit straight in our chairs, left hand in the lap. No reaching, no stooping or slurping, and every request prefaced by "please." Mother believed in the old saw: "Always eat as if you were dining with the king, then you'll never be embarrassed if the king comes to dine."

After manners, we shed all pretense of trying to please

the king. We were noisy—oral, vocal, clamorous, everybody trying to tell what had happened to *him* today. "Don't talk with your mouth full," Mother kept admonishing. "Don't all try to talk at once." It was futile; good or bad we were dying to spill it at the family table, where we knew reactions would be fervent. The best times were when everybody was in a good mood and the tales were funny. We laughed, sometimes so hard we had to be excused. Dad and my brothers were all incurable clowns; given the slightest encouragement they did what they could to bring this about. Sometimes we burst into song. "Now we don't sing at the table" was another somewhat futile admonition. When people who enjoy each other's company get together it's hard to curb such a spontaneous expression.

Not that harmony always prevailed. The king would have been shocked at the vehemence of our arguments, the sound and fury of our quarrels. When the yelling got too bad Mother would simply say firmly, "I think you'd better be excused." The only things we were not free to discuss at the table were matters which might turn the stomach. No gory details of accidents or operations, no mention of creatures that crawled. If anyone slipped, Dad would pale slightly, clap a napkin to his mouth and flee without even asking Mother.

Other than this, the family's evening meal was a kind of funfest, open forum, wailing wall, and free-for-all. A place where you laughed or complained about your unfair teacher or got very mad and had things out with somebody without missing a bite, or, as far as I know, getting indigestion. A place so lively and filled with possibilities, in fact, that nobody wanted to miss it . . .

Today's experts warn that only agreeable subjects should be discussed at the family dinner table. I suppose I must agree. If and when you can *find* a table with an entire family gathered around it of an evening, the occasion is so rare it ought not to be marred with dissension. I have also read articles describing a kind of protocol of participation. Mother or Father suggests, "Now let's all go around the table and each of us tell the most interesting thing that happened to him or that he's learned today." This too I have tried, with discouraging results. "Aw, nothing much," one child will shrug. Or another, "Sorry, I've got to get going, Mike's picking me up—" While another is intent only poking down the absolute minimum required before escaping back to his programs.

No, the call "Supper's ready!" doesn't echo through neighborhoods much any more. It's dinner now in most places, and it's seldom ready for everybody at the same time. In the first place, Mother's not always there to get it. She's not home from work yet, or the golf course or her club; but there's plenty of food in the refrigerator, or the kids can heat up a nourishing four-course TV dinner, they won't starve. Or Dad's late getting home, and what with bucking traffic after a hard day he needs to unwind a bit. So the clever wife already has the martinis ready, and they share their Happy Hour while the kids eat in the kitchen or the rec room in front of the TV set.

In fact a lot of young wives recommend this as one way to keep a good marriage going. "I always feed the children first; then Jim and I can enjoy a quiet dinner without all that confusion. We need to be able to talk to each other, we need adult conversation."

Well, fine, good—don't we all? But aren't we already reaping a sorry but logical harvest of kids who were herded off the scene to communicate only with each other, and so can have no meaningful dialogue with adults now? Or who sat transfixed (as children are squatting still) before cartoons and Westerns and wars. No wonder so many of them are violent and destructive, so many of them rude. And how about their manners? How can you learn to sit or stand up straight while slouched on the floor? Who teaches you not to slurp or behave crudely or refrain from discussing the dissection of a worm while eating, if at the same time you're downing a solitary dinner to the accompaniment of pools of blood in living color?

Suppertime . . . That final meal when the day was almost over. The tradition of the family table. In letting it slip away from us I'm afraid we've lost something precious. We've cheated our children, stunted their social growth, gagged their articulation, cut off too early those ties that nature meant for us. The ties that bind us to people in the same family, people who represent comfort, security, nourishment, not only of body but of spirit. Ties that used to be gathered up at the close of day and drawn together, if not always in peace, at least in fellowship and caring. . . .

I wish that by some magic I could step to the door and hear it echoing from every house for blocks. *"Suppertime! Come on in, supper's ready!"*

GOING TO CHURCH WITH A DAUGHTER

How nice it is to go to church with a daughter, Lord. What a lovely thing, whether she's two or ten or twenty.

What a blessing, the Sunday morning rites of dressing. Even the inevitable commotion about what to wear. Even the inevitable men's scolding about being late.

Thank you, Lord, for the pleasure of setting off at last and of slipping into a pew feeling—pretty. For a daughter is like wearing a personal adornment, a piece of shining jewelry or a living flower.

People smile upon us. They pay her compliments, which are in essence mine too. For a daughter is a kind of special tribute, an achievement, a joyous adjunct and projection of mother.

Thank you for the privilege of kneeling beside this daugher, reading the responses together, finding the place for her. Or when she's older and I can't find my glasses, having her sure finger find the place for me.

What a blessing, to sing the hymns together. To join voices in the old familiar tunes, or struggle with the new ones. To have eyes meet sometimes, puzzled or in amusement, and remember how my mother and I used to exchange these glances in church together long ago.

Thank you for the special harmony there is between mothers and daughters in church together, Lord, whatever our differences at home. Thank you for this wonderful way to begin the week.

THE SON WHO WON'T STUDY

Lord, help me to be more understanding of my children's limitations. Guard me against demanding more of them than they are equipped to give.

This son, so bright about anything mechanical, who's up half the night with his ham radio, and is always grubby from rebuilding cars. He's failing in school because he simply won't study. Except for motoring magazines, he won't even *read*.

You know how hard I've tried. Trips to the library, books of his own. I've nagged, scolded, coaxed, pleaded, threatened, offered rewards. And now that they say he's not going to pass, I've stormed.

I shudder at that memory, Lord. My yelling—and his furious, half-bitter, half-bewildered retorts. And that last accusation before he slammed off: "I can't help it, Mom. Stop trying to make me into something I'm not!"

Something he's not . . . and never will be. A professional man like his father. A lover of books and language like me . . . How much he'll *miss*, my very soul grieves. But am I grieving so much for him as for myself?

How can he "miss" something that's alien to his nature, that he's never enjoyed? Any more than I "miss" the things so vital to him? I'm lucky to get a car started, let alone cope with its insides. The very idea of greasy engines is revolting to me . . . What if somebody tried to force me to build a radio?

Help me to see his side of it, Lord, as I sit now in what seems the wreckage of my dreams for my son—and yes, my pride. Help me not to consider what *I* want for him, but what *you* want for him. Since you made him so different from us you must have had your reasons. Help me to understand those reasons and release him to go his different way.

Maybe he's meant to go to trade school instead of high school or college. If so, let me remember how many bright and wonderful people have worked with their hands and haven't gone to college, and how much they've done for the world.

Dear Lord, instead of bemoaning my son's lacks, let me be grateful for his accomplishments. His excellent mind that comprehends things I can't. His skillful hands. Thank you for these gifts, God. Give me new pride in them, and help me to convey that pride to him.

I now accept my son for what he is and can be. I affirm and claim a happy, productive life for him.

A MOTHER'S WISH-GIFTS FOR CHRISTMAS

The family has all scattered on errands, Lord, and at last I can wrap their presents. But now, as I sit in this bright clutter of paper and ribbons, I keep thinking of other things, better things, I wish I could give them.

First, I'd love to put peace, world peace in a package. (What a marvelous present for all families everywhere that would be.) But since I can't, maybe I can try even harder to keep peace within this house. To manage less-hectic meals and bedtimes, to prevent or calm down its arguments and conflicts.

Help me in this, Lord.

And this fishing rod I'm struggling to make look nice for my husband, without revealing its secret. What would I like its clumsy package to include?

Freedom to *go* fishing more often, for one thing. But mostly freedom from worry. Worry about mortgages and car payments; about our health, the children's future, our happiness.

But as I sit pondering this impossible gift, you make me realize I *can* give him something very important that will help achieve that very thing: My consideration. Doing everything within my power to spare him.

* * *

Our sons, Lord. What would I like to tuck into their boxes along with the boots and shirts and football gear? For one of them, self-confidence, belief in his own abilities, more ease with girls. For the other, better grades so he'll get into the college he wants to attend.

How can I compensate for these gifts that I can't bestow? By more encouragement, more praise, by showing them every day how much I believe in them.

And my daughters, Lord. As I wrap the sweaters and tennis rackets, the books and records, the doll clothes I stayed up so late to finish for the littlest one . . . I can think of so much more I'd hand them if I could.

I'd like to give them poise and graciousness. Kindness and compassion. Courage for all occasions—for tests and dates and interviews, but especially the courage to be themselves whether it makes them popular or not.

Above all, I'd like to say, "Open your eyes and your arms to the priceless present: the wonder of being a woman today when so many careers are calling and you can still be a wife and mother if you want."

The list of my longings for my family is endless, Lord. I can't wrap up the things I really want. But one thing I can give all of them—though no box would ever be big enough to hold it. Something that's mine alone to give, as often as I want:

My love.

SHOPPING WITH A DAUGHTER

Lord, please give me strength for this shopping trip with my daughter.

Bless us both and let your love shine through us as we set off on what should be so pleasant, but is generally such an ordeal.

First, fortify me with thanksgiving. I realize I am lucky to have a lovely, healthy daughter who really enjoys clothes. And lucky to have enough money (if we don't go overboard) to provide the things she needs.

But I'm going to need some extra fortifying, Lord, with the following:

Please give me patience as we trudge from store to store, parade in and out of fitting rooms. (Ease my aching feet, soothe my frazzled nerves, keep sweet before me the picture of that hour when she finally finds *something* that meets with her approval.)

Give me will power. Don't let me show enthusiasm (if I like anything she's sure to shudder). Help me refrain from even making suggestions. No, however difficult, help me stand quietly by and let her choose.

Above all, don't let me talk her into things. And if I have to talk her *out* of things, please give me tact, let me be kind but firm. And let her accept my reasons without being too disappointed or resentful.

Give me good sense about price tags, God. Don't let me spoil her. But don't let me spoil our relationship either by being a pinchpenny mother.

Remind us both to smile at each other. To discuss instead of argue. To laugh when we're practically on the verge of blows. And to take time out for lunch or a cup of coffee. (It's when we both get tired that nerves and tempers flare.)

Thank you for giving us both strength for this shopping trip. For the joy and anticipation I suddenly feel. I'm smiling at her already, and she's smiling back! We do love each other enough to overcome our problems and appreciate our good fortune. We're setting off today to discover new delights.

Thank you that I can go shopping with my daughter!

A BOY'S FIRST CAR

Dear Lord, please bless this boy and his first car.

Bless his pride in it, his joy in it, his plans for it.

Let it be whole and sound and right and good for him. Let it carry him safely.

Lord, bless his energies—may they be equal to cope with it (and pay for it).

Bless his mind—may it learn from the mechanical experiences he will have with this car. And may he learn from the emotional experiences this car is going to bring.

Oh, God, give my son judgment in operating this car.

Give him joy without recklessness, power without folly.

Give him generosity and dignity and decency and common sense.

Lord, I offer them up to you for blessing and safe-keeping: This boy. This car.

I CAN'T UNDERSTAND MY DAUGHTER ANY MORE

I just can't understand my daughter any more, God. And she can't understand me.

We used to be so close, we used to be such friends. Even when we had our differences she'd come flying back to me.

But now, though there are still moments of sweetness and laughter, times when we can talk, those times are so few. I don't understand her silences, Lord, her locked door, the secrets she keeps from me. And when we do talk there is so much crossness and tension and criticism. Often outright hostility.

Where has my little girl gone, God? What have I done to drive her away?

And you, Lord, seem to tell me:

She's going where you went, where all girls go: To find herself. And you haven't driven her away. Life is beckoning to her, and she must follow. This is what you've really been preparing her for, isn't it? To be strong enough to find her way.

But it hurts, God. I love her so much. Why must she make it so hard for me?

And clear and true I hear the answer. The only possible answer: *Because it is so wonderful having a daughter. Otherwise, you couldn't bear to let her go!*

THE LOVELY ALIENS

Oh, Lord, please bless these lovely aliens, my children.

They seem so strange to me at times, not even resembling me in face or traits or body.

It is sometimes hard to believe that I had anything to do with producing them, these vigorous strangers going their own way with such vigor and independence.

The fact that I even clothe and care for them seems an anomaly, as if I am just some loving outsider attending their needs.

At times I protest this, Lord. I don't want to be an outsider.

I am lonely for the deeper attachments we had when they were small. I feel a hungry desire to know more truly what they think, to share their lives.

A kind of righteous indignation rises up, demanding, "See here, if it weren't for me you wouldn't *be* here! Pay attention to me, draw me in. Darnit, I'm your *mother*."

Then I am reminded of my own, often inconsiderate youth.

You help me to see that this is nature's way, however cruel, of cutting natal strings. I cannot carry them forever in my womb, or on my lap. (Only in my heart.)

The burden of it would be intolerable. For my sake as well as theirs, I've got to let them alone, let them go.

So bless them as they make these fierce, sometimes foolish, sometimes faltering strides toward independence. Give them strength—they're going to need it!

Don't let my self-pity sap their progress. God bless these lovely aliens, my children.

RESCUE THIS CHILD

Oh, God, please help my child. He has no direction, no goal. He's wandered away from so much that he used to be, or that you, his creator, would have him be.

And I am not only worried sick about this, God, I feel guilty. I search my own behavior asking, "Why? Why? What have I done to bring this about? Where have we, his family, failed?" That he, with all his goodness and beauty, his brains, his tremendous potential, should be so lost. Right now it's as if he's nobody going nowhere, at a time when the rest of the world is on its way.

Dear God, please find and restore my wandering child. Arouse in him a sense of purpose, steady him, set him upon his rightful path, and walk with him.

We who love him can't do it. Only you who love him even more can do it.

I offer him to you now, whole and beautiful and filled with promise, the way you sent him to us. Thank you for helping him become the person you meant him to be.

RESPITE

Oh, Lord, thank you for this little space between crises in our family. Thank you for this probably brief span of peace.

Right now nobody is ill. Thank you. Right now nobody is in trouble. Thank you. Right now I am coasting, resting. It is as if I am walking across a pleasant meadow with only the happy chiming of birds in my ears and the sunlight as of some wondrous love upon my face.

The familiar cries of sorrow, distress, imploring pleas, and arguments are still. Thank you. The familiar burdens seem to be lifted, the problems for the moment all resolved. I rejoice in this sense of lightness and release.

It is common sense that tells me that this lovely respite cannot last, and not really my lack of faith.

For now, let me simply be thankful for this respite. Let me be revitalized by it. Let me draw from it physical strength and spiritual resources for the inevitable crises and conflicts to come.

Thank you, God, for this precious span of peace.

PSALM FOR A SISTER

I will lift up my eyes and smile as I give thanks for my sister. My radiant, complicated sister, who is more than a sister—who is my friend. (Blessed is the woman who has one like her, and thrice blessed if she has more than one.)

I will thank the good Lord that we were children together, sharing the same room and for years the same bed.

I am grateful for the memory of her small body warm against mine. I rejoice to remember our playhouses and paper dolls and plans. Our secrets and surprises. Even our quarrels.

I feel a deep and poignant longing for those days when we were girls together. Life-hungry, love-hungry, each fighting her own battle, yet supporting each other against parents and the world.

My sister, oh Lord, my beautiful sister, often maddening, always understanding, always fun.

Thank you for this woman who shares my parents, my past, my blood; who sees me whole—the beginning, long ago, and the person I am now. My sister, whose faults are so clear to me—and dear to me, just as my faults are to her. Yet for all our differences, and the miles that lie between us, we would still battle the world for each other.

I laugh for the joy of my sister, all the comedy, the gaiety. And I sometimes weep for my sister. I long to comfort her, to hold her close, as we held each other for comfort or for courage as little girls.

Dear God, please take good care of her, this sister I love so much.

THE EARTH'S HEART BEATING

How can I find you, God? How can I claim your strength?

I am tired, so tired . . . tense, so tense. And my nerves are screaming. Now, if ever, I need you. I need your reassurance and your peace.

Yet there is only this raw trembling vacancy inside me. This sense of emptiness and futility.

Come back to me, Lord. Calm me, quiet me, for I am indeed weary and heavy-laden and I need your promised rest.

"Stop going so hard, Mother," a daughter says. "Lie down a few minutes, relax."

I flop on the floor and she kneels beside me, long and lithe and fair, and deftly massages my neck and back. "Let yourself go. Be like the cat."

It dozes on the arm of a chair, eyes half closed. I stretch out . . . and out . . . trying to emulate its yawning movements. . . . How utterly cats yield every muscle and nerve, how sweetly they sleep. But how do they occupy themselves all day? I wonder. Nobody to play with, nobody to talk to, nothing to think about. Yet this cat of ours goes outside and vanishes for hours . . . must surely occupy itself with something for hours. Chases a bird or a rabbit, suns itself, prowls the woods . . . How stupendously boring—unless you are a cat.

I ponder some of this aloud, and my daughter, who has left my side, looks up from the jeans she is mending.

"She's in tune with the universe," she says. "God keeps her happy."

"Why? I wonder. Why a cat at all?"

"God put her here to be company to us, and perhaps to teach us that. That the way to be happy is just not to worry, to relax, to flow with the universe."

"But people can't do that. We have too many problems, things to worry about."

"Yes, but the animals have their problems, too," she says. "Most of them. The mere problem of survival. And they're calm about the whole thing, they trust nature—their own nature and the larger nature all around them."

"People are different. We can't be like that."

"Yes, we can. Some people do. People who take up the religious life and just meditate, or take vows of silence. It's the same thing, just merging with the universe."

"That seems selfish. It's escaping responsibilities to other people."

"I think nature meant us to be more selfish than most people are. What's really more important than the self, Mother? You yourself? The problems go away, most of them, but you remain. You stay *you*. You shouldn't let yourself get so damaged and divided up by responsibilities and problems."

Thoughtfully she bites a thread. "I pray about things, so many things, so many problems. I know I don't have half so many responsibilities as you—yet I think I have a lot, for my time of life I do. And I pray about the people and the problems, and then I try to meditate, but that takes mental effort. It's better when I just let go, just relax and let myself flow into nature—the rain, for instance. The rain speaks to me almost as if it's trying to tell me something. Last night it was raining and I prayed and pretty soon it was the rain praying with me, and almost the rain praying *for* me. I could just lie there and listen.

"And there are times when I have just lain out in the sun and on the grass and flowed into it, the universe—and I could hear the earth's heart beating."

"The earth's heart?"

"Yes, don't you think God put some of his own heart into the earth when he made it? And gave it a heart, too?"

(Out of the mouths of babes, I think . . . or a daughter twenty-two . . . No, wisdom is not reserved solely for the old.)

The earth's heart beating . . . and my own. Yes.

For now as I lie here resting, yielded as the cat, it comes to me through my own hand, that steady pulsing . . . and hers . . . and that of the quiet cat.

For are we not all one? Linked to the same rhythms, we three creatures within this room . . . and all those beyond. Seen and unseen, the blood flows, life-sustaining.

Within the very earth itself the currents flow. The vital life forces of all its inhabitants and the saps and juices of all its vegetation reaching down and up. And in and through and deeper, ever deeper, the ceaseless silent pounding of energies undreamed.

A sense of joyous discovery fills me.

For I realize now that to sense it and become one with its source I must stop struggling. To fight with life is to fight off God!

Now I feel his presence, his reality, his strength.

Now I hear the quiet rhythms and am cradled in those rhythms like a child being rocked to sleep. . . . Now I can truly rest.

WE ARE MOVING AGAIN, AND I DON'T WANT TO GO

We are moving again, God, and I don't want to go.

I am sick and tired of moving.

I resent the time that must be squandered in packing and unpacking. In house selling and house hunting.

I don't want the children to have to change schools anymore. I don't want to have to make new friends anymore. I don't want to have to explain myself anymore, or try to find myself (or even my way around) in a new setting.

The adventure of moving has palled, Lord.

Setting off for a new city I used to think, "Somewhere out there it lies waiting for us. There in its vastness stands the place that will become home to us. There, right now, laughing and talking, are the people who will become important to us."

But now, oh Lord, this same prospect fills me only with a sense of being lost. Wanderers, strangers, with no real home to go to. Not really belonging anywhere, to anyone.

I have a sudden shocked awareness of how Mary and Joseph must have felt that night when they faced the careless crowds of Bethlehem and were told to be on their way.

I want to be able to put my roots down. Deep, deep.

How can I ever find out who I am if, so much of my life, I don't even know *where* I am?

On, God, hang onto me once more as I face the chaos and confusion of moving.

Help me to realize that you will go with us again, you will be with us again. I can talk to you wherever I am; I have a friend I can never lose in you wherever I am.

God, sustain me as I face this move.

THE FAREWELL PARTY

Thank you, God, for all these people who have gathered to tell us good-bye.

The ones we've been so close to and the ones we've rarely seen. The ones we've liked so much and even the ones who've been sometimes hard to take.

Now curiously, they are all dear to us as we come together for the farewell party. Now suddenly I see who they are in relation to us—and who we must be in relation to them.

They are the living embodiment of time and place—our time in this particular place. They are themselves, yes, but in large or small ways they are changed because we came together. And we are changed because of them. We have interrelated; the precious stuff of our lives has touched.

What a miracle this is, what a blessing. That you created us, not to live alone or behind closed doors, but to brush against and help to color other lives.

And when this time is over, the parting hurts.

Friends taken for granted become strangely precious when it is time to separate.

Perhaps this is why these partings must come. To make us aware of each other, to realize our identities as characters in each other's life stories. To give us a little glimpse of who we are in the eyes of those who are our friends.

A farewell party—what a joy, however it hurts. What an honor. They love us enough to wish us well. "Fare well wherever you go," they are saying.

And we can only answer in kind, "Good-bye. Fare . . . well."

Thank you for all these dear people, Lord. And bring us together again in another place, another time.

"GIVE ME A BRIGHT WORD, MOTHER"

Our daughter has always loved words.

From the time she was beginning to talk she was forever chanting them, trying out strange combinations, as if fascinated by their very sound. And when she had started to school and was learning to read and write words of her own, words assumed some lovely new significance.

She was impatient because her vocabulary was still too small to express all the things she was discovering, and so she began asking for words as she might ask for cookies or a hug. Words became a form of favor, a kind of little gift that only I, who used them in my work, could bestow.

Waking up in the morning, or rushing in from play, she would ask: "Give me a bright word, Mother."

And I would answer with a little string of words—object or adjective—that called up brightness to the sense or the mind: "Sunshine . . . Golden . . . Luminous . . . Shiny, like a fire engine that's just been polished. Or jewelry . . . Sparkling . . . Diamonds sparkling in a golden crown."

"Is luminous bright and shiny like a pan? Is that why they call some pans *aluminum?*"

"It could be, but I don't think so. Aluminum is a little too shiny for luminous. I think of luminous as more like moonlight shining on a lake or through the leaves."

"Oh, I love luminous!" she would cry. Decisively, like a shopper: "I'll take luminous."

Or the request would be: "Give me a soft word, Mother."

"Velvety," I'd begin. "Velvety soft like a blackberry or a pony's nose. Or furry, like your kitten . . . Or how about lullaby? That's a nice soft word . . . Or soothing . . . Gentle . . . Dreamy."

Her own eyes would go soft and dreamy with listening. She would try them on her tongue, murmuring, "Gentle . . . velvety . . . soooothing." With a little sigh—"That's nice—soooothing. That's my word!"

Or, perhaps cross or frustrated, she would come storming in from play. "I need a glad word right now!"

"Glad? All right, let's see. Circus is a glad word. Circus clowns, parades . . . Or how about birthday? Presents. Surprises. Party . . . And some glad words to go with them are joy, excitement, laughter, fun."

"No, no, I already *have* those words," she would sometimes protest.

"Well then, jubilee. That means a glorious celebration. And another glad word that sounds a lot like it is jubilant . . . Or maybe you'd like elated?"

Taking them in, savoring them, her face would brighten. "Oh," she would marvel, "it must be wonderful to know so many words!"

She outgrew all this, of course. Before long words had ceased to awe her. She has acquired plenty of words of her own, a whole vast treasury of words to use as she needs or pleases. Words for diaries and letters and to spill to friends on the phone. Words for school reports and tests. Words in books that she has to read or wants to. And if the meaning of any of these words eludes her she has a dictionary handy, she can always look them up.

No, my daughter no longer must come rushing to me like an eager little shopper seeking words to fit her moods.

And yet, in another far more vital and challenging sense she still turns to me, expectant, convinced I'll be able to provide the words she needs:

"I want to be in with these kids, I want to be popular, but I still want to be myself. How can I do both, Mother? . . ."

"Is there any way I can make this teacher *believe* I didn't cheat? . . ."

"How can I tell Daddy what I did to the car? . . ."

"Why won't you let me go? Everybody else is allowed. . . ."

"I don't care what she's done or what they say, she's my friend and we've got to help her, Mother. . . ."

"Why doesn't he call? Oh, Mommy, what'll I *do* if he doesn't like me any more? . . ."

The times when she's puzzled or tempted or troubled, the times when her heart is breaking. The times when she can't understand. Then, in spite of all the words I've read and said and heard and think I know, I find myself groping desperately for the right ones. I feel like the child she used to be, running up to me with her demands.

I too need a source that is older and wiser. And I find myself imploring: "Give me a hope word. Give me a sure word. Give me a bright word, God!"

HE WAS SO YOUNG

He was so young, God.

So young and strong and filled with promise. So vital, so radiant, giving so much joy wherever he went.

He was so brilliant. On this one boy you lavished so many talents that could have enriched your world. He had already received so many honors, and there were so many honors to come.

Why, then? In our agony we ask. Why him?

Why not someone less gifted? Someone less good? Some hop-head, rioter, thief, brute, hood?

Yet we know, even as we demand what seems to us a rational answer, that we are only intensifying our grief.

Plunging deeper into the blind and witless place where all hope is gone. A dark lost place where our own gifts will be blunted and ruin replace the goodness he brought and wished for us.

Instead, let us thank you for the marvel that this boy was. That we can say good-bye to him without shame or regret, rejoicing in the blessed years he was given to us. Knowing that his bright young life, his many gifts, have not truly been stilled or wasted, only lifted to a higher level where the rest of us can't follow yet.

Separation? Yes. Loss? Never.

For his spirit will be with us always. And when we meet him again we will be even more proud.

Thank you for this answer, God.

FOR A DAUGHTER ABOUT TO BE MARRIED

Listen, Lord, please listen . . .

I am very conscious of you as I stand beside my daughter's bed. She is tired from all the preparations; she has turned in early. But I can't sleep. I have slipped in to tuck up the covers about her one more time. And to just stand here a moment absorbing her loveliness.

Tomorrow she is to be married—this baby that came to us at such an inconvenient time.

I know you have long since forgiven me for how dismayed and resentful I was then. I know you have been with us since, sharing our almost passionate pride and pleasure in her accomplishments. (You heard my thanks, you know my sense of blessing.)

You have been close to us too in the times of anguish, the illnesses, the arguments, the problems. (You heard and answered my prayers.)

Now I want to thank you once again for all those years that she has been a part of our family and has meant so much to us.

* * *

Bless her tomorrow as she stands beside the young man who is her final choice. Be with her as she makes her solemn promises. Stay close to her as she begins this new life that is her own, separate and apart from us.

Give her joy and pride in her husband; and him in her.

Lord, I could ask so many things for both of them. I could ask that you spare them trials, hardships, differences, sorrows. And I do ask that—yes, I suppose, even knowing that they will have their share.

Now I ask only that the companionship surpass the conflicts, the happiness far outweigh the hurts. And that whatever they face, they both stay close to you.

And oh, yes, one final thing, Lord, as I tuck her in this last time and turn away: May every child she bears bring her the delight that she has brought to us.

DON'T LET ME CRY
AT THE WEDDING

Oh, Lord, don't let me cry at my little girl's wedding.

Don't let me cry as she comes down the aisle.

Let the radiance she has given our lives shine on my face now, to match the radiance on hers.

Let her feel, not my aching sense of loss, but my joy that she has found so fine a man to take care of her for us.

Oh, Lord, don't let my husband hurt at our daughter's wedding.

That arm that she's clinging to as proudly, trustingly, as when she was a little girl—thank you for it.

Let this be truly a moment of communion for them, a happy summary of all their memories as father and daughter.

Thank you for the steadiness of his step and the pride in his eyes as he gives her away.

* * *

Thank you for his smile as he takes his place beside me. For permitting us to come to this hour together, surrounded by so many people dear to us, to witness this beautiful ceremony.

My heart is full of thanksgiving. Almost too full of wonder and blessing. I love her so and rejoice so for her.

Lord, don't let me cry at my little girl's wedding.

GIVE ME THE LOVE
TO LET THEM GO

Lord, sometimes I love my children so much it seems I can't ever bear to let them go.

"Hurry back!" my heart cries after them almost every time they leave, whether for camp or a date or just the daily trudging off down the walk for school.

No matter what the confusion we've just been through— the frantic scramble for books or money or a missing sweater, no matter the chaos, the noise, even the quarrels, something inside me goes scurrying after them with last minute words of love and warning. And the urgent unspoken plea: "Come back soon."

And when they are all gone at once, God, like right now . . . Though you know how I revel in the peace and freedom, yet there is this aching emptiness inside me too.

And sometimes, alone with their father, I have this sense of some awful preview: Of loneliness and boredom. Of a life without purpose and meaning. Of two people haunting the mailbox for letters, or waiting for the phone to ring . . . Or worse, a couple clinging to an unmarried son or daughter, unwilling to let the last one leave.

Lord, thank you for making me aware of this dread presentiment. It's like a signal telling me I've got to start weaning myself from my children. Not loving them any less, but ceasing to feast so continually on all they do. I realize I've got to start nourishing myself in other ways. New interests apart from them—help me to find them, God, starting now. Spur me to call that class I've been thinking of joining, that volunteer service that needs me. Things that will help me to grow as a person. There are a hundred unlocked doors and opportunities in my life, things I want to explore, things that challenge.

Now is the time to anticipate them. Now is the time to start finding them. Don't let me make excuses for myself— how busy I am, how much the children still need me. And guard me from these guilty, doubtful feelings already beginning to stir.

Brace me with the knowledge that the kindest, most generous thing I can do for my family is to begin to prepare for the time when they won't be coming back. A time when they won't have to feel guilty or selfish about poor old Mom whose world has collapsed.

Thank you for this insight, God. Give me the love to let my children go.

BRING BACK THE CHILDREN

Lord, it seems sometimes that my arms aren't long enough or my lap isn't big enough. I wish I could stretch my arms out and out to embrace all my children. These, here about the table now, and those who are away, off to their meetings or their dates or far away in their own homes.

I am suddenly aware of them, all of them wherever they are, and the excitement and wonder and pain of their lives are almost too much to comprehend.

I am so thrilled about them, so proud of them, and so worried about them too—all at once. I want suddenly to reach out and touch them, the warmth of their flesh, the feel of their hair, to draw them physically in.

I want to hold them on my lap again, the big ones and the little ones, all at once. I want to tuck them in their beds under the same familiar roof. I want to lock the door and go to sleep knowing they're all safe in the shelter of this house.

Lord, I wish I could have all my children back—now, this moment, at once. But since I can't, you who are everywhere reach them for me, keep them safe in the shelter of my love.

FIRST GRANDCHILD

Thank you, God, that it's here, it's here, our first grandchild!

I hang up the telephone, rejoicing. I gaze out the window, dazzled and awed. "Just a few moments ago," he said. "A beautiful little girl."

She arrived with the sunrise, Lord. The heavens are pink with your glory. Radiance streams across the world.

The very trees lift up their branches as if in welcome, as if to receive her. And I want to fling out my arms, too, in joy and gratefulness and welcome.

My arms and my heart hold her up to you for blessing.

Oh, Lord, thank you for her and bless her, this little new life that is beginning its first day.

THE LETTER HOME

All over the world tonight women sit writing: The brides, still a trifle self-conscious as they perform this new domestic task; the wives so long married it has become second nature—writing the letter home.

"Dear Mother and Dad— Well, we made it. It was a long hard trip, but so wonderful I want to tell you all about it. Jim was so sweet. No girl ever had a lovelier honeymoon."

Or, "Dear folks: I'll try to snatch a little time while the baby's napping, to report on what's been happening." Or, "Dear Families—including Margaret and Elmer, Grandpa and Grandma, Bob and Uncle Mac: Please forgive me for the carbon copies. Have been so frantically busy that the only way to catch up on our correspondence is to write to everybody at once."

And typed or handwritten, on finest stationery or the back of a child's wobbly drawing, they have a quality all their own—a woman's letters home.

For she has left her own people to follow her man. And whether they have moved just a few hundred miles away or across a continent, an ocean, her letters trace the course of her new life. A life filled with all the incidents, great and small, that go into the fabric of a family: The first tooth and the first operation. The raise in salary, the Couples' Club they've joined, the church, the grocery story, the neighbors. The hopes, the prospects, the aspirations; and often— though these are touched on lightly, if mentioned at all— the disappointments and worries.

For slowly, subtly, a woman senses that this is a record of happiness, actually, her letter home. Not that she is expected to write only of sunshine and roses. Nor that she's too proud to complain. No, it's something deeper, more significant. A gradual recognition that, however she may put it off, a wonderful thing happens when she sits down to write that letter home.

For this is her journal, her account. And strangely, it is the good, the gay, the funny things that come swimming to the surface of the chaos of raising a family. By a kind of magic, in the sheer act of recollecting and recounting, her own appreciation takes over, her confidence in the future, her gratefulness. Seldom does she consciously think: "I won't write that. It would worry them." Rather, the problem doesn't seem so bad in retrospect—and less interesting than Sue's first formal and Ted's paper route.

Her words are awaited hopefully all over the world, on farms, in cities, in little towns. No author, however famous, has an audience more eager, more faithful. Day after day, parents watch for the letters, fret when they don't arrive, wondering what's wrong. And oh, the rejoicing, the lift of the spirits when they do. "Here it is. Well, it's about time! Let's see what Alice has to say."

So women sit writing. Up and down the street, in the big

cities and the small towns, all over the world. Writing that diary of their destiny, making their entry into the account books of their lives: "Dear Folks . . ." "Dear Mother and Dad . . ."

MOTHERS KEEP ALL THESE THINGS

But Mary kept all these things, and pondered them in her heart.

—*St. Luke*

You make your annual pilgrimage to the attic to bring down the decorations from the family Christmas box. The long ropes of tinsel for the tree. The fragile colored balls, a few always shattered. The faded big red stocking that's hung on the front door how many years? The crèche and its figures—Baby Jesus in the tiny cradle that the youngest ones love, the wise men, the shepherds—they are getting grubby, you notice, and one of the kneeling camels has lost an ear.

Really, you should replace so many things. Take this stable, just a rough box on which one of the boys nailed a clumsy roof. Or that angel—too big for the scene; an awkward plaster angel your little girl made and painted with watercolors in second grade. Surely you should throw it out—she'd never miss it. You reach for the wastebasket, drop it in. But suddenly, with the compulsion that makes you rush back to the fireplace to rescue their papers or drawings, you haul it forth again. You can't do it. Because, though its creator would never miss her lumpy angel—you would.

Mary kept all these things, and pondered them in her heart—

How many things a mother keeps, you think as you look about . . . Battered little first books. Baby shoes. Scrapbooks stuffed with their pictures and souvenirs. A daughter's first prom dress . . . Such foolish things that only a mother would cling to. All mothers. Mothers like Mary, who have gone before—and mothers to come.

"Keepsakes," is written on a large box on the shelf. And in it, lovingly labeled by fingers long still, is a yellow sailor suit that belonged to the child who grew up to be your husband. His own first laboriously printed Christmas cards. And his first pair of red boots. His mother, too, kept all these things. When we were first married I used to wonder why. Then I had a child, and I understood.

Mothers keep all these things. Because they are the physical reminders of our children, the shed garments of a time that, however hectic it may be now, will someday seem precious.

Mary kept all these things . . .

You feel a renewed kinship for that girl-mother. You wonder what reminders of His childhood did she perhaps save. His first little garments, or the sandals in which He learned to walk? A wooden toy cart perhaps, that His father had made for him in the carpenter shop? And what memories did they bring back to her later to ponder in her heart?

You take up the bulging box. This year, as usual, its contents will all make the journey into the holiday with the family. The lumpy angel, the battered bells, the beloved red stocking, mended and refurbished with a bright new bow. It wouldn't be Christmas otherwise.

Because Christmas is for keeps. It comes every year and will go on forever. And along with Christmas belong the keepsakes and the customs. Those humble, everyday things that a mother clings to with her hands, and ponders, like Mary, in the secret spaces of her heart.

GOOD-BY, CHRISTMAS TREE

Taking down the Christmas tree is like stripping the feathers from some beautiful bird. Even the children, so eager to do the adorning, escape this chore if they can. And after a dutiful insistence on a mother's part: "You can at least take the ornaments off the lower branches," and (visualizing havoc): "No dear, I'd rather you didn't climb the stepladder to get the angel off the top," you shoo the children off, privately relieved. Like many another rite of womanhood, this one seems to be a solitary task.

You go about it with vigor, wrapping the bright baubles and stowing them in their boxes; efficiently winding the prickly strands of tinsel; and, with the probable foolish thriftiness that men seldom understand, plucking the frail silver icicles to save them too—as many as you can. How they dance in the still staunchly shining lights! How they cling to the brittle branches and your hand. Small though their actual value, you feel their growing weight like a tangible treasure that is too precious to throw out.

Too precious. The branches reach out their arms. Even the dry tick of their falling needles does not mitigate the sense of some gentle imploring: "Stay, stay!" And though you yourself have said, in the hectic rush of holiday preparations, "Christmas comes too often. I wish we could just skip it every other year," and, in the chaos of papers and presents, "I'll be glad when we can get out of this mess," now you stand haunted by it. The whole of it, from the very beginning. From your first shocked protest, seeing the decorations and hearing the carols in the stores: "No, no. It can't be Christmas. Not again! Why do they have to start it so early?" to this moment.

For there was scarcely time for Christmas, after all. The shopping, the cards, the baking, the parties, the programs at church and at school. Almost before you knew it, it was Christmas Eve—and you stand remembering the children's anticipation, so intense it was akin to anguish. And the rattle of wrappings, the squawk of a doll, as you and your husband stuffed stockings, laid out gifts, in the ancient, thrilling parental conspiracy. And the focal point of it all—this lovely tree. Like a queen, the tree graced the window, pouring its rainbow lights upon the snow and welcoming you when you returned from midnight services. And then it was morning, and the youngsters were shouting, "Wake up, wake up! Merry Christmas. Come see!"

How festive it all was, the tree reminds you—the dear,

still shining tree. How joyous. Belatedly, you stand there, wanting to stop its plunge into the past. Not let Christmas truly be over—as it will be over and done with, once the tree is down. And with the going of that tree, another year in the life of your family.

Never again will things be just as they are now, with the children just this age. A toddler, a second-grader, a Cub Scout, and a son who has known the thrill of shopping with money from his first paper route. Next year Jimmy will have abandoned his bike for a car, and the daughter who wanted one final doll will be asking for clothes, instead, and be interested in boys.

There will be other gifts, you know, the pleasures and the problems of other stages. But with each passing holiday the children are growing away from you—and, like this tree, will eventually be gone. And you can't wrap their bright, insistent lives in tissue paper and store them in a closet. All you can wrap, to treasure and hold fast, are your memories.

But now, this very Christmas—which you approached with such resistance and found at times so trying. How could I? a mother wonders, standing there alone, gazing at the lights. They are almost more lovely shining on the bare uncluttered branches. Their strings are like living eyes, blinking merrily. Flooding the tree now in scarlet, now turquoise, gold, and a merry fountain of winking hues.

It is time to hush their bright clamor, time to silence and darken their gay reign. Come now, unplug them. Just a touch of the hand. And as you reluctantly reach out, you bid the tree good-by: "It's been wonderful, hasn't it? Why, it's the very best Christmas we've ever had!"

MOTHER, I'M HOME!

"Mother, where are you? I'm home!" Day after day you hear that call. Over and over. When the littlest bounces in from kindergarten, proudly bearing his crayon drawing: "Mommy, here I am. Look what I made today. Mommy, I'm home!" At three o'clock when the older ones begin to streak in: "Hey,

I'm home." Sometimes on weekends or holidays, the ones away at college. "I'm here! It's me. I'm home."

And with that cry come both responsibility and rejoicing. As life begins to surge through the house you take up the tasks it brings. The sandwiches they demand before tearing off for football practice, the money for Cub Scout dues, the things to be found: "Honey, those shoes are right under the bed where you left them." The phone calls: "Mary wonders if Jeanie can stay awhile."

And the day's adventures to be listened to, its triumphs and its disasters: "I made it, I made it. I'm a cheerleader!" "Mom, Miss Johnson promised I could wash the board, but she chose Marie." "Mother, I've just got to talk to you about this boy."

It's a signal that peace is ended, that cry "I'm home." With the banging of the door, your day is stirred once again to action. No longer are you your own person. You belong to them.

Yet, in the confidence of that cry, you feel a surge of pride. They want you; they seek you out. However poorly equipped you may feel for the job at hand, at least you're available and willing, and to them you're invaluable.

"Mother I'm home!" Oh, the ego in that announcement. Oh, the glorious awareness of love. "How important I am," it seems to say, and you laugh sometimes at its brashness. But your heart is tender too, even as you realize that they take you for granted—the fact of your presence and your delight in *their* presence.

"I'm home." They rap softly on your door at night, tip-toe in.

"You can go to sleep now, Mother. I'm home." And oh, the relief of that voice, the comfort of that good night kiss, for the long vigil is ended, the hours of worrying. They're safe; the last one's in.

They grow up so fast; they go away one by one. After a while only on their visits does that glad cry come. Hectic visits, filled with their outside concerns—dates, parties, or the turmoil of families of their own. The cribs are put up, the high chairs produced, and you know that you are no longer the center and hub of their existence, no matter how joyously they proclaim their own homecoming, bursting in. Home is somewhere else. A different job, a different life, a different love to follow yours, a different person to greet them when they return.

And that once-familiar cry has taken on a new significance. It means that you don't have to watch the clock anymore when they're late. You don't have to worry. They have reached their destination. Each one is safely in. In a new and much more wonderful way, each voice is assuring you: "I'm home, Mother. I'm home!"

Life Love

DON'T LET ME TAKE IT FOR GRANTED

*L*ord, don't let me take this wonderful gift of life for granted.

What a miracle it is just to wake up in the morning—to be alive another day!

Just to be able to get breakfast: to crack eggs into a sizzling skillet, to pour milk for the noisy horde. Just to feel myself *functioning*—muscles and mind and voice. (A voice the rest of the family probably wishes *didn't* work quite so well!)

Remind me to stop sometimes in the midst of it—the often chaotic, maddening midst of it—and touch it, taste it, love it, feel very grateful for it. Let my heart pause to utter a little secret prayer of thanks.

* * *

Lord, don't let me postpone my appreciation until all this may be threatened. Don't let me wait for a time when I might be ill—hurt, afflicted, in traction—and out of circulation before I realize it could be taken away.

Don't let me wait till it's over—as I know one day it will be—and I look back, perhaps alone. Don't let me wait till I'm desperate, Lord. Don't let me wait till I'm dying.

Help me to be fully awake and aware of the wonders of my life *now*, while I'm healthy and agile and able. Let me appreciate it while my family is all about me, in spite of the work and the worries they cause.

Let me keep my rejoicing current. As fresh as the eggs, as new as the morning paper, as bright as my children's faces or the sunlight dancing at the door.

Thank you for each day of our life together. Don't let me take it for granted.

MY BODY

Thank you, God, for this body.

For the things it can feel, the things it can sense, the wondrous things it can do.

For its bright vigor at the day's beginning, for the hard sweet satisfaction of it walking, working, playing. For its very weariness at the day's end, and the dear comfort of it sleeping. Sometimes for even its pain—if only to sting me into some new awareness of my own existence upon this earth.

I look upon it sometimes in reverent amazement—for we are indeed fearfully and wonderfully made. All its secret silent machinery meshing and churning, all its muscles coordinating, the whole of it so neatly functioning.

Lord, don't let me hurt it, scar and spoil it, overindulging it or overdrive it, but don't let me coddle it either. Let me love my body enough to keep it agile and able and well, strong and clean.

*   *   *

Thank you that I live within this body—the real, external, forever existing me. That it has been made to serve me so happily, so well, so long. And until the day comes when I'll have no further need of it, let me appreciate it to the fullest and be grateful for it: my body.

SPRING WIND

Your spring wind, Lord, is a bullying boy.

It snatches the clothes I am trying to pin on the line and whips them about my face.

It grabs the lids of trash barrels and sends them spinning like silver hoops.

It yanks the vines like a little girl's braids.

It shakes the blossom-laden trees, and the sweet confetti of their petals rains down upon me.

Your white clouds rush headlong before it. Your great trees bow and sway. Your flowers bend to its caprice.

The wind is a rollicking peddler, crying his wonderful wares, browbeating the world to buy.

I love your spring wind, Lord.

Its bright prancing. It makes me want to dance too, to roll a hoop, throw confetti, gather armloads of flowers (instead of clothes).

Your vigor is in it. Your joy is in it. Your infinite lively artistry is in it.

Thank you for spring wind, Lord.

THE LADDER OF STARS

On some nights the stars are simply there, brightly scattered. Distant, serenely shining, to be enjoyed but not remarked. Yet going to bed in the cool of a sweet spring night, what is it about the sky? Some feeling of expectancy, some secret withheld.

"Don't draw the shades," it seems to advise. "Don't shut out even an inch of this quiet, calmly shining night."

And so you fall asleep with the draperies still parted, and dream and rouse and dream again that the stars have come down to stand beside your bed. That somewhere near, almost near enough to climb, there rises a ladder of stars.

And you wake and sit upright . . . for there it is! Just beyond the windows and across the stream . . . The sky has sought and found some secret source of stars. Little stars in a mad multiplication, and big ones—enormous flowerings. From somewhere in the heavens they are bursting, gay little storms of unsuspected stars.

And the stars have come down, have indeed come down, and scurried about and rearranged themselves to stand at the stream's very edge. Or to hover just above it, while a few more keep fiery guard above the trees. They have become a ladder of diamonds, winking and beckoning.

All you have to do is to throw off the covers and fly off the balcony to grip their rungs. It must lead straight to heaven . . . surely you could climb it straight to heaven, this fire escape of stars.

"GARDEN'S UP!"

The other day I saw a cartoon in which a little girl in a market was tugging at her mother's sleeve and exclaiming, "Look, Mommy—vegetables you don't have to defrost!"

I laughed, but it also gave me a pang. I grieve for children who grow up missing gardens: the springtime thrill of spying in the dark earth the first pinstripe of green that signals "seeds are up!"; the Halloween glory of lugging their own pumpkins in from among the cornstalks; most of all, the long, luxuriant feasts of the summer in between.

Nowadays, even in my small Iowa hometown, patios have replaced the potato patch, and supermarkets boom where the old orchard used to be. Here and there, like some wistful monument to the past, an iron pump still stands. But its slender arm that you used to yank so vigorously to wash the garden stuff is rusted fast. Vines claim the pump shaft—or a housewife has decoratively enshrined its feet in petunias.

When I was growing up, the garden was as much a part of a child's world as his mother's apron—a kind of character symbol. The bigger and neater it was, the more worthy of respect. To have a little, scrabbly, half-hearted garden, or a big, unkempt one, was to be labeled shiftless. And not to have a garden at all—well! You were either so impressively rich you could afford to buy from others, or so downright lazy you were probably on relief.

Gardeners, whatever their era or locale, are of-the-earth earthy. They garden out of love. Such was my Grandpa Griffith. His garden was his passion and his pride, neat as a Grant Wood painting, its products blue-ribbon winners at the county fair. So, since Mother did not inherit his earthy fervors and Dad was a traveling salesman, it was generally Grandpa who saved the family honor by lining up Nate Mitchell and his horse, Daisy, to plow our back yard.

As Nate bellowed, "Gee-yaaap!" or "H'yaaar!" and Daisy began her jingling journey, the soil that rolled and billowed so magically from beneath the great silver blades was pitch-black. We darted behind, stamping its chocolaty richness under our feet, crumbling its clods in our hands (or throwing them at each other).

When the entire back lot had been transformed into a black and stormy sea, and we'd all had a turn at petting Daisy (the velvety prickle of her nose, her sweaty, sour-sweet flanks, still shaggy with their winter coat), the real business of gardening would begin. Dad always managed to be home for this event. Plotting and conferring as to where to put what, he and Mother would drive the stakes and stretch the cords, chalk-white against the black, so that the rows would be straight. Meanwhile, all of us clamored, "What can *I* do? Let *me* help! I want *this* corner. . . . No, that's *mine*. Mama *promised* me!"

They were remarkably patient with us. Dad, balding young, chewing gum in his chipper way, would be both funny and tender as he adjudicated claims, guided wobbly hoes, and squatted to help eager fingers shake seeds into trenches.

Then, after days of anxious watching, the miracle occurred. You rushed out one morning to discover a few beady trails of green. "Garden's up!" First, the round pushy radish leaves; then the tiny points of onions, followed by a delicate dance of lettuce sifting through. Astoundingly soon, Mother was sending us out to see if anything was big enough.

Each day we were learning a lesson no child of the supermarket can appreciate: that nature, for all her bounty, gives you nothing scot-free. Soon we were being ordered forth to keep the weeds at bay. Or to chase off the rabbits, little hide-and-seek enemies that you couldn't hate even when they sheared off an entire row of your very best broccoli. And though we fretted and fussed about aching backs and blisters, we found the garden a humming, pungently sweet and tantalizing place.

The peas had an air of precious superiority, their tendrils winding gracefully up the props and clinging with delicate fingers, their blossoms like tiny white bows. Then the green pods formed, at first flat as a girl's bosom, but swelling, ripening against the day when you would descend, banging a pan, to find the pods had become long and fat, some full to bursting.

Sitting on sunny back steps, you shelled them. Birds sang, mothers worked in kitchens, screen doors banged. There was the crisp snapping of the pods. With a sensation vaguely sensuous, your fingers rooted out the emeralds they contained. Some you ate raw—juicy, flat, faintly sweet. The pods piled up on a newspaper, like the wreckage of mighty fleets. You saved a few for little boats and sailed them later across a puddle or a big tin tub.

Potatoes were a lustier vegetable, and Grandpa used a pitchfork to dig them. I can see him yet, tall and handsome and white-mustached, the clods raining softly through his lifted tines, a few potatoes clinging to the parent root like small gnomes. The rest were buried treasure scattered about, and you hunted them as you hunted eggs. These first little new potatoes had skin so fragile it could be scrubbed off with a stiff brush. The flesh underneath was rosy, like that of children whose mother has scrubbed their faces.

Sweet corn was royal fare. It grew tall and stately, hobnobbing with the hollyhocks and sunflowers. On hot nights you could sometimes hear it crackling as it stretched its joints toward the stars. We watched its development with hungry eyes, measuring our own growth against it, standing on tiptoe sometimes to pull aside the rosy silks and test the kernels with a fingernail. When the ears were ready they spurted milk, and off you streaked with the news. In blissful suspense you waited while Father or Grandfather came to check; and what joy when he broke the ear free, stripped the husks aside and waved the nude ear aloft like some triumphant offering. "Sweet corn for supper!"

Almost everything that could be eaten raw rated high with us: carrots wrenched out of the ground, orange and crisp, and washed under the pump; turnips so white and purple they looked like painted clowns; muskmelon (or cantaloupe) split open with a jackknife, the seeds scooped out, the sweet, pale flesh engorged clear down to the lime-green rind.

But nothing could surpass a tomato picked and eaten, still sun-hot, on a drowsy summer's afternoon. And no fragrance is more pungent than that of tomato vines when you brush against them in the dusk playing run-sheep-run. You gathered the scarlet globes into bushel baskets and lugged them into the kitchen. A big fire would be burning, and on the back of the stove Mason jars would be clicking and whispering like a crowd of gossips. Dad would tighten the jars at night when he was home, while Mother took proud inventory: "Fifteen quarts of tomato sauce, nine jars of catsup and five pints of piccalili!" As this provender joined the glassy ranks that marched across our dampish, moldy-smelling cellar shelves, a feeling of peace and plenty would overtake us: a snug and squirrel-like sense of conquest and provision against the winter's cold.

Vegetables weren't all that made summer such a halcyon time. There was the fruit, as well, which progressed through tantalizing stages to clot the fences, burden the trees and rain in wanton plenty upon the ground. And we children were greedily in tune to every stage: "There's cherries big as acorns on the tree!" "The apples are getting ripe!" While parents admonished, "Not yet—it'll be another week at least. Now you kids be careful. Remember how sick you got last year."

We ate our way through summer. No competition from Good Humor men, no adult voices urging, "Now eat your vegetables, get your vitamins." Blissfully unaware, we gorged ourselves on nature's raw, fresh offerings and were as healthy as colts. When there was a pump handy we washed our plunder. If not, we ate it anyhow. ("You've got to eat a peck of dirt before you die.") There was little danger, for nobody sprayed against rivals then. Just as we didn't begrudge the bees their honey, we didn't begrudge a few apples to the worms. If we found an intruder, biting down, we simply threw the fruit away, and reached for more. . . .

I dream sometimes of those abundant summers in memory's lost emerald land of Oz. I wish my children could make little boats out of new-picked pods, and eat green apples, and raid a melon patch. I want them to know that fruits and vegetables don't grow on supermarket shelves, to be had solely for money and the opening of packages. That somewhere fruits and vegetables are being born and harvested by human hands out of God's own earth and sky and sun and rain.

A SONG OF PRAISE FOR SPRING

This is just a little song of praise for spring, Lord, and the wonders it works in me. The way it makes me want to rearrange things, clean and decorate things—the house, the garden, myself!

It's as if your sunshine, spilling across the waking earth, spills through a woman's spirits too. Why else should I feel this mad urge to paint the bathroom (forsythia yellow), tidy up closets and cupboards, add more purple cushions of creeping phlox to the driveway?

There's a touch of April, Lord, in the lift all this bestows. To see shelves lined with gay new paper, canned goods in near array, shoes submissive on their racks, garments weeded as neatly as the first daffodils.

I'm even inspired to "houseclean" in the manner of our mothers. Literally strip a room down to its bare branches and scrub it until it squeaks and gives off a tang as exhilarating as rain on little new leaves. Then haul (or browbeat men into hauling) furniture back—but all in new places so as to be surprised each time we sail in . . .

Or to get clothes in shape. Fix zippers, alter skirts, add or subtract belt, buckle or bow. Or to make the sewing machine sing into the night; or come home from shopping with a sense of beauty and bargains that make me feel in style with the shining new wardrobe of the world.

Best of all, Lord, spring inspires me to do some neglected housecleaning and refurbishing of my spirit.

Out with self-pity, old grudges, regrets. In with self-esteem . . . To refresh my own interior with a new supply of forgiveness and understanding, of goals and delights and dreams. To scatter these like seeds in the soil of myself and literally feel them grow.

Thank you, Lord, for all these sources of sunshine for a woman—all these ways to feel and celebrate spring.

HEART FRIENDS

How generous is God that he has given me these few and special women who are the true friends of my heart.

How he must love me that he has let us find each other upon this crowded earth.

We are drawn to each other as if by some mystical force. We recognize each other at once. We are sisters of the spirit, who understand each other instinctively.

There is no blood between us, no common family history. Yet there are no barriers of background, or even age. Older, younger, richer, poorer—no matter. We speak the same language, we have come together in a special moment of time, and the sense of union we feel will last throughout eternity.

How generous is God that he has given me so many other women I can call friends. Dear, good, life-enriching women who add flavor, value, delight. I would be the poorer without them.

Yet surely the Lord's true concern for us, his children, is to lead us to these rare and special few. The ones who call out to us from the crowds, who hold fast to us through trials, triumphs, long separations.

The friends with whom the heart feels joyfully at home.

THE GENEROUS ARTISTRY

How generous is your artistry, God, that you made all things in creation to be enhanced by other things.

Leaves—how lovely in themselves.

How marvelous that they sprout like tiny parasols in the sweet spring air, are opened by the heat of summer, and turned from green to crimson and gold by the tangy chemistry of fall. But no, that is not enough. You have added the sun and the wind and the rain to toss them about, adorn them with bangles, make them dance and shimmer.

And the trunks of trees.

How stately they rise, strong and sufficient with their rough dark bark. They reach for the sky, making a mighty harmony of their own. Yet their beauty too must be heightened, given an added dimension by the silver brush strokes of sun and rain.

And the rain itself.

It is not just falling water to quench the thirst of the earth. It too is enhanced by all it touches—rooftops or leaves or lake. It runs across the water before the wind like an advancing army, shields flashing. Or it falls gracefully, each drop a dancer spreading her skirts on the shining surface of a ballroom floor.

Your rocks would not need to be embellished, God.

Their gray-white stolidity, often glittering from their own white substance . . . their pure raw sculpturing. Yet even a rock is endlessly resculptured in sun and shadow and storm. Or a mantle of moss is tossed across its shoulders, or a meandering vine. Or flowers creep from a crevice. Or a bird's nest is tucked there, from which music spurts, and brisk bright wings.

For creatures too participate in this constant interplay of loveliness.

Dogs and cats and butterflies. Squirrels and people and children and all wild things. Life . . . life . . . all dipping and darting about together, or only just pausing to observe. But all adding myriad varieties of radiance and color.

How marvelous, this ever-changing pattern of the world's beauty, God. How you must love us to create for us such interlocking loveliness.

Don't let us ever be indifferent to it. Let us always see in it your generosity, your tremendous artistry.

THE REFRIGERATOR

Oh, God, how I dread cleaning the refrigerator. And I mean that not as an oath, but a prayer.

There it stands, singing away so faithfully, keeping our foods fresh for us. Reluctantly I open it, and instead of being grateful for its overflowing plenty, I want to back away and slam the door.

Instead, let me pause a moment and thank you. How generously you provide for us. We are never hungry. There is more than enough to go around—there are even leftovers.

Leftovers. A nuisance, yes, but also a symbol of your bounty. Quite literally our cups "runneth over."

And these cups, Lord. These chill bright bowls. Thank you for them and for all the foods they hold. What an infinite variety of things are here to please and nourish us. The eggs, so delicate and white in my hands. The milk, rich and heavy in its cartons. The bins of vegetables and fruit. The tangy globes of oranges, the moist green lettuce, the red meats, and yellow cheeses.

Everything that we need to survive you quietly put upon this earth for us, and the proof is here before me. Here on these crowded shelves.

Lord, forgive me for even a moment of irritation. Flood me with thankfulness.

Bless these shelves that I scrub and restore to order. Bless my hands as I work. And bless this task; make it no longer a source of dread, but a humble form of woman's worship— cleaning the refrigerator.

MORNINGS ARE SPECIAL

My mother always loved the morning.

I know a lot of people do. But with her morning was special. I can't say that she never woke up cross or troubled, I'm sure she often did. But what I remember most are those mornings when she was so full of hope and joy and enthusiasm, bubbling with bright plans for the day.

"Get up," she would call from the foot of the stairs. "Oh, do get up now, come on—it's such a beautiful day!"

And as we burrowed deeper, she would launch into a veritable paean of description: "The sun is shining so brightly and the birds are singing. Just listen to them, I can hear a mockingbird. And there's a nest of orioles in the lilac bushes, there goes one now!"

She would then produce more practical reasons: "I'm going to bake and clean and that garden needs weeding, so come on, you can help, I need you. But really it's so lovely out it'll be a pleasure, a person can accomplish so much on a beautiful day!"

By noon her enthusiasm had begun to wane, by midafternoon her hopes and energies were definitely dragging. No doubt her offspring's failing to share her zest to get up and enjoy the world (and its jobs) had a lot to do with this. But she was definitely what would today be labeled "A Morning Person."

And so am I. Morning is so new, unshabby and unsoiled. Morning is like a brand-new garment fresh out of the box. You want to try it on. To wear it! No matter what its color—sunny or gray—garbed in morning nothing seems impossible. By afternoon you're used to it, the day seems adequate, it covers you, but is no longer exciting.

By evening you're tired; the day's score is being tallied up, and sometimes you're not sure it was worth it. What did you accomplish? Nothing. Or seldom as much as you intended to. Sometimes you shrink back in dismay from the errors you have made, the miseries endured. (How could morning have so betrayed you—morning with its promise!)

Or if the promises have been fulfilled—your achievements please you, there has been excitement, unexpected pleasure—then, yes, evening can be lovely, looking back on it. But it's over when you go to bed. There's no calling back the day—the bad of it to be somehow changed, or the good of it either.

For morning people it is only in the morning that life is so entirely yours, unused, unspoiled, filled with the thrilling mystery of what lies ahead; and yet that is, right now, this moment, so beautiful, so intensely satisfying.

For me heaven will be like that. And when a voice calls, "Get up now, come on, it's morning!" I won't mind a bit.

UNEXPECTED COMPANY

They'll be here soon, the company I wasn't expecting and really don't want very much—but thank you for them.

Bless this house (and help me to get it cleaned up in time). This kitchen (and help me to find in it something worthy of guests).

Bless my dear foolish husband who invited them, and me as I strive to be a good hostess and a good wife to him.

Bless this table that I'm preparing; these linens (thank you that they're clean); this china and silver, these candles, wobbly though they are. This room, this meal—may it all turn out to be shining and good and lovely, to compensate for my sense of distress, ill humor, of not wanting to bother.

Oh, Lord, thank you for these guests as they drive toward us (and make them drive slowly, please).

I send out thoughts of love toward them, I send out welcome, and these thoughts ease my nervousness and make me genuinely glad inside.

Thank you for their friendship. Thank you that they have called us and can come. Thank you for the greetings and the news and the ideas that we will exchange.

Fill us all with rejoicing. Make us feel your presence among us. Bless our coming together in the warm hospitality of my house.

MOON SHADOWS

The moon will not let you sleep. It is huge and brightly burning. Round, intense, it pours its white fire upon all the hushed yet night-singing earth. . . .

It powders the outlines of the trees in the distance so that they melt into ghostly shapes. Yet those that branch across the window are etched by its silver tools into blackest clarity. . . .

It trembles upon the black satin surface of the lake. It pours into the room. And the beams across the ceiling are repeated in shadows drawn by the moon. . . .

Across these double lines lean the dark shadows of the window frames, making soft shifting plaids. And mounting these crossed ladders of shadow are a host of shadow figures; dark trembling shapes that march as mysteriously as spirits on some eternal journey—washing, leaning, trembling against each other. Overlapping, never still. . . .

At first you cannot imagine their source. The leaves outside? But no, the leaves are still. And then gazing down, down, you see the moon reprinted upon water that shifts, trembles, glances in its light. . . . The figures that walk your walls by moonlight are water shadows!

SCRUBBING A FLOOR

Thank you for the privilege of scrubbing this floor.

Thank you for the health and the strength to do it. That my back is straight and my hands are whole.

I can push the mop. I can feel the hard surface under my knees when I kneel.

I can grasp the brush and let my energy flow down into it as I erase the dirt and make this floor bright and clean.

If I were blind I couldn't see the soil or the patterns of the tile or the slippery circles shining.

If I were deaf I couldn't hear the homely cheerful sounds of suds in the bucket, the crisp little whisper of brush or mop.

I would miss the music of doors banging and children shouting and the steps of people coming to walk across this bright expanse of floor.

Lord, thank you for everything that has to do with scrubbing this floor.

Bless the soap and the bucket and the brush and the hands that do it. Bless the feet that are running in right now to track it. This I accept, and thank you for.

Those feet are the reason I do it. They are the living reason for my kneeling here—half to do a job, half in prayer.

A floor is a foundation. A family is a foundation. You are our foundation.

Bless us all, and our newly scrubbed floor.

THE RUNAWAY CANOE

You regard it rocking lightly at the dock, the just-patched and repainted family canoe.

And you feel you simply must assert yourself, if only for the children's future memories. What if they had to recall, "My mother was a hopeless nincompoop. She couldn't even paddle a canoe."

"Come, dear, how'd you like to take a ride?" you invite the littlest, doubtfully.

"You really mean it? Oh, goody, you gonna drive the boat?"

"No, let's not get too ambitious—I'm going to drive the canoe. And put on your lifejacket," you add nervously.

She scrambles eagerly in, grabs a paddle. "Can I help steer?"

"Well, maybe, after I get used to it."

You too step gingerly into the now drunkenly rocking shell, and ease down onto a cushion. "Well—" cheerily, "here we go!"

Fortified by vague recollections of having helped boy-friends paddle canoes in college, you shove off valiantly. But something seems to be wrong. Instead of heading sensibly toward the island, it rears and roots.

'Saaay, lookit Mother!" Your husband hollers from the shore: "You're sitting in the wrong end, honey."

"What difference does that make?" you demand, faintly irked.

"A lot if you expect to get anywhere. Boys, go help her," he orders. And now all the swimmers are regarding your plight and yelling instructions. To your consternation, a little crowd comes sloshing out to hold the craft steady while you stagger to the proper end.

"Go away, go away!" you order angrily as they stand by in an interested huddle. "I can do it."

"Sure you can," your husband says. "Don't watch her. You kids go on and play."

Self-consciously you keep stabbing at the water. "We'll head over to the islands," you inform your passenger confidently.

But the vessel has a stubborn will of its own. Whenever you gee it seems to buck and haw. "I tell you what—" you announce, as the island backs farther away by the minute— "let's go over to the fishing hole instead."

"Okay, I'll help." Your daughter pokes happily at the amiably nibbling waves. With growing confidence you bounce and struggle toward the sufficiently indefinite spot on the silvery platter.

Then a shrill whistle from shore. "Telephone, honey. You're wanted on the phone."

"Okay, I'll turn around, I'll be right there."

But the more fervently you lash the water, the more earnestly the vessel turns its snout toward the opposite bank and dedicates itself to the cause of taking you there.

"Hey, we live over this way, remember?"

"I know, smarty, I know, but it won't *cooperate*."

"Stick your paddle way out and pull back—"

"Turn it a little as you stroke—" "Try the opposite side—" Everybody wants to get into the act. Calling directions, the kids streak down the sand. And somebody suggests brightly, "Get out and shove."

Thoroughly flustered now and mad at the whole bunch, you try to do everything they say, only to find yourself tacking more wildly toward the wrong bank.

"Lassie, come home." A witty neighbor has joined the rousing little group.

"Oh, go drown yourself," you mutter. He's the least of your worries, however. For now, to your horror, you realize you are about to be cast up on the lap of total strangers having a cocktail party.

They look up from their float at all the commotion, and even your little girl inquires in troubled tones, "Mother, where we *going*? Do we know those people?"

"We're about to," you sputter, through set teeth. "I—seem to have lost the hang of it," you announce in what you hope are charmingly helpless tones.

"Here, let me help." A handsome male squats on the dock; holds out a hand. "We're neighbors? Won't you join us?"

"Heeeey!" Bewildered shouts still echo from the opposite bank. "What's the big idea? Where you going? Hey, telephone!"

THIS HOUSE TO KEEP

Sometimes my home just seems so cozy, God. For no special reason it suddenly seems warm and dear—as if it had put sheltering arms around me. I feel snug, protected, like a mole deep in its burrow, or a bird in its nest.

This kitchen with its clutter . . . This bedroom with its tumbled beds . . . The family room, deserted now but warm with the memories of last night's music, last night's fire.

I feel shielded by these walls, and yet in charge. So joyfully in charge. They are mine, to do with what I please. I want to spread my wings, to draw them a little closer to my heart.

Deep instincts stir. Half-buried recollections . . .

Of childhood playhouses of the past . . . In a garage. Under the attic eaves. Or down in the ravine, with tall ferns for curtains, and fallen logs and rocks for furnishings. How snug and secret it felt and yet how free, especially when raindrops spattered overhead.

You know, Lord, how often I hate this house. Mourn its defects, deplore its confusion, want to flee its confining walls. Yet on some days love rises up to compensate—like the guilty, almost overpowering love I feel when I've been cross or unfair to the children. I want to hug it as I do them, to wash its face, straighten its clothes, tuck it in. To make it as clean and sweet and charming as I possibly can.

Because it's a part of my life, even as they are. It echoes

my tastes, reflects my character, and for all its imperfections, it is warm and dear to me.

Thank you, Lord, that I have this house to keep.

THE BUFFET DRAWER

Here's to that great repository of American living, the buffet drawer!

Even if you eat at a breakfast nook or a coffee bar in the kitchen, you must pass it, usually, on your countless travels throughout the house. And as you do so it awaits you, silent-mouthed but ever ready to open and gulp the flotsam and jetsam that nobody knows quite what to do with:

The door keys. The Charge-a-Plate. The school papers, the safety pins, the bargain soap coupons. The pencils, the notices, the pamphlets that nobody reads but somebody might want to, so you'd better not throw them out.

What housewife is so equipped with will power that, dizzily viewing the constant accumulation, she doesn't shut her eyes and simply scoop it into the blind relief of the buffet drawer?

What female is so firm in her demands that she can enforce a more orderly disposal of possessions upon her progeny? "These are your ball and jacks, take them to *your own room!*" . . . "This is your party invitation, put it where you can find it, for goodness sake." Thus though we chant in a kind of dutiful recitative day in and day out, who heeds, pray tell? Who obeys?

No, there exists a kind of common understanding: If you don't need it but want to keep it, where more safely can it go on deposit than in the buffet drawer? We even answer all inquiries thus ourselves: "Where can you find some bobby pins? Look in the buffet drawer." . . . "Has anybody seen your Scout knife? It's probably in the buffet drawer."

And even if the missing object isn't at once unearthed, how often other treasures are: "Hey, here's that cowboy wallet Grandma gave me for Christmas two years ago." . . . "I only scared up three bobby pins, but I found this jeweled barrette and this rabbit's foot and it's already brought me luck—look, here's a movie pass and it's not even dated and there's a neat matinee this afternoon."

Betimes, of course, you clean it. When it reaches the point of sheer satiety. When its jaws are so bulging full they're beginning to show leakage and you can scarcely shut them. In a burst of reform you dump the entire contents on the dining room table and sort. The tacks, the lipsticks, the buttons, the jewelry—each in its proper heap to be tidily distributed or filed away in boxes and jars. A lot of the papers can be burned—the notices of a citizens' meeting four months ago, the homework; yea, though you feel guilty twinges, those unredeemed soap coupons.

My heavens, how bare it is. How neatly compartmental-ized, you gloat. This section for school tickets and such. This for the circulars. This one for combs. "And there's simply *no excuse* for its getting into such a mess again," you lecture with fervor and hope. In fact it's so clean it intimi-dates you. For a little while you actually refrain from the daily sweep yourself.

But soon—just when one cannot say—you too know the sweet relief of its all-embracing vaults. Of answering the inevitable, "What'll I do with this?" by the equally inevita-ble, "Well, for now—put it in the buffet drawer." And the queries, "Where can I find it?" with that comfortable, de-pendable prediction: "You know very well where it probably is—the buffet drawer!"

WHAT IS A CAT?

A cat is first of all a kitten, to be cuddled and adored. Kittens have baby-blue eyes and plaintive, comical little mews. They have to be mopped up after and trained. Their tiny tongues lap milk like pink flags flying. They chase balls or string or their own tails, in fact anything that moves.

Kittens are gay and tender and funny and charming.

But kittens grow up to be cats.

Now their eyes have turned a bland, enigmatic green. A

cat gazes directly at you, with something profound and superior in its eyes. A cat's gaze is as ancient and secretive as the sphinx.

And the things cats chase now are alive! Mice or chipmunks or bunny rabbits or birds. At this point cats cause awful conflict in the bosom of any owner. "Hooray, go after the mice!" we encourage the helpful hunter. But we want Cat to spare the birds and the little wild furred things. "You bad, you wicked creatures!" we scold, regarding the offering that Cat has proudly deposited at our feet.

Chasing the bewildered villain away, we try to mend the victim, or feeling guilty, bury it tenderly. Yet reason informs us that this is Cat's nature. No amount of punishment or protest can alter the instinctive machinery that makes him a predator. How sad, how strange.

Cats also have strange and noisy courtship customs.

Males fight, and females move constantly from litters to lovers. Even trotting them to the vets seems to make no difference to courting Toms. They still come caterwauling under windows, with noises that put a banshee or a colicky baby to shame.

Cats also enjoy a good snooze in unlikely places—the buffet, a dresser drawer, a closet shelf, your husband's hat. They enjoy sharpening claws on the furniture, and kneading them on anything soft and woolly, such as blankets or your best sweaters.

A good way to lure them from the sofa is by providing them with a scratching board covered with burlap and baited with a dash of catnip. (For some reason they go mad when they sniff catnip, rolling and squirming as if intoxicated. It is the cat's LSD.)

Cats *don't* suck baby's breath, as is maliciously rumored; but they are curious about anything that moves, attracted by the smell of milk and softness, so they can wake him up and disturb him. Ernest Hemingway says, in *A Moveable Feast*, that during those early Paris years their cat, F. Puss, served as their son's baby-sitter.

Cats are very loving. They will wind between your legs when you are trying to get dinner on the table. They will plop on your lap when you're reading or sewing, and want to cuddle. Their purring is steady, insistent, and as comforting as a kettle boiling joyously on the hearth.

Cats, like people, have personality. Some are gentle, some gay, some solemn, some bold, some are cowards. All are a nuisance. And we bother with them for simply one reason: We love them!

MORNING BIRDS

How impudent are morning birds! How annoyingly gay. Tired, needing sleep, you hear them starting up sometimes outside your window, like insistent little alarm clocks that you can't shut off or hurl away. Trilling and cheeping and shrilling their glad little cries. Running scales. Ringing bells of brightness. Chiming.

How they carry on, unaware of the head that plunges into the pillow. Or the being who rises, stalks to the window, prepared to shoo or shout "Oh, go away!"

Only you cannot. No, you cannot. For the day itself is too giddily joyful too. Fresh, untasted. New and sparkling. The sky a cool pink-tinged blue.

The trees are all atwinkle in the coming sun. Their branches dip slightly under the fragile singers. Leaves tremble as, with a spurt of wings, a glimmer of color, an oriole or a cardinal soars away.

By contrast—how silently. How effortless the lift of wings. How totally unresistant. Their motion is like the spontaneous spill of music from their throats. Birds are so relaxed. They sound and seem so free, so happy, because they don't fight their surroundings. They simply flow into them.

And now you think: How peaceful are morning birds. How restful.

For their joy is contagious. You feel it beginning to dance and sparkle within you as your own resistance gives way. You want to laugh. You want to join their bright chorus and go singing into the new day.

Oh, but you're not a bird, remember? The day will be

complex. Filled with phone calls, duties, problems, jobs that nobody, man, or bird, could effortlessly fly through. But maybe the birds have been little emissaries to prepare you. "Sing if you can" they may have been saying. "But when you can't, remember our silence too."

FORTIFY ME WITH MEMORIES

Sometimes life seems almost too wonderful, Lord.

My husband's arms around me. A new baby kitten-soft on my shoulder. A son who (after all that trouble) is turning into a bright and handsome boy. A daughter who's witty and lovely. A new puppy to be gathered around and adored.

Friends calling their good nights after an unusually happy party. A moment of rare understanding with another friend on the phone. An hour of high excitement when the mailman brings wonderful news.

There are times when all these things seem to shout and sing within me, Lord. To merge into something almost too beautiful, like a sunset or a symphony. Fused into some instant or hour of perfection. At times I can scarcely bear it, Lord—this beauty, this benediction.

Oh, help me to remember it, please . . .

When the baby screams all night with the colic. When the pup throws up on the kitchen floor. When my husband is cross and discouraged. When the son fails me and the daughter becomes a blind fury against me.

Gird me with the shining moments, God. Fortify me with memories.

Help me to realize during the pain and the petulance and the anguish that life *is* truly wonderful, Lord. And it takes the grim moments to enhance the ecstasy.

THE ANGEL BIRD

Each year the herons come—stately steel-blue beings who nest in the rushes across from the cabin, and stalk the fishes on slender legs. They fly with their long necks arched inward, emitting their curious cry, "Frahnk, frahnk!"

There is always mystery and excitement about any large bird. These almost people-sized creatures who can lift themselves so magically and soar off into the sky. As if they could carry you with them if you made your longing clear and they so willed.

Then there are the bitterns, a chunkier small species, the brown of the weeds. But loveliest of all the herons is the white one which descends once a season, like a visiting celebrity, and usually alone.

"Mommy, guess what? An angel flew by my window this morning!" a child exclaims. And so it seems. For there is something unearthly about that white span of wings against the vivid blue sky. Something that speaks of purity, joy and peace, coasting down.

How placidly it perches upon the piece of driftwood it has chosen; the silver of the sun-bleached wood, the snowy body, a statue reflected on the water. How patiently it stands in the shallows, or walks the sands with slow elegant grace. It is oblivious to our admiring gaze. Yet sometimes the children are convinced it dips its wings to us, going by. And sometimes it cuts so close to the cabin you could reach out and touch it, so it seems.

You know better. It would be like trying to touch an angel. It would be like holding in your hands for one brief, enthralling instant the bright bird of happiness. It would be too much.

But whenever anyone announces its arrival, or calls out, "The white heron's still here," it is like a good omen. You feel that for a small and lovely while you have a heavenly guardian.

HIS VERY WORLD DANCES

To me, no art form speaks more eloquently of my Creator than the dance. His very world dances! Almost everything in nature that he has made.

* * *

Look out the window, now, right now. Whatever the season, look out upon the vast living stage of the world. How hard it is for nature to be still; even on the stillest summer days the squirrels leap and scurry, the streams cavort, ballets of tiny butterflies dip and swirl. And when the wind stirs—! Even now, November—a chill bright golden day. The grass has nearly lost its green, the trees are almost bare. Yet lean and stripped, those trees lift their arms to the sky as if in worship, and dance. The few remaining leaves do a happy roundelay as they come skirling down. They are little girls in dancing class, skittering this way and that. They skip across my window as I write, land briefly, pirouette on.

Below is the water, sequin-skirted in the sun. Moving, ever-moving to the cadences of its currents and the wind. The waves keep time. Like a perfectly trained chorus, a line of them swings forward arm in arm, white-plumed; bowing their heads in unison they break, rise, surge shoreward, regroup. There with another little bow they disperse, reach toward me, then retreat to dance again.

Soon winter will stop their performance, polish the stage. But then the snows will come dancing down, weaving and twining like Maypole streamers as they fall. . . . Then spring and the triumphal melting, the dancing of rain, the dance of buds on the boughs and petals on the breeze.

Lord, how you must love dancing to put its rhythms into all these things. And into your creatures—insect, bird or beast. To equip them with such grace.

MORE STATELY MANSIONS

"Build thee more stately mansions, O my soul!"—Another of Mother's favorite quotations. From *The Chambered Nautilus*, by Oliver Wendell Holmes . . . She looks up from the washboard with a twinkle in her eyes, tosses back a lock of her long dark hair, and goes on, as her hands wring out the clothes: "As the swift seasons roll! Leave the low-vaulted past!"

Oh, Mom, that little house where you worked so hard! . . . You could have held your own in any stately mansion, and you set foot in so few during your life. But then why should you? you already occupied so many. Mansions of the spirit, mansions of the mind. The Lord had given you the keys, and you wandered them at will. . . . Through books— of poetry, especially. Through the music you listened to with such pleasure ironing, baking, keeping your family clean. Through copies of famous paintings cut so carefully from magazines.

It was years before you saw the originals of some of those paintings in the galleries. How awed and astonished you were at their size. A gigantic Rubens, I remember, claiming half a wall—though it had hung cozily in its dime-store frame over your bed and Dad's for years. You gasp, then giggle behind your hand—"Suppose Rubens ever dreamed he'd hang in *our* stately mansion?"

Stately mansions . . . the cold marble floors ring beneath our heels as we walk them, Mother and I, under the vaulted ceilings. The flowers are bright in the courtyards, the fountains sing and splash. We wander from picture to picture, sitting often to rest, for she's getting old now and her feet hurt and she has to get her breath. . . . We sit loving the place, its sculpture, its brasses and bronzes and tiles. Then we rise and find the oriental wing. . . . How she loves the Chinese porcelains. Getting her big round reading glass from her bag, she studies each huge vase or urn carefully, remarking the exquisite detail, the intricacy of design. And now she alludes to "Kubla Khan": "'Through wood and dale the sacred river ran, Then reached the caverns measureless to man.' You know I'd have loved to have a Ming vase, but unfortunately the Jewel Tea man never gave them for premiums, and I doubt if you could get one today with trading stamps."

Even as I laugh and hug her, my heart breaks. I want, with sudden blind passion, to place her in her stately mansion surrounded by all the beautiful things her soul craves.

But later, long after she's asleep, I go outside and gaze up at the stars sparkling so brightly. And the last few lines of her *Chambered Nautilus* come to me:

> *Let each new temple, nobler than the last,*
> *Shut thee from heaven with a dome more vast,*
> *Till thou at length art free,*
> *Leaving thine outgrown shell by life's unresting sea!*

And then the words, from another source altogether: "In my Father's house are many mansions."

Mother will have her mansions.

NEW YEAR'S EVE

It's almost over, Lord. The old year's almost over.

In a few minutes the whistles and bells will proclaim it. "Forget it, it's over. Off with the old, on with the new!"

But I'm already a little homesick for the old year, Lord. I don't want it to be over, not really. I want to hang onto it a little longer. The happiness it held—the joys and surprises. Big important ones, yes, but the little ones too. Delights that were often too small or perhaps too frequent even to realize, to appreciate and savor before they vanished.

Even the pain and problems—somehow I want to cling to them too. I long to rush back, reclaim them. Handle them differently, be more careful, more patient, more generous, more wise. I don't *want* the New Year, Lord. I just want another chance at the old one!

But mostly I don't want to part with it just yet. For we loved it, whatever mistakes we made. It was ours, our life together.

But now the bells are clanging, the whistles are shrieking. People are laughing and singing—and I am caught up in the excitement too. "Don't look back," everything seems to be shouting. "Look ahead!"

And a great exhilaration courses through me as I realize:

Yes, yes, they are right. How wonderful, that every year you present us with this great, new, shining package of time.

How promising its contents. How mysterious. How thrilling, challenging, in some ways almost frightening. Yet mainly how marvelous—that we can discover those contents only as we live them. Until we have stripped off the final wrapping of the final day and another year lies at our feet.

Revealed, completed, endured, enjoyed. But whole at last, and so—wholly and utterly ours.

Thank you that as we put the old year away with all the tattered and treasured Years Past, you always give us a new one to open.

Life is so dear. Each year is so dear. Each *day* is so dear. Thank you for every moment, Lord.

Self Love

WHO AM I?

O h, God, who am I? Where did I come from and where am I going? What am I doing here?

Sometimes, passing a mirror, I am startled by the stranger who seems to be wearing my face. Who is this person who looks like me (poor thing) and rushes around in my body?

She cleans up the kitchen, sorts the laundry, yells at children, loves, worries about and fights with a man who seems to be her husband.

She goes to bed at night, gets up in the morning, cooks, eats, gets other people off to their destinations and then hurries to her job. A job in a sometimes drearily familiar, sometimes startlingly strange place. Or a club where she knows almost everybody—and nobody, actually.

And we are the same person, this woman and I. Yet different, too—as if I am allowed to wake up sometimes in her presence and cry out: "Hey . . . *you!* Who are you, and what are you doing here?" And she can only regard me, stricken and surprised.

Who am I? Who am I, God?

I am alive—I must be. See, I am shaking a hand: I can feel it warm against mine. I am conducting a meeting: I hear my own voice calling for the treasurer's report. I am racing to the car, gabbling with somebody; our heels click on the walk, the door bangs. I am hurtling along a highway to pick up a child and take him to Little League.

But in the very moment of awareness, I am sometimes pierced by the sheer pointlessness of all this.

What does it matter, God? What does it *matter* whether the clothes get sorted, the kitchen cleaned, the treasurer read her dull report? What would it matter if I didn't show up for work? Would the course of human events be altered in the least if my son didn't get to the ball game?

This woman who seems to be doing these things in my body, wearing the label of my name. What has she got to do with *me*?

Forgive me if this sounds frenzied, God. I *feel* frenzied—and frightened sometimes.

It's all going by so fast. Life's rushing past me, time is sweeping me along in its torrent, and I don't know where I'm going, or why. I long to grab something along the way. I can't slow it down, but I feel that I've got to grab something, hang onto something, or I'll be obliterated altogether. The real me (if there is such a creature) will be even more lost than she is now.

Already half-deafened by the demands of other people, half-blinded, desensitized, she will go down to death with her own needs not only unmet but only half-recognized.

Rescue me, Lord. Stretch out your hand to me.

I know you must be out there—somewhere. And if I can only find you, hang onto you, perhaps I can be saved. Not in the sense of an afterlife, but saved from the choking futility of this life now.

I am groping for you, God. Stretch out your hand—and don't let me fight you away. Draw me onto a place where I can at least get perspective. Where I can meet myself on quieter terms and try to figure out who I am, where I am going—and why.

TIME OUT FOR LOVE

Lord, don't ever let me be too busy to love . . .

A child who comes running in for a hug and lavish exclamations of praise because he's just learned to stand on his head. Yea, though I'm trying to make bouillabaisse and to keep the clams from getting all over the kitchen and the lobsters from crawling off, don't let me shoo him away.

Don't let me be too busy to love, Lord . . .

A neighbor who's just had a fight with her husband and needs a shoulder to cry on; or who's just had her first poem published and is dying to celebrate with someone. Though I'm already behind schedule and there's company coming, don't let me be too busy to listen and, in this way, to love.

Lord, don't let me be too busy to love . . .

A son who's home unexpectedly from boot camp with a buddy who hasn't got a home to go to—both starved for some good old-fashioned fried potatoes and corn bread. No matter how hectic my day's program, don't let me be too busy to fix it (well, at least give them a hand). Above all, to show him how thrilled I am to have him back and the other kid with him.

Don't let me be too busy to love, Lord . . .

My husband when he's tired and discouraged, or high from a big deal at the office, or simply wants my attention. Don't let me be too preoccupied with TV or a book or a friend on the phone or my own day's score of frustrations and peaks and valleys to give him what he longs for. Don't let me be too busy to love.

And now, Lord, thank you for giving me so many people, so many opportunities to love. But please forgive me when I fail them; help them to forgive me, and me to forgive myself.

You made me human, and there is only so much of me to go around.

THE NEW OUTFIT

Oh, Lord, dear Lord, I've spent too much on this new outfit. I'm beginning to worry even as I carry it excitedly down the street.

It's so lovely—the most becoming thing I've found in years. I felt I simply had to have it, and in one mad moment I bought it. But now the price tag is like a weight dragging at my steps. Guilt and anxiety are beginning to dim the first high delight I felt.

I see very nice looking things much more reasonable, it seems in the windows I pass. I wince to recall what I paid, I deplore my rash impulse. I think of the bills, the budget, the things the children need.

What kind of mother am I to blow all that money on myself?

Lord, I am hesitating. Perhaps I should turn around right here before I lose my nerve and take it back! . . . Help me to do the right thing now, this minute, while the traffic light still says STOP . . . But no, it's turned to green, I'm somehow being propelled across the street, carrying my lovely box.

And my heart is suddenly lighter as a sweet conviction dawns: Anything cheaper that I didn't really *care* about would be a disappointment, not only to me but to the rest of them. They *want* me to feel and look the way I feel and look in this new outfit!

Thank you, Lord, for making me realize that now and then a woman simply has to be extravagant.

I'VE SAID "YES" ONCE TOO OFTEN

Oh, God, I've done it again, I've said "Yes" once too often and now I'm stuck with this extra job.

How will I manage to accomplish everything? All these committees, all these meetings, all these phone calls.

Right now I don't see where there'll be enough time in the day (or night). I don't see where my strength is coming from.

Only you will help me. You will give me strength. You will give me the intelligence to manage. You, who created time, will even give me that.

Now let me quietly thank you for this challenge. If I'm a fool to take on so much—all right, you, who made me so, will not leave me stranded. You will fortify, you will supply my needs.

Bless the people with whom I'll be involved. Bless the job I've undertaken, and I know it will prove worthy of the efforts I bring to it.

SELF-AWARENESS

What a wonderful thing is self-awareness. It is the touch-stone of a full, vibrant, fulfilling life.

I don't mean self-consciousness in the sense that we have been warned about. A preoccupation with how you'll look and act with other people only makes anyone anxious and ill at ease. No, no, self-AWARENESS is something quite different. It is the ability to appreciate your own being. To realize even in little ways, the sheer magic of being alive.

SELF-AWARENESS is practiced constantly by children. They glory in how fast they can run, how loud they can sing. They rejoice in how they are growing, in whatever dimension . . . We adults lose this natural delight; bogged down with responsibilities and concerns for other people, we go dull and take ourselves for granted. We even begin to fret and stew and harp and complain about the burdens that are the inevitable accompaniment of life.

Yet how glorious it is just to BE here on this planet, able even to cope with and carry these trials. What a marvel simply to exist! . . . To be YOU, right now, this moment, in that body, for all its limitations, is a priceless thing, and it won't last forever. So pause and become AWARE OF IT.

Practice Being Grateful

Practice being grateful for every breath you draw. Whatever your religions or your doubts, each of us has materialized out of a mystery. But one undeniable fact is you are here, constantly breathing and tasting the most precious commodity of all—life. Rejoice in the simple act of getting out of bed in the morning, the night's sleep behind you. Let the hot and cold water of the shower pound down upon you stirring you to the awareness, "Hey, it's me!" Smell the breakfast you are cooking for yourself or other people, hear the sounds of kitchen and family and dogs and cats and cars. Be AWARE of yourself in relation to all these things, an active, vigorous participating being, vital to others—yes, but vital as well to YOU.

Look at every member of your body with wonder. Every finger, toe, elbow, knee. Breast and belly and back. How remarkable their smooth intricate joinings, what a complex package. And these eyes to see, these ears to hear . . . Don't wait until some of these senses are threatened; don't wait till you're in a hospital having a hysterectomy—in pain, in fear, in traction. Bless your body and its creator for its abilities now. Thank God—and it—your SELF—this physical vehicle of the spirit, for serving you.

It Makes You More Attractive

Self-awareness even makes you more attractive. It puts a new spring in your step, a new sparkle in your eyes. And you can't be truly self-aware and let yourself go. The truly self-aware person refuses to submit to anything that despoils his own image. It is self-awareness that makes him step on the scales, do those exercises, brush the hair until it shines. When you're in league with beauty you're in league with one of the nicest aspects of life.

Take time for self-awareness!

THE COMPLIMENT

I want to suggest a new Beatitude: "Blessed are the sincere who pay compliments."

For I have just had a compliment, and it has changed my day.

I was irritated. Tired. Discouraged. Nothing seemed much use. Now suddenly all this is changed.

I feel a spurt of enthusiasm, of energy and joy. I am filled with hope. I like the whole world better, and myself, and even you.

Lord, bless the person who did this for me.

He probably hasn't the faintest idea how his few words affected me. But wherever he is, whatever he's doing, bless him. Let him too feel this sense of fulfillment, this recharge of fire and faith and joy.

GETTING AT IT

Oh, Lord, please help me to stop worrying about this annual bazaar they've put me in charge of, and get *at* it!

You know how weak I am, and what a procrastinator. How I let myself get talked into things I sometimes later regret. How I lie awake nights dreading what I've undertaken, scared I won't be up to it. You know the times I've panicked, even considered making excuses for myself and trying to get out of it.

And the longer I put off getting started the worse it gets.

Now, with your help, this is going to stop. Not only because time's flying by and there's so much to be done, but because I'm ashamed of this self-inflicted suffering.

So here goes, God. Today, this minute. I'm getting at it. (There. The very resolution has a calming effect!)

I'm drawing up a plan of action. I'm calling committee meetings. I'm already getting ideas, exciting ones (what strange things happen once the gates are simply unlocked)!

I know it won't be easy, but you've made me realize it won't be all that hard. You will give me self-confidence and strength—and ultimate success. But you can't do any of these things for any of us until we *start*.

(Come to think of it—if you created the world and its creatures and even the universe in seven days, you must have just made up your mind and *done* it. And maybe even *you* didn't realize how great was your own potential or how vast would be the result.)

I'VE GOT TO TALK TO SOMEBODY, GOD

I've got to talk to somebody, God.

I'm worried, I'm unhappy. I feel inadequate so often, hopeless, defeated, afraid.

Or again I'm so filled with delight I want to run into the streets proclaiming, "Stop, world, listen! Hear this wonderful thing."

But nobody pauses to listen, out there or here—here in the very house where I live. Even those closest to me are so busy, so absorbed in their own concerns.

They nod and murmur and make an effort to share it, but they can't; I know they can't before I begin.

There are all these walls between us—husband and wife, parent and child, neighbor and neighbor, friend and friend.

Walls of self. Walls of silence. Even walls of words.

For even when we try to talk to each other new walls

begin to rise. We camouflage, we hold back, we make ourselves sound better than we really are. Or we are shocked
and hurt by what is revealed. Or we sit privately in judgment, criticizing even when we pretend to agree.

But with you, Lord, there are no walls.

You, who made me, know my deepest emotions, my most
secret thoughts. You know the good of me and the bad of
me, you already understand.

Why, then, do I turn to you?

Because as I talk to you my disappointments are eased,
my joys are enhanced. I find solutions to my problems, or
the strength to endure what I must.

From your perfect understanding I receive understanding
for my own life's needs.

Thank you that I can always turn to you. I've got to talk
to somebody, God.

GIVE ME A GENEROUS SPIRIT

Give me generosity of spirit, God. True generosity of spirit
so that I can be truly glad, and show it, when other people
succeed.

It's not hard to share a recipe or a baby-sitter. Not a bit
hard to lend a neighbor a tablecloth or an egg. It's even kind
of thrilling to come to somebody's rescue with your best bag
or prized (if unpaid for) mink.

And for most of us sympathy comes easy. To lend an ear
to a friend's troubles, be a tower of strength in times of
illness or disaster . . . There's a heady drama about being
needed; the heart feels proud of itself, it receives more than
it gives.

But oh, Lord, how much harder it is to share an hour of
joy, of triumph. To be genuinely proud of somebody else.
To be generous with praise . . . When another woman's
child has made the Honor Society or the football team, or
starred in the school play. When her husband has won a big

promotion. Or when she herself has done something important, something exciting. When the flags of her life are
flying!

That's the true test of friendship, Lord. Not when we feel
luckier and stronger, when we can reach *down* to help somebody. But when we feel less lucky, our importance threatened; when we've got to reach *up* to give.

Guard me against jealousy, God. Free me from envy.
Flood my heart with genuine joy, and help me to show it,
when my friends succeed.

BLESS MY GOOD INTENTIONS

Lord, please bless my good intentions.

I make so many promises to myself about all the nice
things I'm going to do: Have somebody over. Phone, write,
send books and get-well cards and flowers.

You know how often I lie awake at night planning the
delights I want to do for people. Or mentally writing the
most beautiful letters.

You know my heart is full of love—but also how full of
other things is my day. Duties, demands, problems. So that,
all too often, these other things don't get past my mental
gates. Or are hopelessly blocked or detoured when they do.

The get-well cards I buy get lost—or I can't find the right
address. The people I try to cheer up with a phone call are
already on the phone, or out! The budget won't quite stand
the strain of flowers, and there's nothing but a few scraggly
marigolds in the yard.

The cake I bake for the shut-in falls, or the car won't start
to take it to her. When I sit down to write those lovely
letters, the lovely words have vanished—or there's a sudden
immediate crisis to be resolved.

They say hell is paved with good intentions, Lord. But I
wonder if the paths to heaven aren't cobbled with them too?

Surely you give us credit for our kindly thoughts. At least
they're better than critical ones even when, through life's

complications of our own procrastinations, we fail to follow through.

You've shown us that we are more than body, we are spirit. And thoughts are powerful things. Maybe the vibrations of love they release, actually accomplish more than we know!

Anyway, Lord, please bless my good intentions.

THANK GOODNESS THEY STILL LOVE US

The trees stand bare and gray. To see them now you wouldn't dream (if you hadn't seen it) that soon, in a few weeks, they will burst forth in loveliness. And that the earth, now sodden and brown, will likewise become green, and gay with flowers.

But we know that the world is just waiting . . . resting . . . It can't be beautiful all the time. It has to have these periods in which to replenish its juices. To store up, get ready for spring. And we like it anyway. We take this for granted; we forgive it . . .

And it's this way with people. We can't always be beautiful. We can't constantly go through live all dressed up. We've got to take off our makeup, get into comfortable clothes. We have periods, sometimes for days, weeks, sometimes only a few hours, when we too are drab and colorless and plain, not only in our looks but in our performance.

But those who truly care about us understand. They don't mind; they forgive us. Sometimes it only makes us more dear to them, more human in our imperfections. Thank goodness, they still love us!

GIVE ME PATIENCE

Oh, God, give me patience!

With this child who's telling his eager, long-winded story. Let me keep smiling and pretending I'm enthralled. If I don't, if I cut him off he'll not only be hurt, he may not come to me with something really important next time. But, dear Lord, help me to guide him gently to the climax soon.

Oh, God, give me patience!
With this baby who's dawdling over his food. He must eat, the doctor says, and I mustn't coax, threaten, or grab him and shake him as I'm tempted to—even though I know it would only make things worse and damage us both. Help me to sit quietly waiting, waiting, learning patience.

Oh, God, give me patience!
With this boring old lady who wants me to look at all the pictures of her grandchildren and listen (again) to her oft-told tales. Help me to remember that I may be just as difficult some day, and that by showing warm interest I can add a little joy to her few remaining days. Let me love her instead of resent the time she's taking. Let me gain something from enduring this hour with her. Let me learn through her the lesson of patience.

Oh, God, give me patience—as I wait for a friend who is late, or for a line that's busy, or for traffic to clear. Let me be fully aware of my surroundings as I wait—the feel of the chair upon which I sit, the passing parade of people, or the scent and color and sound of the very air. Help me to realize that no time is really wasted in this life so long as we are fully awake to the moment, so long as we are aware.

Oh, God, give me patience—with myself!
Wth my follies, my hasty words, my own mistakes. The times when I seem a hopeless bumbler unworthy of friend or family or the company of any human being, so that I get into a panic and think, "Why am I taking up space on the earth? Why can't I flee, vanish into eternity, simply disappear?"
Help me to stop wrestling with remorse. Taking a futile inventory. Waking up in the night to berate myself for "things I ought to have done and things I ought not to have done." Reassure me, oh God, that there *is* health and hope

and goodness in me, and that if I just have patience they will take over. I'll become the person I want to be and that you expect me to.

LET ME TAKE TIME FOR BEAUTY

Lord, let me take time for beauty.

Time for a jug of flowers on the table, or a plant if flowers aren't in bloom. Time for a dab of lipstick or a fresh blouse before the family comes home. Don't let me settle for the dingy, the shabby, the ugly—either with myself or with my house, just because I'm too lazy to make the effort.

Give me the energy and the will to provide a bit of beauty.

You've made the world so beautiful, Lord, let me take time to see it. Even as I'm rushing to the market or driving children to their destinations, let me be aware of it: the glory of hills and woods and shining water. The colors of traffic lights and yellow buses, of fruit stands and lumberyards, of girls wearing bright scarves that dance in the breeze.

Let me take time for the beauty in my own backyard, Lord.

Let me lift my eyes from the dishes to rejoice in the sunshine spilling through the trees. In the squirrels darting jaunty-plumed along the bleached boards of the fence. In the raindrops strung out on the clothesline like a string of crystal beads.

Let me take time for the children. How quick they are to discover beauty and come running to us with their offerings.

Don't let me be too busy to exclaim over these treasures: a bluejay's bright feather, the first violets and dandelions, a shell, a pretty stone. God, forgive me for the time (I wince to remember) when, involved in some dull task—ironing maybe—I shooed away a child who was begging, "Look, come look. A butterfly!" A cocoon was breaking, I learned later. He wanted me beside him to witness this miracle, this birth of beauty out of its dark cage.

Dear God, to live at all is such a miracle—whether as bug or bird or creature of any kind. To come into existence upon this planet and be able to witness its beauty is such a privilege, especially for a human being.

Help us to cherish and be a part of that beauty.

Let me take time for beauty, God.

THE COURAGE TO BE KIND

Dear Lord, give me . . . them . . . somebody the courage to be kind.

That poor man who just got on the subway is so shabby, so talkative, so obviously confused. He doesn't know where to get off, but the woman he asked just gave him a cold stare and pointedly moved away. The man on the other side of him has turned his back.

Nobody will help him, Lord, and my heart hurts. It hurts so for him, but it's pounding for me too. I don't want to be conspicuous—to have them stare coldly at *me*. But oh, Lord, I know where he wants to go, and I can't stand it any longer. Please give me the courage to lean across the aisle, force a smile and signal with my lips and my fingers: "Three more stops."

And now, oh, Lord, give me even more courage, for he has lurched over to my side. He wants to talk—talk in a loud, eager voice about the job he's going to apply for and why it's important that he get there on time.

Yes, yes, he's been drinking, and he probably won't get it, poor guy. But thank you that I'm able to listen, to offer a little encouragement and to see that he doesn't miss his stop.

Thank you for his grateful handclasp at parting, his smile from the platform, his jaunty yet wistful wave. Thank you that I no longer care what the other passengers think, because my conscience is at rest and my heart is warm.

Please help him, Lord, and bless him. And thank you for giving me the simple courage to be kind.

DON'T LET ME BE SO HARD ON MYSELF

Father, please don't let me be so impatient with myself.

I fret, I scold, I deplore my many shortcomings.

Why am I so messy? Why do I get myself into such complicated situations? Now why did I say *that*? Won't I ever learn?

My mind carries on an idiot monologue of self-reproach. Or I lie awake bewailing the day's mistakes. I wince before them. I call myself names I would never call other people. I am stung and tormented by these self-lacerations.

I know all this is useless. The more I berate myself the worse I seem to become.

And it gets between us. It is unworthy of the trust I should have in you who made me as I am, and who loves me despite my faults.

I know that you want me to be aware of them and to improve as best I can. But help me to forgive myself a little quicker, to be a little kinder to myself.

LET ME GO GENTLY

Let me go gently through life, Lord, so much more gently.

Right now, calm my exasperation as I try for the third time to get that telephone operator to respond. Let me sit gently, think gently, speak gently when the connection is made. (It may not be her fault. Or she may be young and new to the job . . . or older and troubled by the very same problems I have.)

Smooth my sharp edges of person and temper and tongue. Give me gentleness in dealing with people. Strangers like this, who are human too, subject to error and hurt. And gentleness with my family . . . Not softness, no—keep me firm—but gentle of voice instead of shrill. Gentle of movement and manner and touch.

When life frustrates me, delays me, I want to grab it and shake it and rush it on. Or when it comes bashing and battering at me, every impulse yells, "Fight back!" But all this is so destructive, it only wastes more time and burns up precious energy. Remind me that true strength lies in gentleness.

Help me to practice gentleness. In small inconveniences like this as well as large problems with those close to me. If I can just keep gentle, firm but gentle, then I'll be better able to meet life's major crises with dignity and strength.

Thank you for giving me gentleness, God.

"IF ONLY"

Please rescue me, God, from the "if onlys."

If only my husband was home more, helped more, would try to be more understanding . . . If only the children would mind, cooperate, pick up after themselves, study harder, do better in school . . . If only my neighbors were more congenial . . . If only my friends were more considerate . . .

Then—ah *then* I'd be a happier person, able to be more efficient, productive, make my life really count.

Please help me to stop this blaming of outside circumstances, Lord, and start taking myself in hand.

And this includes bidding good-bye to the "if onlys" that keep beckoning me to look back:

If only I'd gone on to graduate school instead of getting married . . . If only I hadn't had my first baby so soon . . . If only I had encouraged my husband to go into business for himself . . . or *hadn't* discouraged him from buying that land (it's worth a fortune now) . . . If only . . . If only . . .

Lord, I know there's nothing more futile than these "if onlys." None of life's choices are guaranteed. The "mistake" of the past may have been a godsend in disguise. And we will never know, so how can we ever judge?

Only one thing is sure—that what we did or didn't do then, or what other people do or don't do now, has very little bearing on me. My happiness today.

So help me to shape up, Lord. To face my problems without the crutch of "if onlys" I've been leaning on.

TALKING TO YOURSELF

They say talking to yourself is a sign of being nutty. Well then I enjoy being nutty and I'd go nuttier still if, when I'm alone, I kept all my lovely words locked away. Talking to myself helps keep my life in order. I'm my own best listener and I'm company for me. I have the best time talking to myself.

I talk to the dog, the cat. I talk to my plants and I often address even such objects as the oven or the piano or my false eyelashes: "Come on now, oven, get going if that roast is to be done by seven o'clock." "Don't feel bad, dear piano, I really love you, and I promise to have you tuned next week." As for what I say to my false eyelashes, especially when they won't go on straight—well, sometimes that's better left unsaid.

The dog's tail thumps in quick response to every word. The cat cuddles up, purring, or caresses my legs. Even the plants perk up at a few kind comments; scientists have proved that, even if I could not see it for myself. As for inanimate objects—immovable, solid, mostly voiceless— how do we know they don't respond in their own way? I like to imagine the oven's heart burns a bit more brightly, and the piano has a happier plink as I run a hand affectionately along its keys. Even eyelashes seem to behave if given a little fond coaxing or scolding.

Talking to myself helps keep my life in shape. I tell myself what I've go to do each day: "First, call the bank, and then the baker and order the cake for the party. Then be sure to put those clothes in the machine before you warm up the car."

I also take oral inventory before going anywhere: "Makeup kit, glasses, notebook, pencil, checkbook, change— and oh, yes, don't forget the slips for the cleaner's and the mail."

I frequently scold myself—especially after hanging up the phone: "What an idiot! Now why did you say THAT?"

And I praise myself, especially for deeds well done: "Gee, what a thrill to see the house looking so nice and clean. A lot of work but it was worth it, hooray for me!"

I sometimes comfort myself in secret when there's nobody else to do so: "Now don't feel bad, forget it, you did the best you could."

Thank goodness I'm not the only one who has this habit. If I were I'd think I was a little nuttier than I am. A lot of other people tell me they're unabashed self-talkers-to, too. Even if they didn't I'd guess it—just observe the lips engaged in solitary discourse in passing cars.

So if you're one of us, admit it. And welcome to the club.

HELP ME TO UNCLUTTER MY LIFE

Help me to unclutter my life, Lord.

Rescue me from this eternal confusion of belongings (mine and other people's) that just won't stay orderly. This suffocation of phone calls, clubs and committees. ("No man can serve two masters." you said. A woman is lucky if she *has* only two!) This choke of bills and papers and magazines and junk mail. I buy too many things, subscribe to too many things, belong to too many things. The result is such confusion I can't really enjoy or do justice to anything!

Deliver me from some of this, Lord. Help me to stop bewailing this clutter and work out some plan for cutting down.

Give me the will power to stop buying things we don't really need and that only become a chore to take care of. Give me more sales resistance when it comes to antique stores and white-elephant sales and supermarkets. And give, oh give me the will power to get rid of a lot of things we already have. To unclutter my cupboards and closets and attic of things hung onto too long.

And oh, Lord, help me to unclutter my life of too many

activities. Give me the self-discipline to stop joining things. And to weed out the organizations that don't really matter to me. (They'll be better off without me.) And the strength to say "No!" more often when the telephone rings.

Lord, show me a way of uncluttering my life even of too many people without being unkind. A way to love and help people without letting them gobble me alive.

There are so many dear, wonderful people I long to see, need to be with for my own soul's growth. Yet we are lost to each other because of this profligate squandering of energy and time. Give me the determination to reclaim these truly life-strengthening friends, at whatever cost to other idle, meaningless relationships.

And while I'm at it, Lord, help me to unclutter my mind. Of regrets and resentments and anxieties, of idiotic dialogues and foolish broodings. Sweep it clean and free. Make it calm and quiet. Make it orderly.

Put me in control of it as well as my house . . . and my calendar . . . and my harried spirit. Thank you. With your help I know I can triumph, I can unclutter my life.

THE STONING

Lord, I detest myself right now.

For I've just come from a luncheon where four of us spent most of our time criticizing a mutual friend. Her faults, her eccentricities, how extravagant and undependable she is. How she spoils her children, how vain and eager she always is to be attractive to men.

And though a lot of these things are true (Lord, they really are) I found myself wondering even as I joined in: Who are we to judge? Isn't every one of us guilty of at least some of the very same things? Was that why we attacked her with such relish? (Dear Lord, I'm so ashamed.) Because it made us feel a little bit better ourselves to brandish the defects of somebody so much "worse."

* * *

Well, I don't feel better about myself now. I keep thinking of what Jesus said to the men about to stone the adulterous woman: "Which of you is without sin?" Yet there we sat, self-righteous, stoning our sister with words.

How, Lord, can I make amends?

I long to call her up and beg her forgiveness, but that would be a terrible mistake. She would be so hurt, so much damage would be done. No, all I can do is to ask *your* forgiveness. And pray for her.

Help her, strengthen her, bless her. Don't let her ever know what we said about her, please.

And oh, Lord, put more compassion in my heart, guard my tongue. Don't let me ever again join in stoning a sister— or anyone—with words.

ORDER

I will trust the Lord to bring order into my life and into my house.

In his presence there can be no real chaos and confusion and dirt for he is peace and purity and order—and he is here.

He lives within these walls as he lives within my heart.

He sometimes stops me as I fret and struggle and scold, and says, "Don't be discouraged." He reminds me that we are all his untidy children, but he loves us all—even as I love these who cause me so much work.

As I move from room to room picking up other people's possessions, he reminds me how abundant is life that it strews in my family's path so many good things.

He bids me look out of the window and see the abundance of the fields, the woods, the water.

The very earth is strewn with the bright ownings and discards of its living things: sticks and branches and leaves, shells, snakeskins, nests and weeds, and feathers and flowers.

The very water carries these things on its breast. The wind blows them about.

Yet Mother Nature does not despair—no matter how many times she must do it all over.

He reminds me that back of everthing, governing all, is order. Absolute order.

I will trust the Lord to bring that order into my house.

LET NO JOB BE BENEATH ME

Thank you, God, for the wonderful gift of work. Humble work. Hard work. Brain work or back work or hand work.

I don't care much for lily-white brains and lily-white hands. I like brains that have been toughened and tried. I like backs that have been strengthened and even bent by their burdens.

I like hands that are tough, too—wrinkled from water, calloused and bruised from rocks and shovels and hammer and nails. I like hands and backs and brains that have wrestled with things, lifted and carried.

Thank you that my parents worked hard and taught their children to work hard.

Help me to remember that no job is beneath me, and with your help no job will be beyond me.

HOW CAN ANYONE BE BORED?

How can anyone possibly be bored?

So the children are grown and gone. Or you never had any children, and you've lost your life's partner. Or the job you had is over, you're retired. Whatever the reason, the days seem bleak and empty, time stretches before you like a vacuum you don't know how to fill. . . . In short, you're BORED.

But how is this possible if you are in reasonably good health, and have all your senses? How can anyone who LIVES be bored? There's so much in the world to be learned, so much in the world to do.

* * *

The ears alone offer so many lively paths to activity and enjoyment one couldn't take them all. Birds singing, for instance, (what a variety of little voices, what a medley of unique and vital tunes). Merely to learn about bird calls and their meaning could furnish an interest for years.

As for music! The infinite varieties of music to be listened to and understood. Blues. Jazz. Rock. Chamber music. Concertos, symphonies, Composers, performers.

When I consider the vast magical world of music and my own comparative ignorance, I am appalled. If I chose but the smallest segment of it to truly appreciate and master, there would not be enough time left in my life for its rewards. . . . While if I decide to create music myself—take up those long-abandoned violin lessons, start over from scratch on the piano, get the kinks and cobwebs out of my voice and sing in a choir.

And who can be bored who has eyes. Art, fine art is everywhere for those not too busy to be aware—from the masterpieces in an art gallery to those in your own backyard. Whether a Raphael madonna—or a young mother bending over her baby's stroller. . . . A Dutch landscape by Vermeer—or the scene from my kitchen window. . . . An abstract by Picasso—or a puddle on a cracked sidewalk, mirroring the sky.

All the art galleries to be visited. All the dances and dramas and films to be seen. . . . And all the books—the staggering number of books, past and present, to be read!

And if you can taste, if you can smell. If you enjoy food— if you can cook. How can meals ever be a bore? Who has enough hours to try all the exciting recipes in newspapers and magazines and the constant parade of new cookbooks? Or to take all the classes in the gourmet arts? Wine tasting, cheese making, exotic fondues and curries and pates. Not to mention the enticing possibilites of organic foods.

Or if you have hands. All the arts and crafts to be explored. Sewing and quilting and macrame. The painting, the sculpture, the ceramics. The gardening, the flower arranging. A myriad of skills that can be yours. How can these hands be idle when there is beauty to be created? Or when there is so much need? Need that cries out for a few days, even a few hours of someone's time.

Abused or abandoned children, the old, the helpless, the blind. Or the young who desperately need a friend. There is so much work to be done, and so many friends to be made, not only among those who need you, but those who are already helping!

How can anyone reach drearily for another cigarette or shuffle a deck of cards another pointless time? How can anyone possible be BORED?

I'M SHOWING MY AGE

Behold, thou hast made my days as it were a span long, and mine age is even as nothing in respect of thee.

Psalm 39:5

Oh, God, dear God, I'm showing my age.

I'm not young and beautiful any more, the way my heart imagines. When I look in the mirror I could cry. For I look just what I am—a woman growing older.

And I protest it, Lord. Perhaps foolishly. I am stricken.

"Vanity, vanity, all is vanity," the Bible says. But is vanity truly such a fault? You, who made women with this instinctive hunger to hang onto personal beauty, must surely understand.

Dear God, if this be vanity, let me use it to some good purpose.

Let it inspire me to keep my body strong and well and agile, the way you made it in the beginning. May it help me to stay as attractive as possible for as long as possible—out of concern for other people as well as myself. For you, who made women, also know that when we feel attractive we're a lost easier to live with.

But oh God, whatever happens to my face and body, keep me always supple in spirit, resilient to new ideas, beautiful in the things I say and do.

If I must "show my age" let it be in some deeper dimension of beauty that is ageless and eternal, and can only come from you.

Don't let me be so afraid of aging, God. Let me rejoice and reach out to be replenished; I know that each day I can be reborn into strength and beauty through you.

KEEP ME AT IT

God, give me due respect for the abilities you have given me.

Don't let me sell them short. Don't let me cheapen them. Don't let me bury my talents through indecision, cowardice, or laziness.

Plant in me the necessary determination. Keep me at it.

Rouse in me the fires of dedication. Keep me at it.

Give me the energy, strength, and will power to bring your gifts to their proper fruition. Keep me at it.

When I falter or fall lift me up and set me back on my destined path. Keep me at it.

Oh, God, when the way seems dark and there is no light there, plant at least one small signal fire at the end of the long black tunnel that I may keep plodding steadily forward toward it.

When friends laugh at me, keep me at it.

When people tempt me away from it, keep me at it.

When others scorn what I have produced, let me not be discouraged. Keep me at it.

When those who have tried and failed or who have never tried at all, those who are envious or indolent, when such people would hurt me by spiteful words or acts, let me not be bothered. Return me to my task. Keep me at it.

Let nothing really matter but these precious gifts you

have entrusted to me. For their sake let me be willing and proud to make the sacrifice. Keep me at it.

THE MISSING INGREDIENT

Lord, I have all the ingredients for happiness in my life. A lovely home, a wonderful husband. Children, friends, health. Why then is there such a sense of vacancy in me? Why this glum feeling of futility, even sometimes despair?

It's as if I keep expecting something glorious to happen that part of me is afraid is never *going* to happen. Some added flavor that's lacking, some challenge. Snug and safe and lucky (oh, so lucky) I press my disconsolate nose against the shining picture windows of my nest.

I want a parade to come by instead of just seeing kids climbing off a school bus. I want a limousine full of mysterious and exciting people to sweep up to the curb instead of a fuel-oil truck. I want the world to cry, "Come out, come out, you brilliant, beautiful thing! Why are you wasting yourself there?"

I want some glamor, some drama, some attention. I want to do something *important*.

I know, Lord—yes, yes, I know that making a home, raising a family *are* important. And that when the house is cold, better a fuel-oil man than a diplomat. So give me a sensible scale of values, give me patience.

But don't make me too sensible either. Don't give me too much patience. Maybe this is a "divine discontent" to keep me from getting sluggish, complacent. Maybe this hunger for some missing ingredient in my life is simply a way of telling me: "If you want something exciting to happen, you've got to *make* it happen." . . . Join a theater group or start one. Take a class or teach one. Find a job or create one. Sing, paint, write, dance. Help others who don't have the things I'm so blessed with and don't always appreciate.

Maybe you *meant* women like me to grow restless, in

order to give our full measure to a world that has been so good to us.

SELF-PITY

Lord, all night I lay awake consorting with self-pity.

Its idiot voice would not let me sleep. It entertained me with its chant of woes.

It pursued me into the pillow when I tried to bury my head. When I turned to the right it was there, insidiously smiling; when I turned to the left it perched upon my bed.

I thrust it aside but it would not leave me; it would not let me go. And though I finally slept, when I awoke this morning, it trailed me into the kitchen triumphant.

It was not satisfied that it had robbed me of rest; it wanted to sit beside me at breakfast, to tag me about all day. It pursues, it clutches at me still.

God, I am asking you to purge me of this awful companion now. I offer it up to you to do with what you will.

Take self-pity away. Banish it. Heal me of its scars.

Please put self-respect, and a vital glowing sense of the many marvels and blessings of my life in its place.

JUST FOR TODAY

Oh, God, give me grace for this day.

Not for a lifetime, nor for next week, nor for tomorrow, just for this day.

Direct my thoughts and bless them.

Direct my work and bless it.

Direct the things I say, and give them blessing too.

Direct and bless everything that I think and speak and do. So that for this one day, just this one day, I have the gift of grace that comes from your presence.

Oh, God, for this day, just this one day, let me live generously, kindly, in a state of grace and goodness that denies my many imperfections and makes me more like you.

TO WITNESS SUFFERING

Oh, God, this suffering ... to be helpless witness to another person's suffering.

It seems that my own I could bear more easily. At least I could cry out lustily, bloodily. I could wrestle it, fight it, put up a mighty battle.

But this—to be whole and strong, every sense vivid and vulnerable, and be forced to attend a love one's agony. To hear the cries and witness the struggle yet be powerless to put an end to it.

Or to have to be brave because the sufferer is so brave. To be cheerful when the heart is breaking. To live within sight and sound and touch of the endless suffering, essential to the victim's very existence.

I cry out against this sometimes, Lord. Even as I beg deliverance for the sufferer, or that some of these torments be put upon me instead. Why do you allow it? What earthly good is such suffering? And why have I been cast in this role?

Then I realize that you are not the author of suffering, but that you alone can take our suffering and turn it to some good purpose. What that purpose is I don't know, only that it *is*.

Surely for that reason you made me unusually strong, resilient, enduring. Able to comfort if only by not breaking down. Able to share some modicum of that strength.

Lord, when I think I can endure this no longer, let me remember those who did not flee the scene of the cross.

Help me to keep my vigil with suffering as courageously as they kept theirs.

THE BOX IN THE ATTIC

This box of college keepsakes, God. I don't know whether to laugh or cry, going through them. I don't know whether to wrap them up tenderly again or pitch them out.

The cups and medals so tarnished, the photographs of glory, hopelessly dated, poor things. And these dry, faded flowers . . . how could I ever have thought their colors would last? They're ghost flowers now. This whole box is filled with nothing but ghost memories, ghost promises . . .

The speaking contests won. The plays when everybody said I had so much talent, ought to go to New York, become a star. Here are some of the old programs, here is the dusty velvet costume I wore as Desdemona. I hold it up forlornly, half amused, half guilty—I couldn't even get into it any more!

"Promises, promises," as the saying goes. Promises unfulfilled. And I wonder—have I failed life, Lord? Or has life failed me?

Or has there been any failure at all?

How do I know I'd ever have gotten to Broadway, if I'd tried? Or become a star? Or been any happier if I had? And isn't the role I'm playing now just as important as any I'd have there? (The work is steadier, that's sure, and the rewards, though less spectacular, are surely a lot more lasting.)

So I wonder, trying to sort out this box in the attic, what should I be feeling—regret, or relief? Should I weep for my wasted talents, or should I be thankful that I've avoided the grim old-fashioned work and heartbreak it takes to succeed on the stage? (Not that there isn't plenty of that in being a wife and mother! And I *am* a star . . . well, anyway a co-star of this family.)

Yet something nags at me yet, Lord. A restlessness I can't rationalize away. These tarnished, tattered, faintly ludicrous souvenirs—they are a kind of mute accusing testimony. I did have talent once. And talent is precious, talent means responsibility. Like that story in the Bible, when you give somebody talent you don't expect it to be buried.

Have I buried my talent, Lord, or only put it away for safe-keeping? Surely there are places where I can use my talent still. And for better purposes now than just to satisfy my own ambition. Surely, without neglecting anybody, I can find outlets right here—little theater, coaching children, helping out with plays for charity.

I can't repolish the loving cups, let out the costumes, refurbish these souvenirs. But I can polish up my own gifts, let out my own horizons, reactivate *me!* Instead of mooning over past triumphs, I can get going on tomorrow's.

Thank you, Lord, for leading me to this box of keepsakes in the attic.

I'M TIRED OF BEING STRONG

Forgive me, Lord, but I'm tired of being some of the things I've tried so hard to be.

I'm tired of being so capable, so efficient. I'm tired of the compliment, "If you want to get something done ask a busy person." (Guess who?)

I'm tired of being considered so patient and understanding that people dump their troubles (and their kids) on me.

I'm tired of being so cheerful. I want to be free to be cross and complain and not get a "buck up, old girl," routine. I'm tired of being my husband's faithful partner and helpmate instead of his playmate.

I'm tired of being considered so independent, so strong.

Sometimes, at least sometimes, Lord, I want to be weak and helpless, able to lean on somebody, able to cry and be comforted.

Lord, I guess there are just times when I want to be a little girl again, running to climb on my mother's lap.

FORGIVING MEANS FORGETTING

I don't find it too hard to forgive, Lord—what's hard is to forget.

When someone is truly sorry I think, "Yes, yes, I forgive you." Just to have the estrangement over, to be relieved of the awful pain of being parted even mentally from someone I love. In sheer self-protection I think I "forgive."

But the memory remains. Deep, buried deep inside me, the deed or the word still lives. And it rises sometimes to taunt me, to wreck the peace I've achieved.

Why, Lord? Why do these memories linger?

Is it because I've forgiven for the wrong reasons? Selfish reasons. Not genuine compassion and love and charity for the other person and his human frailties, but for myself. Me—me—*me*. Because I can't stand to be so hurt.

Help me to change this, Lord. Make me strong enough to forgive people out of love rather than a mere frantic desire to ease my own wounds. Forgive so wholly, fully, in such a flood there is no room for nagging memories.

Thank you for teaching me to forgive this way. True forgiving means forgetting.

POSSESSIONS

Help me not to put too much stock in possessions, Lord. Mere possessions.

I want things, sure I want things. Life seems to be a continual round of wanting things, from the first toys we fight over as children, on through our thrilled counting of the wedding presents . . . Not primarily love and friends and pride in what we can do, but *things*.

Sometimes I'm ashamed of how much I want things. For my husband and the house and the children. Yes, and for myself. And this hunger is enhanced every time I turn on the TV or walk through a shopping mall. My senses are tormented by the dazzling world of *things*.

Lord, cool these fires of wanting. Help me to realize how futile is this passion for possession. Because—and this is what strips my values to the bone—one of my best friends died today in the very midst of her possessions.

The beautiful home she and her husband worked so hard to achieve, finally finished; furnished the way she wanted it, with the best of everything . . . The oriental rugs she was so proud of. The formal French sofas. The paintings. The china and glass and handsome silver service . . . She has been snatched away, while silently, almost cruelly, they remain.

Lord, I grieve for my friend. My heart hurts that she had so little time to enjoy her things. Things she had earned and that meant so much to her. But let me learn something from this loss:

That possessions are meant to enhance life, not to become the main focus of living. That we come into the world with nothing, we leave with nothing.

Help me not to put too much stock in mere possessions.

I MUST DEPEND ON MYSELF

Thank you, Lord, that there are so many people I can depend on for so many things. My husband and children. My neighbors and friends. The people with whom I work. I know I can count on any one of them—most of the time, at least—to do things for me, often without being asked. Just as they know they can count on me to help them.

But there is another person I must learn to depend on even more, Lord: *Myself*. You gave each of us areas of life where we *can't* lean on anybody else.

Nobody else can do our exercises, stick to our diets, study our courses, take our exams. Nobody else can read or write our books, sing our solos, dream our dreams, execute our plans. Nobody else can get our lives organized, productive and moving in the direction of our goals.

In short, Lord, no other person can keep my promises—to others or to me. For that, all that, I've got to depend on myself.

Help me to remember this. God, give me belief in myself and the will power to act on that belief. Thank you for gradually guiding me into habits that fortify that faith, so that at the end of each day I can realize: "I didn't let me down. I did what I promised myself!"

And even when I undertake too much, set my sights too high, project goals a little beyond my reach, help me not to get discouraged. Rather, to realize that delay doesn't mean defeat. Despite a hundred detours, I will keep driving in the right direction.

I will not quit. I will keep my commitments.

Thank you for giving me a clear, honest awareness of this, God, and the courage to live by that truth. Make me always able to depend on myself.

AN AMERICAN WOMAN'S PRAYER

Thank you, God. First and foremost that I'm a woman. What's more, an American woman—that luckiest of all possible beings. For nowhere else in the whole wide world could I be so respected, so cherished, so privileged (some people call it downright spoiled) and yet so free.

Thank you that I can vote or run for office (and win too). That I can marry or not, have children or not, work or not, and it's nobody's business but my own; there's nobody really to stop me but me.

Thank you that, although discrimination dies hard (men have run your world so long, God, and forgive me but you made men proud and slow to change), no doors are really closed to me. I can be a doctor—surgeon, dentist, vet. I can be a lawyer, I can be a judge. I can dance, swim, act—be an artist, drive a truck, umpire a baseball game. I can work in forests or harvest fields as well as offices if it suits me.

But, dear Lord, how I thank you that my government doesn't *make* me do any of these things. I can stay home and be a wife and mother if I please. I can be my own boss as I cook and sew and chase the kids and clean. (And while I'm at it, thank you for the marvelous conveniences that make keeping house in America easier than anyplace else on earth.)

Thank you, God, for the prosperity and plenty of this incredible country. The abundance of our resources—coal and oil and water and grain, and human energy and skill. For you know how hard we've worked to get where we are.

Unlike the skeptical hireling of the parable, we didn't just bury the gifts you gave us, but plowed and sowed and sweat and made them bear fruit. And then, with arms and hearts overflowing, we rushed to the whole world's aid.

Thank you that we inherited not only our forefathers' and mothers' achievements but their generosity, their willingness to share. That never in all our history have we turned our back on another nation in need.

Thank you, God, that my children were born in this remarkable land. *Born free.* Daughters as well as sons, just as free as I am to do with their lives what they will.

Oh, help us truly to value that freedom, God, and guard it well. Don't let us take it for granted. Don't let us become weak, soft, vulnerable. So afraid of being considered old-fashioned, so eager to be sophisticated, modern, that we play into the hands of those who would take it away.

Don't let us discount it, downgrade it. And dear God, make us just as quick to praise our country's virtues and triumphs and blessings as we are to criticize. For who can do his best—man, woman, child or nation—if no credit is ever forthcoming? No appreciation—only blame?

Help us to stop criticizing *ourselves* so much, God. Restrain our own breast beating. Help us to remember that no nation since the beginning of time has ever had even half the freedom and advantages we enjoy.

Light in us fervent new fires of patriotism, Lord.

Patriotism. A word of passionate honor in almost every country except the one that deserves it so much! Make us proud to be American patriots once again. Willing to shout our heritage from the housetops. Let us thrill once more to the sight of our star-spangled banner. May it fly from every flagpole, be honored in every schoolroom. Let us and our children pledge our allegiance to it wherever Americans gather, and sing the words of its anthem with love and thanksgiving.

Oh, Lord, dear Lord, remind us: We are so *lucky* to be Americans. And I'm so lucy to be an American woman.

God Love

TO LOVE, TO LABOR

I am trying to find God.

Secretly, desperately, so many busy people are trying to find God. But we can't, we think we can't because we *are* so busy. Going to church to worship God takes time (precious time when we need to rest from all our busyness); meetings to talk about God take time. Prayers and meditation take time. . . . Peace, leisure, quiet . . . let me alone, give me a vacation away from my job and the family, let me walk along the seashore, climb a mountain, camp in the solitude of a forest. There I'll find God waiting and I can relax and say, "At last. I've been dying to meet you, have you over, come in!"

But the people of life keep clambering all over us, the business of life won't let us escape. Or if solitude, long postponed, is somehow achieved, are we comfortable with this stranger, God, are we sure he's even there?

No, no, if I am to know him, truly know him, neither of us can wait. What then? Take God along to work? *That* rat race? Absurd. Work is the result of God's enemy. Weren't Adam and Eve happy playing in the Garden (and walking and talking with God) until Satan ruined everything? They were driven out for their folly, and their punishment was to labor: "In the sweat of thy face shalt thou eat bread, till thou return unto the ground . . ." (Gen. 3:19).

So labor became a fact of life. The most important fact, actually, for most of us must work to survive. And work can indeed be punishment: work you detest, work that seems to be leading nowhere. But punishment is generally meant not to damage but to strengthen us. And that long-ago Lord of our beginnings knew it: No more handouts, no more child-like idling. . . . Toil, sweat, achieve, *grow.* . . . I made you, now make something of yourselves.

Back of that eviction curse lurked a blessing. The Creator was doing us all a favor, he was enriching the whole human race.

How glorious that you drove man from the Garden, God. How wise of you, how glorious! You saw that they would not have been complete in the Garden, undeveloped as children, playing children's games. You foresaw that they wouldn't have been happy, for there is no real joy in idleness, no challenge, no satisfaction.

Until they were forced to labor, procreate and labor, they could never become true people. Living, breathing, striving people, able to taste fruits far more sweet than that first forbidden apple: the fruits of their labor.

You gave them—and us—the gift of sweat, the salty baptism of our own toil. You gave us the sweetness of rest after a hard day's work. You gave us the satisfaction of accomplishment, the joy of a job well done. And you gave us goals, the dream of greater achievements to come.

And you foresaw that only in labor can there be love, true

love. Man for woman, woman for man, and both of them for their children.

For we labor for those we love. And love sweetens that labor and the labor cements that love.

I can't imagine a world without work. Surely it would be an empty, meaningless world. A world without God in it.

THE TREES

We seek you in people, God. We try to find you in churches; we hunt you diligently in books. And all the while your reality is everywhere around us, simply awaiting recognition. Your messages are written in the landscape if we'll only look.

Brother Lawrence, the seventeenth-century monk who left such a beautiful legacy in his *Practice of the Presence of God*, was converted by the mere sight on a midwinter day "of a dry and leafless tree standing gaunt against the snow; it stirred deep thoughts within him of the change the coming spring would bring. From that moment on he grew and waxed strong in the knowledge and love and favor of God."

Years ago in suburban Philadelphia . . . my tree. A great oak whose branches scraped the attic window where I had fixed up a cubby with books and papers. My cozy high retreat. There I could sometimes flee when the storms of life seemed almost too much to bear. . . . Lie across the couch "having a good bawl," as my mother used to say. Grappling with a woman's private agonies . . . Mine, rejection slips piled as high as the dishes in the sink . . . The daily tearing asunder as children, desperately loved, wove maddeningly in and out of my study with their tears and little treasures and demands . . . A husband I was lucky to see once or twice a week . . . And now this—after three years of editorial encouragement and personal sacrifice, the return of the novel that would (I thought) solve everything.

Rain pouring down to match my tears . . . The plaintive screech and scratch across the glass, then tap-tap-tap as if something was begging to come in . . . Go fling up the window, break off the offending branch. Yet there with the coldness on my face, something held me. Some majesty of motion—this greater thing than I swaying and keening and uttering its own cries into the wind. Its permanence spoke to me, its great age. It had lived long before me and would go on living, no doubt, long after I was gone. Blind, deaf, unfeeling, how could it know anything about me? And yet it spoke to me, comforted me in a way I could not articulate.

Later, when it was dark, I remember going down and putting on a son's old hooded mackinaw and creeping out in the rain to embrace the tree. Self-dramatics? Maybe. But I wanted to put my arms around its great girth, feel its bark against my cheeks. It had something to give me no human being could. Just what, I didn't know. Only that it stirred in me some deep sense of protection and faith. God, my long-neglected God, had created that tree.

If he could do that, he could do anything! He could look after me.

These moments of awareness, Lord. These powerful moments of conviction. Why can't we hang on them? Why do we let them slip away?

Yet they are not in vain. Looking back, we remember them with a kind of puzzled wonder. Looking forward, even during the times when we feel hopelessly lost and groping, something tells us they will come again.

And if we will listen, truly look and listen, there is no stopping them. They will happen over and over.

They will happen now!

God has so much to say to us through the trees. Lie on your back and read his eolquent sermons in the trees. . . .

A chill but sun-gilded February day. I stretch out on a wooden bench in the yard and gaze up at the sky. And all about me rise the trees, naked, stripped, revealed. They are like nude dancers stretching . . . stretching . . . glorying in their lovely bones. How incredibly tall they are and how straight they grow. The trunks in almost every cluster soar unswerving toward the sky, as if intent upon their goal. Yet their branches reach out . . . out . . . a little uplifted as if in adoration or rejoicing. They are in an attitude of dancing or of prayer. And I see that they are open, so very open, as if to give and to receive.

What blessings pour down upon those grateful arms. Sun and wind and snow and rain and lightening wings. They are merry with squirrels; and at night they wear stars in their fingers.

They are open for giving as well. They are lively with birds, they hold their nests for safekeeping. Soon these outstretched arms will be bursting with buds and flowers and leaves. They will spread their fragrance and their shade. Nuts will rain down from the generous arms, fruit will clot their branches and be claimed by other arms, unpreaching. Or the fruit will fall by its very abundance, too much for the boughs, so richly receiving and giving, to contain.

And it is all a matter of the sturdy central trunk, undiverted on its skyward journey, yet accompanied, always accompanied by these happy, open, spreading arms. . . .

The design—the perfect design for tree or man. To be strong in central purpose, heading toward the destination meant for us, but open, always open to give and to receive.

WHY AM I WORKING HERE?

This work you have given me, God. This job I seem doomed, at least right now, to do.

Why do I hate it sometimes, struggle so against its demands? Why do I so often drag myself to the appointed place and anticipate the day I must spend there as a form of penalty?

Why does it sometimes seem unworthy of me and the abilities you have given me? . . . Is this true, Lord? *Is* it unworthy, or am I unworthy of it?"

Help me sort out these confusions, God. To recognize, in

a very practical, earthy sense, why I am performing this particular service during this particular time of my life upon the earth, and if it is really what you want me to do.

For I must find you in my work. Work is a part of life. You are a part of life—the very source of these hands, these feet, this brain.

Whether I am scrubbing a floor, pounding a typewriter, fixing a car, digging a mine, operating a machine . . . whether I am coping with personnel problems or an unruly classroom . . . I am earning my keep upon this planet. I am paying my way in human coin. And quietly, inflexibly back of the whole design, you are.

Is this seemingly empty, disagreeable labor a time of humbling? To show me I am of the selfsame stuff as my brothers and sisters—no worse, no better?

I, too, can lift and carry, argue, cope, hurt, get dirty, do things I dislike or things I consider beneath my so-called dignity.

Am I being tried for self-denial? Self-control? Am I being tested for appreciation? To be thankful that I have the means to earn my daily bread, and the ability to see its small but sure rewards (the shining floor . . . the ledgers that balance . . . the children progressing . . . the nuggets of coal).

Or is this a time of training, Lord? Of preparation for more vital challenges ahead? Of learning—every day, hour by hour, even though I can't see it—the skills and qualities I'm going to need?

This I know, Lord. This much I know and must remember: Nothing is wasted. Nothing is fruitless—no work that you give us to do. If it is of you—decent work, honorable work, work that helps mankind in any way instead of harming it—then that work is effective.

It affects my life's development, body and soul. And it affects everyone around me. My family; the people who work beside me. And all the younger lives it touches, they are marked by my work, too.

Help me to realize this fact, to accept it and even glory in it. For now, for now, for as long as you really want to use me in this manner . . . But let me always be open to change. Alert for the voice that calls, "Come! You're ready for something else." Hopefully, something better. But at least the next step on the ladder of my life.

Until that time comes, I am resolved to return to my job rejoicing.

Giving more to it.
Getting more out of it.
Learning more from it.
And thanking you.

SIGHT ON A MOONLIT ROAD

The leaves are still frail and new, a tremulous green dusting upon these tall old trees. And just below them the dogwoods are a delicate white mist of bloom. Only a red suggestion of buds a few days ago, now the flat, faintly cupped petals are upheld, like some display of precious china in a jeweler's window.

The moon enhances their translucent purity. The very roadway, dark by day, is white with its flooding.

The black and white dog bounding along ahead has a luminous quality. And the cat, which has slipped out and pats silently behind, is also shining. White face and paws echo the Dalmatian's spotted body in tinier dots that weave through the shadows. Like little floating stars or petals in the fragrant chirping night.

A utility pole beside the road is illuminated too, its black spear and crossbar moon-rimmed. Turning, I see its startling shadow lying across the moon-white road.

A cross! A leaning cross, moon-etched. Tender, graceful,

and not really sad. Only poignant. A poignant reminder of suffering. The Lord's suffering and triumph. All human suffering and triumph.

A moving sight on a moonlit roadway.

A POTATO

I am peeling a potato.

What a homely thing it is, this lumpy ellipse in my hand. Brown, earth-brown, with the dust of the earth clinging to it. Yet as my knife strips away its humble skin, how moistly pure and white it is inside. Solid yet succulent, rich with the nourishment drawn from the darkness in which it lay.

Contrasts—all these contrasts. The light and the dark, the buried and the risen. The continuing miracle ready to spring from the ordinary things of everyday . . . How amazing this is. What secret treasures the silent soil holds. And how little we have to know and be to tap them . . . A potato! This potato.

If I were to save even a chunk of it, a piece with an eye in it, and bury it, it would become another plant bursting forth with leaves and flowers to inform me when it was ready, that it had flung about it hidden nuggets to be dug. Offering me more potatoes than I would need for a week . . . Such abundance!

And such magic. That this mealy whiteness soon to feed my family emerged from the mute black stuff beneath my feet. Dirt, plain dirt. Dirt that we get on our shoes and are forever trying to drive out of our houses. Low, common, spurned, yet vital to the whole life plan, and during this existence, at least, never to be escaped. It upholds me every step I take. And though I may fly from it by plane and flee from it by boat, it is the substance to which I must always return. I am earthbound. Chains of gravity hold me to the earth, and the even more powerful chain of life itself. Its grains and its grasses feed me, and so do its trees with their nuts and fruit. Except for fish, every creature that nourishes me likewise must draw its own nourishment from the earth. While deep in its body it carries fuels to warm me, minerals and elements to build and serve me in a thousand ways.

Scientists in their laboratories might be able to duplicate synthetically all its elements. They can and have made artificial substances in which things will grow. Yet what of the organisms that exist in that soil, the microbes, the bacteria, the bugs and worms? Even a teaspoon of soil. A thimbleful, a pinch. In *The Secret Life of Plants* the authors tell how the famous oceanographer William Beebe occupied himself during a long sea journey by analyzing a small bag of earth mold. "And found in it over five hundred separate specimens of life. He believed that more than twice that many remained to be identified."

Soil squirms and breathes and lives, it draws life into itself and gives life back.

And so—this potato . . . Brown with the same earth from which human beings came, and the earth to which we must return.

I think of Genesis. First two chapters. Turn the fire low and read them. . . . The simplicity. The absolute directness and purity of the story of creation. God so busy about his monumental task:

> *And the earth was without form, and void; and darkness was upon the face of the deep.*

Try to imagine. I can't. But God (or something) imposed order. Brought light, divided night from day and sea from land.

> *And let the dry land appear: and it was so.*

> *And God called the dry land Earth; and the gathering together of the waters called he Seas; and God saw that it was good.*

> *And God said, Let the earth bring forth grass, the herb yielding seed, and the fruit tree yielding fruit after his kind, whose seed is in itself, upon the earth: and it was so.*

And the earth brought forth grass, and herb yielding seed after his kind, and the tree yeilding fruit, whose seed was in itself, after his kind: and God saw that it was good.

There is something very tender and moving about that. Someone, or something, wanted things to be so right for us. Everything in readiness and plenty of it—so much, so much. And when every last thing had been done, he took a bit of dust from the ground:

and breathed into his nostrils the breath of life; and man became a living soul.

I once dismissed all this as a pretty myth. But only out of my own ignorance and futility, my helplessness to understand. I tried to replace it with formulas and theory (I didn't understand those either, but I thought they sounded more intelligent). Now I see that it is really more intelligent to acknowledge the marvel as simply beyond understanding. But that someone or something indeed "saw that it was good." Not chaos but order. Not poisonous but life-sustaining. And the most remarkable creation of all emerged from the mystery: man with his mind and his choices and his indestructible soul.

There is something tender and moving, too—and to me almost funny—that this Creator chose the dirt for our source. Why not a drop of water or the petal of a flower? Nothing so delicate or aesthetic—no, a bit of the rich yet humble dust! . . . So I am akin to this potato and everything that grows. For this dust, this very dust that I am rinsing away right now, provides all the building stuff of my body. And when that body is no more use, it will return to the ground.

Strange.

Allegorical language has a way of distilling and preserving deep instinctive truths. We speak of the good earth, Mother Earth. And we call god our Father. The one who created this earth and richly seeded her to produce this whole family I belong to—the family of man. We are indeed children of the earth, as we are children of our earthly parents. And all this makes us children of God.

THE GARDEN

This is my garden, God, this is my garden, my own small precious portion of the earth that you have made.

I will dig and hoe and tend it, I will grub in the soil that is cool and moist and scented with spring.

I will find you in that soil as I crumble its clods or press these small seeds deep into its dark flesh.

What a joyful thing, the feel of your silent soil. It clings to my fingers, it is hard and certain beneath my knees.

It receives my little offerings—these tiny plants, these slips and cuttings, these infinitesimal seedlings, with a kind of blind, uncommenting magnificence. I am a trifle awed before it, I am filled with an amused humility.

How insignificant I am that I should be entrusted with this miracle to come. No, no, the earth will surely reject my anxious efforts, my foolish hopes. Yet I know a happy patience too. Wait—only wait upon the Lord, as the Bible says.

And sure enough. The silent, teeming forces of creation set to work, and soon the miracle has come! Onions and lettuce for the table. Shrubs to be trimmed. The incredible colors and fragrances of flowers.

I think of that first garden where life began.

I think of that final garden where Christ prayed. ("In my father's house are many mansions," he said. I feel sure that among those mansions there are many gardens too.)

How marvelous that man's existence—and woman's—began in a garden. Perhaps that's why we feel so wonderfully alive in a garden. And so close to you.

NEEDLEWORK PRAYER

Thank you for the joy of needlework, Lord. Though I sometimes wonder why I do it. All this time and money to fashion something I could buy far more easily . . . A canvas already painted, an already-woven cover or cushion or rug.

Yet here I sit perserving, inching toward the dream. Drawing these strands of color in and out, watching my own living fingers create the scene.

What deep secret drive impels me, Lord? So that I keep returning to my task, and when it is finished begin anew.

A love of beauty, yes, and the thrill of creating beautiful things. But more, For as I stitch away I feel *in* love, not only with this, my chosen pattern, but people too. My family, my friends, those who will eventually see this work and perhaps love it as well. But in a deeper sense—I love you.

I think of you whose canvas is the universe, and how tirelessly you make it beautiful for us. How you neddlepoint the sky with stars, and cover the earth with fine little stitches of green. How you embroider the fields and flowers, and petit-point the beaches with sand and shells, I think of the brilliant, ever-changing tapestry of the trees.

Thank you for all this loveliness, Lord. For its patient artistry. When I take up my needle and thread the bright yarn, I feel very close to you.

THE COWS

I don't need to seek God in nature, for he is there. Every sunrise testifies to his presence, every rainfall, every flower. It is impossible to stand by the sea and watch the waves rolling in without being almost overcome by a sense of his wonder, or see the wind lashing the trees without feeling his power.

And in nature I have learned lessons about God's own nature. They are written in the landscape, they are hidden yet ready to be discovered in the flight of birds or the very stance of trees. And secrets have been unlocked for me simply by observing his creatures, some of the answers to the eternal riddles of existence have been revealed.

I began to understand free will (at last!) on a creek bank

one day, watching the cows. Five or six stood cooling themselves in the water, jaws busy, eyes bland. What a fixed stare cattle have. A kind of blank brooding. Their tails kept flicking flies off their backs, their jaws never ceased their silent rhythms. As we first approached, a couple of them emitted blasts of sound that sent the children scurrying. (A cow's moo is not a gentle thing, and musical only in stories.) Now they simply stood regarding me where I had stretched out on an army blanket.

The children were off trying to catch crawdaddies in a can. I lay alone resting, reading, gazing into the sky or returning the empty stare of the cows. . . . Overhead, clouds coasted, a hawk wheeled, and to the west I could glimpse a V of geese and faintly hear their honking. . . . How free the geese, I thought, how earth-bound and fated the cows.

Other birds called from the trees. What were they saying? I wondered. And what message had there been in the bellow of the cows? . . . Poor cows, blatting their foolish protests, now resignedly silent. Cows to be milked morning and night, or herded onto trucks and hauled of for slaughter. How sad to be a cow. If I had to be another creature and could choose, I'd join the wild geese flying. How free, how free! . . . But wait, the geese aren't free either. They fly always in formation and to certain feeding grounds at certain seasons. And their entire vocabulary is limited to that honking I hear faintly, thrillingly now. How sad to be a goose, speech-deprived.

And it occurs to me that human beings are the only creatures equipped with words. Why? Why were all the marvels of language reserved for us alone?

These cows. These birds. Not only the geese but the bobolinks singing from the pasture grasses, the turtle doves mourning, the other little voices chipper or sleeping in the trees . . . They are telling each other something, no doubt, they are expressing something. For almost every creature, bird or beast, has a voice with which to court, proclaim hunger, anger, fear, pain, and joy. And so, in a small and limited way they can communicate with each other and with us.

Yet they have no vocabulary, there is no way with which they translate their thoughts, if thoughts they have. They can't read, they can't write. They miss the entire experience of books and poetry and plays. . . . These books I have brought with me, to read or not. A cow couldn't choose; a bird could only peer over my shoulder, a butterfly poise on the pages, not understanding. Why should they? They have no need for the secrets locked in those letters.

The alphabet. Such a tiny package, less than a handful of letters to reveal such vast treasures: Words! Millions of words, not only in my own language but in the languages of the world. All but a few use this same alphabet. This magical key which I, as a person, own as a birthright and can use to my heart's delight. For I have been given the mind to understand it; and I have the sole choice what I shall speak, what I shall read, what I shall learn.

I can turn my back on knowledge and move dumbly through life like a cow, or I can open books and become transported in time and space. I can learn anything I want to in the whole wide world.

So as I lie in the shade beside that stream contemplating our differences—the cows' and mine, the birds' and mine—it dawns on me that herein lies the answer to something that long has troubled me: free will. In creating us as independent beings and sending us into life equipped with one simple tool God indeed made us "only a little lower than the angels." With dominion over the animals—and over ourselves.

That's it. That's got to be it!

For the animals aren't free. "Free as the birds," we say. Yet these very geese, flying in formation, are driven toward their destination by forces beyond their control. The bright singers in the trees—all, all function not from choice but from instinct. Even animals still living in the wild have been programmed to their ways, they needn't choose. Creatures of every other kind are trapped, usually within a single environment, during their brief life-span. Even their journeys, if they make them, are performed by instinct rather than choice, or by the choice of man. Animals can have neither dreams nor aspirations. They can't decide to work or not, or choose between the jobs they have (not even beavers or bees or ants). They can't invent things to make life easier. They can't benefit themselves by education; if they are trained at all, it is by man, and for the use and pleasure of man.

By comparison, how free we are. Trapped between birth and death, yes, but able to make so many choices in between. To do with our lives what we will. Average people—in a free society where there are no human dictators to force us—we can work where we please at whatever we please, marry whom we please, travel wherever we want.

Laws impose a few limits on us, there are social limits of our own devising, and we consider ourselves limited sometimes by lack of money or by the environment that seems wrong for us. But there is no force in existence that keeps us from breaking those limits, even of law. Unlike the animal kingdom, our Creator gave us free will. We can be as good or as bad as we want. As wise or as ignorant. We are free to move about and try things, accepting, rejecting, shaping the pattern of our days.

And when we are tempted to ask why God doesn't step in and intervene to spare us wars and murders and rapes, all the misfortunes that befall us, we must not forget that such intervention would be bought at the cost of forgoing our greatest gift of all.

We would then become as the animals. Free and yet not free. Free from the bother of making choices, from the penalties involved when we err. But herded about like cattle, dumb and wordless about our fate. Isn't it better, surely, to write the story of our own lives in a language freely given us? Our follies, our mistakes, the countless times of anguish caused by our very choices—surely even these are better than to live the bland life of a beast.

And this, too, has drawn me even closer to a personal reasoning God. If I could conceive of a universe populated only by animals—yes, it might possibly be considered some kind of mysterious, still awesome accident. . . .

* * *

But the fact that we, too, are here, Lord, your people thinking, speaking, laughing, choosing, falling, rising, loving—that can be no accident. Thank you for creating us in your image, releasing us on this remarkable planet with complete freedom to live the lives you have given us.

MUSIC

Let me try to imagine a world without music. What if you'd given us such a world, God?

Not a silent world necessarily. Let it have the usual noises—sound of voices, pound of feet, bark of dogs . . . roar of engines, click of dishes and pans . . . bang of hammers and typewriter keys and doors. A busy, efficient world but a world without song . . . I can't bear it, the very concept is sad!

Not even bird song? No, this world empty of music would have to forgo even the belling and trilling of birds; only those with raucous cries could remain. . . . Not even a human whistler? No, because it's hard to whistle even at a girl without musical notes creeping in. Factory whistles, yes, calling people to work. Police whistles, traffic whistles, sirens—whistles for duty and danger. Shrill mechanical whistles—but no human whistles because when a person whistles he or she is glad.

And gladness would have little place in a world bereft of music. We would survive, I suppose. We would eat and sleep and work and mate and die. But would we love? Would we rejoice? Would we grieve? Would we be moved to acts of heroism or even acts of kindness? Would we achieve? . . . How could we? Why should we? For music is such an emotional thing. And doesn't everything in life circle round and round and in and out of us in rhythmic patterns of emotion?

Music stirs us, inspires us, uplifts our spirits or depresses them sometimes. ("Turn that off, it's too sad, I can't stand it!") Music charges our energies, our loyalties, our sense of pride—in a nation or a football team. (The flag is flying, here they come, listen to the band!) Music is "the food of love." We flirt to music, fall in love to music, dance, dream, and marry to music. From the lullabies sung at the cradle, to the taps that hurt so terribly, yet somehow make it all seem so right at the grave, music is inextricably entangled with our emotions. An outward expression of things we feel so deeply yet can't articulate.

How can anything so exquisite, so beautiful and powerful come from any source except the mysterious source of us all?

Come on somebody, show me. Dig up some proof, evolutionist; present me with some fact that will explain music. When and where in the meticulous selectivity of the species did music first begin? What manner of man first felt song sitrring in his heart? Who or what put that yearning there and why? Who gave him the skill to express it? And where do the melodies come from?

Why the infinite variations, multiple as the stars, so that if you composed for a million years you could never exhaust the supply? . . . But no, there's no use trying to grasp the why and how of music, it is the most elusive art of all. A painting or piece of sculpture can be felt and touched. A book you can hold in your hand and read. But music?

Listen! . . . It comes to you across the hill, someone singing and playing. . . . It pours through your house from unseen sources (too many sometimes). . . . It may seem visible to you as the violinist moves his bow, the tympanist beats his drums, yet they are only the instruments; shut your eyes and you hear it in all its glory still. Even when you look at the score, you see only diagrams that the musician translates into these marvelous sounds. Sounds that somebody else first heard in his head . . . How come? Why did he hear them in the first place, and from where? And why, once these silent "sounds" have been set down on paper (and who can explain *that* transition?) and transposed by voice or instrument into what we call music, why should these sounds have an effect on *me*?

No, no, the mystery is too much. I give up, I can find no

other soruce for it but God. No other *reason*. God must have given us music to sweeten life with its burdens, to give us an extra dimension for sharing life's emotions. Otherwise what *good* is it? And if it is good, then it is of God.

There must have been music before creation. (The music of the spheres). There must have been music at the dawn of creation. And when man woke up and found himself upon the earth, I believe he must have heard the birds already singing and uttered his first song. And instinctively he must have reached out for a reed or stick with which to fashion an instrument to enhance and enlarge that song; to express greater feelings than his whistling lips or limited throat could.

The Bible is full of singing and playing . . . of lutes and timbrels and tabrets, of drums and flutes and harps and lyres. "The Jewish nation was a nation of musicians," says Henri Daniel-Rops. They must have music. Music to celebrate harvests and victories and feasts and weddings, music to mourn the dead. And to worship, ah, to worship! . . . David and his psalms. He could never have written those immortal words without the music that accompanied them, and he sang them to both Jehovah and King Saul. . . . The songs of Solomon could only have been born to music, and how much richer our heritage would be if we could know their original tunes. Music pulsates through the whole marvelous, fantastic story of man civilized and otherwise. Pagan, Jew or Christian, Moslem, Buddhist, Hindu, or American Indian, whatever the religion, music enables mortals to call out to the heavens from which we come. To make contact with our Creator. Music is the bridge sublime.

Isn't it significant that angels sang to announce the birth of Christ? "And suddenly with the angel there was a great throng of the heavenly host, praising God and singing: 'Glory to God in the highest heaven, and peace to men . . .'" (Luke 2:13–14, Jerusalem Bible). God himself turns to music. How else announce that tremendous event? Music, the universal language.

Music throughout the world. No words are needed when

great music is played, no translators necessary. Attend an international youth orchestra festival. So many young people from so many countries, different in speech and face and dress. Yet when the conductor lifts his baton and the hands, black or white or brown, lift their instruments, all become as one. And when the strong sweet sounds begin to pour forth, all barriers vanish, the entire assemblage becomes as one. As one they hear and understand this common celestial tongue.

Who or what but an all-powerful common father could be back of such a phenomenon? This, too, a baptism of the Spirit . . .

To be able to hear music, what a blessing. But even the deaf don't miss it altogether. They, too, "hear" the pulsations, feel the rhythms, beat time, often dance. At Gallaudet, famous Washington college for the deaf, they have a robed choir and "sing" with their fingers! . . . The genius of Beethoven, overcoming even the deafness that began at thirty and was total by the time he was forty-nine. Imagine: to hear some of your own masterpieces only faintly, and that great oratorio *Missa Solemnis* not at all. Except in your mind . . .

Except in the mind . . . The miracle of the mind. What is mind but the unseen stuff of God? The ephemeral but potent dust of all creation drifting through our consciousness? Caught, held, transformed into ideas that are in turn transformed into things. Sometimes tangible things like houses and books and colleges and banks and cars. Sometimes that magnificent intangible, music.

How I'd love to be a composer, listening, ever listening for the sound of pianos and strings and brasses in my head, and when I heard them, able to set them down. I know it's not all that easy—but even to wrestle with the sounds, changing and rearranging until I had them meshed into near-perfection. How I'd love even to be a musician, drawing the music from a piano or horn or cello. . . . Observe musicians as they play. They are lost to us, they dwell in another world. They are transported to places where we cannot follow. They are close to the hearts of God.

As for us who sit listening . . . we are given glimpses of the divine. For a little while our own world changes, too, its harsh edges soften, and melt into something lovely; the darks and the grays brighten, take on living colors; the grim gives way to something that shines. We are soothed or enlivened, delighted or profoundly moved. We forget, we forgive, we want to dance and laugh and love and cry.

Nobody can tell me this isn't your doing, God. Your very breath and being entering ours. Speaking to us, calling to us, using music to stir us, comfort us, uplift us. And giving us a foretaste of even more beautiful music to come.

TWO BY THE SIDE OF THE ROAD

Jesus, dear Jesus, I sometimes envy you! When you felt pity for people you had only to reach out and touch them and they were healed. You could make them walk again, you could restore their sight. . . . I feel such pity for people, but so helpless before their plight. Jesus, dear Jesus, show me what to do.

The Good Samaritan. That parable was for all of us. That parable was for me. . . . Oh, but it takes courage to be a Good Samaritan, it can look silly, even be dangerous. It's not safe to go to anybody's rescue any more, not even by daylight on a busy street. New York, especially. People don't pay any attention, just walk on by.

And I'm in New York now, taking a walk before a luncheon appointment, on a bitterly cold day. And across the street, in front of a funeral home, lies a body. Heavens, don't they even pick up their *bodies?* Don't look, none of your business, hurry on by. . . . But what if—? Never mind, look in store windows, beautiful clothes, forget that—*but what if it isn't a body?* None of your business, don't be a hick. . . . Okay, okay, cross the street, walk back just to be sure, it's probably gone by now. . . . Only it isn't, and people are stepping around it, paying no attention, although you see it moving, hear its feeble cries—"Help me . . . some-body!" Okay, *okay,* hick, chicken out-of-towner, break down, make a fool of yourself, ask what's the matter?

He's shaking, haggard, sick. He needs food, something warm in his stomach. If you give him some money will he please go in out of the cold and eat? (You are begging for yourself!) He agrees, sobbing, and you hand him a dollar, escape. (Fool, he'll use it for drink.) When you look back he waves so plaintively you can't stand it. So *go* back, *go* back, idiot. "Your problem is alcohol, isn't it? Will you go to A.A. if I can get you there? They'll help you."

"Lady . . . I'll go . . . anywhere!"

Try to find a phone booth, try to find their number. They say they can't come after him, but if I can bring him by taxi . . . Try to get a taxi. . . . He is sitting up now, and another woman has stopped to talk to him. "Would you like for me to go with you?" she asks. Thank God. Especially since the headquarters prove to be in an undesirable section. (Could you have gotten him safely up those stairs by yourself, hick? Would the cab driver, sweet guy that he seemed to be, have helped you?) No matter, the other Good Samaritan supports his other side. . . . And they welcome him kindly, assure us he will have medical attention, food, a bed.

Leaving, the woman and I agree we, too, will sleep better tonight, knowing that. And that we could use some coffee ourselves. "He was worth saving," she says. "He's an educated man—did you notice his diction? And his manners, even so sick. When he said he'd never forget us he meant it. He's a good but very sick man."

Belatedly, we exchange names—and gasp. She is Ann Williams-Heller, well-known nutritionist. She writes for the same magazines I do, knows the same people! We fall into each other's arms, friends. . . . She came to this country as an Austrian war refugee. Now, years later, love brought us together. Out of all the people swarming the New York streets, the same life line from the same God drew us together at the side of someone who was suffering.

". . . whatsoever good thing any man doeth, the same shall he receive of the Lord. . . ."

It's not always that swift, that clear. Now I must record

by incident of the old woman in Haifa, not to exalt myself, heaven knows, but only to try to understand the peculiar anguish of another love shared. . . .

She was bent over, heavy and stooped, with a homemade crutch under one arm, and in the other hand a knobby stick on which to lean. At her feet, a string bag filled with groceries. Evidently she had been shopping and discovered she could not carry them. She was weeping and making pitiful gestures to people thrusting past on the steep hot street.

I halted, torn. Our bus was making only a brief stop. Long enough to explore some of the art shops. I was rushing up the hill to look at some mosaics glimpsed in a window. But my heart would not let me pass. I halted, picked up the heavy bag, and tried to walk with her a little way.

Then I saw that her poor old feet in their run-over shoes could scarcely make it. She had to pause every few inches and point to one of them, so swollen it had broken through the thin flopping slipper. I set down the bag and knelt to examine it; the shoe was so broken and dusty it had rubbed the flesh raw. How to help, what to do? I tried putting a Kleenex in the sole to ease it a little bit. I caressed her foot with my fingers. Then I stood up and said, "Lean on me." And thus we progressed a little way.

Meanwhile, I was trying to enlist the aid of an Israeli soldier—anyone who might know where she lived and come to her aid. But if they understood they gave no sign; they simply shrugged and went on. All I could do was talk to her encouragingly in a language she did not understand. And when she had to stop again the hurt was too much for both of us, the love; I embraced her and kissed her and we clung together, so at least she realized that somebody cared. And she gazed at me through her tragic old eyes beneath the ragged shawl, and the tears flowed afresh.

The others were returning to the bus, calling, "Come on!" I would have to leave her. In desperation I hailed a boy of about fifteen and pleaded, "Do you speak English? Do you know where this woman lives? Can't you please carry her things home?" To my relief, he nodded, took up the bag, and set off down the hill. Behind him she continued to plod, inching along, halted again and again by the agonies of age. The last I saw was that stooped figure still making its tortuous way downhill in the blazing sun.

And my heart cried out after her. I felt as if I was abandoning her, as if I ought to give up all the comforts and joys of my own life to make her life easier . . . in that awful moment of recognition she was my mother! She was all the mothers who have borne children and grown old and crippled and live in poverty and torment as they struggle through their final days. I wanted to help her. I wanted to know that she lay on clean sheets in a cool house with somebody nearby to soothe her and keep her company.

I wanted to heal her. And to be able to do so little hurt so much.

I said that I sometimes envy Jesus. Now I realize . . . he couldn't heal everyone either, he couldn't provide for all the poor. There were simply too many. He, too, was limited by time and energy. And if *he* had limitations, how much greater are my human limitations. And if I suffer because of them, how much more he must have suffered for those people he had to turn away. (And must suffer still for us.)

But this I must remember. There were and are no limits on his love. All he asks of me is that I put no limits on my love.

FLYING THROUGH FOG

I can barely see the wings, Lord, but they are outspread like arms. Like your everlasting arms.

They hold us up, they reach out like a benediction. "Don't be afraid," they say, and so do the bright little lights. "We are strong, we are firm."

I see the small flaps open and close as we speed steadily forward through the fog. They are like the movements of an enigmatic but reassuring smile.

I am relaxed, I am calm. Who can fear the clouds and the fog which surround us like the very breath of God?

Like homing pigeons we are being led to our destination. Blindly yet surely the instruments lead us home.

Your hand is upon us, your eye is upon us. Though we rise and fall with the currents—on this journey or through the fogs of life, you will hold us up. You will see us through. We reach firm ground, we land.

Oh, Lord, let me remember this later, at the times when I need it, when the fogs of life overtake me and there seems to be no landing place—let me remember this flight through the fog.

POETRY

Poetry . . . its rhythms that echo the rhythms of the universe. This, too, speaks to me of God.

In the beginning, the very beginning, a mother rocking her child to sleep—the songs she croons to him, the little nonsense chantings. All this cradling and loving—there is heartbeat back of it all—her own heartbeat and the great heartbeat of God.

With some of us, once this rhythm begins it never ceases; from Mother Goose to Masefield, we respond. From the little gooseboy wandering "upstairs and downstairs, and in my lady's chamber" to Masefield going "down to the sea in ships . . ." And the sea itself rolls in, the waves never varying their patterns. The very wind cries in cadences, and the trees turn into lovely swaying poems in the wind. While the rain pounds out its measures on the roof.

God puts a hunger in some hearts when we are very small; God puts a pencil in the hand. There is no appeasing that hunger unless the pencil moves, too, struggling with these elusive rhythms.

God, and a good librarian, led me to poetry in the wonderful library we had in Storm Lake, my little home town. The poetry books were few, but their treasures over-whelming. Here it had happened, the miracle had happened—the words had been shaped to their delicate true purpose, people had captured the wind!

God led me to the Psalms . . . I remember almost the very moment as a child in church one morning. The responsive reading. From the pulpit a voice leading: "Thou crownest the year with thy goodness; and thy paths drop fatness." And we, all of us, even those new to the wonder of words, could reply: "They drop upon the pastures of the wilder-ness: and the little hills rejoice on every side."

The little hills! . . . And the rest: "The pastures are clothed with flocks; the valleys also are covered over with corn; they shout for joy, they also sing."

Something shouted for joy within me, too; the Holy Spirit roused me through this poem. . . . And today, read-ing the Psalms today, whatever our age, we walk again on hillsides clothed with flocks and corn, and love God and challenge God and bow down before the mystery and the marvel of his never-ending plan.

For the universe, the whole universe, is one great poem. Day and night, birth and death, winter and spring, blos-soming and withering, sunshine and storm . . . the metro-nome swings, the very stars in their courses have such meter they could be scanned.

And even when God himself seems to have gotten lost somewhere, or we have wandered off like the little boy in Mother Goose and can't be found—we have not been ban-ished, and there is no banishing the patterns. The language of the world is never stilled, the great eternal system with its tireless heart punds on.

And so poetry is of God. True poetry that makes one's own heart leap in recognition. Reading it, poetry that some other tormented or rhythm-rejoicing soul has brought into being, is sometimes as if God himself has struck us down unaware from the printed page.

Yes, oh yes—this is another way to be hurled straight into the heart of God.

WITH THE TONGUES OF MEN AND ANGELS

Jesus said: "Thou shalt love the Lord thy God with all thy heart, and with all thy soul, and with all thy mind. That is the first and great commandment. And the second is like unto it, Thou shalt love thy neighbor as thyself."

The thirteenth chapter of First Corinthians tells us how. The famous chapter on charity, or love. And how that Paul could write! No author, not even Shakespeare, has ever produced anything to surpass that treatise. "Though I speak with the tongues of men and of angels, and have not love, I am become as sounding brass, or a tinkling cymbal."

Read it, oh read it to learn the true nature of love. Some versions, use the word *charity*; no matter, the words are interchangeable, they mean the same thing. (And how significant that is.) Generosity, giving, sharing, having mercy, being patient, showing compassion, understanding. And no matter what I say, or how many people I help, if I go about this bitterly or grudgingly, then "it profiteth me nothing." If I am truly to know and love God, I must have love for his people in my heart.

This means I will be charitable in my spirit as well as my acts. I will refrain from judgments. ("Judge not, that ye be not judged. . . ." Who knows what agony lies behind the locked doors of another person's life?) I will not stone a brother or sister with words. ("Inasmuch as ye have done it unto one of the least of these my brethren, ye have done it unto me.")

I will love my neighbors, and show it whenever I can even though I may not tell them so. I will try to love my God with all my heart and soul and mind—and *tell* him so.

For the very words of love enhance and intensify love. If I want to find God and hang on to him, I've got to thank him for creating me and letting me live. Every moment of my life will be a witness to that wonder. But he will be closer, ever closer, if I love him and tell him so!

* * *

"And now abideth all these things . . ." that have helped lead me back to God.

People and writings and work. Birth and death and nature. The church and prayer and pain and the wonders of art.

". . . but the greatest of these is love."

Part III
To Help
You Through
the Hurting

Contents

Introduction

Thisbook is a collection of things I have written about human hurting. Including that greatest hurt of all, losing someone you love.

I know how it feels. I have been there. And I have shared the terrible hurting of others.

We all need comfort. We all need hope. We all need to realize that "this too will pass." This is *not* the end for us. So long as there is life in our bodies, God wants us to get up and go on. When we do, he often has wonderful things in store for us.

It is my prayer that this little book will not only help you through the hurting . . . but help you to find them.

I

Pain

Out of the depths have I cried
unto thee, O Lord.
Lord, hear my voice:
let thine ears be attentive
to the voice of my supplications

Psalm 130:1–2

THIS HURT

*L*isten, Lord, please listen . . .
    You will help me to bear this hurt. This seemingly intolerable pain.
    You will help me not to cry out in agony. But you will be patient with me too; you will not ask me to be too brave inside.

This hurt, oh God, this hurt.

It is a shock, it dazes and numbs me. So that for a little while I can move blindly, almost insensate, about my duties.

Then it revives, it comes again in waves, rhythmic beatings that seem almost not to be borne. Yet I know that I must bear them, as a woman endures the pains of birth.

I am in labor, Lord. A terrible labor of the spirit. And it is infinitely worse than childbirth because right now I can see no deliverance. And I will have nothing to show for it.

* * *

Or—will I? Will, I, Lord?

Surely I will have new strength in compensation. Surely somewhere inside me there will be some hard sustaining residue, some accretion of anguish like the mineral deposits from water, or rocks hardened out of a volcano's boiling lava.

Perhaps this very pain is building a rock cliff within me that will stand stern against further assaults of pain and grief. And it will be both a protection and a base from which to start anew.

Thank you for this revelation. You who are truly the "rock of ages" will support me and help to build in me this other rock of strength.

BELIEVE AND RECEIVE

I must tackle the subject of suffering, God. I must wrestle with the problem of finding you and not letting go in spite of the awful injustices of your world, in spite of pain.

You know I don't understand it—I don't think many people do, no matter what they claim. I sometimes feel very stupid. Again and again it is explained to me, the purpose and need of suffering. And I listen and nod and agree.

Then I see people who've lived lives of great goodness and sacrifice die sudden dreadful deaths; or trembling through long lonely living deaths in nursing homes. . . . I see the horrible ravages of famine and wars. . . . And the children—O dear God, the little children neglected, abused, raped. Or born crippled, mute, blind.

And my very soul rages. I don't BLAME you, but there is no sure heart-knowledge of mercy or justice within me. I can only accept the fact (and ask you to forgive me) that I can't accept some things.

I can only trust to such sure heart-knowledge as I have: That suffering does not come from you. But it is not in vain. It DOES serve some purpose in the total scheme of things. And you expect us to take it. Take it without too much breast-beating and weeping and wailing, "No fair!" TAKE it and MAKE it work for our own soul's growth.

I can't believe you deliberately send it for that reason, God. But since we are stuck with it (or you are stuck with it) you will see help us through it.

You will help us overcome it, and emerge purer, finer, better because of it. Above all, closer to you.

In personal suffering we can find you. Know you as never before.

As for other people's suffering? The appalling injustices we are forced to witness and before which we feel so impotent? These I cannot and must not ignore. These I must do all that I can to assuage.

Yet I cannot and must not let them stand betweeen me and my God. To do so would only add my own misery to the weight of human despair. I must have you, God, to sustain me. I must have your help if I am to know any happiness as a human being, and so be able to help anyone else.

My choice is this: "To doubt and do without," as someone has said. Or "to believe and receive." I believe, Lord, I believe. And even in times of trouble—yes, even more richly in times of trouble—I receive!

TO SING SO THAT OTHERS MAY HEAR

One of the best articles I've ever read on suffering was written by one of the two Hopes in my life, Hope Good; it appeared in the magazine *Orion*. In it she told of once having a rabbit whose cage was ripped apart by dogs one night and the pet torn to bits. She wept for days, asking, "How could a loving God have permitted such a catastrophe? Suddenly, like a revelation, I concluded that I was to this creature as God is to me, yet I was unable to assist when it needed me. Yes, God loves us with a deep compassion, even when He is unable to come too our aid."

She went on to say, "We must stop asking, Why did this happen to me? Instead, we must ask ourselves: How can I use it creatively? . . . There is no evil so terrible that it cannot, with God's help, be used . . . the challenge to make something of value replace a failure, defeat or disappointment is about the only way man has to answer the problem of suffering."

Another clipping, yellow with age. Written by former Senate chaplain Frederick Brown Harris in his column "Spires of the Spirit." He called this one "Dialing the Man

Upstairs." "The object in dialing God is never to demand, 'Get me out of this,' but 'Save me from surrendering to this.' We haven't mastered the first lesson in the Primer of Life's meaning until we know that the chief end of man is not comfort, but character. . . . If character were the goal, rather than comfort, then a lot of things that otherwise seem to have no business here would make some sense."

To become not bitter—but better. To compensate. To turn the affliction into something fine. Artists always do this; a part of their genius is the ability to translate their sufferings into their greatest symphonies, sculpture, paintings, poems. But one needn't be a genius. "Out of the night that covers me, / Black as the Pit from pole to pole, / I thank whatever gods there may be / For my unconquerable soul," my mother used to quote from "Invictus." And every day, out of the dark night of suffering, shine forth unconquerable souls. With lights so vivid they brighten the way for others.

Following are two of the many I have known personally:

Barbie

Born with a clot which caused the blood to back up, to rupture and hemorrhage in the esophagus and stomach. Years of intense pain and stress, hospitalizations, surgeries—one to remove her esophagus and a third of her upper stomach. A last-ditch life-saving effort, which left a hole in her neck for saliva to drain out, and another hole made directly into her stomach through the abdomen into which liquids could be fed. Agonizing, weakening bouts with hiccuping . . . yet this brave girl donned highnecked dresses, dated, went to school, held part-time jobs, sang in the choir—and wound up cheering those who came to cheer her!

During all this she was writing to her family and friends; remarkable letters which became a journal of courage and faith.

Listen to this, written at fifteen, after hearing a moving sermon about total commitment:

> *I sat in the balcony in the "cry room" (for mothers with babies) where I could hear Pastor Bob but no one could hear me [hiccuping]. I sat up there half-drugged from my tranquilizers, angry, scared, and very discouraged. . . . Afterward, I went up to talk to him. He had told about a lady in his church who had tried to commit suicide before she'd found Christ and turned her life over to Him to control, and I wanted to know what he'd told HER. I told him I didn't understand why this had to happen to me again; and I asked him—if God is such a God of love, then why is He doing this to me? We talked for a while, then prayed together, and I went home to do just what he told me to.*
>
> *I went to my room and I prayed: "God, forgive my anger at You, and my discouragement. I know it's wrong, but I'm desperate, Lord. . . . Father, I give up fighting AGAINST having it—and fighting with You OVER it. If this is what You want for my life, even though I don't understand it, I accept it. So here is my life for You to do with whatever you want to. God, I believe YOU'RE now in control. Thank You!"*
>
> *Man, when you say that, look out—things are going to start to happen!*

She fell asleep without help for the first time in weeks, she relates, and woke up hours later with the hiccups gone.

> *Now no one can tell me there is no God or that God is dead or that He doesn't love and watch over His children.*
>
> *I KNOW I have a God, and that my God is alive, and that my God loves me!*

Barbie's battle was far from over. At sixteen she was forced to write after unsuccessful surgery:

> *"Satan's cause is never more in danger than when a human no longer desiring, but still intending to do God's will, looks around him upon a universe from which every trace of Him seems to have vanished, and asks why he has been forsaken, and still obeys."*
>
> *This quote from C. S. Lewis so perfectly depicts my situation as I*

lay in the Intensive Care Unit. . . . I was disappointed that the surgery had failed, terribly frustrated that I was sick AGAIN, that I was born this way with no hope of ever changing it, that I was missing out on school activities, most of all I was just TIRED of hurting so much!

Then the Lord stepped in and said, "Now wait a minute. What is the last thing you did in that operating room before you went to sleep?" I said, "Well, I committed my life completely into your hands and thanked you in advance for being my Sufficiency. . . ." "O.K. then," He said. "What are you getting so upset about? . . ."

She then prayed the famous Serenity Prayer:

God grant me the serenity to accept the things I cannot change, the courage to change the things I can, and the wisdom to know the difference.

And concluded:

I can't change the fact that I was born with a birth defect, but I CAN change my attitude toward it.

Her high school picture smiles from the letter she wrote shortly before her eighteenth birthday. A radiantly beautiful dark-eyed girl, saying:

It has now been fifteen months since my esophagus had to be removed, and the doctors are still at a complete loss at to how to put me back together again. But in fulfilling His promise—"I can do all things through Christ who strengtheneth me"—it was made possible for me to combine my junior and senior years into one, and with the help of a wonderful tutor, to maintain a "B-plus" average, so I WILL walk down that aisle to receive my diploma with my class!

Barbie was almost nineteen when she wrote her final letter. Still intending to go to college, yet aware that the Lord might have other plans for her.

Oh, Pastor Luther, I do praise and thank Him from my innermost being. Because as one of the verses from your text Sunday says,

"They should SEEK *the Lord, if haply they might feel after Him and* FIND *Him, though He be* NOT FAR FROM ANY ONE OF US. *For in Him we live, and move, and have our being!"* (See—I listened!!)

. . . *John 11:4 says, "This sickness is not unto death, but for the glory of God . . ." But I'm not afraid to die, because if that is His ministry for me, then I am willing. And He* CAN *use me in this way, in* EVERY *way. . . . I am totally, completely His, to do with as He chooses.*

The entire story of Barbie Hertel is being told in a book written by her mother. . . . Meanwhile, a school library building is being named for her, and the impact of her gallantry, her faith in the face of suffering, can never be measured. . . .

Elias

A young Greek musician performing in a strange land. A slight limp, a long history of leg problems. Now—cancer, the doctors say. The limb must come off. . . . The night before the amputation he asks for his guitar. We bring it and he lies in bed tuning it lovingly. Then he begins to play and softly sing. Beautiful, heart-melting Grecian love songs. And it is so poignant and lovely the nurses begin to peer in. And other patients. They stand and listen, young and old. One a very old black man. And a young mother from her vigil in the children's wing.

Can she bring some children to hear him? she asks. Will he share his music with them? He says yes, of course, bring the children. And she comes leading them, three little girls who have had tracheotomies. Their throats are bandaged, none of them can speak. But they gaze at him with awed delight, these silent five- and six-year-olds. They keep time with their hands. And as the music quickens and he nods and smiles at them, one of them begins to dance around in her robe, her little slippers.

He leans toward them, his great dark eyes alight. "I play some songs you know, ha? You know 'Frère Jacques'?" They nod and he begins to sing, urging them to join in: "Frère Jacques . . . Frère *Jacques*—" And though they can't make a sound, their lips move, miming the words. With his smile and his eyes he encourages them.

Then he moves into one that makes them bounce: "This old man, he played *one*, he played nick-nack on my drum. . . . With a *nick-nack*, paddy-whack, give a dog a bone, *this* old man came rolling home!" They are beating time, the tiny one in pigtails tries to dance, too, mute but joyfully they "sing."

A sassy little black nurse pops in, joins the fun, warbling in a high foolish falsetto before ordering, "Now hold still, Mr. Music Man, for your shot." Attention is focused on the doomed leg lying in its heavy white cast. The foot protrudes, and into it the needle goes. Elias takes up his guitar again, finishes the next tune with the brisk familiar rhythm—"Shave and a haircut, six bits!" The children laugh and the one with the huge blue eyes clicks her tongue to echo its beat. Then, thanking him, the young mother shepherds them away.

Lights are being lowered, the others have left, too. We turn to tell him good night, each gripping a hand on either side of the bed. We say a little prayer for him. When his eyes open they are wet, but he continues to smile. "Now don't you worry, I be okay."

The next time we see him the leg is gone. He is in great pain. But he touches the tiny cross around his neck and forms the words silently, like the children—"I'm okay. I'm okay."

GOD ONLY KNOWS

Common expressions have a way of packaging truths.

Consider: "God only knows."

How often we say this when we come up against something we can't explain. Usually something we object to, something of which we despair. "Why did this have to happen? . . . God knows!" Or "God only knows."

Slang, yes . . . but wait, isn't it maybe something more? Can this be the voice of the soul itself speaking? Handing

over to God a mystery too much for us. Saying, in essence—
God knows . . . God *does* know. . . . And only God.

The speaker may not even be a believer, merely someone
resigning the matter to fate. Yet the persistence of the
soul's knowledge is there. . . . For we can't hope to understand all the secrets of the universe or the total nature of
God or even of his complex creation, man.

We are so human. Faulty and finite. Boxed within certain
physical limits, at least during our stay on earth. We can't
fly in the air under our own power, or sustain ourselves
under water unless we have aids. . . . And we have cleverly
invented such aids; things we could not have imagined a few
years ago we have now achieved. . . . Such progress! Yet
how far are we able to progress in the matters of mind and
spirit? How long will it take us to understand God?

Loving God and feeling his presence does not mean for a
minute that we are his equals. . . . The maker of one single
river . . . or the sun . . . or me! How can I hope to comprehend his mystery?

I just know that I am his child. And you are his child. And
no matter what happens in this life or beyond it, he will not
forsake us. . . . Meanwhile, when things occur that are
beyond my feeble comprehension, things that test my faith,
scald my spirit, rend my secret being, I can indeed cry out in
sheer human dismay, resistant and yet resigned—yes, and
reverent:

"God knows why. God only knows!"

While the still small voice of my deeper soul-knowledge
whispers reassuringly: "Yes. God knows."

THE SUFFERING FEW OF US ESCAPE

*You know what a coward I am about suffering, God. My own or other
people's.*

*I would never have made a martyr; once they started to beat me or drag
me to the lions I'm afraid I'd have recanted. If I were imprisoned and they
tortured me for secrets, I don't think I could stand it—I'd tell!*

And I am sickened before the spectacle of suffering, and physical suffering, of man or animal. (How can anyone be entertained by brutal acts? How can anyone cheer at the sight of any creature bruised, bleeding, struggling desperately to escape?)

It's hard for me even to READ about suffering. If I am helpless to stop it, it seems witless to punish my own flesh and soul by drinking in the dread details. . . .

No, no, I must flee from physical suffering.

Yet there is another kind of suffering few of us can flee. And that we cannot stop by a mere act of will: not by averting our eyes, running away, slamming the door.

The agony of love in all its variations.

Man and woman love. The many aspects of love between male and female . . . Anxiety about the one so close to us . . . Long separations . . . Conflicts, quarrels, doubts . . . Husband and wife who've forgotten how to talk to each other . . . Indifference . . . The bitter wounds of unfaithfulness . . . To be denied the person most deeply loved . . . The awful unfulfilled hungers of body and soul . . .

These our private crucifixions.

And children: O God, dear God, the multiple crucifixions we undergo for our children. Nailed to the cross again and again for their shortcomings. Or only waiting at the cross sometimes (which can be worse) forced to witness their suffering.

So I am no stranger to suffering. And I can't honestly call myself a coward before these emotional assaults. In some ways I feel brave before them. I have faced them before, most of them, and will face them again and survive. You give me the strength, you give me the courage.

You make me realize that anyone who drinks from the sweet cup of love must also swallow the gall. But love is worth it . . . ah, but it's worth it! And if you truly love, as Jesus taught, then the price we pay for love has even more value.

In suffering for love of others we are also suffering for love of you. This suffering I welcome, Lord.

IF IT CAN TEACH US TO FORGIVE

My heart broke for this daughter, so young to be suffering so much. The *if onlys* piled up . . . *If only* we could have talked them out of the too-early marriage. *If only* we'd had the right answers or been able to help when the problems got bad . . .

But now the worst of it is over, and she emerges from the years of trial still young and calm and strong and—incredibly—even closer to God: "Mother, listen, just because we love God and he loves us doesn't mean we're not going to have *pain*. Pain is the price we pay on earth for loving someone. But the pain of love—that's the kind of pain that can make us realize the true nature of God.

"How could I turn my back on Jesus just because I have suffered over human love? I understand now how *he*, Jesus, feels. How he must suffer over loving us so much, when so many people don't know or love him."

She speaks of her marriage without regret; they both learned so much from each other. "And who knows what time will bring? Who knows the impact we have on other lives? Who knows what God can do, how much good he can build out of our mistakes? The fact that we could forgive each other for the pain we caused each other, isn't that what Jesus wants? Isn't that a pretty big thing? Yes, of course it hurts, but even hurting isn't in vain if it can teach us to forgive."

THE CROSSES

Morning . . . a broad green Iowa pasture where the children and I used to hike . . . Crawl gingerly under the barbed-wire fence, then up the hill and on through the tall tossing grasses. Lurking among this growth are the lavender thistles, pronged and pert, like imps to be wary of. Birds spurt ahead—quails and blackbirds red-winged and gold. Meadow larks call from the fences. Everywhere the bird cries are ringing and chirring and caroling. How many there are—a bird Paradise.

The green-golding weeds and grasses have a gilded look in the morning sun. They wash and shine and make their own soft music. They bend toward the bank. The ground pitches toward this bank, and at its edge you look down upon the stream, broad and clear and sparkling, winding between these escarpments. In the distance more fields, and the houses of the town Le Mars, and highways where cars and a few trucks race along. Yet here all is wide and vast, peaceful and free.

I walk along the bank and then down its side to be near the water, where there are glittering sandy beaches, and then thick muddy tracks where the cows have been. The mud is very black and rutted from their hooves; it squishes underfoot and sinks softly, and my sneakers turn black at the edge. I plod along until I reach the dry place and then consider climbing back. . . . And standing there wondering which is the least steep, I am aware of telephone poles that swing along the division between pasture and plowed corn-field. Poles standing slender and tall and spread-armed against the sky.

Or are they telephone poles? Utility poles probably, because they have a crosspiece, they make the form of the cross. And at the tip of each arm and at its crest is a small ornament that must have something to do with power. A glass insulator, maybe? Whatever it is, it adorns this cross— these gentle, graceful, stately crosses as they repeat them-selves, at first large . . . then smaller . . . smaller . . . dwin-dling to the eye against the sky.

For some reason I start up the steepest bank, and discover it isn't very steep, after all. Following a slightly zigzag course, I go bounding to the top . . . and stand arrested once more by the sight of the crosses through which the silent power sings.

The image of the cross itself is enhanced. . . . Is man driven, I wonder, to repeat this design in so many areas of his life? Or is it that the cross was and remains a plain, practical arrangement of timbers or anything else, to sup-port death . . . or life? In any case, here are these simple, lovely crosses against the blue morning country sky. And I am held by the sight.

The cross, symbol of sin and suffering—this beautiful geometrical design. And comfort and inspiration to so many

. . . Christ suffered for us and he took away our sins. But he couldn't spare us the suffering; not even he! Yet isn't the empty cross the symbol of suffering that is over and done with? Of the man who died there and then walked free?

I understand now what my friend Hope Applebaum meant when she said once, "You have to suffer. You have to go through Gethsemane before you can rise." At the time I knew what she was saying, but it had no real significance. Now it seems as clear and clean as the country air. . . . All these crosses! They mark the landscape of our lives.

Even as I stand there looking at the utility poles I see that they have double arms. There are crosses piled upon crosses. . . . We often carry several crosses at a time. And yet each is gemmed with its little vital star of power. And the time eventually comes when that particular cross has served its purpose; the hour of suffering is over and the cross is empty. The man or woman walks free.

Now that I have become aware of crosses I see them wherever I am. Fashioning a child's kite, looking up at the mast of a sailing ship—always the central spire and the arms outspread. It is an image of balance and beauty, of both surrender and blessing.

And the crosses in all the windows of the world! The shape of the cross that is made by the central lines of windowpanes. . . . Coming into an English village one night at sunset, the winding streets so narrow you could almost reach out from the bus and touch the cottages on either side . . . and each cottage window ablaze with the sun, as if to illuminate the black crosses that divide the glass.

It was like suddenly seeing a whole forest of small black crosses alight to welcome us. I said to my daughter, "Look, look!" And she, too, saw the phenomenon. Not only here but every place we went—on the streets of London, in the windows of loft or shop or pub, the cross as clearly defined, once you watch for it, as on the spires of cathedrals.

All those crosses, like a silent signal, inescapable, reassuring. Reminding us of the many trials people can endure and yet every day go cheerfully on . . .

But let's not get too poetic about crosses. They are beautiful from a distance, yes. During those times of life when we have put ours down (if only for a little rest); when we've grown enough to know the value, get perspective. . . . But when you're *carrying* one! (Or more.)

The thing to remember is this: We are not alone. Each of us has a cross to bear. The fact that we may not see another person's cross, often don't even suspect it, doesn't mean it isn't there. Hidden, so often bravely hidden behind a smile, a laugh, a proud carriage, a job superably done—hidden behind locked doors—yet the cross is there. Again and again I have been staggered at the eventual revelations. Shocked to discover how many people had been going through their private crucifixions . . .

Crucifixions for others. Parents crucified for their children's mistakes. The husband or wife of an alcoholic crucified hour by hour. Not intentionally—few people deliberately set out to hurt those close to them—yet the inevitable Golgotha is there. So many, oh so many innocent victims! Nailed to the cross of our terrible concern for those we love, we bleed for them, and there is no freedom for our tormented spirits until they, too, are free.

Yet doesn't this, too, draw us closer to God? By sharing Christ's cup of suffering, don't we taste the true communion? And if we can love as he loved, forgive as he forgave, we, too, can be uplifted.

No personal crucifixion need ever be in vain.

THE HEALING

Thank you, Lord, that tonight my heart is light. Like something newly freed. For I have discovered how to heal it of an unexpected wound; one of those slight, seemingly small rebuffs or humiliations or blows that ought not to hurt so much, but for some of us who are unduly sensitive maybe, they do: A bawling out from the boss. A scolding from someone dear. A sharp word from a friend. Even rudeness from a stranger.

Such things can strike the sunshine from the day. The spirit winces, beats a quick retreat. We feel our wet eyes sting.

Then pride urges retaliation. Sometimes we want to turn on somebody else, as if to pass the pain along. Only now, Lord, I know the true way to relief is to cancel out the pain by doing something kind.

Thank you that today, still seething and suffering, I found myself seated on a bus beside a small shabby man. And I realized, as he stared fixedly out the window, that he was struggling not to cry. And my own little hurt seemed to shrink before the enormity of his. I knew I must speak to him—and did.

And he turned to me, Lord, and drew from his threadbare wallet a picture of a bright-eyed little girl six years old. "We lost her yesterday," he said. He was going now to pick out flowers. He wanted to talk about it. He was glad somebody cared. In our few blocks' ride across the city we shared it—his pride in her and his great loss.

And we touched upon the mystery of being born at all, of being parents, of the brevity and beauty of life upon your earth. And when we parted he was actually smiling. "You've made me feel so much better," he said.

"You've made me feel better too," I told him. For my own petty pain no longer mattered. It was as if some balance had been struck between that which is hurtful and that which is healing.

And perhaps that is all that really matters. That the good, the kind, the decent in this world can equal and even surpass the bad.

Thank you that I have learned this lesson, Lord. Next time it surely won't be so hard to overcome an unexpected hurt.

CUT BACK THE VINES

"Go cut back the grapes," I tell my son. "They're too thick, they've practically taken over the garage."

Naturally he has urgent business elsewhere; but after the usual argument he grabs the pruning shears and dashes outdoors. I hear him whacking away.

I look out later, and am aghast. The garage walls are naked. He has severed the lush growth clear back to the ground. "You've ruined them!" I accuse. "We'll never have grapes there again."

Wrong. The grapes came back the following year with an

abundance never known before; great purple clusters, fat and sweet, so heavy they bowed the trellis. It was just as Jesus said: "Every branch in me that beareth not fruit, he taketh away; and every branch that beareth fruit, he purgeth it, that it may bring forth more fruit" (John 15:2).

I thought of the ruthless slashing. The seeming waste. My scolding protests and my son's innocent bewilderment—he'd thought it was what I wanted. Our misunderstanding. The great fire we had to have even to dispose of the old branches . . . and now this! The newer, stronger, invigorated vines. The harvest so plentiful we carried basketsful to the neighbors.

"He purgeth it . . ." Pain and problems, the conflicts and disappointments, the defeats, the tragedies to which we all are subject—are they not purgings? I look back on my life sometimes in amazement before the memories of those terrible cuttings. Those times of trial by fire, it seemed. . . . Intolerable, intolerable. Rescue me, spare me! . . . Yet now I realize they were essential to my growth. How much hostility had to go in the process, how much self-pity, how much pride. A tangle of choking, life-impeding habits threatening to deny all that God meant me to be. I, too, had to be cut back, laid low.

And somehow, in the midst of it, I realized I could not go it alone, Lord. It was too much. I could not handle the weight of it, the people, the problems, the family, my job as a wife and mother, my fate as a woman in this demanding world, without support beyond my own.

Those words in John—all of them—must have been written for me: "Abide in me, and I in you. As the branch cannot bear fruit of itself, except it abide in the vine; no more can ye, except ye abide in me.

"I am the vine, ye are the branches: He that abideth in me, and I in him, the same bringeth forth much fruit: for without me ye can do nothing" (John 15:4-5).

It was like that. I saw that without you I could do nothing. You are the vine, not me. Weak and faulty as I was, I'd been trying to be the vine, holding up all the branches. I was just a branch and I had to be pruned, I had to be stripped if my roots were to be strengthened. Then only then could I bring forth much fruit!

PERSECUTION

It is a common paradox that persecution only intensifies faith. Strange. Why? Does God release some extra dimension of power when things get really rough?

Those early Christians, stoned, whipped, burned . . . what sustained them? What gave them the courage to suffer and die? But more, seeing their fate, what kept the rest of them from turning traitor? Instead, the very blood shed seemed to nourish the Christian soil, new converts sprang up.

What would have happened to Christianity without opposition? I wonder. Supposing the Romans and Greeks and unconverted Jews had said, "Okay, go ahead, don't mind us." Supposing they'd built churches instead of hiding out to worship in caves and homes? Would they have preached with such passion? Could they have drawn others to the cross if they hadn't been forced to carry their own—and to die on them? Supposing it had all been made easy. Would Christianity have become the living force it has been through the ages? Would it even have survived?

In our own time—the persecutions in communist countries . . . the Soviet Union, East Germany, Albania, Czechoslovakia, Yugoslavia . . . people crowd into darkened homes. To share a single Bible, to pray and sing. Sometimes just to listen to someone who *remembers* the Bible. And when he comes, this Dutchman who can be known only as Brother Andrew, with the Bibles he has been able to smuggle across the border, carefully rationing them out—they weep for joy and risk arrest to have one in their possession. . . .

(My church is never locked. There are half a dozen churches within walking distance of my house. I have more versions of the Bible than I can count. What do they matter? Really *matter*? I can go to church or read a Bible anytime I want—so I put it off. . . . No, it isn't ease that intensifies faith, it is desperation and denial.)

God's Smuggler. Richard Wurmbrand's *Underground Saints.* And that other staggering book of Wurmbrand's *In God's Underground.* . . . These modern martyrs—I read their stories of sacrifice, imprisonment, torture, the incredible things they are still undergoing for God, and am ashamed. My own problems pale. I have never been persecuted. I have never suffered, at least not like that.

Could I if I had to, Lord?

This is not to say that you or I or God would willingly inflict such torment on anyone. But we must recognize that good can come of it. That there is no evil so terrible that good can't come of it. And sometimes a stark, bone-deep realization of how much God really means to us can come in no other way.

We turn to God, too, as individuals or en masse when all hope seems lost and there *is* no other way. (Why not *from* God when even he seems unable to deliver us from the tangible evil? Why *to*?)

Stalin's "planned and deliberate famine" intended to break the peasants' resistance to collectivization. . . . Malcolm Muggeridge describes the terrible toll in *Chronicles of Wasted Time*. And how he went to a crowded church one morning in Kiev, after witnessing it.

Young and old, peasants and townsmen, parents and children . . . Never before or since have I participated in such worship; the sense conveyed of turning to God in great affliction was overpowering . . . for instance where the congregation say there is no help for them save from God. What intense feeling they put into those words! In their minds, I knew, as in mine, was a picture of those desolate abandoned villages, of the hunger and the hopelessness, of the cattle trucks being loaded with humans in the dawn light.

Where were they to turn for help? Not to the Kremlin and the Dictatorship of the Proletariat, certainly; nor to the forces of progress and democracy and enlightenment in the West. . . . Every possible human agency found wanting. So only God remained, and to God they turned with a passion, a dedication, a humility, impossible to convey. They took me with them; I felt closer to God then than I ever had before, or am likely to again.

Such reactions are intuitive, leading to truths too profound to question. They go back beyond time, back to Job and Lamentations and the hillsides where David sang his songs of worshipful desperation:

I cried unto the Lord with my voice, and he heard me out of his holy will. Selah. I laid me down and slept; I awakened; for the Lord sustained me. I will not be afraid of ten thousands of people who have set themselves against me . . . (Psalm 3:4–6).

It is as if we are led by strong supernal forces. Driven by the soul's surest wisdom: This way, this way!

Come unto me, all ye that labour and are heavy laden, and I will give you rest (Matt. 11:28).

GOD'S ANSWER TO EVIL

Isn't the strength that is born of suffering God's answer to evil? God does not will the suffering, cannot or does not prevent it, cannot or does not always take it from us. But within each of us he has implanted a precious core of power mightier than the atom. Call it what you will, survival mechanism maybe, the stubborn will to overcome. But trigger it, arouse it, stir it with enough pain and despair and humiliation, enflame it, feed it with human blood, and look out. The explosion can rock the world.

It happened in a mass sense with our black people; and it happens in an individual sense every day. Jaws jutted, teeth bared, eyes flashing, human beings emerge from hell to declare: "Nothing is impossible to me now!"

Somewhere at this moment—on a hospital bed or in a

prison cell . . . at a machine or desk, in a mill or mine where even a job can seem punishment . . . in a divorce court or the purgatory of a loveless marriage . . . in the cruel tearings of family conflict—there are new people being born. Coming forth stronger and finer. Seeing themselves, perhaps for the first time, in all their reality and true potential.

"The best years of your life may be the years of your failure, your heartbreak, your loneliness," wrote Air Force Chaplain Thomas E. Myers before his own death in a crash with his men. "When you discover *why* you have life and go one step further, decide that no matter what cost may be involved, you will follow that *why* until you see yourself the 'man God meant.' . . . You will have found that special thing which the God who made you planned for only you to build, to create, to cause to grow."

That may be one "reason" for suffering. Never God-caused but forever God-used, if we but have the courage to turn to that source implanted within us.

FOR EVERY CROSS I'VE CARRIED

Thank you, God, for every cross I have ever had to carry. For every burden I have ever had to bear. For every honest tear I have ever shed.

Thank you for my troubles—they give me courage.

Thank you for my afflictions—they teach me compassion.

Thank you for my disappointments—through them I learn humility and am inspired to try harder again.

Thank you that in fashioning this world you didn't see fit to spare us from the evil you knew would be there. Thank you for not keeping us like dumb animals in a corral. That, instead, you freed us, gave us the dignity of making our own decisions, even if it also meant we must stumble and fall and suffer in order to rise again.

Thank you that in every aspect of our lives you are always near us. Loving, protecting, helping. Hearing our prayers and giving us the strength to endure what we must for our own souls' growth.

I know you, Lord, in times of peace and plenty. But when life is easy it's too easy to forget you; I don't need you quite so much. When life is tough, however, when I see nothing about me but trouble and torment, then I must find you, I must have you! I go crying to you through the darkness, knowing that though the whole world forsake me you will not turn away. My very suffering brings you near.

LETTER FROM BARBARA

Two of the chapters included in this book ("Pain" and "Death"'), first appeared in *How Can I Find You, God?* Shortly after that book was published I received the following letter. One of the most eloquent and moving I have ever read. I feel this woman's testimony must be shared, not because I had anything to do with it, but solely in the hope her remarkable release will help others.

Dear Marjorie,
May I call you by your first name? I feel like we are friends, even though I haven't finished your book. I am so overwhelmed by what you have to say that I am being compelled to write you at three o'clock in the morning. I have prayed for guidance; please put all else aside and listen to me. (I assure you I have never done anything like this before.)

To begin—I got along just fine with you up to page 18, your chapter called "Birth." It hurt me terribly; I was angry and bitter, because you see I cannot have children. My two sons are adopted. "How dare she infer that only a woman who gives birth is blessed?" (I am sharing these thoughts with you, not as a criticism, but as a witness to how God's love can work a reversal of the soul. I had not yet seen the light, not released these grievous harborings, because I had not yet realized that's what they were!) I love my boys fiercely, as much as any woman who ever carried a child. . . .

But I overcame my resentment and pushed on. Now comes the deeper part. Not my story, and yet it must somehow become my witness to God's great love for each and every human being, no matter what the circumstances. Of course, as you say, God doesn't "allow" terrible catastrophes; they just *are!* Pain is not God's will, God's way, only a fact of life. It is what you do with the pain, with the fact of life and death that is important.

All right, let us say I am still reading your book. I am starting on page 149, "Pain." Thoughts are racing; thoughts like, "You've been pretty terrific so far, but my dear you are not going to tell me a thing about pain. Or death. You see, *my pain has been the death of my loved ones . . .*"

Then, in that chapter on pain, I read: "For every cross I've carried, thank you, God. For every burden I have ever had to bear. For every honest tear I have ever shed . . ." And the rest. Suddenly, overwhelmingly, I realize that *I do not want to give up my pain!* After all, I have had to be a martyr to that pain; my whole family has. Dear Lord! Not everyone suffers the loss of five loved ones, in less than a month!

It began with the fire. My twenty-nine-year-old sister, nearly six months pregnant. (The perfect baby girl was left within her womb. I cannot bear a child; why *her* and not me?) Her two healthy, bright, wonderful daughters, ages six and eight. They weren't only her daughters, they were mine too, in the event anything ever happened to her. Mine because they were the daughters I never had. Mine because I helped raise them during a time all three of them went through living hell. Her husband, the girls' father, was a terrible man; they suffered much before the decision was made to leave him.

How could I release this to the Lord? My family and I paid for this pain ourselves, in agony. And a week after their death, more to come! Bette's husband, the girls' new father who loved them, who was in the process of adopting them. There had been hope for him. He had been badly injured, but was out of the coma. He could sit up, consume some food, communicate even though he had a "trach" tube in his throat. And he had to be told they were gone. We were with him when he printed the word "Wife?" with his fingers. The doctors had decided to tell him the truth.

This great young man, who had shown my sister and her girls what the love of a husband and father was all about, experiencing the pain, literally, of fire and hell and such loss—finally to have his own life taken when it had seemed so sure he would survive. *I must give up this pain too?*

And then, only a week later, my father. *Gone.* Heart attack, my eye! He died of a broken heart.

I wanted to fling your stupid book across the room. Again the words lunged at me, "Thank you, God, for every cross I have ever had to carry . . ." My God, my God, I cannot thank you for this pain! If I thank you for it, then I must release it to you, and this I cannot do! To survive, I must keep it and hug it to me. It is mine! *I paid for it!*

I am by myself still. Again, the Lord's way, for I needed complete solitude for the decision I was about to make. I paced the room, your book in my hand. I went to the kitchen cupboard, laid your book on it, and read aloud again: "Thank you, God, for every cross I have ever had to carry. For every burden I have ever had to bear. For every honest tear I have ever shed." No, Lord, I cannot. But I must. And I did. *I actually did!* I released the whole mess to the Father, the Heavenly Father. Because I was paying for the pain all in vain. *Christ had already done it for me.* How could I not have understood that before? God forgive me.

I knew and loved these people; they loved me. Would I *rather not have known them at all?* Oh, God, of course not! My last living memory of Sherry, the youngest, is running down the hall to me with her arms outstretched, shouting, just because she felt like it, "Auntie Barbie, I love you, I love you!" The tears are streaming down my face as I write this. But for the first time in four years, they are tears of joy and acceptance.

It is nearly morning now. I can hardly wait for the day to begin, for the church to open. The people who attend are my friends. They know of my anguish and have shared it with me. Now they must know of my release. I have never personally witnessed before. But I feel earnestly I now have something to share with many. No more tears of self-pity, only tears of joy for the love of God. *If I can accpet this, I can accept whatever comes. Whenever it comes.*

So you see, this is not exactly my story. It is a story of family, of love, of pain, of loss and unbearable grief, and finally with God's help, joy. I know I want to serve God more from now on. Whether it be witnessing for him, or urging people to cherish life while they have it, or just sharing with a friend, as I have done with you. I don't really know, but I will find out.

Somehow, through all this, I have also released to God the fact that I will never bear a child. Have released all my ill harborings against my sister's first husband (which is a miracle in itself). All the old grudges are just gone.

God love you; I love you; I thank you.

Your friend in the Lord,

Barbara J. F.

II

"Gone Where"

Yea, though I walk through
the valley of the shadow of death,
I will fear no evil: for thou art
with me; thy rod and thy staff
they comfort me.

Psalm 23:4

GONE WHERE?

And now—death.
Doors close, and a visible life disappears. I no longer see that image except in memory.
Has he taken God with him? Have I then lost God?

When someone dies, we say, "He's gone."

It is a hot night in a little Iowa town. . . . Footsteps on the walk beyond the window, a mysterious knocking at the door. . . . My father rises, I hear the murmur of voices. The door slams, footsteps are running. . . . I lie heart pounding, puzzled, filled with foreboding.

At last footsteps return, more slowly. I hear the door open, and my father's voice in the bedroom, saying, oh so gently to my mother: "Dear, your father's gone."

"Gone!" Her awful cry of disbelief . . . the shock of her moaning.

I lie trying to comprehend it. . . . *Gone* is a difficult word for anyone, let alone a child. . . . To vanish, be no more—inconceivable. . . . *Gone. All gone* . . .

But then a simple resolution presents itself, in the form of a question: "Gone where?" Gone usually meant you went someplace. My father was a traveling man, gone lots of times on the road. He came back; he always came home.

And so I remember hopping out of bed and running barefoot to reassure her. "Don't worry, he'll be back."

"No, he won't, honey, Grandpa's *gone!*"

"Gone where?"

And she held me and rocked me as she wept, she told me Grandpa had gone to heaven. But it didn't seem to comfort either of us. . . . *Gone* in death meant the trip from which there is no return. I would never see my adored Grandpa Griffith again, not on this earth, and I began to whimper, not because I really sorrowed yet, simply because I could not believe it. . . .

Now I realize the validity of that child's question: "Gone where?" For if we believe the promises of Jesus, we do go somewhere.

We, who are God's dearest creation, cannot simply be stamped out, canceled, obliterated. We are not sticks or leaves to be consumed in the fire, clouds to vanish in the wind; we are so much more than bodies, we are miracles of mind, emotion, spirit! It is this that distinguishes us from all else on the face of the earth, animate or inanimate. We are God's children, his companions, angels (fallen angels, yes, but still his angels).

When one of us leaves the earth, it is for another destination. As surely as if he had climbed on a train that becomes just a plaintive wail in the distance, or a plane that dwindles to a speck in the sky. The rest of us can no longer see the plane or train or bus or car, or its occupant. But we know it is taking him somewhere.

"All aboooard! Let's go!" . . . Whether we are prepared for that summons or not, we all know it's coming—to us and everyone we love. And its very inevitability bespeaks as a God firmly in charge. When our time on earth is up (whatever the circumstance, even time foreshortened), God wants us back. He has other plans for us. And no matter how smart we think we are, how independent, how accomplished . . . no matter about our books, speeches, inventions, musical compositions, cures . . . no man or woman is able to say, "Sorry, not me, forget it."

When death says, "Let's go," you *go.*

Good-bys are always hard. Separations always hurt—whether short or long or final. . . . The vacancy, the emptiness, the loneliness, the longing . . . But it helps, how it helps to know that the one we miss so acutely has not ceased to exist, but simply lives in a place where we can't join him yet.

DAD'S ROSES

Death can be a bridge that leads the living to God as well as it leads those who have left us.

Our love wants to follow, our love refuses to let go.

Our hearts go crying after the dear ones. . . . "Wait for me, wait for me!" . . . But they can't, they must continue on their journey and we know we can't follow, not yet. We can only look up, earthbound.

And yet we sometimes feel their presence so powerfully there is no mistaking it. And with it, the presence of God.

For a long time during the first year after my father died, I was aware of him standing among roses, many roses, on a lovely slope of hill.

He had always loved roses. Those he raised were a source of great pleasure and pride. I can see him yet going out to trim them, wearing a beaten-up old sweat-stained hat that Mother deplored . . . his blunt, work-scarred hands arranging them so gently on the trellis, his ruddy face filled with such pleased affection. Sometimes he'd pause to sniff deeply of their fragrance, then remark to anyone who happened to be near—"Pretty, ain't they?"

Now here he was among the roses, many roses. . . . No, I didn't have a vision, and yet the lovely picture would come to me. He was always smiling faintly, with the familiar twinkle in his eyes, as if there was something delightful he wanted to say. And I knew without question what it must be: "Pretty, ain't they?"

Then he would turn and trudge away.

That was the only sad part of this image. That after it he must go without a backward glance for me.

And yet I did not protest it, for I realized he was in your keeping, God. You had your hand on his shoulder. You would stay close to him and close to me.

This awareness . . . sensation . . . define it as you will, came less frequently after the first hard weeks and ultimately came no more. Yet I remember it vividly, and even the memory gives me reassurance. My bright-eyed dad, always so vitally active, had not only gone, he was still going! Though without haste now, without worry or urgency.

He had time to pause and admire the flowers. Time to console me by sharing the wonder. To marvel in his old way—"Pretty, ain't they?"

MOTHER'S BIBLE

Death can also bridge the estrangements between people.

For twelve years my mother lived on alone in their little house with its roses. . . . Then one day when she was eighty-four . . . one bright day after serving lunch for my two brothers who often popped in for a bite and one of their lively debates on how best to improve the world . . . she hung her apron behind the door and went to join God and Dad.

I wish this were quite as idyllic as it sounds. She had not been feeling well for weeks and I'm sure she sensed that she was going. She had made quite a few little preparations, including leaving instructions, written in her familiar tiny script, in the Bible she always used, on her dresser where we'd be sure to find them.

But one thing uppermost on her mind she had been able to do little about. There had been a feud in the family. One of those agonizing conflicts between grown children that tear a parent apart. She had wept over it, prayed over it, but the wounds were far from healed.

But now that the house was silent and we all came rushing back, everybody forgot. People ran sobbing into each other's arms. And there was so much to be done. There was simply no time for hostilities. . . . Yet they refused to vanish altogether even in the face of death. Though proprieties were maintained, even an extra show of courtesy, after that first surge of emotion you could feel them quivering, threatening.

Then, that second night, we saw her Bible on the coffee table.

Not the "new" one given her on some anniversary years ago to replace the heavy, cumbersome old one with its family records. We had already consulted the "new" one. This was the old one so long ago relegated to the top shelf of the bookcase. Yet here it lay, on a table that had been cleared and dusted several times! Who had gotten it down? . . . Mystified, we consulted each other.

No one else had been here, at least no one who would have known or cared about that particular Bible. Yet none of us had done so, and each of us was as puzzled as the rest. . . . That Bible simply appeared; there is no other explanation for it.

Without a word everyone sat down while my sister opened the book at its marker. It opened to the thirteenth chapter of John. In a second she began to read aloud:

"'Now before the feast of the Passover, when Jesus knew that his hour was come that he should depart out of this world unto the Father, having loved his own which were in the world, he loved them unto the end.'"

She paused and looked around. All our eyes were wet. Hers went back to the page. "It goes on to tell the story of how Jesus washed the disciples' feet," she said. "And there's this—this place is marked! 'Little children, yet a little while I am with you. Ye shall seek me: and as I said unto the Jews, Whither I go, ye cannot come; so now I say to you. A new commandment I give unto you, That ye love one another; as I have loved you, that ye also love one another.'"

She couldn't go on. She didn't have to. The two who had been so tragically separated groped out for each other's hands. Then they embraced, holding each other as if never to let go.

The peace they made that night was to last. The bridge of death had become the bridge of love that is also God.

THE MESSAGE

Oh, God, my God, you have taken my mother away and I am numb with shock.

I see her apron still hanging behind the kitchen door. I see her dresses still in the closet, and her dear shoes there upon the floor.

Her house is filled with her presence. The things she so recently used and touched and loved. The pans in the cupboard. The refrigerator still humming and recent with her food. The flowers she had cut still bright in their bowl upon the table.

How quickly you called her, how mercifully. She simply stopped what she was doing and looked up—and you were there.

She was ready. She was always completely ready. Yet she must have known that she was going soon. There were bookmarks in her Bible at these passages:

"Though I speak with the tongues of men and of angels and have not charity . . ." Surely this was her message to us—to be at peace between ourselves. And:

"When Jesus knew that his hour was come that he should depart out of this world unto the Father, having loved his own, which were in the world, he loved them unto the end."

To the end. She loved us too to the very end.

Help us, who were her children, to draw near to each other now. And near to her. And through her, nearer to you.

FACE TO FACE

I am searching for you, God. I am trying to find you.

Sometimes you are close, as close as my own hand, my own breath. Again you disappear. I get too busy to pray, too busy sometimes even to think.

And though I feel a vague loneliness, unease, it doesn't seem to matter too much. I have all these other people to talk to, warm living people to work for and love and touch.

Then one of them is torn from me. . . . The phone rings. Or an ambulance comes screaming to my steps. . . . A doctor beckons, looking grave . . .

Then I cry out to you, "My God, my God!" . . . Whether in sheer anguish or anger, I call out to you. Then, as never before, I find you.

Death brings us face to face.

When this happens, all those things I have read or been told—how easy they are to forget. This is not somebody else's concept or philosophy of death. This is *my* death. My flesh-and-blood death to deal with. And now, as at no other time, I must decide whether or not I want any part of God.

But I must realize: If, in my agony, I turn away from God, then I, too, go down into death. The death of all hopes ever to see the one I love again (for I cannot reject God and still claim his promises). And the death of my own spirit. For life can never again have the meaning it had when both he and my God were in it.

If, as I must say good-by to the one who meant so much to me, I also abandon God, then I am doubly bereft.

If, in my pain, my almost intolerable sense of loss, I blame God, I am destroying myself. The words in Job, "Curse God, and die," mean exactly that. To curse God *is* to die in the vital core of self.

Have I ever found God? Do I truly know him? Death puts us to the test. And sometimes the closer we think we have been to God, the more severe the test. . . .

I though you loved me! I prayed, I had such faith—and now this!

I feel sure God understands. For we are only human, bound to those we care about with such fierce hot human ties. It is natural to weep, protest. (Jesus wept, too, at the death of his friend.) And we are like children; all of us are really children inside these grown-up bodies, especially when we lose someone. Like children we lash out at what we can't understand. Then, when the storm has subsided, we must be comforted. We plunge gratefully into the arms of the person we trust.

This is the time for God. Our own Creator. The one who not only gave us life but created and shared with us the life we loved so much. Where else can we turn for any real assurance that that life or our own lives have any meaning? God alone knows the answers, and in God alone can we find them, through his son.

Living in a time of slavery and slaughter, when life was considered cheap, Jesus told us over and over how precious life is. That not one sparrow falls without God's knowing and caring, not one hair of our head is harmed. . . . Living in a hot and arid country, where only the winter rains fill the cisterns or there is a single well for the town, he knew how constantly people were thirsty. Yet he spoke of the deeper thirst, the thirst for God. He told us to drink of the well of living waters, that we might have life everlasting. He told us that our time here is but the flick of an eye compared to eternity, and actually only preparation for the richer life beyond.

We hear those words so often at funeral sermons we forget they were not preached as funeral sermons. Jesus was speaking to people in farms and shops and homes, on busy highways and village streets. Not in hushed chapels with organ music playing and the heavy fragrance of floral wreaths. Not simply to comfort the bereaved. What he was telling those people, and us, was meant as a challenge to a more abundant, generous, God-trusting life here that would lead to an even greater life.

THE LESSON OF LOSS

Thank you, God, for the wonderful lesson of loss.
The arms of my friends console me, the love of my family surrounds

me. *The goodness and kindness of my neighbors sustain me like a staff.*

Though I am prostrate with grief I am supported, as by a great shining column that rises up within me. I can lift up my head, I can walk upright. I can even smile.

For their sympathy is also like a lovely pool in which I see glimpses of goodness and beauty never revealed before. In it my agony is soothed, the ache of my heart becomes bearable and will, I know, one day heal.

Surely if human beings can surround and help and support each other in such times of sorrow, then your love, oh God, must be even more great.

I feel your kind hand upon me through the touch of theirs. I feel your promises fulfilled.

I see my dear one fresh and new and whole, free of pain and problems, spared of all distress. I see that dear one lifted up into some new state so joyful and free and ongoing that excitement fills me.

I sense that blessed presence saying, "It is true! It really is. Believe this, oh believe this and don't grieve."

I am enriched by this loss. My faith is renewed. I am a better person for it.

God of our creation, God of our ongoing, thank you for this wonderful lesson of loss.

PROMISES TO KEEP

"The Lord gave, and the Lord hath taken away. . . ."

That familiar quote from Job. Mr. Malone (the minister in our little Christian church at home) used to challenge this. Got almost angry when he heard people speak of God's "taking" someone. "The Lord didn't take that child," he said. "A germ did." "The Lord didn't strike that man. A car did."

We are all subject to natural laws. When something goes wrong, when a law is broken, disaster follows. . . . But God is the author of the universe, source of those natural laws. Can't he change things to please us? What about miracles? What about prayers?

It is all such a mystery; we study and speak and search

and discuss and know so little. Erudite as we try to sound, we know, actually know so little.

That's got to be where faith comes in. . . . Do we ever need faith quite so much as when a life is snapped off unexpectedly? Suddenly, shockingly, one day here, the next day gone. A young life, especially, so full of joy and promise . . . faith, no matter what. The deep wordless recognition that what *is* must be accepted and does not mean God has abandoned us, nor intentionally done that young life in. . . . But God's *will?* No, I don't think we'd better get faith fouled up with God's will. . . .

The little girl rushing home from school eager to show her mother her drawing and a report card full of A's. . . . How can I believe in a God who would decide: "Aha, I shall cheat that mother of even that brief happiness, I won't even let her reach the doorstep, I'll take that child right now!"

Or my friends Frank and Sara Foster, en route to a Baptist convention with another ministerial couple, Joe and Diane Wortman. Beautiful parents with two children apiece; both had built flourishing churches; they'd witnessed in the streets and were planning a camp for homeless boys. . . . So much accomplished already, so rich a harvest ahead. . . . "The convention is waiting for them; Sara is supposed to sing (I gave her the voice of an angel). Nobody doubts they'll get there, but I've got other plans for them. I'll send a storm to bring that small plane down. . . ."

No, I don't even want to find a God like that. Any god worthy of my worship at least has common sense. And my God is a god of mercy, of fair play and compassion as well as a god of power (who can and continually does work miracles and answers prayers). My God would never deliberately bring harm to anyone. But if it happens—if it simply happens due to wind and rain and weather and man's own mistakes, then God has promises to keep:

Life continuing. An even richer, fuller, brighter ongoing life to compensate.

Lord, dear Lord, I will hold fast to you and remember:

You did not take those young lives, but you received them. (How gently and how generously you received them!)

You did not will their going, but you accept their return.

You did not cut short their time of growth and happiness on earth, but you will enhance and enrich their time of growth and happiness where they have gone.

I will not grieve for what they have lost, I will rejoice for what they have gained.

I will not blame you for what happened; but I will thank you for what is happening now. To them, as they know you in person. To me, as I know you in spirit.

Thank you that your love can turn tragedy into triumph.

SO SHORT, BUT OH SO SWEET

And I must remember this about the death of the young. Sometimes a mission on earth can be accomplished in a very few years. (Jesus didn't live very long either.) Isn't it possible that the work someone may have been sent to do is finished?

Not in the case of those young ministers. No, no, that seems senseless; they were all set to help so many more, to do so much more *good*. But others? At least some others?

One thing is certain: A short life can be an intensely sweet one; almost always sweeter and purer than a life prolonged. Any parent who has lost a child acknowledges this. You sorrow for the joys of life that child has missed, but you recognize the pain and problems it has been spared. It goes back to its maker unembittered, unscarred, leaving only the most beautiful memories behind.

And we know—every instinct knows with some deep knowledge—that life does not stop, whatever its stage of interruption; it continues to develop in perfection. And usually far happier than it could possibly be in this precious but battle-wracked existence.

Quite a body of evidence is accumulating about the life experience beyond. Repeatedly, people who have been close to death, or who have actually died according to medical tests, who remember actually crossing over before being brought back by modern scientific technics, such people insist they experienced such joy, such unimaginable peace and transport that they didn't want to return.

HE WAS SO YOUNG

He was so young, God.

So young and strong and filled with promise. So vital, so radiant, giving so much joy wherever he went.

He was so brilliant. On this one boy you lavished so many talents that could have enriched your world. He had already received so many honors, and there were so many honors to come.

Why, then? In our agony we ask. Why him?

Why not someone less gifted? Someone less good? Some hop-head, rioter, thief, brute, hood?

Yet we know, even as we demand what seems to us a rational answer, that we are only intensifying our grief. Plunging deeper into the blind and witless place where all hope is gone. A dark lost place where our own gifts will be blunted and ruin replace the goodness he brought and wished for us.

Instead, let us thank you for the marvel that this boy was. That we can say good-by to him without shame or regret, rejoicing in the blessed years he was given to us. Knowing that his bright young life, his many gifts, have not truly been stilled or wasted, only lifted to a higher level where the rest of us can't follow yet.

Separation? Yes. Loss? Never.

For his spirit will be with us always. And when we meet him again we will be even more proud.

Thank you for this answer, God.

THE PROCESSION

The more people I lose to death, the nearer to God I am. I had not realized this until recently, and yet it's true.

When I was young, death was a terrifying stranger who snatched one of my playmates one night. I wept wildly and strove to join him by climbing as high as I dared in the maple tree.

Later, impossibly, the town lifeguard and hero drowned, and we were all in a state of shock; but it was mass emotion and unreal. Our grandparents died, but that was the way of the old. Our parents frequently mourned for friends and relatives and went to funerals, but what had that to do with us, the young? For we were, of course, immortal. . . . And yet, in the haunted catacombs of our souls he lurked, that threatening stranger. "No, no, he dare not touch us, we were too young, we hadn't lived yet, and besides we would live forever!"

Then Tommy crashed. My aviator cousin with his grand helmet and goggles, who was going to teach me to fly. And I knew then it wasn't the old and tired and life-used that death relished and stalked, it was the young. And I was horrified and frightened. It was all wrong and cruel, it had nothing to do with God.

But death becomes less of a stranger as we grow older. No less cruel when we have to give up somone we love. But a force we can accept. Now we are the ones attending the funerals while our immortal young run free. We have learned how to say good-by to people, so many people, and go on from where we were. (Sometimes straight from their services to a party.) Besides, death has been all doctored up now, as if you're not supposed to notice. People don't carry on the way they used to, at least when they can be seen; sometimes they don't even have funerals. It's more as if the one who's died has just moved away.

Yet if you care . . . if you truly care.

The pain that seems at times beyond bearing. The aching vacancy that begs somehow to be filled. Speak of him, oh speak of him—reminisce about him with others, talk about the good times, laugh so you won't cry. . . . And this is good for a while; it helps to be with people who knew him, who can share the memories. But watch out lest you try to make their company a substitute for the one who can't return. No other living person and no amount of talk can recreate him for you. So let go of them, let go as quickly as you can.

And the letters, the pictures, the garments hanging mute in the closet. The records you listened to together, the little jokes and souvenirs. What of these? What of these? . . . Let go. Gradually, little by little, let go; for we must stop reaching backward toward the places our dear ones have left before we can reach out and upward toward the place where they *are*. Stop hugging them to your breast in grief. Open your arms to embrace them in prayer.

Back in those days when I was so young I remember a minister's saying we ought to pray for the departed. I couldn't imagine why. They'd lived and died, for them it was all over, I thought, their fate was sealed. How could they possibly need or want my prayers?

But when you are older and have lost someone, you don't have to ask. You find yourself praying, not so much for them as for yourself, because it seems the only way to make contact. . . . "Oh, Cindy—" . . . "Oh, Mother—" . . . "Oh, John—" . . .

Dear God, let them know I love them and am thinking of them. Please take care of my darlings.

And gradually the tone of the prayer changes—at least it did for me. I found it became less a cry of desperate longing than a prayer of loving release. A message of blessing. A time to remember those I loved and to rejoice that they were safely in God's gardens. Like my dad.

You get used to anything, even intense personal loss. And you get used to the more and more frequent departures. This relative. That. A close friend. Another friend. A neighbor, a beloved teacher, your boss. . . . You even get used to receiving that first shock. *No.* I can't believe it—not him! . . . There seems no rhyme or reason so often, no special order, only that there are always more. And more.

Until after a while it dawns on you how many there are. It must be getting crowded in heaven! When you try to remember them in prayer, you have to call the roll. But there is something actually joyful in the thought. . . . They are not alone up there. They have "the blessed company of heaven."

And quietly, steadily, all unseen, this procession of departures has been leading you closer to God.

At least so it was with me. With everyone who leaves, I am being drawn, without knowing it, just a little nearer to the original source who designed their destination. And my own.

For as surely as he sent me to this earth, he has given me a return ticket. I know that one day I, too, will be in that same procession. I will join them. . . . And the mere fact that I call their names in prayer, lifting them up, asking for them peace and joy and all of God's blessings, comfirms the fact that they are *there*. As I, too, will one day be there.

And so I don't fear death any more, or doubt God any more.

Death has helped me to find him.

THE NEW DIMENSION OF LOVE

I know that they live again, that they live again, my dear ones whom I no longer can see.

You have not taken them into a kingdom—they wouldn't be happy in a kingdom—but you have opened wide for them a place of joy and peace and challenge, where their dreams can be fulfilled.

And this place somehow includes my own small portion of the world. They have not really left me, my dear ones, they are close by me in a way they could never be before.

They know how much I miss them, they know how much I love them. They understand about all the things I meant to do for them and didn't, the words I failed to say.

They put their arms around me to comfort me. They tell me, "It's all right, human love is faulty but for all its faults enduring. It goes beyond such things, it goes beyond even this separation. The loss of the body does not mean the loss of that love. There is a new life in which that love is even stronger. For God is love, remember. God is truly love."

And this I know. This, God, I know: They are with you now— forever. And so with me forever—in this new dimension of love.

"WE'LL COME"

It seems such a pity that the scattered members of families almost never get together except in times of loss.

Someone dies. Someone dearly beloved. And suddenly the telegrams and letters begin to fly, the phone calls are being made. People who correspond only at Christmas now send wires, special deliveries. People who haven't heard each other's voices in months, even years, are communicating: "Oh, no! I'm so sorry—when did it happen? We'll come. We want to come." . . .

We'll come. We want to come. . . . Suddenly it seems imperative. It is a compelling desire. For the news that has summoned us in the cause of sorrow has warm and quite wonderful overtones. We must go, we must draw together in this hour when one of our own has passed. We want to, for the sake of that person, but also for our own. To comfort and support each other. And oh, to see each other again—brothers and sisters long apart. Aunts and uncles and cousins. Yes, and second cousins, too. The whole clan.

So many of them, arriving so unexpectedly from so many places. It is a revelation, sweet and rather startling. Not only that they are so numerous, but that they too should want to come. And that in this busy world where distances are great and relatives tend to become strangers, blood ties still are strong.

How good it is to see them. How consoling. And despite the sadness of the occasion, how pleasant in so many ways. The visits so solemnly begun drift off into laughter and good talk: "I hadn't realized you had so many children. That makes me a great aunt, doesn't it? And they're so pretty— whose side do they take after, ours or Mac's" . . . "Now let's see, whatever became of Lou's girl, Irene?" . . . "Remember the time Dad spanked all of us for going swimming that day the waves were so big?"

Reminiscences. The matching of statistics. News. And the old family friends who are so much a part of the past that they too belong: "Your papa came running to our house the night you were born." . . . "Your mother and I went to school together—" The family doctor who saw you all through so many illnesses is there. The neighbors from the old house on Seneca Street.

They too wanted to come. Out of respect to the one who is gone, yes, that is their excuse. But mainly to claim their own memories of the lost days once again, days in which he played a part, the precious days that are past.

And as you all sit around laughing, talking, eating the food the neighbors have brought in, you remark: "How Dad would have enjoyed this. Oh, how happy he would have been to be with all of us." And you add, "If only people could have get-togethers like this when we're all alive!" And everyone agrees.

But we can't. This too we acknowledge. We are so busy, so far apart. It takes the deep seriousness of death to draw us, to make us realize that all lives that relate to us are dear—these scattered lives. And when it is all over, though you rejoice at having claimed them once more, it is sad to say good-by. Then a dear little woman, strong in faith, says simply: "We'll meet again. Don't worry, it's all right. We'll all meet again."

Again something warm and wonderful comes over you. You realize, "Why, yes, that's right. He'll be there too—and we'll all be together again!"

III

When Loneliness Is New

I call to rememberance my song in the night:
I commune with mine own heart.

Psalm 77:6

GOD SAYS, "GET UP!"

*A*gain and again God says, "Get up!"

Sometimes he speaks through people, and it seems a harsh, unfeeling physical command. .... I am ill. Pain-wracked. Anyone can see I'm in no condition to leave my bed. Yet the doctor and the nurses enter, and to my astonishment say, "Let's get you up awhile today. You must get up."

Sometimes it is but the voice of the stern but loving command of the God without and within. . . . I am prostrate with grief, my life is in shambles, there is nothing left for me now but the terrible comfort of my tears. . . . Dimly, beyond drawn shades, I realize the world is going on heartlessly about its business. People pass by, some of them even laughing, outside on the street. . . . The telephone rings. There is a knocking at my door.

I stuff my ears, try to burrow deeper into my awful loss. Then the voice comes strong and clear: "Get up."

"I can't, I can't. . . . O God, I can't."

It comes again. This time more imperative than the telephone or the doorbell or the awareness of duties to people who need me. *"Get up!"*

Startled, I stagger to me feet . . . grope protestingly for some means of support—and find it. A chair to lean on, or unexpectedly the arm of a friend. . . . But in a few minutes I realize I won't need them, for there is another support beside me. God has provided the brace. He would not call me back to action otherwise. He will sustain me.

It is so easy to "quench my thirst with tears and so learn to love my sorrows," as the Paulist priest James Carroll wrote. So easy, and often so tempting, to fall in love with our own misfortunes. For that way lies sympathy (if sometimes only self-sympathy) and possible escape. . . .

We're tired, fed up with this rat race, this drudgery; we don't want to work. . . . "Get up. Do it!"

We are ill and nurturing our own illness. . . . "Get up. Get well."

We are stricken with sorrow or shame; our troubles overpower us, we long only to sink into the slough of our despondency behind locked doors. . . . The command rings loud and clear: "You cannot bury yourself any longer. Get up! Get on with living."

Again and again Jesus said those words. To people lying in sickbeds or even on deathbeds: "Arise! Get up." And they did, and were well and lived again. He is saying them still to anyone who will listen: "Don't give in to your pain and problems. Don't nourish your grief. Get up."

Thank you, Lord, for never failing to say them to me.

Life is too short and too sweet to squander in the darkness, crying. Thank God, thank God you always get me up and back into action. This, as nothing else could, proves how much you care for me.

WHEN LONELINESS IS NEW

Loneliness is so new to me, Lord. I need your help in handling it.

Help me to be a little more proud. Not aloof, but a little less eager for human contact. Let me remember that other people are busy with their friends and families. Don't let me overwhelm them with invitations.

I don't want them to feel obliged to come, out of concern for me. And certainly under no obligation to "do something for me" in return.

This is a delicate area, Lord—help me to handle it sensibly and cheerfully.

Please guide me too when it comes to accepting invitations.

My loneliness is sometimes so acute I feel I'd go almost anywhere at any time with anybody. This is an affront to my self-respect.

Don't let me be too proud, too choosy, but don't let my desperation show or get me into situations I'd regret.

Lord, help me not to talk too much when I do go out. Especially about myself—my problems, my grief.

Let me remember how I've dreaded seeing other lonely people who pinion friends to hear their tales of woe. Don't let me cheapen my sorrow by wearing it on my sleeve.

Lor, make me such good company that I will still be wanted. Help me to remember that I'm not the first person to face loneliness, and I won't be the last.

Thank you, Lord, for giving me the grace to handle loneliness.

THE LONELY WOMEN

God bless lonely women.

All lonely women who come home at night to find no man there.

No scent of smoke lingering. No ashtrays overflowing. No exasperation of men's dear strewings—socks, papers, coins, keys. No sweet tang of shaving lotion and cigars.

God bless all lonely women who will not leap at the sound of a strong male step on the stairs.

God bless women, all the lonely women who lie mateless in the night, hungry for the comfort of arms around them. A strong shoulder to rest on (and cry on and complain on). A male presence to depend on, sensible or brave when threatening noises pierce the dark.

God bless women without men to solve things, fix things, find things—bills and problems and toasters and washing machines and missing fuses so there will be light.

Women who have no man to zip them up, repair an earring, run an errand, share a hope, a dream, a memory, a surprise.

God be gentle with women who have loved men, lost men, or missed the marvel of being with men.

And put gentleness in the hearts of all women who still have men—that they may be kinder to the lonely women, and infinitely more kind to the men who share their lives.

SHE SITS IN DARKNESS

I thought I was lonely, Lord, until I found this woman.

She is blind, quite blind; she sits alone in the darkness.

She is deaf, quite deaf; she sits alone in the silence.

She is ill, quite ill; it is difficult for her to move.

I cannot speak to her, I cannot let her know who I am. I can only press her hand and try to comfort her by my presence, so that she will not feel quite so alone.

Lord, I know now what loneliness is. I have been in its presence. I know that I am not truly lonely, after all.

I can see—I have the company of magazines and books.

I can hear—I have the company of my radio, my telephone, my TV set.

I can move, Lord. I can go about my work, my errands, and go to call on this woman.

"Who am I?" I have often asked of you, and of myself. How much more this question must torment anyone lost in the silent darkness.

I must help her to find an answer to that question. I must let her know, somehow, that she is real and important. Very important. Very real.

She has deeply touched another human being. And because of her I am less lonely and less lost!

God, convey this to her. Help me to make her aware of this.

THE LOVELY SOLITUDE

I've just come from visiting a big noisy family and I'm exhausted. Filled with happy memories yes, but glad to get home.

And now seems a good time to realize that instead of lamenting my loneliness, I should be singing the blessings of solitude!

Thank you for silence, Lord. Sheer silence can indeed be golden. And so can order. I gaze about this apartment with new respect; it seems beautiful right now, and simple to keep it so with nobody to pick up after but myself.

And independence—how divine. The freedom to do what I please.

I can listen to the kind of music I really enjoy or watch the kind of television show. I can read, write, sew, paint or just think without being interrupted.

I can read in bed at night as late as I want without disturbing anybody. I don't have to worry about anybody else's feelings, or have my own unexpectedly hurt. I don't have to argue or pretend to agree when I don't.

I don't have to be bored. I can give a party. I can call up a friend for lunch.

And even if all the people I know are busy, I have only to dial a few numbers, travel a few blocks to be in the thick of those who'll welcome me with open arms. My clubs, my church—hospitals, the Y, the Salvation Army.

More places than I can count, where there are always vital, joyous, stimulating people; and people whose loneliness and needs so far surpass mine that I feel richly endowed and aglow.

Lord, let me remember all this when loneliness gets me down.

And let me remember it also when I get too enamored with solitude. Don't let me become ingrown and selfish.

There is so much work to be done and so many people to be helped and enjoyed. Especially for the woman who lives alone.

PSALM FOR DELIVERANCE

I pleaded with God to deliver me from trouble.

My brain was bruised from seeking solutions. My body

ached from the effort. My nerves were strung tight; they would break, I knew, something would break if I forced myself to go on.

"Help me," I kept crying to my God. "Give me answers. Deliver me from this torment." But my own voice seemed to despair of such deliverance even as I called.

Then a strange quiet came upon me. A kind of divine indifference. I knew without words or even thoughts that I could only withdraw and wait quietly upon the Lord.

And he did not forsake me.

He came in the quiet of the night; he was there in the brilliance of the morning. He touched my senses with hope; he healed my despair. And with the awareness of his presence came the deliverance I sought.

The answers would be provided. Quietly, and in God's own way, they were working even as I waited.

THE RADIANT COMPANY

The Lord has led me into the radiant company of his people. Praise the Lord.

The Lord has given me the fellowship of others on the selfsame journey to find him.

He has given me a spiritual family. He has given me sisters in the dearest sense of the word. He has given me brothers.

We worship together, work together, pray together. And are as richly rewarded in the praying as those we pray for.

I can worship the Lord alone. I can pray alone.

I can know him fully and completely in total solitude. And this is good. For most of our lives we are alone. Despite the presence of many people, we are alone.

But to pray and worship the Lord with others who earnestly, honestly seek him, is to add new dimensions of strength and joy.

Praise the Lord for this gift of fellowship and friendship. For the miracles of work and happiness and healing that burst like stars and change the course of lives when people come together who truly love the Lord.

IV

When the Heart Is Ready

Thou shalt show me the path
of life; in thy presence is
the fullness of joy, and at thy
right hand there is pleasure
for evermore.

Psalm 16:11

THE ADVENTURE

*O*h, *God, I rejoice in the sheer adventure of living.*

Just to wake up in the morning and face the bright mystery of the day!

Even though I think I know, I can't possibly know what will happen before it's over. How many times will the telephone ring, bringing me what voices? What news will come int he mail?

Whom will I meet? Whom will I see? What good friend, what exciting stranger? And no matter how familiar the people who share my hours, what will they do or say?

All these people in the wings of my life waiting to make their entrances. Waiting to speak their lines, to engage me in dialogue that will affect each of us in so many ways.

Words of love, anger, argument, merriment, persuasion, praise—an infinite variety of lines unwritten, unrehearsed, full of pain or promise, or the simple small exchanges of everyday.

How wonderful this is, God. How endlessly intriguing this daily drama of living.

Now a comedy, now a tragedy, but always, always full of expectation. Always a mystery!

LET ME SAY "YES" TO NEW EXPERIENCES

Lord, don't let me be afraid to say "Yes" to new experiences. New places to go, new people to meet, new things to learn. Don't let me be a coward about trying things—new friends or new foods, new books or new music, new inventions, new ideas.

Sure, it's safer and a lot less trouble just to chug along in the same old rut. But that way lies age and stagnation. The young are so willing to try things. And while you didn't design us to stay young forever, if I'd created a world so gloriously full of creatures, places and adventures, I'd be sad to see my children cowering in corners, refusing to discover its surprises—at least until they had to.

Lord, thank you for helping me overcome sheer laziness and dread:

DREAD OF TRAVEL Half-eager to go, half-miserable before the complexities and problems any trip presents. How much easier not to have to shop, pack, cope with tickets and arrangements. Just to stay home where things are familiar. Yet how grateful I am for having made the effort. My life's store of friendships, knowledge and memories is enriched because of every trip I've taken.

DREAD OF SPORTS, PHYSICAL CHALLENGE Learning to swim and dive and skate, learning to ski and ride and play tennis. The voices that whimper and warn, especially as we get older: "The water's cold," or "You might get hurt," or "Stay here where it's warm and cozy. Who needs this?" Lord, don't let me give up the things I already can do, or give in to the voices that would stop me from at least attempting new ones. The back porch may be more secure, but the fun is in jumping the fences . . .

* * *

DREAD OF MEETING NEW PEOPLE *Even the friends now so dear to me were once sometimes frightening strangers. Yet you led me to them, Lord, often against my own resistance. And my life would be empty without them.*

God, don't ever take away my courage to try things.

Guard me from recklessness and folly, from foolishly sampling something just because it's "in" but that I know is wrong. Yet with that sole exception, keep alive my enthusiasm, my curiosity and daring. Let me say "Yes" to new experiences.

DON'T LET ME STOP GROWING

Don't let me ever stop growing, God. Mentally growing.

This mind you have given me (any mind!) has such marvelous potential. Why should I hobble it to a house, shackle it to a kitchen sink, cuddle down with it behind a coffee clache?

It's tempting, Lord, and all too easy to give up, make excuses, do the most comfortable thing. To settle for small talk, small interests, small horizons. I've seen this happen to so many women, some of my brightest friends. No wonder they're bored, God. Restless and bored . . . and boring.

Don't let this happen to me. Let me learn at least one new thing about something important every day. (Well, at least every other day.) Let no day pass without reading. Keep my mind always open, lively, reaching out for new interests, new knowledge.

Don't let me stop mentally growing.

Keep me always growing, God. Emotionally growing.

Help me outgrow my tears, my sometimes childish tantrums. The periods of self-pity when I tell myself nobody loves me, like I used to as a little girl. Please rescue me whenever I revert: steer me firmly forward into the calm waters of mature behavior. Let me feel the thrill of self-command, the dignity of self-control.

I want to keep emotionally growing.

Help me to keep growing, God, in relation to others.

So many people need me, depend on me, look to me for help, for answers. And I so often feel inadequate, unequal to their demands. Sometimes I even feel impatient and resentful, not wanting to be bothered. (Why should they drain my time and energy?) Forgive me for this feeling, Lord, and fortify my reserves.

Broaden my understanding. Deepen my compassion. Give me more wisdom and joy in sharing when I can.

As a wife, mother or friend, help me to keep growing.

Don't let me ever stop growing, God. Spiritually growing. Drawing ever closer to you, the source of it all: The universe. The world and the life upon it. The people . . . the person . . . myself.

I want to know you better, tune in more truly with the harmonies of all your creation, including the life that is my own.

Thank you for this person that you made in your image, Lord. Don't let me ever stop growing.

MYSELF

Thank you, God, for the dignity and beauty of self.

The precious, innate self. The only thing that can't be taken from us. The only thing we really own.

Not selfishness. Not self-seeking, self-will, self-gain. But the wonder of being, simply being—oneself.

God-created, God-watched, God-known.

Accountable, actually, only to you who made us. Shaped each of us outwardly so much alike, and yet made each of us so different in the vital, secret self.

You, who expect of each of us different things. You alone can go all the way with us. Take the final journey with us, and be there when we arrive. You will ask the final accounting of this self and its mission upon the earth.

In knowing you I need no longer question, "Who am I?"

I know. Insofar as it is possible, I know. Through you I know the true dignity, worth and beauty of my own being. For whatever my failings, I am a part of you who made me.

In knowing you, I know myself.

WHEN THE WINDS CRY I HEAR YOU

Oh God, my God, when the winds cry I hear you, when the birds call I hear you, when the sea rushes in it is like the rushing of my being toward yours.

You are voice of wind and bird and beat of sea. You are the silent steady pulsing of my blood.

I would know you better, I would taste your essence, I would see your face.

Yet these few small senses of mine cannot do more. You have defined their limits, you have set them within a framework from which we can only see and touch and hear and attempt to know these marvels that you have made.

But this too is the marvel—that you are within each of us as well. As we are drawn toward your greatness we are drawn toward the greatness within ourselves.

We are larger beings, we are greater spirits.

The hunger for you kindles a holy fire that makes us kinder, gentler, surer, stronger—ever seeking, never quite finding, but always keenly aware that you are all about us and within us.

You are here.

V

"Come Home"

He that goes forth weeping,
bearing the seed for sowing,
shall come home with shouts of joy,
bringing his sheaves with him.

Psalm 126:6

AT CHRISTMAS THE HEART GOES HOME

*A*t Christmas all roads lead home.

The filled planes, packed trains, overflowing buses, all speak eloquently of a single destination: home. Despite the crowding and the crushing, the delays, the confusion, we clutch our bright packages and beam our anticipation. We are like birds driven by an instinct we only faintly understand—the hunger to be with our own people.

If we are already snug by our own fireside surrounded by growing children, or awaiting the return of older ones who are away, then the heart takes a side trip. In memory we journey back to the Christmases of long ago. Once again we are curled into quivering balls of excitement listening to the mysterious rustle of tissue paper and the tinkle of untold treasures as parents perform their magic on Christmas Eve.

Or we recall the special Christmases that are like little landmarks in the life of a family.

One memory is particularly dear to me—a Christmas during the Great Depression when Dad was out of work and the rest of us were scattered, struggling to get through school or simply to survive. My sister Gwen and her school-teacher husband, on his first job in another state, were expecting their first baby. My brother Harold, an aspiring actor, was traveling with a road show. I was a senior working my way through a small college five hundred miles away. My boss had offered me fifty dollars—a fortune!—just to keep the office open the two weeks he and his wife would be gone.

"And boy, do I need the money! Mom, I know you'll understand," I wrote.

I wasn't prepared for her brave if wistful reply. The other kids couldn't make it either. Except for my kid brother Barney, she and Dad would be alone. "This house is going to seem empty, but don't worry—we'll be okay."

I did worry, though. Our first Christmas apart! And as the carols drifted up the stairs, as the corridors rang with the laughter and chatter of other girls packing up to leave, my misery deepened.

Then one night when the dorm was almost empty I had a long-distance call. "Gwen!" I gasped. "What's wrong?" (Long-distance usually meant an emergency back in those days.)

"Listen, Leon's got a new generator and we think the old jalopy can make it home. I've wired Harold—if he can meet us halfway, he can ride with us. But don't tell the folks; we want to surprise them. Marj, you've just got to come, too.

"But I haven't got a dime for presents!"

"Neither have we. Cut up a catalog and bring pictures of all the goodies you'd buy if you could—and will someday!"

"I could do that, Gwen. But I just can't leave here now."

When we hung up I reached for the scissor. Furs and perfume. Wristwatches, clothes, cars—how all of us longed to lavish beautiful things on those we loved. Well, at least I could mail mine home—with IOUs.

I was still dreaming over this "wish list" when I was called to the phone again. It was my boss, saying he'd decided to close the office after all. My heart leaped up, for if it wasn't too late to catch a ride as far as Fort Dodge with the girl down the hall! . . . I ran to pound on her door.

They already had a load, she said—but if I was willing to sit on somebody's lap . . . her dad was downstairs waiting. I threw things into a suitcase, then rammed a hand down the torn lining of my coat sleeve so fast it emerged mittened and I had to start over.

It was snowing as we piled into that heater-less car. We drove all night with the side curtains flapping, singing and hugging each other to keep warm. Not minding—how could we? We were going home!

"Marj!" Mother stood at the door clutching her robe about her, silver-black hair spilling down her back, eyes large with alarm, then incredulous joy. "Oh . . . *Marj.*"

I'll never forget those eyes or the feel of her arms around me, so soft and warm after the bitter cold. My feet felt frozen after that all-night drive, but they warmed up as my parents fed me and put me to bed. And when I woke up hours later it was to the jangle of sleigh bells Dad hung on the door each year. And voices. My kid brother shouting, "Harold! Gwen!" The clamor of astonished greetings, the laughter, the kissing, the questions. And we all gathered around the kitchen table the way we used to, recounting our adventures.

"I had to hitchhike clear to Peoria," my older brother scolded merrily. "Me, the leading man . . ." He lifted an elegant two-toned shoe—with a flapping sole. "In these!"

"But by golly, you got here." Dad's chubby face was beaming. Then suddenly he broke down—Dad, who never cried. "We're together!"

Together. The best present we could give one another, we realized. All of us, just being here in the old house where we'd shared so many Christmases. No gift on our lavish lists, if they could materialize, could equal that.

In most Christmases since that memorable one we've been lucky. During the years our children were growing up there were no separations. Then one year, appallingly, history repeated itself. For valid reasons, not a single faraway child could get home. Worse, my husband had flown to Forida for some vital surgery. A proud, brave man—he was adamant about our not coming with him "just because it's Christmas," when he'd be back in another week.

Like my mother before me, I still had one lone chick left—Melanie, fourteen. "We'll get along fine," she said, trying to cheer me.

We built a big fire every evening, went to church, wrapped presents, pretended. But the ache in our hearts kept swelling. And, the day before Christmas, we burst into mutual tears. "Mommy, it's just not right for Daddy to be down there alone!"

"I know it." Praying for a miracle, I ran to the telephone. The airlines were hopeless, but there was one roomette available on the last train to Miami. Almost hysterical with relief, we threw things into bags.

And what a Christmas Eve! Excited as conspirators, we cuddled together in that cozy space. Melanie hung a tiny wreath in the window and we settled down to watch the endless pageantry flashing by to the rhythmic clicking song of the rails.

. . . Little villages and city streets—all dancing with lights and decorations and sparkling Christmas trees . . . And cars and snowy countrysides and people—all the people. Each one on his or her special pilgrimage of love and celebration this precious night.

At last we drifted off to sleep. But hours later I awoke to a strange stillness. The train had stopped. And, raising the shade, I peered out on a very small town. Silent, deserted, with only a few lights still burning. And under the bare branches, along a lonely street, a figure was walking. A young man in sailor blues, head bent, hunched under the weight of the seabag on his shoulders. And I thought—home! Poor kid, he's almost home. And I wondered if there was someone still up waiting for him; or if anyone knew he was coming at all. And my heart cried out to him, for he was suddenly my own son—and my own ghost, and the soul of us all—driven, so immutably driven by this annual call, "Come home!"

Home for Christmas. There must be some deep psychological reason why we turn so instinctively toward home at this special time. Perhaps we are acting out the ancient story of a man and a woman and a coming child, plodding along with their donkey toward their destination. It was necessary for Joseph, the earthly father, to go home to be taxed. Each male had to return to the city of his birth.

Birth. The tremendous miracle of birth shines through every step and syllable of the Bible story. The long, arduous trip across the mountains of Galilee and Judaea was also the journey of a life toward birth. Mary was already in labor when they arrived in Bethlehem, so near the time of her delivery that in desperation, since the inn was full, her husband settled for a humble stable.

The Child who was born on that first Christmas grew up to be a man. Jesus. He healed many people, taught us many important things. But the message that has left the most lasting impression and given the most hope and comfort is this: that we do have a home to go to, and there will be an ultimate homecoming. A place where we will indeed be reunited with those we love.

Anyway, that's my idea of heaven. A place where Mother is standing in the door, probably bossing Dad the way she used to about the turkey or the tree, and he's enjoying every minute of it. And old friends and neighbors are streaming in and out and the sense of love and joy and celebration will go on forever.

A place where every day will be Christmas, with everybody there together. At home.

"COME HOME"

What is this strange compulsion to go home again? The place you were so anxious to leave, yet can never leave altogether. Too much of you is rooted there. You thought that you were tearing yourself free, bloodily by the roots, yet fragments always remain tenaciously. They are stronger than you think. They tug at you when you go back, they tease and torment you. They people the streets with ghosts, one of them yourself. "This is where you began, where you belong. Come back!" they seem to call.

Yet as Thomas Wolfe said, "You can't go home again." The change is almost too much to bear. And yet the sameness, the sweet tantalizing sameness . . .

When I was home the spring before Mother died we all piled into the car one night after supper and went for a ride. It was sunset, one of those dazzling, burning sunsets that turn the lake into molten gold and stirred me so as a girl. The same docks jutted, the same gulls wheeled, the same droves of little black mudhens were riding, plunging, riding their crests as the same tireless waves foamed in. The lake, mysterious, old, gray-green friend, was rolling in as it has for generations. Grandpa Giffith was chased across it by the wolves one winter. Grandpa and Grandma fished here, Mother and Dad courted in its shady parks. And so did we. Every walk and bench and statue is a silent shout of memories.

But change has disturbed its shores. Manawa Beach, where we used to hike and drink the cold spring water, is now suburbia. Even the farms whose pastures went down to the water have been broken up for handsome new homes. Showplaces all, straight out of magazines. My brother pointed them out: "The Schallers built that place. Next door is Dick Richardson. That's Zene White's—" On and on. He and his wife know them all, and the names they recite are often familiar but just as often strange. "The Hershbergers? Oh, he's the new coach at Buena Vista college. The Dyvads built that one—Harry's on the city council now." My brother and his wife never left our little town, and its occupants and alterations are as familiar to them as the doings of their own family.

There are other changes more staggering. Gone is Curt Bethard's huge old weather-scarred boathouse where we learned to swim and hung around all summer, savage-brown, always in love, waiting for life to happen. Now a cement hole in the ground attracts the kids instead. You hear them laughing and shouting, catch a whiff of chlorine from the pool, and feel a kind of affront for the fishy old lake still bashing bravely in. (What's the matter with kids today? We were never daunted by its mighty muscles, we loved its cold embrace. Even on the roughest days or when it was paint-green we went in!)

But branching up from the parks in all directions are many of the selfsame houses on the selfsame streets. There is solace in this, and a curious pain. How can they be here exactly as when you passed them on your way to school or played in them as children? Like the lake, they seem time-less, rooted in sameness forever, totally unaware that you have left and spent a lifetime elsewhere. And it seems that if only you would get out and go to them, you too would be the same. Back someplace in time again, safe with vigorous young parents who loved you, and your heart was not yet broken.

As we drove idly up and down it became a sentimental journey, for we began to call out the names of the people who once lived in these houses. "Redenbaughs were on the corner, the Beattys next door, then the Pattees—she was always so pretty—"

"Then the Crowleys," another voice would say, "and across the street the Sheffields. Remember how Gordon Sheffield used to hang around wanting to play with us older kids?" It became a kind of contest to see who could re-member first. Up and down the streets we cruised, piecing the past together through these names. Sometimes arguing, "No, the Roops *didn't* live there, it was the Ringenbergs. I oughta know, it's where I broke my arm when their bag-swing broke."

Laughter, a merry uniting of memories along with that dull ache . . . Our pilgrimage draws us even farther into the past. There stands the house where my parents were mar-ried. There, even, the small white cottage behind a hedge "where Dad and I met," Mother says. "At a church party. I'd come with another boy, but he walked me home."

Incredible! It mustn't be there any more in its prim white

dignity, looking as it must have looked that night. For now, impossibly, one parent is gone and the other is old and must soon be going. "Come back!" the mute houses are crying. "Nothing is different, nothing is changed. Come home.". . .

A few months later the phone rang: it was the call I'd been expecting, and it said, "Come home."

A hometown puts its arms around you when a parent dies. It gathers you to itself like a child. It feeds and comforts you. People surround you, warm living people, and they too say with their food and flowers and their eyes: "Stay. Oh, don't go away again, stay home." Sometimes they even say it aloud.

Church, the Sunday after the funeral . . . and she wasn't in her usual pew. She wasn't leading the dwindling Bereans (the "old people's class") downstairs clutching their worn Bibles. Mother played the organ for years when we were little; and she taught from the Beginners through Teens, Young Marrieds and finally these chipper but faltering few. "Where do they go when they graduate from your class now?" someone once asked her, and she laughed, "To heaven, I hope!" There were so few of them left to gather in that little classroom with its nostalgic smell of all church basements—coffee, hymnals, crayolas. And they looked so lost without her.

But it was Dick, a boy I grew up with, who put it into words after the sermon: "Come back, Marj. We need you. This is where you belong."

I felt strangled. There had been nothing for me here in years; why now? Why this strange compulsion now? For the temptation, however absurd, was intense, and the rejection violent.

"You don't understand. I couldn't" . . .

We spent days breaking up her home. Boxing up memories, keepsakes, and photographs that we'd probably never look at again but couldn't bear to part with. Dividing things, giving things away, cleaning. I walked across the backyard to throw out some trash. The arbor needed painting but still supported the torrent of red roses Dad had set out years ago and took such pride in. They climbed all over the garage and trailed the ground, greedy with life. They were almost too fragrant in the hot sun, their petals spilling. Great trees still arched the yard as if still waiting for family picnics on the grass, great gatherings of the clan. Mother's bag of clothespins was still hanging on the line.

My sister came out and we maundered about the place, remembering. And I said, "Why is man the only creature to experience this awful tie with his past? Memory is both a blessing and a curse, it hurts to recall the days which are over."

"That's because we remember only the good things about them. Looking back it always seems so much better." Then she said, "But man needs memory. Without memory there wouldn't be any painters or writers—no doctors to help us, no engineers, no architects. Memory is what enables man to survive and progress."

And this is true, but it's more than that. Man is the only creature whose emotions are entangled with his memory. And the anguish of memory is what we probably must pay for its pleasures, or whatever progress we gain from it. Bitter or sweet, we don't want any part of life to be really over; it should always be available, if only through people who have shared it. When they go they take a part of you with them. Even when something goes that has been a part of your life story—even that old wooden boathouse.

But the roots remain. The roots that will forever keep calling you back, begging. *"Come home!"*

VI

Beginning Again

O sing unto the Lord a new song;
for he hath done marvelous things!. . .

Psalm 98:1

BEGINNING AGAIN: A TRUE LOVE STORY

This is a true love story. A story of the miraculous way God brought together two people who needed each other, and turned their tragedy into happiness.

It bagan, for me, with a phone call one bright February day, and the words from a total stranger: "I love you. You have saved my life!"

I listened. As a writer you learn to listen, sometimes puzzled, always expectant, never shocked. You learn to recognize those whose need is real. This was no kook. The voice, as it went on, was rich and refined. He was a doctor from suburban Pittsburgh, he told me, absolutely devastated by the loss of his wife. Unconsolable, however desperately his family, friends and patients tried. Lonely, wild with grief, suicidal. When, on New Year's night, only a few weeks ago, God put into his hands a little book: *I've Got to Talk to Somebody, God.*

"It was at the very bottom of a pile of her things. I read it that night, and it saved my life. I read it over and over. But I never even write to authors, let alone try to contact them," he said. "I had no idea I would ever be talking to you. After all, the book was published years ago; I had no idea where you lived, or if you were even alive." Until yesterday, while visiting his son in Silver Spring, Maryland, on the way to Florida. He didn't remember even packing the book, but incredibly there it was at the very top of his case. And there, for the first time, he read the information on the jacket: The author lived not far away, somewhere in the Washington, D.C., area.

"I knew I *had* to call you," he said. "But trying to track down your number took hours." Finally, and again incredibly, he found himself speaking with a pleasant man who said, "Yes, of course. Her husband was my cousin. He died last year.

"Somehow, I knew before he told me," George said. "If you are still free, I would like to come to see you."

Yes, I was free, I said, pleased and touched; but unfortunately I was leaving on a two weeks' speaking trip. By that time he would be in Florida.

"I'll wait," he insisted. And, unlikely as it seemed at the time, he did. When I returned, the mailbox was stuffed with notes, all postmarked Silver Spring. And when I called, simply because I'd promised, he whooped for joy. The next night, though I suggested we meet somewhere nearer, he drove sixty miles to the lakeside cottage at the end of a bumpy country road, where I didn't think anybody would ever find me.

I gasped when he walked in the door, this handsome six foot man, with his arms full of roses. For suddenly, and quite clearly, a small voice informed me: *"You will marry this man before Christmas."* Preposterous! I am not one of those people who say, "God spoke to me, God told me this or that." I can't honestly remember ever hearing such a voice before. Absurd.

It seemed even less possible as the evening progressed. True, an enchanted evening: all the way to and from the cozy restaurant for dinner he sang to me, in the most beautiful male voice I have ever heard. He was poised and gallant and funny, and for real. He had brought along his little black doctor's bag to prove it—filled with pictures, clippings and other credentials. We talked for hours. Here are some of the things I learned about George that night, and later from his family, his nurses and patients and others who loved him:

George and his wife had that rarity, a perfect marriage. "In fifty years neither of us were ever untrue to each other." From the beginning they agreed their relationship would take precedence over everthing else in life. As a young physician he prospered early. Leaving the youngsters with willing grandparents, they vacationed together in Florida two months of every year. A third month was spent with the family at their summer cottage on Lake Erie. In September or October they traveled, generally just together again. But between times, he says, he worked long and hard, making house calls and keeping office hours till after midnight, "to put the kids through college and grad school."

Meanwhile, his wife was not only his sweetheart and companion but housekeeper, secretary, bookkeeper, nurse. "She handled everthing. I never wrote a check or paid a bill. I didn't even answer the telephone." Keeping their social life at a minimum, they spent fifty beautiful ardent years living only for each other.

Thus, when his wife died suddenly one morning, almost in his arms at their Lake Erie cottage, he went into shock. "My whole world collapsed. I was like a child turned out in a strange city in the dark. I didn't know what to do, how even to dial for help. I just stood there and screamed. Then I grabbed a bottle of sleeping pills. I could not imagine life without her; I had to die too, I couldn't go on." The sounds of his agony so frightened one dog, a poodle, it dived straight through a screen and ran. The other, a big golden Labrador retriever, hurled himself against his master's chest, knocking the pills from his hand. "I owe my life to that dog."

Neighbors came. Sons were summoned. He was taken home. From that day on he was like a zombie, a man literally ill, almost autistic with grief. To keep his sanity, he continued to practice, but gone was his laughter, his wit, his songs. Again and again I have been told by his nurses, patients, other doctors, 'You wouldn't have known it was the same man. Before he was always so merry, always singing. You know that beautiful voice of his? We could hear it the minute he entered the hospital, it cheered up the patients, the whole staff. Now he was silent, absolutely broken, and nobody could reach him. Everybody tried but it was useless, he wouldn't accept invitations, go anyplace. He was losing weight, dying himself and nobody could help."

This was the state George was in that New Year's night he had briefly described to me. Alone in the bedroom they had shared, cursing God and wanting to die, he told me, when for no logical reason a picture, his own picture, standing on a dresser clear across the room, suddenly pitched forward and crashed to the floor. No wind, no bolt of lightning, just that sudden crash. "Curiously, the picture didn't even break, although a little china dog sitting in front of it was shattered."

Shaken, George fell to his knees. "Forgive me, God," he begged. "But oh, help me, *help* me."

It was at this point something urged him to open the door to the closet beside the bed. "A white door, whose panels make the sign of the cross—it was the first time I'd ever noticed." Behind it a huge pile of his wife's things were stored. "Not books, I'd gone through all her books the day before, and never even looked at a title. Just dresses, purses, knitting materials, you name it. But something told me to reach down, clear down under the pile. And what my fingers found and brought out *was* a book—your book with a title that went straight to my heart. A book that told me you had suffered too, a lot of people suffer, but with the help of God they can and must go on."

It helped, he said, it helped. But no words, whether written by strangers or spoken by caring friends, can fill an empty house or bring back the voice and touch of the beloved. Still George knew, if only to please his frantic family, he must make an effort to come out of his personal tomb. He was finally persuaded to accept the repeated invitations of a Florida couple who had been very close. "We'll give a big party for you," they pleaded. "We'll even send your plane ticket."

No, he would drive, he told them. So he started out one day, with an intended overnight stop at the home of his lawyer son in Maryland. Halfway to Silver Spring, however, another incredible thing happened. George found that his car had somehow crossed a high, impossible embankment and was heading down the superhighway in the wrong direction! With two huge trucks bearing down on him. He managed to swerve out of their path and smash into a tree on the embankment. Nobody was hurt, although a wrecker had to be called to free the car.

The experience was so unnerving, however, he yielded to his son's advice not to drive on to Florida for a few days. It was at this point he discovered the book in his luggage. "I knew then that something strange was going on. If you were alive and still lived in the area, I had to find you."

I was deeply moved by his story. But when, hours later that first night, he kissed me and asked me to marry him, I gently but firmly said No. "Not because 'this is so sudden.' You're still in love with your wife, George. And from all the things you've told me, I know I never could be the kind of wife she was to you."

"But I love *you* now! The past is gone, it's all over. Something happened the minute I heard your voice, it was like waking up from a long nightmare. And when I actually saw you—! It's not your book, it's you, the wonderful time we've had together just in these past few hours. We need each other. God himself must have brought us together. Please say you'll at least make an effort to know me."

Patiently I explained how difficult that would be. He was still practicing in Pittsburgh. I was busy researching a new book, while winding up promotion commitments on the one just published. "I'm really not right for you, George. A large part of me will always be married to my career."

He looked so crestfallen I groped about for a gift. Perhaps a copy of my latest, *God and Vitamins*. As a medical doctor he would probably disagree with its major premise, that for most of us vitamin supplements are necessary. But so be it. Signing it, I thought regretfully, "Well, that's that. I'll probably never hear from him again."

The next morning the telephone rang. To my amazement it was George, announcing in a voice charged with excitement, "This is fantastic, I just can't believe it. Your book about vitamins—I stayed up and am about halfway through it and I agree with everything you say! I've been using vitamins with my patients for years! In fact, at Pitt I worked with Dr. King, one of the early pioneers in vitamin C."

Could he come down again to see me? No, I was sorry, I was packing for a trip to Israel. Perhaps when I got back.

But turning away from the phone I remembered hearing somewhere: "There are no coincidences. Only Godincidences." Adding them up, I could not but marvel: The falling of the picture. The finding of the book. The accident that could have been fatal, but instead only kept him from going on to Florida. His finally dialing a number that proved to be that of my husband's cousin. And now this.

"You will marry this man," the voice spoke again. *"You will marry him before Christmas."*

My own marriage was a different story. Good, but like most, far from perfect. The Great Depression was less kind to engineers and free-lance writers than it was to doctors. During our years of struggle my husband and I encouraged and supported each other, but there was no one with whom to leave our four children for vacations, and no time. It was almost ten years before my husband took even a week away from his work, and many more as chief executive with a large corporation in Washington before he managed a month's vacation, let alone four. He was a wonderful man, successful, generous, admired by everyone. "The best boss we ever had," his people said. But desperately driven, partly to compensate for the time he must spend in hospitals.

He had been cruelly burned with X-ray as a boy. Huge draining ulcers on his back showed up while he was still in college. These had to be dressed every night, and frequently cut out, followed by painful skin grafts. Diabetes and three heart attacks took their toll. Eventually cancer began to ravage his body. The last few years of our forty-eight together were torture for him, and agony for those who could not help him, however desperately we tried. Though the children and I moved heaven and earth to save him, and held his hands to the very end, we could not wish him back.

I missed him and mourned him. But for the first time, almost since our marriage, I felt at peace for him—and for myself. God had blessed me with wonderful health. I still swam, danced, water skied and felt about twenty years old. I still had many things to write. And perhaps, after a period of adjustment, there would still be time for love. "Mother, pray for someone special," my daughter Melanie advised. "That's what I did after I got over my divorce from Rick. Two or three times a day I just asked God to send me somebody special. And along came Haris!" She smiled at her beautiful Greek husband, with whom she was now so happy.

Why not? It had worked for her. So each morning after my shower, or in summer my cold swim; and each night, standing on the balcony at bedtime, I would lift my arms and pray: "Please, God, send me a wonderful man who will love me, and whom I can love."

I wasn't in any hurry, I just felt if this were God's will, it would happen. But the man would have to have certain qualifications if I were ever to consider marrying again. On New Year's night, trying to map out my life a year after my husband's death, I half-whimsically wrote them down. Such a man would have to be: 1. A believer, devout. 2. In good health. 3. Successful professionally. 4. Intelligent, well read. 5. A good talker, but also a good listener. 6. Sexy, ardent. 7. A good dancer. (Not absolutely essential, but why not ask for what you want?)

Six weeks later George called me.

I had forgotten all about the list, however. And it was months before I thought of it again.

Meanwhile, George stormed the gates. He did return and saw me off to Israel. And he met the plane three weeks later, again with his arms full of flowers. A bombardment of letters and phone calls followed, along with gifts and more flowers. Easter week he appeared with his dogs, including Ben, the lab who had saved his life. Into his jeep we piled and drove to Ocean City, Maryland, for a week at his son's. A glorious carefree week of running the dogs on the beach, swimming, dancing. He was a marvelous dancer, a magnificent swimmer—a former lifeguard and captain of the champion Pitt swimming team, I discovered. Also one of the most eloquent and entertaining persons I have ever met. Never had I enjoyed anyone's company so much. And so on Easter Sunday, kneeling together in church, when he squeezed my hand and again asked the crucial question, I could resist no longer.

"Yes, oh, yes!" I whispered. Never mind that here was a man who would never get over his wife (I thought). Never mind that I couldn't balance a checkbook, let alone fill the multiple roles she had for him. What really mattered was that God *had* sent me "a wonderful man who loved me and whom I could love." And did!

Thrilled, we rushed home from church and called his family. "When?" They asked. "June," I heard him reply. "No, no, no!" I rushed onto the scene. I had commitments in Canada this summer, a book to finish, things to settle and dispose of before our lives could be joined. "We can't possibly be married before Christmas."

"*Christmas?*" he gasped. How could we endure being separated again so long? We had to, I insisted. After all, we weren't a couple of kids who couldn't wait. "That's exactly it," he said soberly. "We're *not* kids. We don't have that much time."

I was so adamant, however, he had to yield . . . Daily letters and phone calls. Two weekend visits. Then he was putting me on a plane for Allentown, Pennsylvania, where my granddaughter was dancing in the ballet. He would drive on to Maryland to help celebrate his own granddaughter's birthday. We were in tears at parting, but also cheerful, mature. I was making progress, time was flying. We had so much to look forward to. Keep your sights on Christmas.

This was the mood I was in when I reached my son's house and collapsed, from sheer joyous exhaustion. The week before had been spent in New York doing newspaper interviews and talk shows about *God and Vitamins*. On each I worked in the fact that at seventy I was about to become the bride of a vigorous, swimming, dancing doctor, seventy-one. A man who had himself pioneered in the use of vitamins. How remarkable that seemed, falling asleep. How good God was . . . Then I heard it again, the small voice speaking: *"Don't wait!"*

I smiled, overtired, dismissing it; but it wouldn't be still. *"Don't wait,"* it went on and on, all night it seemed. *"Don't wait!"*

I heard it again the next morning, dancing in the shower. I know it's foolish to dance in the shower, but I always have, especially when so happy. I thought of Kathy, dancing tonight in the ballet. I thought of George. In sheer exuberance I kicked as high as I could, trying to touch the shower head. Suddenly, I was grabbing space. *"Don't wait!"* the voice reminded, as I skidded across the slippery tub, and crashed against its rim.

For an instant I was too nauseous, shocked and pain-assaulted to think. Yet the voice would not be still. Clutching my chest, I crept downstairs. An ambulance was called, the four fractured ribs were taped. I was given pain killers. Somehow I sat through the beautiful ballet. But pain and those incessant words gave me no peace for the next three days. To my dismay, there was no call from George. I was hurt, bewildered, and for the first time afraid. What if his love were cooling? What if his family were urging him to think it over, advising *him* to wait? I had not fully realized how great was my need for him until then.

Finally, on the third night, the call I had been praying for came. My son Mark explained about the accident and handed the phone to me. I was crying so hard I couldn't speak. "Darling, I'm so sorry!" George said. "I didn't want to bother you, I wanted you to be free to enjoy your family."

"Let's not wait!" was all I could think to say. "You were right. Something tells me we shouldn't wait."

"Thank God! I've been in misery."

He would have come at once; he thought I meant now— or next week. Consulting the calendar a few days later, we chose the Fourth of July. Our honeymoon would start in Canada, where I still had engagements to fill. Meanwhile, six weeks to get ready for the wedding.

With the help of sons and daughters, all was achieved. They even shooed me off for a college class reunion one week before. The ceremony, for family and a few close friends, was to be at six o'clock on the patio beside the lake. The weather had been glorious all summer. But we awoke that morning to a raging rain. "Don't worry," the bride-groom said when he called. "I promise you a beautiful day." The blinding rain was still falling, however, when he and his entourage set forth at four o'clock. There were times when the cars had to stop. Yet he kept confidently praying: "Lord, you parted the Red Sea, I know you can part these clouds for Marjorie. She has worked so hard, please do it for her, not for me." And lo, as they turned down that bumpy country road, the sun broke through!

People were mopping up the chairs, bringing out the flowers. The minister arrived, the music began to play. I wore a pink dress the color of the sunset. And as George and I joined hands to repeat our vows, the most beautiful rainbow I've ever seen arched the sky.

We had returned from our honeymoon, and I was packing up books and papers for the move to Pittsburgh, when I came across that forgotten list. "George, listen, you won't believe this," I gasped, and read him those qualifications. "You fill every single one—and more. I didn't even ask God to also make this man handsome. And a great swimmer, with a sense of humor, and a fantastic voice!"

"Who is this guy?" he grinned. "If I ever meet him, I'll kill him." Then, taking that list of specifications to see, himself, he too exclaimed. For it was dated New Year's Day, 1981. "No, I *don't* believe it. Six months ago, to the very day!" He was gazing at me, incredulous. "About what time was it when you wrote this?"

"Around ten o'clock, as I recall. I'd gotten ready for bed. Why?

"That's when it happened. When the picture fell—I remember thinking at first it was the clock. When I was in such terrible despair—until something told me to reach into that closet, where I found your book!"

The book that was to bring us together . . .

George went back to his patients and I to my writing. We are both convinced that the best way to live vital, enthusiastic lives, is to keep on doing the work we love. And no two people on this planet could be happier.

Even so, I must try to answer an important question: Is it possible to take the place of a mate who has been loved so long? No. That place will be separate and sacred forever. What the second husband or wife must realize is that a *new* place has been created. No less thrilling, beautiful and enduring simply because this new door to the heart has been opened later. And the richer and finer the love that has gone before, the greater this second love can be.

Patiently, fervently, George had to convince me of that. "Which would you rather marry—a pauper or a millionaire?" he reasoned. "Love is like a bank account. It builds, draws interest. If a man was poor in love before, he would surely have less of love to give now. The fact that I was always so rich in love only means that now I have a greater store of love to lavish on you."

And again: "See that lake, how its waves are rolling in, how it's sparkling with life? But in the winter it's covered with ice too thick too break. I was like that—frozen, cold and dead. You gave me life! You were the sun, melting everything else away. It was all over—the winter of my soul was over and done. And the past went with it. All that matters is *now*, this wonderful joy you and I have in each other today."

It is a joy beyond anything either of us could have imagined. A bountiful harvest reaped after suffering. A wine that is finer and sweeter with age. Nothing has expressed this better than a beautiful card we received from a dear friend. Citing the miracle of the wine at the Marriage Feast in Cana, it concluded: "May it be said of your love in years to come—'You have kept the best until last.'"